The Political Economy of International Trade

The Political Economy
of
International Trade

Essays in Honor of Robert E. Baldwin

Edited by

Ronald W. Jones and Anne O. Krueger

Basil Blackwell

First published 1990

Basil Blackwell, Inc.
3 Cambridge Center
Cambridge, Massachusetts 02142, USA

Basil Blackwell Ltd
108 Cowley Road, Oxford, OX4 1JF, UK

Library of Congress Cataloging in Publication Data
The Political economy of international trade/edited by Ronald W. Jones and Anne O.
  Krueger.
        p.   cm.
  Essays in honor of Robert E. Baldwin
  Bibliography: p.
  ISBN 1-55786-026-2
  1. International trade. 2. Commercial policy. 3. Baldwin, Robert E. I. Jones,
Ronald Winthrop, 1931–. II. Krueger, Anne O.
III. Baldwin, Robert E.
HF1379.P65   1990
382—dc20   89-31765
                                                                    CIP

British Library Cataloguing in Publication Data
A CIP catalogue record for this book is available from the British Library.

Typeset in English Times Compugraphic on 10/12 pt
by Colset Private Limited, Singapore
Printed in Great Britain by Billing and Sons Ltd, Worcester

Contents

Introduction

This volume of essays has been written and collected in honor of Robert E. Baldwin on the occasion of his sixty-fifth birthday. Few economists have made significant contributions at the leading edge of research in as many areas or over as long a time span as he has.

It has been over 40 years since his first diagrammatic analysis of international trade equilibrium was published in the *Quarterly Journal of Economics*. While steadily continuing his investigations in the realm of pure international trade theory since that time, he has also written extensively in the area of economic development, explored empirical bases for trade in both less developed and advanced economies, and analyzed the political economy rationale of protectionist policies, revealing how such policies have led to the increasing use of sometimes subtle non-tariff barriers to the international exchange of goods and services.

It is altogether appropriate that at this stage of his career he be honored with a collection of essays from colleagues, former students, and professional admirers just as the world at large is engaging in the Uruguay Round of trade negotiations, attempting to cope with many of the issues which Baldwin has so carefully and ably analyzed.

Perhaps the basic theme underlying Baldwin's many contributions is his belief that good economic theory and empirical research can and should contribute significantly to policy formulation. As such, he has been equally at home in clarifying important theoretical issues, in estimating the quantitative importance of the various factors that theory points to, and in analyzing the effects of alternative policy instruments on economic welfare.

His initial publication in the *QJE* was two years before he received his PhD from Harvard.[1] It was followed a few years later by his contribution of what has since been referred to as the Baldwin envelope. This 1952 piece remains a classic, and an important tool learned by all graduate students in international economics. In the next several years, research continued on welfare aspects of trade, but also broadened to cover such topics as the secular behavior of the terms of trade and other issues in economic development. This interest culminated in his text, jointly with Gerald M. Meier, on economic development. It was one of the first in the field, ahead of its time in many of its foci and concerns, and was subsequently translated into six different languages, including Vietnamese and Indonesian.

Bob's interest in the process of economic development could not be sated by mere armchair speculation. Instead, he took to the field for a closer investigation and analysis of the interactions between economic development and international trade and investment. A year spent in the Federation of Rhodesia and Nayasaland – in what is now Zambia – led to his now-classic study, *Economic Development and Export Growth: A Study of Northern Rhodesia, 1920–1960*. Bob was aware at the time that the Federation's days as a political entity were numbered, but the focus of his investigation proved invariant to such political change: a thorough analysis of the manner in which heavy foreign contribution to an economy's export sector (copper), reflected in staggeringly high ratios of foreign investment and exports to GNP, does and does not infiltrate and stimulate development in other sectors of the economy. The book was supplemented by a series of papers on wage structures, export technology, investment, and exchange rate policy in developing countries. A decade later, he followed his interest in trade regimes and exchange rate policy with his NBER study of the Philippines.

By the mid-1960s, Bob's attention was also turning to issues of trade and exchange rate policy in the United States, as he began analyzing the issues associated with tariff-cutting in the Kennedy Round. He was among the first to recognize that the successes of the GATT in tariff-cutting might lead to a proliferation of nontariff barriers, which would be more difficult to deal with through multilateral trade negotiations. The culmination of this line of research was his *Nontariff Distortions of International Trade*, published in 1970. Typical of Baldwin's style, his effort to examine NTBs and their importance antedated by almost a decade the focus of the policy community on this set of issues.

However, interest in issues relating to developing countries did not disappear. Not only did he pursue his empirical investigations in the Philippines, but in 1969 he published perhaps his most famous theoretical article – a thorough examination of the infant-industry argument. The infant-industry argument for protection had been highly attractive to policy-makers in developing countries, arguing that a government can, through its commercial policy, protect "infant" industries under certain conditions and encourage their longer-term emergence as thriving competitive firms on the international market. Baldwin carefully examined those conditions, scrutinizing the circumstances under which they were likely to be correct, and demonstrated that the conditions were far narrower than had earlier been thought.

At about the same time, Baldwin's empirical work on the determinants of the commodity composition of US trade began to appear. Thus, during the 1970s, Bob was continuing to contribute to the literature on economic development, on the multilateral trading system, on commercial policy, and on the determinants of commodity trade flows.

As if these interests were not enough, Bob continued to recognize new issues as they arose, and was not content to rely on received doctrine. By the early 1980s, in addition to his already full research agenda, he added an interest in the political determinants of protectionism. His *Political Economy of US Import Policy* focused on a range of issues which is increasingly under scrutiny: why, when economic theory informs us that protection is almost always Pareto-inferior to alternative policy instruments, do politicians continue to be attracted to protection? The work is quintessentially Baldwin: he sets out conditions under which all would vote for free trade, and then examines the effects of relaxing these conditions one by one. He then proceeds to empirical estimates of the determinants of protection, analyzing the available data with admirable detachment.

More recently, Bob has continued his work on political economy, but also continued older themes including US trade policy, the Uruguay Round, and economic development. His methodology represents a splendid combination of good theory, careful empirical research, and a keen sense of the policy relevance of his analysis.

Given Bob's range of interests, it is no surprise that the chapters in this volume focus on subjects to which Bob has contributed much. Some are theoretical, some empirical, and some policy oriented, but all focus – at varying levels of proximity – on issues of concern in the current international trading system.

The GATT system of open multilateral trade is without doubt one of the major successes of the postwar era, and certainly was an important pillar of the rapid growth of the world economy that was experienced in the first three decades following the Second World War. As tariffs have reduced in importance – at least among the developed countries – nontariff barriers have raised a number of difficult issues. Just as multilateral trade negotiations earlier resulted in a reduction of tariffs, so now the major trading nations must find ways of agreeing on mutual reductions of nontariff barriers. The problem is complicated still further by the emergence of some developing countries as important international traders on the world scene.

With the emergence of these developing countries – primarily the NICs, or newly industrializing countries of East Asia – and the increasing integration of the world economy, protectionist pressures have increasingly challenged the GATT system in recent years. It is no exaggeration to state that the current Uruguay Round of trade negotiations, under which the 103 member nations will either find means of furthering trade liberalization or will plunge into increasingly protectionist policies, is one of those pivotal points in history that represents a significant crossroads.

The contributions to this volume reflect that concern. The first set of four essays focuses on the theory underlying some of the issues crucial to the Uruguay Round. Avinash Dixit examines trade policy in a world of imperfect information, focusing on some recently advanced arguments for "strategic" protection of industries. These arguments have centered upon imperfectly competitive market settings, and have suggested that countries protecting their own industries might give them a headstart in the world market, thereby enabling domestic nationals to earn monopoly profits that would otherwise accrue to businesses in other countries. Dixit, in the spirit of Baldwin's classic infant-industry paper, critically examines the likelihood that policy makers could indeed pinpoint industries for which strategic arguments apply.

The second paper is by Gottfried Haberler, who was Baldwin's professor at Harvard. In his paper, Haberler also examines the strategic trade arguments, and concludes that they do not overturn the traditional case for free trade on welfare grounds.

In the years prior to the Second World War, most international trade consisted of trade in commodities, almost all of which were transported by ship. With the informatics revolution, however, and the increasing differentiation of inputs, trade in services has become increasingly important to the international economy. Finding a mechanism for liberalizing trade in services is also one of the key items on the agenda of the Uruguay Round. Services are, however, different from trade in commodities in a variety of ways, and therefore call for a different analytical framework if progress is to be made. In their paper, Ronald Jones and Henryk Kierzkowski attempt to sort out the issues, by focusing on the ways in which services relate to the production process and enter into international trade.

In the final theoretical paper, James Anderson and Peter Neary focus upon finding a theoretically acceptable basis for measuring reductions in nontariff barriers, and especially quantitative restrictions, upon trade. Recognizing that one of the stumbling blocks to multilateral negotiations for the removal of nontariff barriers is the conceptual and practical difficulty of estimating how much reduction each nation is committing itself to (whereas it is straightforward to know how much of a tariff cut there is), Anderson and Neary propose a "coefficient of trade utilization" as such a measure – relating their measure to the Baldwin envelope.

The next set of papers constitute analyses of policy questions. The first, by Arnold C. Harberger, attempts to reconcile the precepts underlying commercial policy with those underlying taxation theory. It has long since been argued by most policy analysts that, in the absence of entirely free trade, a uniform tariff is to be preferred to tariffs of varying heights. In the literature on public finance, however, theory suggests that a nonuniform commodity tax structure would be optimal. Harberger examines these two, apparently conflicting, views, and shows that there are a number of policy considerations – including the role of traded commodities as intermediate goods – that lead to the conclusion that uniformity is desirable. The second essay in the policy section is by Gene Grossman – Bob Baldwin's son-in-law – and Judith Chin. They examine the benefits and costs to developing countries of agreeing to an international code of intellectual property rights, which has been one of the issues in the Uruguay Round. Surprisingly, they find that it may be directly in developing countries' interests to protect the intellectual property rights of those in developed countries, quite aside from any bargaining that might be done over other issues.

The third policy essay is by Richard Baldwin – Bob Baldwin's son – and focuses on tariff retaliation rules. Among the arguments that have been put forward in the current protectionist environment has been the argument that the United States, if it wants free trade, must be willing to adopt protectionist measures for retaliation as a means of inducing other countries to lower their own tariff barriers. Richard Baldwin's paper examines retaliation rules, under circumstances in which lobbyists in each country are influencing the tariff-setting process, and develops rules of thumb that might be used for retaliation. The final paper on trade policy is by David Burgess, who examines trade in services once again. In Burgess's view, many services are intermediate goods, and he scrutinizes the ways in which protection of services trade may distort countries' comparative advantages. When liberalization in services trade occurs, that may enable countries to shift their commodity production in ways more consistent with their underlying comparative advantage.

The final policy essay is by Rachel McCulloch and David Richardson. They examine the underlying theory of the determinants of the current account balance and capital flows in light of a model first developed by Baldwin in the 1960s. They then use the model to examine US–Japanese trade, a crucial issue in terms of current protectionist pressures. They focus on differences in savings behavior that affect the current account balance, and argue that these differences may be at the heart of the large surpluses generated by the Japanese. In light of the importance attached to the Japanese current account by policy-makers, an adequate understanding of its determinants will be essential if policy mistakes, and protection based on inadequate premises as to the underlying causation of the current account deficit, are to be avoided.

The next set of papers deals with issues in political economy. Krueger asks why import-competing interests, and not export interests, are protected in most countries, and looks at asymmetries in the political process and in policy-making that lead to that result. Gerald Meier examines trade policy in developing countries and its political underpinnings. In the light of the importance of the developing countries in the Uruguay Round, understanding the political pressures making trade liberalization difficult is essential. He notes the lessons that have been learned since the Baldwin and Meier book was first published, especially regarding gains from outward-oriented trade strategies, and then examines those elements in the political process that may make adoption of those strategies politically infeasible.

The final political economy paper is by André Sapir, who examines some of the issues arising from the European Community's intention to remove internal trade barriers among themselves by 1992. As Sapir points out, an important question facing the international economy is whether European integration will consist primarily of measures that are trade-liberalizing, or whether it will take forms that insulate their economies from those of the rest of the world. An important determinant of the outcome will be the ease with which internal liberalization can be achieved, and Sapir examines this question.

The final set of papers represent empirical contributions. Edward Leamer estimates the structure of trade barriers in 1983 for 14 developed countries, and then attempts to assess the impact of these barriers on their trade volumes. Robert Stern and Alan Deardorff use their model of international trade flows to compute the effects of alternative safeguards policies. In the GATT, there are provisions under which countries may reinstate trade barriers if damage to their domestic economies resulting from trade liberalization is deemed unacceptable by GATT criteria. One of the issues surrounding future trade liberalization efforts through GATT has been how these "safeguards" might be strengthened in ways that would make trade barrier reductions more acceptable. Stern and Deardorff apply their model to examining the likely impact of some of these proposals.

The last paper, by Seiji Naya, focuses upon trade and investment in East and Southeast Asia. As already mentioned, that burgeoning region is increasingly important in the international economy, and its role in the Uruguay Round will be much greater than any group of developing countries has previously had. Naya examines the links in those countries between direct investment and the growth of exports, concluding that openness of the economies was essential to encouraging direct foreign investment and that it has significantly contributed to their growth and especially the growth of exports, but that other factors were helpful as well.

Many economists attract attention not only by the quality of their work but by the decibel count of their own self-proclaiming trumpets. In Bob Baldwin's case the latter has always been absent. It is thus even more appropriate that this volume substitute our praise for that which he does not himself provide and thus compliment him at this mark in his on-going career.

Ronald W. Jones and Anne O. Krueger

Note

1 See pp. 313–20 for a complete list of Baldwin's published work.

Part I

Theory of Trade Policy

1

Trade Policy with Imperfect Information
AVINASH DIXIT

Introduction

The principle of targeting is perhaps the most important general result concerning trade policy. It states that any departure from the optimality conditions is best countered, or if desired as a "non-economic" objective, is best introduced, by employing an instrument that acts most directly on the relevant margin. This principle emerged in the early 1960s from several papers by Bhagwati, Ramaswami, Srinivasan, and Johnson, and was discussed in full generality in the well-known synthesis by Bhagwati (1971). In my view the most striking and memorable application of this idea is Baldwin's (1969) demolition of the infant industry argument for protection. The traditional story dates back to List and Hamilton, and was given a partial endorsement by none other than Samuelson (1948, p. 567). It posits some vague dynamic economies of scale as the source of market failure, and argues that protection, by inducing a higher level of production, would lead to the internalization of this externality. Baldwin took the argument apart with surgical precision. First, the spillover may be internalized privately, for example by groups of firms financing joint R&D or workers financing their own on-the-job training. Second, if capital market imperfections prevent such solutions, then the remedy lies there. Indeed, tariff protection will have no leverage at all on externalities of the free-rider type. Finally, in cases where a tariff has some beneficial effect, it will be inferior to other better targeted instruments such as production or credit subsidies. The analysis left the infant-industry protection argument greatly weakened, and in many cases, moribund.

I hope to pay tribute to Baldwin's achievement by attempting a similar analysis in another area of trade policy, namely its role in responding to market failures caused by uncertainty. I must begin by examining more closely the nature of these problems, just as Baldwin found it necessary to pin down more precisely the dynamic externality of learning by doing in order to reach valid policy conclusions.

Contingent contracts

The essence of uncertainty is that at some branching-point, the economic world may take any one of a number of paths. Individual choices, market relations, and government policies then split into those that must, or can, be taken before the course of the world is known, and those taken after.

Some decisions *must* be made ex ante for technological reasons, even though it would be better to postpone action and respond flexibly to each realized circumstance. Sunk investments, occupational choices, and trading commitments are cases in point. Other decisions *are* made ex ante precisely because they provide mutually beneficial ways for individuals to deal with the uncertain future. These are usually contractual relations between named parties, or in an anonymous market. Such contracts specify what each party is to do in each contingency that can arise. Insurance is of course the prime example of such a contract.

The technological and contractual reasons for making ex ante decisions are in principle distinct, but they can also occur together. For instance, if the supplier of sunk capital is also a good bearer of risk, then the payment for this capital can be made contingent upon the realization of the output or the revenue, to the mutual benefit of the supplier and the user of the capital.

It is well known that if a complete set of contracts to cover all conceivable contingencies is available, then the market equilibrium under uncertainty is Pareto efficient. Most economists dismiss this as an abstraction, and irrelevant for practical policy. However, some jump from this to the advocacy of all manner of government intervention. Early literature on trade policy under uncertainty simply omitted all mention of contingent contracts, and was replete with claims that free trade may not be optimum, and indeed may be worse than autarky. Examples are Batra and Russell (1974) and Turnovsky (1974). More sophisticated analyses such as Newbery and Stiglitz (1984) and Eaton and Grossman (1985) recognized the theoretical possibility of contingent contracts or markets, but immediately proceeded to assume them away as being unrealistic. Helpman and Razin (1978) ruled out complete contingent markets, but allowed one simple type of contingent contract, namely real equities, which are claims on a stated proportion of the firm's profit in each contingency.

Almost all previous research in this area has a fundamental flaw. It defends the absence of contingent contracts as a *realistic assumption*. While this may be a *feature of reality* in many situations, it has no business being an *assumption* in an economic model. We must search for the underlying reasons for the absence of such contracts. Failure to do so may sometimes be excusable in a positive model, but it is fatal in policy analysis. This is because the underlying reasons for market failure will also affect the feasibility and the desirability of various policy interventions. Neglecting the fundamentals and making ad hoc descriptive assumptions will yield falsely optimistic results about the potential for policy. This point is well known as the Lucas Critique in the context of macroeconomic policy, but is no less important for tax and tariff policies.

I shall therefore begin with an overview of what contingent contracts try to do, and of the basic reasons why they may be missing or imperfect.

The most important factor that governs what contingent contracts can accomplish is the correlation between different sources of uncertainty in the economy. The simplest is the case of individual risk, where the outcomes for different people are independent. Many personal accidents or illnesses are of this kind. With a large number of persons, the average outcome is risk free. That is to say, pooling yields perfect insurance. More generally, if risks from different sources (for example industries) are less than perfectly correlated, then an individual can reduce his exposure by holding a diversified portfolio. This leaves a component of risk that is common to all, or aggregate risk. Of course the breadth of diversification that is available determines aggregate risk. The terms of trade risk facing a small economy is aggregate if assets cannot be traded, but if such trade is possible, the risk can be reduced further by holding a portfolio that includes equities in foreign firms that produce the country's importables. Aggregate risk must be borne by someone. The only question is how to allocate it among different people. With perfect contingent contracts, an efficient allocation can be achieved; those more willing to bear the risk end up bearing more of it.

Let us turn to a brief review of the reasons for the absence of, or imperfections in, contingent contracts. The simplest is that the contingency itself may not be publicly observable. Then one of the parties to a potential contract generally has an incentive to renege on what is required of it and, knowing this, the other party does not enter into such a contract. If there is crop failure insurance, for example, a farmer may hide some of his crop, publicly show a low output, and make a claim on his policy. Anticipating this, no rational company will provide such insurance. More generally, it may be costly to observe the contingency. Actually, even this does not automatically imply a complete absence of a market – insurance contracts with some costly monitoring may emerge in equilibrium.[1]

The second reason for market failure is that the contingent contract may have to specify some actions to be taken by the parties, and those may not be observable. It may be efficient for a life insurance contract to specify that the insured should not eat excessively fatty foods or smoke, but if compliance cannot be observed, the insured is tempted to cheat. Therefore the contract cannot be so conditioned. This is the problem of moral hazard. Note that there must be some overlying "noise," else the action can be inferred from the outcome. For example, if no non-smoker ever got lung cancer, then life insurance contracts could simply exclude coverage for deaths from this disease.

Third, it may be important to make the terms of a contingent contract depend on some innate characteristic of one of the parties, and this may be its private information. For example, suppose some car drivers are just naturally more careless than others, and know themselves to be so. They have no incentive to tell the insurance company if it cannot otherwise find out. Then an insurance policy that would be actuarially fair for the average driver will attract the worse-than-average driver. This is the problem of adverse selection.

Many other reasons are advanced for the absence of, or imperfections in, contingent contracts and markets, but on closer scrutiny they reduce to one of the above three. For example, administrative costs are really costs of observation and enforcement, while transaction costs arise from asymmetric information and the resulting incentives for opportunistic behavior.[2]

All three kinds of asymmetric information are potential causes of market failures when the risk in question is individual rather than aggregate. First consider the problem that the outcome is not observable to outsiders. If the risk is aggregate, the outcome is the same for all individuals. Then a differential reward scheme can create sufficiently powerful individual incentives to reveal a good outcome, thereby solving the problem. Turning to moral hazard, if one farmer's crop depends on his own effort and the general weather conditions, without any individual source of uncertainty, then his output being less than that of another farmer is conclusive evidence of his shirking. A reward scheme based on relative performance can induce optimal effort. Similarly, with adverse selection, a farmer's relatively low innate ability is revealed by his relatively low output if the only source of noise is common to all farmers. Then adverse selection can be overcome by conditioning insurance on relative yields. More generally, when risk has both aggregate and individual components, contracts can be conditioned on the former, while the latter may remain subject to problems of asymmetric information. In other words, when we seek reasons for the failure of contingent markets or contracts, we must be confined to situations of individual risk.[3]

The information asymmetries that are the putative causes of market failure must be taken equally seriously when we conduct policy analysis. This should be the ground rule of fairness in comparisons between markets and governments; see the excellent discussion in Stiglitz (1981). When we oberve some failure of contingent markets or contracts, and seek policies to remedy the situation, we should begin by identifying the source of the problem, and imposing the same informational restriction on the set of available policy instruments. Where we are not sure of the precise source of the problem, we can try out the various usual suspects for this role.

In the following sections I shall consider in turn each of the three categories – unobservable outcomes, moral hazard, and adverse selection – mentioned above. For each, I shall examine its effect on contingent contracts, and the possibility and the nature of policies that improve upon the laissez-faire outcome. The discussion is based on more formal treatments in a set of papers (Dixit 1987, 1989a, and 1989b). The models in those papers have a common and simplified general structure that I shall outline first, but my informal discussion often steps beyond those special assumptions.

The general simple structure is chosen because it is familiar to trade theorists, and because it focuses on issues of uncertainty and information by removing other reasons for trade restrictions. Consider a small open economy with just one mobile factor of production, labor. The ownership of the other specific factors is shared equally by all workers. Thus there is no monopoly power in trade, and no ex ante distributional conflict. There are two goods, X and Y, and there is individual risk in the production of X. Each worker must allocate all of his labor to the production of one good or the other before the uncertainty is resolved. For expositional simplicity, I suppose that each X-sector worker gets just one of two outcomes, high (X_H) and low (X_L). The outcomes are independent across workers, is to say, the probability that one worker gets high output is the same irrespective of the output realized by any other worker. In the case of unobservable outcomes, this probability is exogenous. With moral hazard, it is a function of the amount of effort made by the worker, and effort is not observable by others. While adverse selection, the probability is the worker's privately known innate characteristic. In each case, the aim is to see how well or poorly private markets or contracts can cope with the uncertainty, and whether and how trade restrictions and other policies can improve upon the performance of the markets.

Unobservable outcomes

After occupational choices are made and production starts, some workers will get the high output and others will get the low output. Since the probabilities are exogenous and the risk is individual, the ideal risk-bearing is perfect insurance. All X-sector workers should have the same disposable income irrespective of their personal good or bad luck. A contingent contract can achieve this – all workers agree in advance that they will pool their outputs and share the result equally. The effect is the same as if each worker held a fully diversified portfolio of equity positions in all workers' enterprises. A more familiar form of insurance contract would ask all X-sector workers to pay a premium in advance, and use the pooled premiums to compensate just the low-output workers.

Neither of these contracts will work if each worker's output cannot be observed after the fact. Under the contingent contract, the lucky ones will have the incentive to withhold their promised payments into the redistribution pool, while under the insurance scheme, they will have the incentive to pretend bad luck and put in claims on the premium pool. Thus voluntary risk-pooling arrangements based on outputs will fail.

Remember that the constraint on information is to be taken seriously, and imposed on the government as well as on private insurers. Therefore the solution of publicly provided insurance is not feasible. We must circumvent the problem by using an observable magnitude that is related to the realization of high or low output. Market transactions are the most plausible candidates. An X-sector worker who realizes a higher output will consume more of the X-good, but if the Y-good is normal, he will have larger net sales of the X-good on the market. How this can be used depends on the detail with which market transactions can be observed.

If each individual's net sales are separately observable, then private insurers can condition contracts on this. A more likely scenario is that the volume of transactions can be observed at some point in an anonymous market, but individual sellers cannot be identified. Now a tax on such sales, whose proceeds are rebated in equal lump sums to all workers in the X-sector, replicates the effect of insurance. Before the disbursal of the revenues, the tax lowers the real incomes of all X-sector workers, but those with high output lose more. When the revenue is returned, those with low output are net gainers and those with high output remain net losers. Disposable incomes move the same way as they would with insurance.

If this policy can be pushed to the limit where the producer price of good X goes to zero, then all X-sector workers will have the same disposable income irrespective of their output realization, that is, insurance will be perfect. In practice, three considerations will prevent the attainment of this limit. First, at a low enough price, even the high-output people will become net buyers of good X. Second, even before that point is reached, smuggling or other tax evasion activities are likely to emerge and restrict the tax possibilities. Third, if X_H and X_L depend on effort or on purchases of other inputs, then the tax will create a distortion of the usual kind.

Even though a perfect policy solution in unlikely, a small tax will be an improvement over laissez faire. As usual the harmful by-products of a small tax are of the second order, while the primary beneficial effect is of the first order. Then a more elaborate exercise can determine the optimum tax rate by balancing the two effects at the margin. Here I focus on the general nature of the policy.

The tax applies to net sales; thus X-sector workers face equal net-of-tax price in their twin roles as consumers and produces of good X. However, consumers of this good who do not produce it themselves should face the tax-inclusive price, and there is no justification for having any tax wedge between this and the world price. In other words, there is no reason to interfere with free international trade.

If domestic net trades are not observable, but those with rest of the world are, then trade taxes or subsidies are the only available instruments. In this case, keeping the domestic price of good X below the world price has the same insurance effect. Now there is an additional distortion, namely in the consumption decision of Y-sector workers, but once again it is of the second order for the first little bit of the policy, and some action in this direction is better than none.

A policy of keeping the domestic price below the world price amounts to an import subsidy if we are importing good X, and an export tax if we are exporting it. The policies that are commonly advocated for insurance purposes in public discussion are ones that favor the producers – production subsidies or price supports. We see that logical analysis of the problem supports exactly the opposite kinds of policies.

What if a person's output realization can be observed at a cost, for example by monitoring, auditing, or detective work? It turns out that competition forces private insurers to use these in an efficient way, so public insurance cannot do any better. But there remains a correlation between net sales and income, which a producer tax can exploit in the same way as above. The details are in Dixit (1989a).

Moral hazard

In my two-sector framework, moral hazard is captured most simply by making the probability of achieving the high output a function of a person's effort. This effort is not observable by others.

In this setting, consider a competitive insurance market. The price is the ratio of premium to payout, and each insured chooses the amount of coverage. Competition will enforce an actuarially fair price. Then a risk-averse worker will choose full coverage, and will have no incentive to make any effort.

To see this a little more formally, suppose an X-sector worker's utility function is $V(I, p, e)$, where I is income in units of good Y, p is the relative price of good X, and e is effort. Let R be the equal per capita rental income arising from each worker's ownership of the specific factors in the economy. Let $\pi(e)$ be the probability of high output. Actuarially fair insurance means that $\pi(e)/[1 - \pi(e)]$ units of low-state income can be purchased by giving up one unit of high-state income. If the individual purchases z such contracts, then the low and high state incomes are

$$I_H = pX_H + R - z, \tag{1.1}$$

and

$$I_L = pX_L + R + z\pi(e)/[1 - \pi(e)]. \tag{1.2}$$

Then z and e are chosen to maximize the expected utility U_X of each X-sector worker

$$U_X = \pi(e)V(I_H, p, e) + [1 - \pi(e)]V(I_L, p, e). \tag{1.3}$$

The first-order condition for z becomes

$$V_I(I_L, p, e) = V_I(I_H, p, e),$$

which implies $I_L = I_H$, and so $V(I_L, p, e) = V(I_H, p, e)$, that is, full insurance. Then, since effort causes disutility, the worker chooses $e = 0$.

Suppose the economy is in such an equilibrium. What role can various policy instruments play? Public insurance or grants add to, or subtract from, I_L and I_H. Trade or tax policies charge p. But none of these can alter the outcomes of zero effort and full insurance. The situation is formally like an economy in which there is no moral hazard problem, the effort level being simply fixed at zero, a fixed probability $\pi(0)$ of getting high output, and full insurance. Standard Arrow–Debreu theory tells us that such an equilibrium is Pareto efficient (conditioned on the effort level), so none of these policies can improve upon it.

What the situation needs is a different kind of policy – one that *reduces* insurance coverage and *increases* effort levels. An example is a tax at the rate τ on a unit insurance policy. Now giving up a unit of high-state income yields only $(1 - \tau)\pi(e)/[1 - \pi(e)]$ units of low-state income. Workers purchase incomplete insurance, and have an incentive to make some effort.

Such an outcome is a Pareto improvement, so there is an ex ante unanimity that it is desirable to achieve. We can think of private contractual arrangements to bring it about. The problem with the zero-effort, full-insurance case is a kind of externality – insurance sold by each firm reduces the workers' incentive to make effort and therefore worsens the odds on all insurance contracts. This can be internalized by making each unit of insurance conditional upon the total insurance purchase of a worker. In practice, firms attempt to do this using clauses that make each insurer's liability subordinate to that of all others. In theory, the simplest way to capture the effect is imposing an exclusivity requirement – each worker must purchase all of his insurance from just one firm. There is still competition among the insurers as they try to attract the would-be exclusive clients. The feasibility of such a scheme depends on the observability of insurance purchases; let us examine the consequences of exclusivity assuming it to be feasible.

Each insurer can now offer a contract that fixes the quantity as well as the price of insurance. This amounts to fixing the worker's net receipts from the insurer, say Z_L and Z_H, in the two states. The expressions (1.1) and (1.2) for incomes change to

$$I_H = pX_H + R + Z_H, \tag{1.4}$$

and

$$I_L = pX_L + R + Z_L. \tag{1.5}$$

The expression (1.3) for the expected utility U_x is unchanged.

Competition forces each firm to offer a level of utility matching that available in the market equilibrium. Each firm also realizes that, given Z_H and Z_L, the worker is going to choose effort e to maximize U_x; call this the moral hazard constraint. Subject to these two constraints, the firm seeks to maximize its expected profit:

$$\Pi = -[1 - \pi(e)]Z_L - \pi(e)Z_H. \tag{1.6}$$

Since there is free entry of insurance companies, in equilibrium U_X adjusts until $\Pi = 0$. Then we can think about the process in reverse, and say that in equilibrium, e, Z_L, and Z_H are chosen to maximize the expected utility U_X of each X-sector worker subject to a zero-profit constraint and the moral hazard constraint.

It can be shown that the equilibrium will have *some* insurance ($Z_L > 0 > Z_H$), but *incomplete* insurance ($I_H > I_L$); see Shavell (1979), Dixit (1987). The fact that some insurance is offered in equilibrium says that moral hazard is not a cause of a complete collapse of the insurance market. Note that *some* incompleteness of insurance is a good thing – it preserves some incentive for effort and raises expected utilities all round. It remains to see if the market provides the *optimal* degree of incompleteness.

The simplest kind of policy intervention is to offer a reward (penalty if negative) for working in the X-sector. Starting from laissez-faire, give a small amount dg to each X-sector worker, and finance it by a tax dt on all workers. Suppose there are N workers in all, and in equilibrium N_X have chosen to work in the X-sector and N_Y in the Y-sector. Then

$$N \, dt = N_X \, dg. \tag{1.7}$$

In response to this subsidy, workers move to the X-sector, and the Y-sector wage rises, until the utilities in the two sectors are balanced again in the new equilibrium. As the Y-sector wage w rises, the per capita rent R falls.[4] With competition in the Y-sector, we have

$$w = F'(N_Y), \qquad NR = F(N_Y) - wN_Y, \tag{1.8}$$

where F is the production function in the Y-sector. The envelope theorem links the changes in w and R:

$$N \, dR + N_Y \, dw = 0. \tag{1.9}$$

Now we can calculate the changes in utilities of the typical worker in each sector:

$$dU_X = \lambda_X[dg + dR - dt], \tag{1.10}$$

and

$$dU_Y = \lambda_Y[dw + dR - dt] \tag{1.11}$$

where λ_X and λ_Y are the respective marginal utilities of income. Since we are moving from one equilibrium to another, these two utility changes must be equal. Using the expressions for dt and dR in (1.7) and (1.9) above, we have

$$\lambda_X[dg - (N_Y/N)dw - (N_X/N)dg] = \\ \lambda_Y[dw - (N_Y/N)dw - (N_X/N)dg].$$

This simplifies to

$$dw[\lambda_X N_Y + \lambda_Y N_X]/N = dg[\lambda_X N_Y + \lambda_Y N_X]/N,$$

or

$$dw = dg,$$

Using this in (1.10) and (1.11), we have

$$dU_X = dU_Y = 0.$$

Thus the policy has no first-order effect on utilities. If we consider larger magnitudes of the subsidy g, there will be an additional tax burden arising from the need to pay g to the marginal workers in the X-sector. Therefore (1.7) will change to

$$N\,dt = N_X\,dg + g\,dN_X.$$

The effect on the utilities U_X and U_Y will be positively harmful.

Very similar calculations hold for other policies, such as publicly provided insurance, or production or trade taxes or subsidies that alter p and therefore the incomes of low and high state producers differently. In other words, and laissez-faire equilibrium is a Pareto optimum, constrained by the moral hazard applied symmetrically to markets and policies. Of course this is not the ideal first-best in a hypothetical full information setting, but that is not the relevant standard for comparison.

In this analysis, moral hazard arose because of unobservable effort. There was no market transaction that could offer a point of leverage. But moral hazard can arise in other ways. For example, a farmer's probability of achieving high output, π, may be a function of his purchase of fertilizer. If this is observable, an insurance contract can be conditioned on it. As mentioned before, a more likely case is that transactions cannot be attributed to specific individuals, but the aggregate volume can be observed. Then tax or subsidy policies come into play. In an equilibrium without full insurance and with some purchase of fertilizer, a subsidy can increase fertilizer use. As usual, a small subsidy is desirable, because its direct effect on the margin of fertilizer use is of the first order and any by-product distortions are of the second order. For a rigorous treatment of this, see Greenwald and Stiglitz (1986).

Note that such a policy has no reason to treat domestically produced fertilizer any differently than the imported kind. That is, trade taxes or subsidies are not the right way to deal with the problem. Only if a transaction were to affect π by its inherent cross-border nature would there be an argument for trade policies to alleviate moral hazard. But such a situation is hard to imagine.

Adverse selection

As with moral hazard, I shall begin with the simplest model of adverse selection. In the same general setting as above, suppose the probability π of achieving high output differs across people. For simplicity of exposition, let there be just two types A and B, with values π_a and π_b. Each person's type is an innate attribute that is not observable to others. Choose the labels so that $1 > \pi_a > \pi_b > 0$, and suppose there are N_A and N_B workers of the respective types in the total labor force N.

With adverse selection, it is simpler to begin by finding the policy optimum, and then comparing the performance of markets against this standard. This is because informationally feasible policies can be completely characterized using the Revelation Principle. This states that any such policy can alternatively be implemented using a direct or revelation scheme. Here the government simply asks each person to report his unobservable attribute, and commits itself to a policy rule that specifies how this information is to be used. This amounts to specifying each individual's labor and consumption allocation as a function of his reported type. The rule must be such that it becomes optimal for each person to report the type truthfully; this is the "incentive compatibility constraint." That is, the utility from pretending to be some other type should not exceed that from answering truthfully.[5]

The familiar constraints of resource availability and technological feasibility are now augmented by those of incentive compatibility. Subject to all these constraints, we look for efficient or optimal policies. The important point to note is that the incentive compatibility constraints involve the utility levels that result from the proposed allocations. The exact consumption bundles that achieve these levels are of no concern as far as the incentive compatibility constraints are concerned. Therefore the standard reasons for achieving these utility levels at the least resource cost remain in force. In our small economy model, this efficiency requirement implies that consumers should go on facing the given world prices. In other words, policies that cope with adverse selection in the best possible way do not include tariffs.

So let us keep the relative price p fixed at the world level, and consider a range of feasible policies and their outcomes. The exposition is simplified by consolidating the economy's budget constraint, so let the government levy a 100 per cent tax on the pure rent in the Y-sector. In the revelation mechanism, the government asks people to report their types. The adverse selection issue is of interest only when there is a mixture of the two types of workers in the X-sector. Therefore let us suppose that $N_Y < N_B$. All those reporting type A are placed in the X-sector, where they receive income I_H or I_L, with $I_H > I_L$, depending on their output realization. All those reporting type B get income I, but N_Y of them are designated to work in the Y-sector and $(N_B - N_Y)$ in the X-sector.

The consolidated budget constraint is

$$N_A[\pi_a I_H + (1 - \pi_a)I_L] = F(N_Y) + p\{[\pi_a N_A + \pi_b(N_B - N_Y)]X_H + [(1 - \pi_a)N_A + (1 - \pi_b)(N_B - N_Y)]X_L\}.$$
(1.12)

The incentive compatibility constraint for type B workers to report truthfully is

$$V(I,p) \geq \pi_b V(I_H, p) + (1 - \pi_b)V(I_L, p).$$

In an optimum this will hold with equality

$$V(I,p) = \pi_b V(I_H, p) + (1 - \pi_b)V(I_L, p).$$
(1.13)

Since $\pi_a > \pi_b$ and $I_H > I_L$, the corresponding constraint on type A workers will be slack and we can forget about it.

The utility levels of the two types are

$$U_B = V(I, p),$$
(1.14)

and

$$U_A = \pi_a V(I_H, p) + (1 - \pi_a)V(I_L, p).$$
(1.15)

Let us look for a Pareto improvement on an initially given situation of this kind. It is simpler to try to increase U_A keeping U_B fixed. This fixes I from (1.14). Differentiating (1.12) gives

$$N_A[\pi_a dI_H + (1 - \pi_a)dI_L] = [F'(N_Y) - M_b]dN_Y,$$
(1.16)

where I have defined the expected marginal product of a type B worker in the X-sector as

$$M_b = p[\pi_b X_H + (1 - \pi_b)X_L].$$

Differentiating (1.13), we find

$$\pi_b \lambda_H dI_H + (1 - \pi_b)\lambda_L dI_L = 0,$$
(1.17)

where I have defined the marginal utilities

$$\lambda_H \equiv V_I(I_H, p), \quad \lambda_L \equiv V_I(I_L, p).$$

The two equations (1.16) and (1.17) leave one degree of freedom among dN_Y, dI_H and dI_L. Let us take dN_Y as exogenous and solve for the other two. We find

$$\begin{pmatrix} dI_H \\ dI_L \end{pmatrix} = \frac{F'(N_Y) - M_b}{\Delta} \begin{pmatrix} (1 - \pi_b)V_I(I_L, p) \\ -\pi_b V_I(I_H, p) \end{pmatrix},$$
(1.18)

where

$$\Delta \equiv \pi_a(1 - \pi_b)V_I(I_L, p) - \pi_b(1 - \pi_a)V_I(I_H, p),$$

which is positive since $\pi_a > \pi_b$ and $I_H > I_L$. Finally,

$$dU_A = \pi_a \lambda_H \, dI_H + (1 - \pi_a) \lambda_L \, dI_L$$
$$= \frac{(\pi_a - \pi_b) \lambda_H \lambda_L}{\Delta} [F'(N_Y) - M_b] \, dN_Y. \tag{1.19}$$

Thus the direction in which N_Y should be changed depends on the comparison of the marginal products of the type B workers in the two sectors, $F'(N_Y)$ in the safe sector, and the expected value M_b in the risky sector.

Now consider the performance of private risk markets in this setting. The problems are well known from Rothschild and Stiglitz (1976). There cannot be a "first-best" equilibrium with full and actuarially fair insurance for each type. The contract that is fair for type A is also preferred by type B. They cannot be observed and excluded, and their infiltration makes the contract a losing proposition. Nor can there be an equilibrium with a single pooled contract that breaks even over the whole population. A competing contract that offers less than full insurance but at better than average terms can be designed to attract just the type A. This leaves the original contract with only the type B clientele, and makes it unprofitable. A competitive equilibrium, if it exists, must have two contracts, one that offers type B full and fair insurance, and the other that gives type A fair but partial insurance, in such a way that each type prefers the contract designed for it. This is the self-selection property or constraint. More specifically, it turns out that type A strictly prefer their own contract, while type B are just at the point of indifference between the two contracts. If the proportion of type B workers in the population is small enough, then such a set of contracts can be upset by a pooled contract; no competitive equilibrium exists in such a case.

If a competitive equilibrium exists, the insurance contract will give type B workers in the X-sector a sure and fair sum Z:

$$Z = \pi_b p X_H + (1 - \pi_b) p X_L.$$

Note that the right hand side is just the M_b defined above. The total income of these workers will be $(Z + R)$, where as before R is their per capita rent income. The total income of type B workers in the Y-sector will be $(w + R)$. Equating these two for indifference, we have $w = Z$. But $w = F'(N_Y)$. This chain of equations establishes $F'(N_Y) = M_b$. Using this in (1.19) above, we see that $dU_A = 0$: if a competitive equilibrium exists, it is constrained Pareto efficient.

If a competitive equilibrium does not exist, various outcomes are conceivable. One is that the insurance market fails completely. If no insurance is available, then the indifference of risk-averse type B between a sure wage w in the Y-sector and their output lottery in the X-sector requires $w < M_b$. From (1.19), a Pareto improvement can be achieved by decreasing N_Y. That is, the safe sector is too large in equilibrium.

Under competitive conditions, an insurance company thinking of introducing a new contract calculates its profitability assuming no other change in the set of contracts available in the market. But the new contract can make some existing ones unprofitable, causing them to be withdrawn from the market. This can in turn make the new contract unprofitable. If the firm looks ahead to such repercussions, it will not introduce the new contract in the first place. The equilibrium under this alternative behavioral assumption is labelled "reactive." It turns out that a reactive equilibrium always exists, but that in it the Y-sector is generally too large; see Dixit (1989b) for details. Remember that the right policy for changing N_Y in the desired direction is a subsidy or a tax on the choice of occupation, not a trade intervention.

Adverse selection can enter the model in more complex ways just as moral hazard could. The probabilities π_a and π_b may not be exogenous, but may depend on the purchase of some relevant input. Thus type Bs may succeed in imitating type As only by purchasing and using an ability-enhancing good. Then a tax on this good makes the imitation harder to sustain, and reduces the force of adverse selection. This is again an application of the general theory of Greenwald and Stiglitz (1986). But, as with moral hazard, there is no reason to distinguish domestically produced and imported units of this good, unless they affect the probabilities differently. One can think of a scenario where the more able can do mental arithmetic, and the less able need hand-held calculators. If Japanese calculators are more efficient than American ones, then they should be taxed more heavily to have equal effects on the adverse selection problem. But this is a contrived picture. Finally, it is worth emphasizing that if such a good is also purchased for other reasons, then the tax that improves the information problem has a harmful distortionary effect on the other uses, and in practice the latter is likely to overwhelm the former except near the zero tax rate point.

Concluding comments

I began with the observation that the causes for the failure of private markets to deal with uncertainty should be explicitly specified, and the informational constraints should be equally imposed on policies. When this is done for the three general causes identified, namely unobservability of individual outcomes, actions (moral hazard) and characteristics (adverse selection), in many cases it turned out markets coped with the problems as well as one could ask – the competitive market equilibrium was Pareto optimal given the constraints of information as well as resource availability. In other cases, a beneficial tax or subsidy could be identified, but it was very difficult to conceive of circumstances in which the right policy was to act on the margin of international transactions. This contrasts with earlier literature which imposed the absence of private risk markets as an ad hoc assumption, failed to consider the underlying causes as possible limitations on policy-making, and failed to consider the whole range of policies and the relative merits of alternative instruments.

These developments retrace the evolution of views on markets and policies that took place after Lipsey and Lancaster's (1956) discovery of the general problem of the second best. The initial reaction was that now anything went; since at least one of the many conditions for the first-best was sure to be violated in practice, the government had a license for violating the rest. More careful research qualified this nihilism. It was shown that with certain kinds of separability, it remained desirable to adhere to the remaining conditions. More generally, there were good policy responses and bad ones; attempts to rank and classify them led to the principle of targeting.

In the same way, uncertainty was initially thought to be this general force that paralyzes the markets, and justifies any and all policy interventions. I have argued that more careful analysis qualifies or reverses such presumptions. Of course this is not the end of the story. Researchers will go on to examine more subtle kinds of market failures caused by incomplete and asymmetric information, and find the appropriate policy responses. A particularly interesting possibility is that information asymmetries come not singly but together. Then private contracts or government policies that help solve one problem can exacerbate another.

I recognize that future research in more complex settings may yield different conclusions. But I hope such work will respect the rule of the game, namely the general principle of fairness in comparing markets and governments: the causes of any market failure should be specified explicitly, and the effect of these same causes on the feasibility, and the absolute and relative efficacy, of various policy measures should be considered carefully.

Notes

I am grateful to Robert Trevor for useful comments, and the National Science Foundation for financial support under grant SES-8509536.

1 Cunningly structured contracts can create the incentives to reveal the truth; see Hart and Moore (1988) and D'Aspremont and Gerard-Varet (1979). But these imply a particular allocation of risk, and therefore work to ensure production efficiency under risk-neutrality, not insurance.

2 Some costs of both types consist of laws or taxes imposed by governments. But the question here is whether and how a government should respond to market failures that arise for other reasons, not the analysis of market failures caused by the government.

3 Eaton and Grossman (1986) and Newbery and Stiglitz (1984) appeal to background reasons of moral hazard and adverse selection as justifying their assumption of market failure when the uncertainty lies in an aggregate variable like the world price. Of course they ignore the possibility of contracts based on relative performance to solve the problem. There is also the point that the world price is a very easily and publicly observable variable.

4   Labor has stochastic constant returns in the X-sector, therefore there is no rent there.
5   See Harris and Townsend (1985) for an exposition of the Revelation Principle.

References

Baldwin, Robert E. 1969: "The case against infant-industry protection," *Journal of Political Economy*, 77, 295–305.

Batra, Raveendra N. and Russell, William R. 1974: "Gains from trade under uncertainty," *American Economic Review*, 64, 1040–8.

Bhagwati, Jagdish 1971: "The generalized theory of distortions and welfare," in J. Bhagwati et al. (eds), *Trade, Balance of Payments, and Growth*, Amsterdam: North Holland.

D'Aspremont, Claude and Gerard-Varet, Louis 1979: "Incentives and incomplete information." *Journal of Public Economics*, 11, 25–45.

Dixit, Avinash 1987: "Trade and insurance with moral hazard," *Journal of International Economics*, 23, 201–20.

Dixit, Avinash 1989a: "Trade and insurance with imperfectly observed outcomes," *Quarterly Journal of Economics*, 104, 195–203.

Dixit, Avinash 1989b: "Trade and insurance with adverse selection," *Review of Economic Studies*, 56, 235–47.

Eaton, Jonathan and Grossman, Gene M. 1985: "Tariffs as insurance: Optimal commercial policy when domestic markets are incomplete," *Canadian Journal of Economics*, 18, 258–72.

Greenwald, Bruce and Stiglitz, Joseph E. 1986: "Externalities in economies with imperfect information and incomplete markets," *Quarterly Journal of Economics*, 101, 229–64.

Harris, Milton and Townsend, Robert 1985: "Allocation mechanisms, asymmetric information, and the Revelation Principle," in G. Feiwel (ed.), *Issues in Contemporary Microeconomics and Welfare*, Albany, NY: SUNY Press, 379–94.

Hart, Oliver and Moore, John 1988: "Optimal contracts and renegotiation," *Econometrica*, 56, 755–85.

Helpman, Elhanan and Razin, Assaf 1978: *A Theory of International Trade Under Uncertainty*. New York: Academic Press.

Lipsey, Richard G. and Lancaster, Kelvin 1956: "The general theory of the second best," *Review of Economic Studies*, 24, 11–32.

Newbery, David and Stiglitz, Joseph 1984: "Pareto inferior trade," *Review of Economic Studies*, 51, 1–12.

Rothschild, Michael and Stiglitz, Joseph E. 1976: "Equilibrium in competitive insurance markets," *Quarterly Journal of Economics*, 90, 629–50.

Samuelson, Paul A. 1948: *Economics*, New York: McGraw-Hill.

Shavell, Steven 1979: "On moral hazard and insurance," *Quarterly Journal of Economics*, 94, 541–62.

Stiglitz, Joseph E. 1981: "Pareto optimality and competition," *Journal of Finance*, 36, 235–51.

Turnovsky, Stephen J. 1974: "Technological and price uncertainty in a Ricardian model of international trade," *Review of Economic Studies*, 41, 201–17.

2

Strategic Trade Policy and the New International Economics: A Critical Analysis

GOTTFRIED HABERLER

In two recent articles[1] I have argued that, using the tools of classical trade theory and making certain unrealistic or even broadly realistic assumptions, it is possible to develop theoretically valid arguments for protection which in actual application are most likely to have negative or even disastrous consequences. Concretely, assuming inelasticities, rigidities, externalities or irrational behavior of certain groups, especially of lowly farmers in less developed countries, the optimum tariff argument for protection can be developed along with the external economies argument for protection which covers the classical infant-industry argument.[2]

In the present article I discuss a new argument for protection which goes under the pretentious name of "strategic trade policy and the new international economics." This theory has been developed in the last five years or so in an extensive and interesting but diffused and excessively repetitious literature.[3]

The proponents of the "new" international economics point out, correctly, that the basic model of classical and neoclassical trade theory on which the case for free trade is based, assumes perfect competition and, therefore, excludes increasing returns to scale. Increasing returns that are internal to the firms in any industry are incompatible with competitive equilibrium; they would lead to monopoly or oligopoly, implying persistently higher profits than in the competitive rest of the economy.

Free traders argue that the existence of local imperfectly competitive firms greatly strengthens the case for free trade. The reason is that the larger the market, the less scope there is for monopolies and oligopolies, and free trade greatly increases the size of the market. In fact, freer or free trade is a potent antimonopoly weapon. Although proponents of the new economics are aware of all that, they evidently believe that many oligopolies would survive under free trade. It would be interesting to have a few plausible examples. But as far as I know, very little has been done on that in the voluminous literature.

I now state briefly the principal conclusions and policy prescriptions of the "new" international economics, their novelty and validity. I take my cue from the latest authoritative summary by Paul Krugman in his paper "Is Free Trade Passé?"[4] which takes into account some of the criticism of the theory. Krugman cites three papers, one by himself, which, written "simultaneously and independently," demonstrate how "economies of scale lead to arbitrary specialization by nations on products" of industries that operate under monopolistic conditions because they enjoy increasing returns. "These models immediately established the idea that countries specialize and trade, not only because of underlying differences, such things as different endowments of factors of production that are mentioned by traditional trade theory) but also because increasing returns are an independent force," determining the international division of labor.

All this is true, but it is now new. Krugman himself says that it was a major theme in Ohlin's *International and Interregional Trade* and in an earlier paper he says that the importance of economies of scale has been "widely recognized" and he mentions especially Bela Balassa and Irving Kravis who have argued that scale economies have played a crucial role in the growth of trade of the industrialized countries after the Second World War.[5]

What, then, is new in the "new" economics? The short answer is: the protectionist policy conclusion. The "new" economics has added one more item to the list of theoretically valid arguments for protection. How important is the new argument for protection from the economic point of view and can it be efficiently implemented? – that is the question to which I turn now.

According to Krugman the new economics holds that international "trade is to an important degree driven by economies of scale." This surely is true in the sense that economies of scale give rise to international trade. "That international markets are typically imperfectly competitive" must be strong doubted, but will not be discussed here. Krugman continues that the new view has suggested two arguments for protection, a wholly new one and an old one. The old one is the external economies argument. It has been reemphasized by the "new" economics, but hardly improves it and need not be further discussed here.

The new idea is that if there are increasing returns and, therefore, monopolistic or oligopolistic firms enjoying excess profits, the government is in a position to shift excess profits from foreign to domestic firms by deviating from free trade, to wit either by imposing import restrictions or by subsidizing domestic firms.[6] Krugman sets up a very simple model that puts the central proposition of the new economics into sharp focus. Suppose there is an industry, say aircraft production, where increasing returns to scale leaves room for only one firm, say Boeing in the United States or Airbus in Europe, to supply the world market profitably. Now suppose Boeing has plans to start production. If it is carried out, it will make large profits and Airbus will be shut out. But, if Europe is alert, it will subsidize Airbus to get ahead of Boeing; the profits will go to Europe and Boeing will be shut out.

The real world is, of course, much more complicated. There exists no industry with only one firm in the world market; there is, after all, McDonnell-Douglas and the Concorde in addition to Airbus and Boeing. Furthermore, there are many industrialized countries, and at this point let us recall that their number has increased since the Second World War. In addition to North America, Western Europe, and Japan, there are now the so-called NICs (Newly Industrialized Countries), Taiwan, South Korea, Hong Kong, and some of the "middle income countries," Argentina, Brazil, have developed industrial centers. All this has intensified international competition and reduced the scope for monopolies and oligopolies.

A serious complication of the new economics mentioned by Krugman and other proponents is, in Krugman's words, the fact "that economists do not have reliable models of how oligopolists behave. Yet the effects of trade policy in imperfectly competitive industries can depend crucially on how [oligopolistic] firms behave."

The most serious difficulty of a successful strategic trade policy mentioned by Krugman is what he calls "the general equilibrium" criticism of the policy. "Interventionist policies to promote particular sectors [for strategic reasons], must draw resources away from other sectors. This substantially raises the knowledge that a government must have to formulate interventions that do more harm than good." A policy aimed at capturing external economies runs into the same difficulty. Favored sectors draw resources from other industries. "Again, the government needs to understand not only the targeted sector but the rest of the economy to know if a policy is justified."

Is there a country in the western world that knows all that, one may ask? Krugman is rather vague about that. He ends the discussion by saying "Governments may not know for sure where intervention is justified, but they are not completely without information. However, the general equilibrium critique reinforces the caution suggested by the other critiques." Amen, one is tempted to say.

Be that as it may, Krugman insists that the difficulty – or impossibility, we may add – of formulating the correct policy is not a "defense of free trade." However, he thinks that it is possible to make "a political economy case for free trade," as distinguished from the purely economic case made by traditional trade theorists.[7]

There are two political economy arguments for free trade. The first is the risk of retaliation and trade wars. Every protectionist move risks retaliation, but in the case of strategic policy protection, the risk is very high, because the country in effect tells its trade partners: "We restrict imports from you in order to shift excess profits from your firms to ours." That clearly makes retaliation almost inevitable.

To guard against this danger, Krugman suggests that some simple rule of behavior should be agreed on. Free trade is such a rule. True, the new "theory suggests that [free trade] is unlikely to be the best of all conceivable rules." But since "it is very difficult to come up with any simple rule that would be better, there is a reasonable case for continuing to use free trade as a focal point for international agreement to prevent trade war." Fine, but what is then left of the strategic trade policy?

Krugman's second political economy argument for free trade comes under the heading "Domestic Politics." "Governments do not necessarily act in the national interest . . . Instead, they are influenced by interest group pressures. The kinds of interventions that the new trade theory suggests . . . will typically raise the welfare of small, fortunate groups by large amounts, while imposing costs on larger, more diffuse groups. The result . . . can easily be that excessive or misguided intervention takes place because the beneficiaries have more knowledge and influence than the losers . . . How do we resolve the problem?" The answer, he suggests, "is to establish a blanket policy of free trade, with exceptions granted only under extreme pressure, [that] may not be the best policy that the country is likely to get." Again – what is left of strategic trade policy?

In his last section, "The Status of Free Trade," Krugman comes out strongly for free trade. His last words are: "Free trade is not passé – but it is not what it once was."

What, then, is the difference between the old and the new doctrine? I take it for granted that the proponents of the new doctrine agree that the international division of labor along the line of comparative advantage is enormously important and we have seen that traditional economists are fully aware of the importance of increasing returns to scale. On the relative importance of the two factors the opinion of the two groups may differ. I confine myself to saying that the answer depends on how many monopolies or oligopolies remain after free trade has whittled them down.

It will be said that the difference between the old and the new creed is that for the former free trade is the best policy while for the latter free trade is merely a second best. For them the best policy is a policy of active strategic protection. Only if governments are weak and too much under the pressure of special interests to conduct a policy of "sophisticated intervention" – only then can the free trade rule be defended as a second-best.

Actually, there is no difference here between the old and the new creed. The traditional trade theorist, too, knows that there are theoretically valid arguments for protection – the external economies argument and the optimum tariff argument. The latter is akin to the strategic protection argument, because it too is a beggar-thy-neighbor argument that invites retaliation and can lead to trade wars. The classical infant industry argument was dealt a severe blow in Robert Baldwin's reappraisal.[8]

I repeat what I said earlier, the only thing that is new in the "new" economics is that it has added another item to the list of arguments for protection, namely the alleged possibility of shifting "excess" returns or profits from foreign to domestic firms. The appraisal of the new economics must then depend on our judgement about the new importance of this new item.

My conclusion is that it is a very weak argument for protection. We have seen that Krugman himself mentions several serious difficulties of strategic import restrictions which makes one wonder what is left of it. All that applies with equal force, sometimes even with greater force, to strategic subsidies. Retaliation is a good example. It is easier to respond to subsidies of a foreign country by imposing countervailing import duties than to respond to foreign import restrictions.

All this leads Krugman in the end to a strong endorsement of free trade. "Free trade is not passé." Krugman starts his last paragraph by saying "it is possible, then, both to believe that comparative advantage is an incomplete model of trade and to believe that free trade is nevertheless the right policy." Absolutely true. Who would doubt it?

I repeat, all that is new in the "new" economics is to have added one more item to the list of theoretically possible exceptions to the free trade rule, to wit the possibility of shifting, under certain circumstances, excess profits from foreign to domestic firms. But as Krugman himself has shown, this in practice is of very dubious value and should be ignored: "Free trade is still the right policy."

However, all that does not mean that there is nothing the government can and should do to help industry to do better in the world market. On the contrary, in all countries, also in the United States, there is a lot to do in the domestic area to foster innovation and entrepreneurship, for example in the area of education and industrial R&D, removing restrictions and rigidities in the labor market and elsewhere, not to mention taxation and macroeconomic policies. In brief, governments should concentrate on their own functions, which are of vital importance for prosperity and growth of the whole economy. Governments should not squander their limited human and material resources on such dubious policies as strategic and other kinds of protection.

Notes

1 "Liberal and Illiberal Trade Policy: The Messy World of the Second Best," in Wietze Eizensa, E. Frans Limburg and Jacques J. Polak (eds), *The Quest for National and Global Economic Stability*, The Netherlands: Kluwer Academic Publishers and Cambridge, Mass.: MIT Press, 1988, and the "Introduction" in Gottfried Haberler (ed.), *International Trade and Economic Development*, San Francisco, Calif.: International Center for Economic Growth, 1988.

2 Robert E. Baldwin, "The Case Against Infant Industry Tariff Protection," *Journal of Political Economy*, May–June 1969, 77, 295–305, gives a masterly criticism of different versions from Alexander Hamilton and Friedrich List to Gunnar Myrdal and Paul Rosenstein-Rodan.

3   I list some publications which I have found especially useful. Gene M. Grossman and J. David Richardson, "Strategic Trade Policy: A Survey of Issues and Early Analysis," *Special Papers in International Economics*, No. 15, Princeton, NJ: Princeton University Press, 1985. Paul R. Krugman, "Strategic Sectors and International Competition" in Robert M. Stern (ed.), *US Trade Policies in a Changing World Economy*. Cambridge, Mass.: MIT Press, 1987. Elhanan Helpman and Paul R. Krugman, *Market Structure and Foreign Trade: Increasing Returns, Imperfect Competition, and the International Economy*. Cambridge, Mass.: MIT Press, 1985. Paul R. Krugman (ed.), *Strategic Trade Policy and the New International Economics*. Cambridge, Mass.: MIT Press, 1986. This last is a collection of the most important papers of the new trade theory with a critical analysis by Gene M. Grossman, "Strategic Export Promotion: A Critique," pp. 47–68.

4   Paul R. Krugman, "Is Free Trade Passé?," *Journal of Economic Perspectives*, 1987, 1(2), 131–44.

5   See Paul Krugman, "Increasing Returns, Monopolistic Competition, and International Trade," in *Journal of International Economics*, 1979, 9(4), 469–79.

6   See James A. Brander and Barbara J. Spencer, "Export Subsidies and International Market Share Rivalry," *Journal of International Economics*, 1985, 18 (1), 83–100.

7   Traditional trade theorists, too, have put forward political economy arguments for free trade. See, for example, Robert E. Baldwin, "The Political Economy of Protectionism," in *Import Competition and Response*, J. N. Bhagwati (ed.), Chicago, Ill.: University of Chicago Press, 1982.

8   Robert E. Baldwin, "The Case Against Infant Industry Protection," *Journal of Political Economy*, May–June 1969, 77, 295–305.

3

The Role of Services in Production and International Trade: A Theoretical Framework

RONALD W. JONES AND HENRYK KIERZKOWSKI

1 Introduction

International trade in services is currently the subject of intense scrutiny among academics. Whereas most contemporary discussions of services attempt to uncover an all-encompassing definition of tertiary activities, in the present paper we deliberately avoid this issue, asking instead what services do. We share in common with other observers the conviction that it is important to liberalize regulations covering services and international trade, but depart from the dominant focus on establishing the determinants of comparative advantage in services. Instead of trying to ascertain which countries will end up exporting or providing services, we concentrate on the manner in which developments in the service sector have encouraged and promoted the general level of international trade in goods.

In asking what services do, we acknowledge the importance of retail activities in facilitating the absorption of the nation's output by its consumers. Other activities, such as those provided by the medical and legal professions, link in a more direct fashion producers and consumers of services. In the present paper we shift attention from these consumption activities to the way in which services are involved in the production process. Two key concepts are introduced: *production blocks* and *service links*. The paper discusses how, with growth of a firm's output level, increasing returns and the advantages of specialization of factors within the firm encourage a switch to a production process with *fragmented* production blocks connected by service links. These links, bundles of activities consisting of coordination, administration, transportation, and financial services, are increasingly demanded when the fragmentation of the production process allows joint use of production blocks located in different regions.

Such fragmentation spills over to international markets. The greater disparity in productivities and factor prices found between countries (as compared to within a country) may encourage, via the Ricardian doctrine of comparative advantage, the use of several international locations for production blocks comprising a given production process. This dispersion is aided and abetted by the possible existence of increasing returns within production blocks.

It seems to us that one of the stylized facts characterizing recent developments in world trade is the fall in relative prices of many services, especially those found in the transportation and communication sectors.[1] This relative price change further encourages the process of fragmentation, whereby increasing use is made of disparate locations in which parts of the production process take place, with more intensive use required of connecting service links. Furthermore, it can be argued that technological advances in the provision of services lower especially the relative costs of international coordination and communication. As services become cheaper, service links at the international level become more frequently and intensively utilized as integral ingredients in the production process.

Section 2 introduces our framework in the context of an economy trading only final commodities. The use which can be made of international markets earlier in the production process and the importance of recent developments in major service industries is spelled out in more detail in sections 3 and 4. In section 5 we relate our framework to Vernon's concept of the product cycle (1966), the importance of national and international returns to scale analyzed in two basic papers by Ethier (1979, 1982), as well as to a recent contribution by Markusen (1986) applying Ethier's model to the issue of trade in services. In our concluding section we discuss a number of policy issues: liberalization under the Uruguay Round, fragmentation and North–South trade, and the role of government policies in influencing absolute advantage and attracting internationally mobile service inputs.

2 Services in the process of expansion and fragmentation

Our framework is best revealed by considering an initial early stage in a production process, in which an integrated activity exists in a single location. Figure 3.1a depicts this early mode as a single *production block*. Service inputs are not absent at this early stage; they are required to coordinate activities within the production block as well as to connect production and consumption via distribution and marketing operations.

We assume that technology within the production block contains elements of increasing returns to scale. Although such scale economies may take many forms, we shall assume in our diagrammatic exposition that productive activities require fixed, or set-up, costs, and that marginal costs of operation are constant. Thus in figure 3.2, line 1 depicts the manner in which total costs expand with scale of output. Vertical intercept Oa represents set-up and other fixed costs associated with the production block while the slope of line 1 shows marginal costs of the production run.

As production expands, alternative techniques embodying a greater

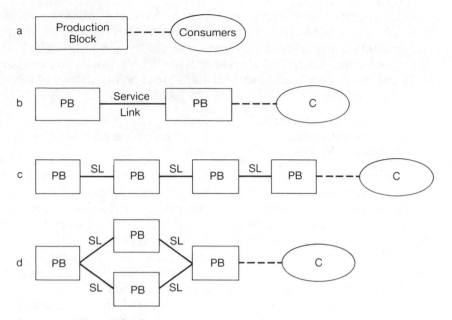

Figure 3.1   The production process

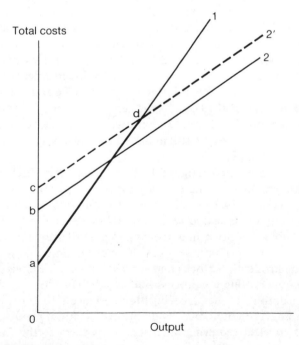

Figure 3.2   Total costs and output

division of labor may emerge as superior. Increased specialization of productive tasks and division of labor of the kind envisaged as early as Adam Smith could result in a *fragmentation* of the production block as illustrated in figure 3.1b. In his classic presidential address, Allyn Young in 1928 emphasized the importance of Smith's views on the division of labor and remarked that

> . . . over a large part of the field of industry an increasingly intricate nexus of specialized undertakings has inserted itself between the producer of raw materials and the consumer of the final product. (p. 538)

We assume that such fragmentation alters the trade-off between fixed and variable costs; lower marginal costs of output are obtained at the expense of a greater total sum of fixed costs in the pair of production blocks. An illustration of the relationship between total costs and output for this fragmented technology is depicted by line 2 in figure 3.2.

At this stage a new role emerges for service activities. The two production blocks pictured in figure 3.1b need to be co-ordinated and linked by use of service resources. The activities of the two production blocks cannot be combined without cost. *Service links* are required to join *production blocks*. These may include transportation costs if the separate physical locations of production blocks warrant. At the minimum, there is a need to plan and synchronize the two streams of production with respect to timing, size and quality. These service links represent inputs additional to any service resources required within each production block. The total costs of production with fragmented technology, represented by line 2 in figure 3.2, need to be augmented by the costs of the service link joining the two production blocks (to yield total cost line 2′). In figure 3.2 we have illustrated these service costs as being somewhat independent of the scale of output (the vertical intercept is shifted from Ob to Oc and line 2′ is parallel to line 2). However, if the costs of the service link are driven up with the level of production, line 2′ could be drawn steeper than line 2. Marginal costs inclusive of services are still assumed to be lower than with the more concentrated techniques (1).

The process represented in figure 3.2 can be repeated to higher orders (see figure 3.3a), creating an increasing number of production blocks and connecting service links. Indeed, the process of industrial development has been historically documented to be one of increasing specialization and division of labor, resulting in a growing degree of fragmentation and an increasing role for producer services. Numerous patterns of interdependence among production blocks and service links can be envisaged. Figure 3.1c represents a production process whereby each production block utilizes as inputs the outputs of the preceding block. Figure 3.1d illustrates an alternative grouping: the simultaneous operation of a pair of production blocks, the outputs of each requiring an assembly process at the final stage of fabrication.

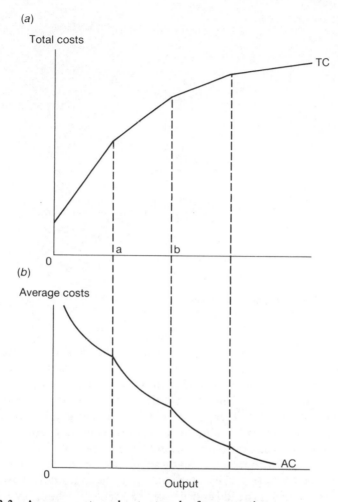

Figure 3.3   Average costs and output under fragmentation

This process of development, as illustrated in figure 3.3 over several stages of fragmentation, embodies two sources contributing to continuously decreasing average costs. For any degree of fragmentation the combination of fixed costs and (fairly) constant marginal costs within production blocks (coupled with a relatively heavy fixed cost component in each service link) ensures that average costs decline with output. This rate of decline is accelerated at every point at which a switch is made to technologies incorporating a higher degree of fragmentation.

Figure 3.4 illustrates the dependence of marginal cost upon output as production growth encourages a switch to more fragmented technologies. Assuming production remains within the confines of a single firm and that

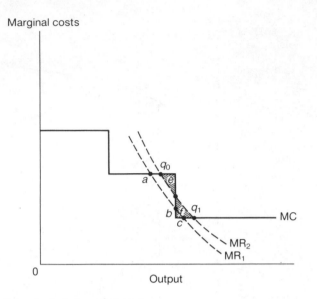

Figure 3.4   Marginal costs and output

market demand is less than infinitely elastic, the firm would maximize profits by selecting an output level at which marginal revenue equals marginal costs. However, there may be multiple intersections for any given marginal revenue curve. Consider that demand has grown sufficiently to support the MR_1 curve in figure 3.4. Point b shows marginal revenue equal to marginal cost, but is a point of local profit minimization – a small contraction or expansion of output would increase profits. The contenders are points a and c. Profits at a are clearly superior to those at c – a movement from a to c involves primarily marginal losses as marginal costs exceed marginal revenue with the lower order of fragmented technology, and fall short of marginal revenue only for the small stretch (from b to c) where the firm adopts the more fragmented technology.

If we envisage a smooth growth of demand, and with it an associated growth in marginal revenue schedules, at the critical MR_2 curve (when shaded area e equals area f) the firm could produce either q_0 or q_1. For a slightly higher level of demand, output level slightly exceeds q_1. The range q_0q_1 is never observed. That is, a smooth growth of demand leads to gradual transitions to more fragmented technologies, but the price drops corresponding to such transitions lead to jumps in output volumes. Such jumps are more noticeable if marginal revenue (and associated demand) are more elastic.

Little has been said so far about the role of firms and the relationship between the number of production blocks and service links and the number of firms. The idea that firms may wish to incorporate functions which might otherwise be provided less efficiently or at higher costs by market transactions has been stressed by Ronald Coase (1937) and his followers. However, the evolution of the production process, with its increasing complexity, opens up the possibility of vertical specialization and the appearance of new firms. In the limit every production block and service link might represent a separate firm. The producer of the final good located at the end of a production chain might rely completely on the market to supply necessary intermediate products and services.

The process of spinning off new firms could be reinforced if various production blocks and service links can be utilized by more than one sector, or by more than one firm producing a differentiated product in the same sector. Telecommunication services, with high fixed costs, provide a good example of an activity which would be too costly to develop by a single firm in a different industry. The firm would rely on the market. It is, on the other hand, possible that the emerging new production blocks and service links will be retained within the firm.

In our view the process of increasing fragmentation and use of service links is consistent either with patterns of development involving a greater scope of activity by a single firm or with heavier reliance upon the market to co-ordinate activities of newly emerging independent firms. For example, Stigler (1951) cites the case of the small-arms industry in Birmingham in 1860. The master gun-maker engaged in market transactions with independent manufacturers, each performing separate, differentiated tasks. An alternative is exemplified by a typical large US corporation, with its own legal department, a fleet of corporate jets, publishing facilities and an internal transportation network. Even such a large corporation, however, is likely to rely on the market for some major inputs such as tele-communications and financial services.

Fragmentation involves extra costs. Recently firms have become more aware of how expensive it is to hold inventories. "Just-in-time" technology has been shown to be effective in holding down production costs.[2] Improvements in computer technology and telecommunication have allowed a greater degree of reliability of deliveries and synchronization of output streams required by "just-in-time" inventories strategy.

3 International markets and the production process

International markets have not been excluded from the account of the development process described in the preceding section. Heretofore we assumed that goods appearing at the completion of the production process were traded on world markets, but that intermediate products and service inputs were not. The array of goods selected for production at home already reflected positions of comparative advantage and the further bias towards concentration encouraged by increasing returns to scale. As compared with complete autarky, the extent of specialization brought about by allowing free trade in final goods itself promotes welfare gains; the cut-back in the number of different production processes undertaken allows a higher degree of fragmentation in each.

The new possibility for international trade which we now wish to consider involves the role of services in linking production blocks across national boundaries. If the assumed overall position of comparative advantage in a particular good does not imply lower national costs for each production block and service link used, efficient production processes may involve a mixture of domestic and foreign activities. Recent developments in the world automobile industry have encouraged widespread trade in components. For example, in 1986 Japan ran a surplus in car-components trade with the United States to the tune of $5.6 billion. Bosch of West Germany has captured 75 percent of the world market for anti-lock braking systems.[3] In 1983 around 60 percent of imports and exports for the United States and the Economic Community consisted of intermediate goods; consumer goods and capital goods counted for roughly 20 percent and 10 percent, respectively.[4]

Figure 3.5 displays cost comparisons for the same degree of fragmentation – two production blocks connected by a service link. Line *H* shows fixed and variable costs when both production blocks are located at

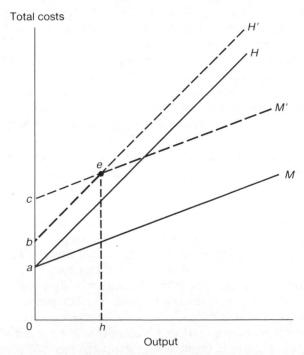

Figure 3.5   Total costs and output: effect of foreign service links

home, and H' adds in the costs of the required service link. Suppose that in comparing each production block separately, the foreign country would have a lower marginal cost for the second block and the home country for the first. The combination of home first production block and foreign second block is represented by line M, and we assume the same fixed costs are involved as for line H. However, we also assume that the service costs of linking a domestic and a foreign production block are greater than those required if both blocks are nationally based. (In figure 3.5 distance ca exceeds distance ba.) The possibility of service inputs linking internationally dispersed production units lowers the best cost-output line from beH' (i.e. line H') to broken line beM'.

In our framework, production blocks are each located entirely at a single location, but service links may involve inputs from more than one country, or, indeed, inputs from a third country. (Lloyd's of London could provide insurance for shipments of automobile parts from Canada to the United States.) In our illustration (figure 3.5), we have assumed that the fixed costs associated with domestic production blocks are equivalent to those found abroad. This assumption was purely arbitrary. If the foreign country possesses a cost advantage in the second production block, it might have been embodied in elements of fixed costs as much as in variable costs. What is less arbitrary is the assumption that the service costs of linking production blocks in more than one country exceed those involved in purely domestic links. However, even in this respect there could be exceptions. In the case of Canada, for example, connecting production blocks in British Columbia and Ontario may involve higher-priced service links, e.g. transportation, than required for British Columbia and the State of Washington.

Further insights into the manner in which international trade involving fragmented production blocks yields extra gains to producers can be obtained by looking at two basic models of trade, viz. Ricardo and Heckscher–Ohlin.

(i) A Ricardian framework:

In the Ricardian context suppose that initially the home country uses two production blocks with the marginal labor input coefficients in each block denoted by a_{Li}. (Comparable input coefficients abroad are denoted by a_{Li}^*). Assume that units of output in the two blocks must be matched one-for-one to obtain a unit of final output. Further assume that fixed costs within production blocks and between countries are identical. If no trade in producer components were allowed, let us assume that the home country possesses an overall comparative advantage in producing this commodity. Letting w and w^* represent wage rates in the two countries, such a ranking according to comparative advantage implies that:

$$\frac{a_{L1}^* + a_{L2}^*}{a_{L1} + a_{L2}} > \frac{w}{w^*}.$$

Our assumption of the foreign country's superiority in the second block, and the home country's in the first block, is captured by the Ricardian inequality,

$$\frac{a_{L1}^*}{a_{L1}} > \frac{w}{w^*} > \frac{a_{L2}^*}{a_{L2}}.$$

Allowing the foreign country to take over production of the second block would lower marginal costs and thus allow gains. For such rationalization of production to be undertaken, the scale of output would have to be large enough for lower variable costs to outweigh the extra costs of international service links.

(ii) A Heckscher–Ohlin model:

Whereas a Ricardian framework allows us to focus on the possibility that the relative efficiency of labor varies among countries and commodities and, further, from one production block to another, a Heckscher–Ohlin framework recognizes the use of many factors in the production process. The factor intensities required in one production block may differ from those in another. (We ignore, here, the further possibility that service links as well require factor proportions which might differ from country to country. Indeed, one possibility is that service links are provided by the lowest-cost source in world markets.)

To take an example, suppose that the first of a two-part fragmented technology for producing a certain commodity is more capital intensive than the second. Factor endowments differ between countries, and suppose the foreign country is relatively so well endowed with labor that even with free trade allowed in parts of the production process factor prices are not equalized. If international service links can be forged, relatively cheap labor abroad and cheap capital at home could establish the basis for an internationally mixed production process. The international market place, with its variety of factor productivities (Ricardo) and factor prices and factor intensities (Heckscher–Ohlin) provides the richer possibilities associated with trade in production blocks according to comparative advantage to add gains to those associated with increasing returns and fragmentation as the scale of output expands.

The hypothetical comparison which we have been making is between trade patterns in a world in which trade takes place only in final commodities, with each country responsible for the entire integrated production process involved in its final exports, and those in which the production process can be fragmented so that production blocks for a given final output can be located in a number of countries. If each production block is identified with only one final output and if each final output is produced in only one country, allowing trade in components of the production process could be expected to yield gains from world resource reallocation more closely corresponding to lines of comparative advantage. However, the potential for gain is even greater if final goods trade reflects a sizeable degree of intra-industry trade and/or if production blocks can in principle be used to support output of completely different industries. In such cases the existence of service activities providing international links for production blocks opens up the possibility of an even greater degree of international specialization, with concurrent gains from increasing returns to scale and greater degrees of fragmentation. The automobile example cited previously illustrates how the output of one component (antilock braking systems) can be used in a number of differentiated products. Furthermore, some service links, e.g., those exemplified by telecommunication, may be required by production blocks used in a wide variety of different industries.

Whatever the sources of comparative advantage, the possibility that separate production blocks can be dispersed in their geographical location increases the chances for less developed countries to participate to some extent in the industrialization process. In a world in which all production blocks must be located in a single country in an integrated process, less developed regions always have a comparative advantage in some commodities. But these may represent agricultural or raw-material extraction activities in which, we suppose, labor does not possess the opportunity to acquire sets of skills which are associated with certain types of learning-by-doing. The role of services in fostering the fragmentation of the production process over a number of different countries becomes important. Through such fragmentation countries may partake in some part of industrial activity even when a comparative advantage in the integrated process is still out of reach.

4 Price changes and the role of services in trade

Recent decades have witnessed a technological revolution in service sectors. This would certainly have surprised Adam Smith. The very man who brought us the concept of gains from the division of labor viewed services as being "unproductive of any value." A more muted modern view would still claim that services tend to get left behind in society's steady march on the technological front. The source for such a view stems in large part from identifying service activities as extremely labor intensive. Furthermore, services tend to be associated with sheltered non-traded sectors.[5]

The type of inputs required for service links in the production process shares few of these characteristics. Foremost among these inputs must be ranked telecommunications and financial services. Rapid technological change has increased the ease and reduced the cost of linking different production blocks. Furthermore, domestic deregulation pursued by governments in countries such as the United States, Canada, and the United Kingdom has accelerated the pace of these cost reductions.

Economies in the cost of providing service links promote the process of fragmentation. Total production costs fall for any given level of output, and a switch to a more diversified production process can be attained at lower levels of output. This is illustrated in figure 3.2. Lower service costs shift line 2' downwards, moving switch-point d south-westwards along line 1.

We would argue that the type of technological breakthrough and innovation that has characterized sectors such as telecommunications, transportation and financial services has had especially pronounced effects in reducing the relative costs of *international* service links. A bank manager in New York can communicate with an associate in Hong Kong as rapidly and almost as cheaply as he can with a colleague in Chicago. National boundaries scarcely impede transmission of large bodies of data. By utilizing recent innovations such as FAX machines, a fashion designer in Paris can transmit graphic details and instructions to cutting-room floors in Taipei instantly and at a fraction of the costs of international courier service.

The clothing industry provides an interesting example of how relative costs, reliability and speed of providing service links influence the internationalization of the production process. Spurred by the US offshore assembly (807) scheme, the American textile industry profited from a finer international division of labor by reallocating some production stages to developing countries. As pointed out by Morawetz (1981), Colombia and several Far East Asian countries were in direct competition for the task of assembling fabrics which had been cut in the United States. Colombia was a winner in this competition in the early 1970s, with the outcome largely determined by its favorable geographical location which resulted in relatively low costs of airfreight and telecommunications service links. Morawetz points out that ill-advised national macro and exchange rate policies soon reversed the Colombian cost advantage. In any case, technological advances in transportation and telecommunications since that time have done much to remove the advantage which proximity to markets brings.

Service links have benefited from learning-by-doing at the international level. Decades of rapid growth of international trade and expansion of foreign investment resulted in an accumulation of a wealth of knowledge about foreign countries, their markets, and their political systems. Business firms are especially concerned with property rights and procedures for contract enforcement available to non-nationals. The legal climate in which international transactions are undertaken now seems less hostile and more predictable. As a consequence of these developments, the scope for international participation and interpenetration of markets at the production level has been greatly expanded. The reduction in the cost of services generally has fostered increased fragmentation and division of labor in production; the greater relative cost reductions for services linking international operations have had a profound effect in stimulating the use of international markets at every stage of the production process. This, we would claim, is the primary connection between services and international trade. One of the stylized facts of international commerce is the increasingly large share of trade represented by exchanges of producer goods and middle products.

We would further argue that the reduction of uncertainty regarding foreign production activities and the greater reliability provided by international service links are especially important in encouraging trade within the production process. The precision of delivery dates, for example, is of much more concern to producers weighing the possibility of repeated reliance on foreign components than it is to individuals who are engaged in one-shot purchases of the final consumer good.

Just as in the domestic sphere, we emphasize that the process of increasing fragmentation and use of international markets does not preclude a variety of organizational structures for firms. Although it may be in the firm's interest to avoid arms-length international transactions in favor of establishing a multinational presence, our framework encompasses as well interconnected production processes involving many firms. Certainly many of the service links could be provided by outside suppliers, perhaps some of them multinationals in their own right.

5 Comparisons with existing models

Currently it is fashionable in discussions of international trade theory to elevate the phenomenon of increasing returns to scale to a level of importance at least equal to that of comparative advantage in explaining sources of gains from trade. We have described a framework which highlights the role of services in encouraging international trade. In this framework the traditional grounds for international trade based on the doctrine of comparative advantage have been supplemented by two ways in which production processes exhibit decreasing costs. Our treatment of increasing returns to scale owes much to Ethier's (1979, 1982) fundamental papers. However, we have pursued a less formal modelling strategy and differ in the manner in which we interpret the relationship between international trade and increasing returns.

National increasing returns to scale in Ethier's 1982 paper are embodied in cost functions which relate bundles of factors linearly to levels of national output. These functions can be interpreted as combining elements of fixed and variable costs, a procedure we adopted in modelling increasing returns within a production block.[6] Each such process yields as output a "component" which differs from any other "component," albeit produced in an entirely symmetrical fashion. These components, some of which (in a trading context) will be produced abroad, are combined in a production function for "finished manufactures" which allows for increasing returns from the use of a larger array of components. The form of this latter function is similar to that presented by Dixit and Stiglitz (1977) in a different context – one showing how an individual can benefit from having access to a wider variety of consumer goods.[7] Ethier's production function for finished manufactures expresses what he labels international returns to scale.

There is no analog in Ethier's formulation to the role of services in linking production blocks, with or without international trade. Instead, his components are costlessly assembled. International increasing returns are introduced by allowing trade in components, thereby increasing the variety of components available to any given producer at any output level. By stark contrast, in our framework it is an expansion in the scale of output encouraged by growth in demand (whether domestic or international) which leads to an increased degree of fragmentation in the production process. The consequences of opening trade in producer components in our model and in Ethier's are thus fundamentally different. In the Ethier formulation, producers seize upon the possibility of utilizing a greater variety of components in order to expand output because his international increasing returns depend on the extent of variety and not, as in our treatment, on the scale of output and the attendant degree of fragmentation. In our framework the potential for international dispersion of production blocks, made possible by connecting service links, yields gains to the extent that a finer degree of disaggregation and specialization according to comparative advantage results in traditional fashion in greater efficiency in resource allocation. This is a feature absent in Ethier's model.

Markusen (1986) builds directly upon the Ethier framework in his discussion of services and trade. If trade in producer goods is allowed, it *must* be trade in services, for the "components" in the Ethier model are redefined as producer services. This interpretation of the role of services differs sharply from ours. In our treatment services may or may not be traded; their main function in trade is in allowing fragmentation over production blocks located both at home and abroad.

Some of the concepts underlying the "product cycle" introduced by Ray Vernon (1966) are present in our formulation. Early stages in the cycle of development of a product are located in a country having available a host of potentially usable factors and skills, because the techniques required in product development are still uncertain. As this uncertainty is resolved, and production techniques simplified, the location of production may shift abroad if a foreign source has a comparative advantage with the new, simplified, techniques.[8] As in our treatment, Vernon allows for the international relocation of a production process. Missing, however, is the same use of comparative advantage to argue that *part* of the production process be located at home and part abroad. Our framework, focusing on the development of separate production blocks connected by service links, opens up a scenario in which the production process can be finely divided into stages. The international location of each block (or stage) is heavily influenced by international comparisons of factor prices and productivities, with the scale of output indicating the extent to which the entire process can be fragmented.

6 Concluding remarks

Our framework can shed some light on issues under discussion in the Uruguay Round and in particular on consequences of international trade liberalization in services for North–South trade. Countries such as India and Brazil have expressed fears that comparative advantage in service activities resides in more highly developed countries. Even if one is willing to assume that the most efficient providers of service links are all located in the developed countries, it has to be realized that liberalization of services and a subsequent fragmentation of production could result in a finer international division of labor in which developing countries could actively share. Certain production blocks, especially the ones requiring labor-intensive techniques, could be more cheaply produced in LDCs. The gains from liberalization of trade in services would then manifest themselves in a greater participation of developing countries in goods trade. It is therefore important that the participants in the Uruguay Round see gains and losses in the overall context rather than in the context of service sectors alone.

Consider the position of a country which does not have a comparative advantage in supplying services on the world market. What should its stance be towards negotiations aimed at liberalizing service trade? We have already emphasized that such a country's export activities can gain by virtue of less expensive service links which allow some production blocks within the country to be made part of an international production process. Furthermore, the literature on the Dutch Disease alerts us to the consequences for trade in traditional export sectors of technological progress in one sector – in this case a service sector. If services become freely tradeable, they are available not only in the source country but in others as well. However, the extra activity in the source country could, by raising wage rates or other input prices, hurt the relative international position of other industries in the source country compared with similar industries abroad. That is, less developed countries may think they will not succeed in the competition for internationally liberated service activities, but as consumers they may have relatively more to gain in service-using sectors than do the developed countries.[9]

Even if trade in services is opened up, a less developed country may deal with outside service activities more harshly relative to other countries vis-à-vis domestic regulations (e.g., concerning banking or the financial sector) or levels of taxation or of uncertainty in terms of governmental attitudes towards private business activity within its borders. Here it is important to emphasize that differences between nations in governmental policies, domestic regulations and levels of taxation all bear upon patterns of international trade in a manner which is absent if international exchange is limited to final consumer goods. Trade in the latter instance is governed by comparative advantage; high business taxes, for example, may hit all local activities fairly evenly and thus not affect the comparatively best assignment of resources and factors which are trapped behind a nation's boundaries. But once trade seeps down into factors and inputs utilized in the production process, *absolute* levels of government interference bear upon the ability of one country's production blocks to come in at a lower cost than those of another country. The traditional question, what should a nation's own immobile resources do (answered by criteria of comparative advantage), needs to be supplemented by asking where internationally mobile service inputs are employed (answered in part by criteria of relative attractiveness of one country versus another as a stable locale to host internationally connected productive activities).[10]

We conclude by emphasizing what we stated at the outset. We are concentrating on one of the things which services *do* in the production process: Service links have the function of connecting production blocks in separate locations, perhaps among several countries. But other roles are available for services. Aside from those mentioned earlier, whereby services are utilized within production blocks and aid in marketing the product for consumption, we should note the role of services in research and development. More broadly interpreted, services may be used to explore future possibilities for fragmentation and re-alignments within the production process, in a manner going beyond their operational role in bilaterally linking pairs of production blocks. In all these uses, services are important for the manner in which international commerce is encouraged, whatever their direct status in trade.

Notes

This project has been undertaken under the auspices of the Institute for Research on Public Policy (IRPP), supported by a research grant from the Department of Regional Industrial Expansion (DRIE), Government of Canada. The authors wish to thank Elias Dinopoulos, Howard Gruenspecht, Douglas Irwin, Ulrich Kohli, Anne Krueger, Gustav Ranis, John Richardson, Paul Romer, Frances Ruane, and Frances Stewart for helpful comments. Jones's research was supported in part by the National Science Foundation Grant No. SES 8510697.

1   Transport costs have been steadily declining for decades. North (1958) cites ocean freight costs in 1910 as one-thirtieth of their level in 1800.

2 For an alternative view of the significance of "just-in-time" technology see Kumpe and Bolwijn (1988).
3 These figures come from the *Economist*, December 17, 1987, p. 57.
4 These figures are cited by Kol (1987).
5 See Balassa (1964) and Bhagwati (1984), as well as the literature on the so-called Scandinavian model of inflation.
6 Earlier use of this simple method of capturing increasing returns to scale can be found in Krugman (1979).
7 Romer (1987) gives a continuum version of the Dixit–Stiglitz function and applies it to growth in a closed-economy context.
8 It is perhaps tempting to use the Dixit–Stiglitz formulation to model the advantages which having a wide array of productive factors available conveys when uncertainty exists as to technology.
9 This argument is described in further detail in Jones, Neary, and Ruane (1987).
10 This issue is discussed in more detail in Jones (1980).

References

Balassa, Bela 1964: "The Purchasing-Power Parity Doctrine: A Reapparaisal," *Journal of Political Economy*, LXII(6), 584–96.
Bhagwati, Jagdish 1984: "Why are Services Cheaper in the Poor Countries?," *Economic Journal*, 94, 279–88.
Coase, Ronald 1937: "The Nature of the Firm," *Economica*, 4, 386–405.
Dixit, Avinash and Stiglitz Joseph 1977: "Monopolistic Competition and Optimal Product Diversity," *American Economic Review*, 67 (June), 297–308.
Ethier, Wilfred J. 1979: "Internationally Decreasing Costs and World Trade," *Journal of International Economics*, 9, 1–24.
Ethier, Wilfred J. 1982: "National and International Returns to Scale in the Modern Theory of International Trade," *American Economic Review*, 72(3), 389–405.
Jones, Ronald W. 1980: "Comparative and Absolute Advantage," *Swiss Journal of Economics*, 3, 235–60.
Jones, Ronald, Neary, J. P., and Ruane, F. 1987: "International Capital Mobility and the Dutch Disease," in Henryk Kierzkowski (ed.), *Protection and Competition in International Trade*, Oxford: Basil Blackwell.
Kol, Jacob 1987: "Allyn Young Specialization and Intermediate Goods in International Trade," Mimeo.
Krugman, Paul 1979: "Increasing Returns, Monopolistic Competition, and International Trade," *Journal of International Economics*, 9(4), 469–79.
Kumpe, Ted and Bolwijn, Piet 1988: "Manufacturing: The New Case for Vertical Integration," *Harvard Business Review*, March–April, 75–81.
Markusen, James R. 1986: "Trade in Producer Services: Issues Involving Returns to Scale and the International Division of Labor," Discussion Paper, Series on Trade in Services, The Institute for Research on Public Policy.
Morawetz, David 1981: *Why the Emperor's New Clothes are Not Made in Colombia*. Oxford: Oxford University Press.
North, Doug 1958: "Ocean Freight Rates and Economic Development 1750–1913," *Journal of Economic History*, 18(4), 537–55.

Romer, Paul 1987: "Growth Based on Increasing Returns Due to Specialization," *American Economic Review*, 77 (May), 56–62.

Stigler, George 1951: "The Division of Labor is Limited by the Extent of the Market," *Journal of Political Economy*, 59(3), 185–93.

Vernon, Ray 1966: "International Investment and International Trade in the Product Cycle," *Quarterly Journal of Economics*, 80, 190–207.

Young, Allyn 1928: "Increasing Returns and Economic Progress," *Economic Journal*, 38 (Dec.), 527–42.

4

The Coefficient of Trade Utilization: Back to the Baldwin Envelope

JAMES E. ANDERSON AND J. PETER NEARY

Quantitative restrictions have become the principal means of trade distortion in developed countries in the last 30 years. The vast literature on the measurement of trade inefficiency has nevertheless focused almost exclusively on tariffs. Treatment of quotas[1] is basically an afterthought, covered by equivalence. The theoretical foundation for the usual measure is the expenditure function. Its value has the welfare interpretation of a lump sum transfer of income and its arguments are prices. In this essay we propose a more appropriate measure, the *coefficient of trade utilization*. Its value has the welfare interpretation of a lump sum transfer of quota licenses and its arguments are quantities. The coefficient of trade utilization is in the class of distance function measures (Debreu, 1951; Deaton, 1979) extended to close the general equilibrium. It is the natural approach to the contemporary situation in developed countries where quotas are the main ingredients of protection, is simpler to use, and has numerous operational implications for the evaluation of trade reform and of growth in the presence of fixed trade policy. We present some of the principal trade reform results of our companion paper (1988) below.

The subject matter of this paper is especially appropriate in a collection of essays honoring Robert Baldwin. He has been a leading figure in documenting the rise of quantitative restrictions (1971), and has spent much of his career advising on and evaluating trade reform. Moreover, his best-known analytic contribution, the Baldwin envelope (1948), is, like ours, a tool which focuses on quantity rather than price space. We show below how its depiction of the set of maximum attainable consumption bundles given foreign behavior can be related to distance function concepts appropriate to a trade reform. Baldwin's focus on treating the opportunity to trade as an alternative technology is captured in our treatment. A useful parallel is that the rate of change of the coefficient of trade utilization is conceptually akin to the rate of change of total factor productivity used in growth accounting.

The new measure has both theoretical and practical advantages over the standard approach in a quota-ridden world. In practice, investigators analyze discrete changes in policy with a potentially erroneous conversion of the quota to tariff equivalence. Any correct version of welfare measurement must at least implicitly use the coefficient of trade utilization because its derivatives are always the correct shadow prices of quotas, which must be integrated over the interval of change. The conceptual steps leading to the appropriate treatment of quotas with expenditure function methods are slippery and some investigators have fallen. The coefficient of trade utilization also may have a practical element of superiority in reduced information requirements for its rate of change form. This is certainly true when the trade control system approaches being a pure import quota system, with rents retained at home. Reduced information requirements are especially useful in allowing a feasible emphasis on the inefficiency of the detailed mis-allocation of resources involved in quota systems.[2] Standard methods impose a high degree of aggregation due to the infeasibility of calculating a large number of demand parameters.

Theoretically, the new measure has advantages in interpretation. The standard measure of inefficiency is a compensating variation in income, assumed to be collectible (payable) as a lump sum. This is a convention of such long standing in public finance that it is difficult to remember how artificial it is to assume the presence of an implicit extra instrument, the lump-sum transfer. The representative consumer analysis shared by both approaches is sustained by background transfers between dissimilar consumers; but the coefficient of trade utilization has the virtue of working exclusively with the actual instruments of distortion, hence it implicitly achieves the transfers by assignment of the quota rights. A related advantage is that the coefficient of trade utilization is appropriately scaled by trade; whereas the usual compensating variation is scaled by total expenditure, necessarily implying trivial proportionate changes. Some investigators find it expedient to report the compensation measure scaled by base expenditure in the controlled category; the coefficient of trade utiliza-tion is the rigorously based counterpart to this procedure.

The quota reform theorems we state to illustrate uses of the new concept are substantial extensions of the quota reform theorems of Corden and Falvey (1985) to allow for international sharing of the rent. They show that if pure import quotas (100 percent rent retention) are the only means of protection, all quota increases are welfare improving.[3] If rent is shared, however, the domestic prices of quota-constrained goods will change, which alters the amount of rent transferred abroad. Our approach shows that nevertheless the Corden–Falvey result goes through under implicit separability between the quota goods and the remaining goods. We also give useful expansions for the case where some quotas decrease, and where some non-quota goods have tariffs.

I Outline of the paper

The subtitle of this essay is "Back to the Baldwin Envelope," and is the organizing theme relating our work to the earlier literature.

Part II first develops the consumption space analysis where imports and domestic goods are perfect substitutes, the subject of Baldwin's original analysis. Inefficiency can result from domestic distortions which drive production below the domestic frontier, from wedges between the marginal cost of imports and their marginal production cost, or from transfers of quota rent. This paper is concerned only with the latter two, and it is very convenient to shift the analysis to the trade space, since this is the space of the instruments. For the small country case of constant marginal cost of imports, the main focus of the present paper,[4] a pure import quota (with 100 percent rent retention) does not shift a country off the Baldwin frontier, since it does not change the equality of foreign and domestic prices which are parametric to the Baldwin problem. Pure import quotas are a rarity, however, with the norm being a mixed instrument in which the rent is shared. The empirically very significant inefficiency due to rent transfer is analyzed in terms of the *coefficient of rent utilization*, the fraction of frontier consumption of the import good which is achieved by the initial bundle.

The remainder of the paper works in trade space with two additional inefficiencies of distorted trade. For trade in final goods we add a consideration of the exchange inefficiency (operation at the wrong point on the Baldwin frontier). For trade in inputs, quotas result in inefficient production, hence operation off the Baldwin frontier. Either case closes the analysis by endogenizing the domestic prices of the quota-constrained goods. For trade in final goods in part III we measure the proportionate expansion from an initial bundle to a Meade trade indifference curve in the subspace of controlled trade. Following the results of our companion paper (1988) reviewed in appendix 4.1 we develop the general equilibrium reduced form budget constraint which supports the reduced form trade utility level and derive the shadow price of a quota. It is the unit quota rent retained at home plus two additional terms involving respectively the marginal revenue gained from less rent transfer abroad and the marginal tariff revenue lost from taxed non-quota goods. For a pure import quota system the latter terms are zero. Shadow prices are associated with distance functions, so on this base we build an operational general equilibrium distance measure of trade inefficiency, the *coefficient of trade utilization*.

Part IV develops the case of trade in inputs, where the imported inputs are subject to quotas. The coefficient of trade utilization is the ratio of initial inputs to the inputs needed to achieve the maximal consumption on the Baldwin envelope, available with free trade. It has an entirely parallel development to part III.

Part V applies the new concept to the topic of trade reform. Section V.1 presents powerful new theorems on the direction of welfare-improving quota reform in terms of the coefficient of trade utilization.[5] Section V.2 turns to its practical application in terms of operational measures. For the case of implicit separability, the coefficient of trade utilization measure is operational, and requires less information than what appears to be required by expenditure function methods. The latter are shown to be erroneously applied in standard text treatments, with a correct version requiring use of the coefficient of trade utilization in any case.

II The Baldwin envelope and trade efficiency

Robert Baldwin's best-known analytic contribution is the Baldwin envelope of maximal consumption bundles. If all other distortions are suppressed and all controlled traded goods are final goods which are perfect substitutes for domestic goods, we have Baldwin's original case. Figure 4.1 depicts the Baldwin envelope of maximal consumption bundles given optimal utilization of both home and foreign production possibilities for the small country case. The Baldwin problem is to maximize the value of consumption at any given consumer price ratio. Maximal consumption possibilities lie on the tangent lint at E with slope equal to minus the foreign price of good 2 in terms of good 1. This tangent reflects the first-order condition of the Baldwin problem.

Inefficient trade policy results in operation below the frontier. Alternatively, trade reform can be evaluated in terms of approaching the frontier. For the small country case shown, quotas only restrict the length of the line segment achievable for consumption above or below E, such as at $\bar{Q}$. Trade remains efficient. For the large country case the foreign offer curve is placed at E (located at the maximal production income point given the domestic price), and a point like $\bar{Q}$ is not on the envelope, since it does not equate the slope of the offer curve with the slope at E; the foreign

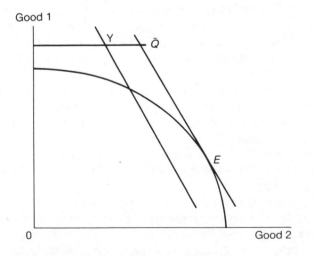

Figure 4.1 The Baldwin envelope and trade efficiency

marginal cost of imports varies with Q. A point on the foreign offer curve between $\overline{Q}$ and E will be efficient for the given prices. To find points superior to $\overline{Q}$ it is necessary to trace out the remainder of the Baldwin envelope, involving different domestic prices and the corresponding optimal settings of trade *and* domestic production. Fortunately this elaborate structure can be avoided in the small country case, and in the large country case when the market clearance link between domestic prices and trade controls is established. A trade space analysis of productive and exchange inefficiency is then possible.

Evidently a pure import quota cannot be inefficient in the Baldwin sense. But rent sharing involves a lower budget line in figure 4.1, or operation below the Baldwin frontier, such as at Y. Alternatively, trade is below the foreign offer surface in the trade space analysis. We now develop a general formulation for measuring such inefficiency.

II.1 The coefficient of rent utilization

There are two classes of traded goods, Z and Q. We suppose that only the Q goods are subject to government control. We shall follow the convention that Q denotes a scalar quantity and P a scalar price for a traded good, while $\mathbf{Q}$, $\mathbf{P}$ denote vector quantities and prices respectively. Other scalar magnitudes shall be in plain text. For simplicity we develop only the small country case of fixed foreign prices, $\mathbf{P}^*$ for the Q's and π^* for the Z's. In the vector case, $\mathbf{P}$, $\mathbf{Q}$, π, $\mathbf{Z}$, π^*, $\mathbf{P}^*$ are vectors with, for example, $\mathbf{PQ}$ denoting the inner (dot) product of the vector $\mathbf{P}$ and the vector $\mathbf{Q}$. The quota $\mathbf{Q}^0$ gives rise to total rent $[\mathbf{P} - \mathbf{P}^*]\mathbf{Q}^0$, which is split between the two nations with $\omega[\mathbf{P} - \mathbf{P}^*]\mathbf{Q}^0$ going to foreigners and $(1-\omega)[\mathbf{P} - \mathbf{P}^*]\mathbf{Q}^0$ going to home residents. This is consistent with an award of $\omega\mathbf{Q}^0$ worth of licenses to foreigners, or with a VER of $\mathbf{Q}^0$ supplemented by a vector of home specific tariffs at rate $(1 - \omega)[\mathbf{P} - \mathbf{P}^*]$, which retain $(1 - \omega)[\mathbf{P} - \mathbf{P}^*]\mathbf{Q}^0$ of the total rent.

In figure 4.2 the initial distorted trade consumption bundle lies at C on the Meade trade indifference curve U^0. The budget line supporting U^0 at domestic prices has a horizontal intercept at E with value OE = $(1 - \omega)[P - P^*]Q^0$ (in terms of Z), while the budget line through C at foreign prices has a horizontal intercept at D with value of $-\omega[P - P^*]Q^0$, representing the transfer to foreigners. The *coefficient of rent utilization* is δ = BA/BC, the ratio by which the potential consumption at A must be deflated to reach U^0. With a pure import quota, 100 percent of the rent is retained, ω equals zero, δ equals one, and trade is efficient (although exchange may not be; the marginal rate of substitution on the indifference curve through the intersection of Q^0 with OA may not equal the slope of OA). This possibility is illustrated in figure 4.2 as equilibrium trade at point F, where an indifference curve not drawn passes through the intersection of Q^0CG with OA. The slope of the indifference curve gives the domestic price.

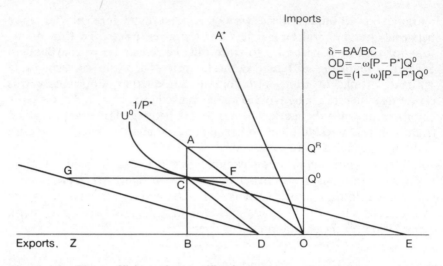

Figure 4.2   The coefficient of rent utilization

The other extreme possibility is a pure VER in which none of the rent is retained, ω equals zero, and the equilibrium trade bundle G is found by the intersection of an indifference curve (not drawn) with Q^0CG such that the tangent line to it at G passes through the origin O (so that trade balance is imposed in terms of domestic prices). A value of δ greater than one implies inefficiency. So the coefficient of rent utilization serves to measure the inefficiency arising from the gift of rent to foreigners.

More subtly, a quota system usually involves non-competitive allocation among suppliers, and in a multi-country world is equivalent in terms of figure 4.2 to picking an average ray OA which is less favorable than the least cost ray. δ can be refined to measure the distance from the least cost ray OA* down to point C, in which case it picks up the (empirically very significant) additional trade inefficiency arising from misallocation among suppliers.

We now formalize the development of δ. Q^0 is the vector of controlled trades. Z is the vector of unconstrained trades, assumed to have zero tariffs for simplicity.[6] P^* and π^* are the associated fixed foreign price vectors. The trade balance for the small domestic economy is

$$P^*Q^0 + \pi^*Z + \omega[P - P^*]Q^0 = 0. \qquad (4.1)$$

In forming (4.1), ω is taken to be the same for all controlled trades for simplicity. The generalization to differential rent retention (different ad valorem tariffs in each controlled sector) involves composition effects which we ignore to start. In terms of moving in the Q direction, Q^0 differs from the point $Q^R = Q^0\delta$ on the foreign offer surface as the implicit solution to δ in

$$\mathbf{P}^*Q^0\delta + \pi^*\mathbf{Z} = 0. \tag{4.2}$$

The domestic price expenditure at the initial equilibrium is $\mathbf{PQ}^0 + \pi^*\mathbf{Z} = (1 - \omega)[\mathbf{P} - \mathbf{P}^*]\mathbf{Q}^0$. The initial amount of revenue $G^0 = (1 - \omega)[\mathbf{P} - \mathbf{P}^*]\mathbf{Q}^0$ supports utility U^0. Now consider an alternative feasible Q, such as Q^R. The domestic price expenditure at A is $\mathbf{PQ}^R + \pi^*\mathbf{Z} = (1 - \omega)[\mathbf{P} - \mathbf{P}^*]\mathbf{Q}^R$.

Definition 1: The *coefficient of rent utilization* is

$$\delta(\mathbf{Q}, G^0) = \frac{[\mathbf{P} \ \mathbf{P}^*]\mathbf{Q}}{G^0}. \tag{4.3}$$

That is, the value of δ is the rent at Q normalized by the rent at Q^0 which supports U^0.[7] $\delta(\mathbf{Q}, G^0)$ is a general function, but when $\mathbf{Q} = \mathbf{Q}^R$, δ measures the inefficiency of the current allocation relative to the Baldwin envelope. (4.3) appears to be unnecessarily elaborate as a means of expressing the value of δ, but in fact it has a very useful similarity to the coefficient of trade utilization used in succeeding sections of the paper.

II.2 Applications

Note that $\delta_{\mathbf{Q}} = [\mathbf{P} - \mathbf{P}^*]/G$; increases in the quota increase efficiency in proportion to the normalized unit quota rent. The unit rent is properly regarded as the shadow price of the quota. *All quota reforms in the half-space above the quota revenue budget line with slopes equal to unit rents are efficiency increasing.* For nonuniform rent retention the corresponding derivative expression is

$$\delta_{\mathbf{Q}} = \frac{(\mathbf{I} - \mathbf{\Omega})[\mathbf{P} - \mathbf{P}^*]}{G^0},$$

where $\mathbf{I}$ is the identity matrix and $\mathbf{\Omega}$ is the diagonal matrix of rent shares $\{\omega^i\}$.

Quota reform can be evaluated generally in terms of moving toward the Baldwin envelope. In percentage change form the coefficient of rent utilization moves by:

$$\hat{\delta} = \Sigma\theta_i\hat{Q}_i, \tag{4.4}$$

where $\theta_i = \dfrac{(1 - \omega_i)[P_i - P_i^*]}{\Sigma(1 - \omega_i)[P_i - P_i^*]}$, the retained rent share of quota i.

It is simple to derive from (4.3) analogous expressions to (4.4) for changes in the rent retention shares ω_i and for exogenous shifts in P^* or other factors affecting the initial position. One important implication of this paper is that the measurement of $(1 - \omega_i)$ is a very significant empirical issue, since its magnitude is critical to the efficiency (and in the remainder of the paper welfare) effects of tariff and quota reform.

A significant alternative use of (4.3) takes account of inefficient allocation of quotas by country. The vector $\mathbf{Q}^0$ may contain country-specific elements which are perfect substitutes for domestic use. Let Q_i be the ith country's export to the home country, and let $\Sigma Q_i = \bar{Q}$. A reallocation of the Q_i's subject to the same $\bar{Q}$ will not affect the common P. Sugar is a good example, with trade for which the P^*s are very widely dispersed among supply sources. It is clear that a reallocation of $\mathbf{Q}$ to cheaper sources acts as a reduction in the price index $\mathbf{P^*Q^R}$ in (4.3), with no effect on $\mathbf{P}$ or G^0. Then δ rises to reflect this accounting for the additional source of inefficiency. In figure 4.2, the refined measure involves the distance from C to a point not drawn on OA* due north of Q^0.

III   The coefficient of trade utilization

Now let us turn to focus on the production-cum-consumption inefficiency in the trade space. The conceptual elements are illustrated in figure 4.3. As in figure 4.2, C is the initial trade bundle, associated with Meade trade utility U^0. C is created by a quota Q^0. Total rent in terms of the export good is DE, the difference between the value of Q^0 at domestic prices, BE, and at foreign prices, BD. The fraction ω of total rent is given to foreigners, OD in figures 4.2 and 4.3. Then $(1 - \omega)$ percent of total rent is retained at home, OE. At free trade the utility level U^* is attainable, with imports Q^*, lying on the foreign offer curve.

Now consider the measurement of inefficiency of the trade equilibrium.

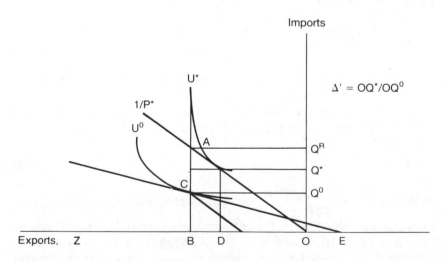

Figure 4.3   The coefficient of trade utilization

Distance measures (Hicks' (1944) "quantity-variations") specialized to the trade case involve movements in the Q direction toward a reference utility. How is the distance from U^0 to U^* to be measured? As in the income compensation case (Hicks, 1944), there is generally a "compensating" and an "equivalent" quantity-variation measure. For the case shown, these coincide, since the amount of Q which yields U^0 or U^* under the budget constraints and the optimizing behavior of agents is unique. The (equivalent variation) factor by which Q^0 must be expanded to yield U^* is $1/\Delta'$, where $\Delta' = Q^0/Q^*$; the (compensating variation) factor by which Q^* must be contracted to maintain U^0 is $1/\Delta$ where $\Delta = Q^*/Q^0$. In higher dimensions we develop the appropriate generalization of this almost trivial accounting. For more than one import, the compensating and equivalent variation measures are not coincident. Generally the new reference utility will not be at the free trade level, and for trade reform theorems we shall be concerned with local changes in Q.

The key ingredient behind all the applications below is the general equilibrium shadow price of a marginal change in a quota. This is derived for the final goods case in our companion paper (1988) and summarized in appendix 4.1. Shadow prices are always the derivatives of distance functions, so on this base we can construct the coefficient of trade utilization. Part IV shows that the same structure goes through for traded inputs as well.

In general, we solve for Δ, the coefficient of trade utilization, using the distorted trade utility function derived in the Appendix. We define the distorted trade utility function, a reduced form general equilibrium function relating the realized utility to the trade instruments:

$$U = v(\mathbf{Q}, t; \omega; \mathbf{P}^*, \boldsymbol{\pi}^*), \tag{4.5}$$

where t is the trade tax on the unconstrained group, set at zero for convenience here (appendix 4.1 and Part V develop the complete version which also allows for differential rent retention). The key shadow price of the quota is proportional to v_Q and is shown to be:

$$r = (1 - \omega)[\mathbf{P} - \mathbf{P}^*] - \omega \mathbf{P}'_Q \mathbf{Q}, \tag{4.6}$$

where ' denotes the transpose of a matrix and $\mathbf{P}_Q$ is a matrix expression developed in appendix 4.1. Under weak separability, the second term is positive. Also, let $v(\mathbf{P}^*, \boldsymbol{\pi}^*)$ be the general equilibrium reduced form utility for free trade. Δ is a radial expansion or contraction factor for either the old bundle $\mathbf{Q}^0$ or the new bundle $\mathbf{Q}^*$. Generally, Δ, the *compensating variation* form of the coefficient of resource utilization, is implicit in:

Definition 2 The *coefficient of trade utilization* is

$$\Delta(\mathbf{Q}^*, U^0; \omega; \mathbf{P}^*; \boldsymbol{\pi}^*) = \{\Delta \mid v(\mathbf{Q}^*/\Delta; \omega; \mathbf{P}^*, \boldsymbol{\pi}^*) = U^0$$
$$= v(\mathbf{Q}^0; \omega; \mathbf{P}^*, \boldsymbol{\pi}^*)\}. \tag{4.7}$$

We assume $v_\Delta = -v_Q Q/\Delta^2 < 0$, which means $v_Q Q > 0$. That is, the aggregate shadow value of quotas must be positive. The assumption is required for Δ to be defined, since the global version of the implicit function theorem can not applied to (4.7) if the derivative v_Δ is not one-signed.[8] The condition is analogous to the familiar condition in the analysis of trade distorted by taxes that the aggregate revenue be positive, and reduces to it in the case of pure import quotas, but it is obviously more restrictive. A rise in Δ then measures a welfare increase. The *equivalent variation* form is implicit in:

$$\Delta'(Q^0; U'; \omega; P^*, \pi^*) = \{\Delta' \,|\, v(Q^0/\Delta'; \omega; P^*; \pi^*) = U'\}. \tag{4.7}$$

A rise in Δ' again measures improvement in the utilization of the trade opportunity. $\Delta' < 1$ when $U' > v(Q^0, .)$. Δ' is not generally defined when U' is the free trade level, since the maximal U^* is achieved uniquely with Q^*, which is not generally a radial expansion of Q^0.[9]

Evidently a single coefficient of trade utilization function yields the values of Δ or Δ', with the difference lying in the function being evaluated at different points. Henceforth we will refer to the function as $\Delta(Q, U; \omega; P^*, \pi^*)$. Δ is a quantity index closely related to those analyzed in the productivity literature. We list some properties of Δ in Q for reference; see our companion paper for details:

   (i) Δ is homogeneous of degree one and concave in Q.
   (ii) Δ', the equivalent variation form of Δ, is a quota-metric utility function.

Calculation of Δ for evaluation of the initial point compared with free trade requires solution of a general equilibrium model to obtain Q^*, defined by $v_Q(Q^*, .) = 0$. Either form can also be used, however, to compare *local* changes in the efficiency of trade policy, as when Q' is the reformed bundle. The compensating variation form is especially easy to compute in this case, as we develop in Part V.

IV Imported inputs

While it is obvious to an economist that taxes on imported inputs are inefficient, trade policy does in fact often have such controls. For example, in 1988 the US VER controls on imported DRAM chips led to production delays for computer manufacturers and high spot market premia for DRAM chips. The coefficient of trade utilization will be extended in this Part to the case of imported inputs. Inefficiency occurs for a small country even with 100 percent rent retention, due to the production inefficiency, while there is no exchange inefficiency.

Figure 4.4 illustrates the conceptual issues for the case of one imported

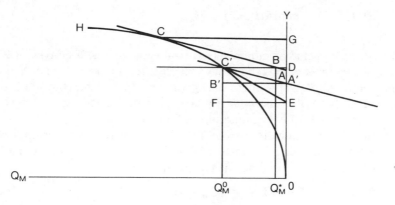

Figure 4.4 The coefficient of trade utilization: imported inputs

input Q_M and one (composite) output Y. The production function is OH, and Q_M trades for Y at the fixed world price P^*/π^*, with the free trade solution being production at C, with GA of Y trading for GC of Q_M. OA is left for domestic consumption. The feasible set of consumption bundles is on the line segment OA, with A the maximal point. A quota $Q_M{}^0$ results in production at C', with C'B' of Y traded for A'B' $= Q_M{}^0$. With 100 percent of the revenue A'E assumed to be retained at home to simplify the diagram,[10] consumption is at A'. The coefficient of trade utilization is $\Delta =$ C'D/CG, the proportion of actual input use to efficient input use.[11]

We now develop general expressions for Δ, first constructing some necessary building blocks. The development is entirely parallel to that for the final goods case reviewed in appendix 4.1. We first derive expressions for optimal expenditure or revenue associated with quantity-constrained and "free" categories as functions of the trade control instruments, the quotas. Then these are substituted into the general equilibrium budget constraint to obtain the reduced form consumption as a function of the quotas. Finally, we define the coefficient of trade utilization as the distance in quota space from an arbitrary quota vector to the quota needed to sustain a target consumption level.

To proceed formally, we define the maximal *domestic product function* as:

$$R(P, \pi) = \max_{Y, Q_M} \{\pi^*Y - PQ_M \mid T(Y, Q_M) \le 0\}, \tag{4.8}$$

where $T(Y, Q_M) \le 0$ is the domestic production possibilities frontier. R is the domestic value-added. Any imported primary factor services appear as elements of Q_M. R is the standard dual function in general equilibrium production theory (see for example Dixit and Norman (1980)). It is convex in prices P, π^*; with first derivatives $R_P = -Q_M$ and $R_{\pi^*} = Y$. Next we define the *gross revenue function*:

$$\tilde{R}(Q_M, \pi^*) = \min_{P} R(P, \pi^*) + PQ_M \qquad (4.9)$$

(4.9) is a well behaved minimization problem, since R is convex in $\mathbf{P}$. By (4.8) we know $\tilde{R}$ equals the gross value of output, π^*Y, where Y is at a maximum and $\mathbf{P}$ is at a minimum, given (π^*, Q_M). $\tilde{R}$ has first derivatives $\tilde{R}_Q = \tilde{P}$ by (4.9) ($\tilde{P}$ = the value of marginal product) and $\tilde{R}_{\pi^*} = Y$ by (4.8). $\tilde{R}$ is concave in Q_M by the minimum in $\mathbf{P}$ property of (4.9).

Now we are ready to define Δ. The net value of consumption is $C = \pi^*(Y + Z)$, where exports $\pi^*Z < 0$ must be given up to pay for imports Q_M. The external payments constraint is:

$$P^*Q_M + \pi^*Z + \omega[P - P^*]Q_M = 0. \qquad (4.10)$$

Using (4.9)–(4.10)

$$C = \pi^*(Y + Z) = \tilde{R}(Q_M, \pi^*) - (1 - \omega)P^*Q_M - \omega PQ_M. \qquad (4.11)$$

The first order condition for efficient use of imported inputs Q_M is

$$-R_P(P, \pi^*) = Q_M.$$

This in inverted to form the domestic price of inputs function:

$$P = P(Q_M, \pi^*).$$

We now define the *distorted trade consumption function*:

$$C(Q_M; \omega; \pi^*) = \tilde{R}(Q_M, \pi^*) - (1 - \omega)P^*Q_M + \omega P_M(Q_M, \pi^*)Q_M. \quad (4.12)$$

The critical property of this function is the implied shadow price of quotas:

$$r_M = C_{QM} = (1 - \omega)[P - P^*] - \omega P'_{QM}(Q_M, \pi^*)Q_M.$$

Note that it is entirely parallel to (4.6), the shadow price of quotas for the final goods case.

The maximal value of consumption is

$$C^* = \pi^*(Y^* + Z^*) = R(P^*, \pi^*),$$

since (4.10) at free trade is $P^*Q_M^* + \pi^*Z^* = 0$.

Definition 3 The *coefficient of trade utilization* is implicit in:

$$\Delta(Q_M^*, C^0; \omega; P^*, \pi^*) = \{\Delta \mid C(Q_M^*/\Delta; \omega; \pi^*) = C^0\}. \qquad (4.13)$$

The equivalent variation form is:

$$\Delta'(Q_M^0, C'; \omega; P^*, \pi^*) = \{\Delta'/C' = C(Q_M^0/\Delta'; \omega; P^*, \pi^*)\}. \qquad (4.14)$$

We assume $r_M Q_M > 0$, so that Δ is defined, since the implicit function theorem requires

$$C_{\Delta'} = -C_Q Q_M/\Delta'^2 = -r_M Q_M/\Delta'^2 < 0.$$

If $C' = C^*$, the free trade level, the equivalent variation form is not defined, as in the case of final goods quotas. (4.13) is defined everywhere, and is the form used below for local evaluation of quota reform. With sufficient information the maximal domestic product function or the gross revenue function, equations (4.13) or (4.14) are operational globally.

V Applications

The coefficient of trade utilization will now be applied. In section V.1 it yields theorems on partial quota reform which are much more general than any available in the past. In section V.2, we discuss the operationality of the new concept.

V.1 Evaluation of trade reform

Typical trade negotiations concern partial moves toward free trade with possible backsliding in some categories. The regressive motion is pronounced at periodic renegotiation of VERs, such as the Multifiber Arrangement. The standard gradual reform theorems in the literature concern tariff reform, and are highly restrictive. Welfare improves if all taxes are cut equiproportionately, or if the highest taxes are cut first provided that all goods are substitutes.[12] This meager harvest can be greatly extended for the case of quotas when their full implications are utilized.

We present here some of the reform results of our companion paper. Quite generally, quota increases are locally welfare improving if they move in the half space above the initial shadow budget value of the quotas: $rQ \geq G^0$, where r is the shadow price of the quota. Special cases allow ready calculation of r and very useful theorems on partial reform. We show that all quota increases are welfare improving under implicit separability and uniform rent retention, since r is positive in this case. In fact r has a particularly simple form which is operational, so the full space of welfare increasing reforms is readily characterized. One implication is that some regression is permitted in the reform (some quotas may decrease), so long as the rent on quota goods rises and the foreign price value of quota goods rises. Outside these cases we must either do more work to calculate r, or restrict the domain of reforms.

For restricted domain reforms, making no restriction on substitutability or tariffs, all uniform quota increases are welfare improving quite generally (assuming the total shadow value of quotas is positive).[13] This is a counterpart to the uniform-radial-cut-in-taxes rule, but is much more general in that a number of embedded distortions are left alone. With differential rent retention and no tariffs, the space of guaranteed-welfare-improving reforms widens to any convex combination of Q and ΩQ where ΩQ is the total of licenses given to foreigners. Our companion paper also has useful results on quota reform in the presence of tariffs on the non-quota group and tariff reform in the presence of quotas. Using the coefficient of trade utilization, we put these propositions into a constructive form easily calculated by trade negotiators.

How does (4.7) translate into an *operational* measure for evaluation of trade reform? A change in **Q** accompanied by a change in Δ so as to hold U constant at U^0 yields a compensating variation measure. If the coefficient of trade utilization rises due to trade reform, the reform is welfare improving, with the calculated increase in Δ being a surplus in the form of a proportionate expansion in consumption of the constrained categories. In the equivalent variation version, where the reform shifts U to U', Δ' is a *quota-metric* utility function.

Using the implicit function theorem applied to (4.7), a change in Q_i alters Δ by

$$\Delta_{Qi} = -\frac{v_{Qi}}{v_\Delta} = -\frac{r_i/\Delta}{-rQ/\Delta^2} = \Delta\frac{r_i}{rQ}. \tag{4.15}$$

(4.15) implies that the elasticity of Δ with respect to a change in quota i is the quota value share of quota i, $\theta_i = r_iQ_i/rQ$. In rate of change form a quota reform alters Δ by

$$\hat{\Delta} = \Sigma\theta_i\hat{Q}_i, \tag{4.16}$$

where a circumflex denotes a percentage change. The case of imported inputs is essentially identical. Note that the local change form of Δ (holding C constant at C^0 by shifting Δ as $\mathbf{Q_M}$ changes) from (4.13) is:

$$\Delta_Q/\Delta = -\frac{C_Q}{C_\Delta} = \frac{r}{rQ_M}.$$

This is identical to (4.15) in the final goods case. Then by similar steps:

$$\hat{\Delta} = \Sigma\theta_{Mi}\hat{Q}_{Mi} \geq 0, \tag{4.17}$$

Then we can state:

THEOREM 1

(a) *Under a quota system with 100 percent rent retention, all quota reforms raise welfare at the rate of increase of normalized quota rent.*

(b) *With uniform rent retention and implicit separability, all quota reforms raise welfare if normalized rent rises (condition (a)) and if the external value of Q rises, P*dQ > 0.*

PROOF: In appendix 4.1 we show that in case (a) $\mathbf{r} = \mathbf{P} - \mathbf{P^*}$; in case (b) $\mathbf{r} = (1-\omega)[\mathbf{P}-\mathbf{P^*}] - \omega\mathbf{P'}_{Q}\mathbf{Q}$ which we show under implicit separability is $\mathbf{r} = (1-\omega)[\mathbf{P}-\mathbf{P^*}] - \omega/\epsilon\,\mathbf{P}$, where ϵ is the aggregate compensated import demand elasticity for Q goods, necessarily negative.

A reform is welfare improving if it raises $\mathbf{rdQ}$, which in case (a) means raising the normalized quota rent, $\mathbf{PdQ} > \mathbf{P^*dQ}$. In case (b)

$$\mathbf{rdQ} = (1-\omega)\{\mathbf{PdQ} - \mathbf{P^*dQ}\} - (\omega/\epsilon)\mathbf{PdQ}.$$

This is positive if both terms are positive. If in addition to $\mathbf{PdQ} > \mathbf{P^*dQ}$, positive normalized rent increase, we stipulate $\mathbf{P^*dQ} > 0$ we are sure that $\mathbf{PdQ} > 0$. Then both terms are positive.

Note that Theorem 1 generalizes the Corden–Falvey result that all northeast moves are welfare-improving to the case where some quota decreases are permitted. All quota reforms in the half-space above the initial quota rent budget line are welfare improving:

$$[\mathbf{P} - \mathbf{P^*}]\mathbf{Q} \geq G^0 = [\mathbf{P} - \mathbf{P^*}]\mathbf{Q}^0$$

For the pure import quota case, (4.16) implies Δ moves proportionally to the quota rent. Theorem 1(b) generalizes Corden–Falvey to allow rent-sharing.

(4.16) measures the improvement in the productive efficiency of trade (movement toward the Baldwin envelope) combined with the improvement in the exchange efficiency (moving to the right point on the envelope). The coefficient of rent utilization measures the productive efficiency of trade, equation (4.4) in rate of change form. The improvement in (4.16) can be decomposed into the productive efficiency and exchange efficiency components in

$$\hat{\Delta} = \hat{\delta}\frac{\mathbf{rQ}}{(\mathbf{I}-\Omega)[\mathbf{P}-\mathbf{P^*}]\mathbf{Q}} + \left(\sum_{i=1}^{N} \frac{(-\mathbf{P'}_{Qi}\Omega Q)Q_i}{\mathbf{rQ}} \hat{Q}_i \right). \qquad (4.16')$$

For the pure import tariff case $\hat{\Delta} = \hat{\delta}$ as the second order term vanishes. The interpretation is that an initial equilibrium at a point like A on figure 4.2 still has a binding quota, with less than the free trade Q. A relaxation of the quota is feasible by travelling out along the foreign offer curve OA; the percentage improvement in the coefficient of trade utilization is simply the percentage improvement in the Q direction.

Now we consider non-uniform rent retention, consistent with non-uniform tariffs in the quota-constrained group. The shadow price of quotas becomes:

$$\mathbf{r} = [\mathbf{I}-\Omega][\mathbf{P}-\mathbf{P^*}] - \mathbf{P'}_Q\Omega\mathbf{Q}, \qquad (4.19)$$

where Ω is the diagonal matrix with the ω_i's on the diagonal, differing across quota categories and $\mathbf{I}$ is the identity matrix. (4.16) is still the formula for $\hat{\Delta}$ with (4.19) used for the prices. The implications for quota reform are severe. The new rent transfer term in the shadow price has essentially the same properties which are so troublesome to tax reform propositions, and it requires strong restrictions on either preferences or the admissible reforms to overcome it. It is possible for a shadow price to be negative, so that some quota increases could be welfare-decreasing. In the tax reform literature this has led to the *uniform radial cut* rule of equiproportionate cuts in taxes. This has an analogy for quota reform: an increase in all quotas in proportion to ΩQ will guarantee that the rent transfer effect is positive: $-(\Omega Q)'P'_Q(\Omega Q) > 0$ since P_Q is negative semidefinite, as shown in appendix 4.1. This is the exact counterpart to the reason for the uniform radial cut rule in the tariff case. We have also assumed, in order to define Δ, that the aggregate shadow value of all quotas is positive. Then trivially, a uniform proportionate increase in all quotas raises Δ in the same proportion, which is welfare increasing by assumption. Then it is also true that any quota increase which is a convex combination of the two rules will guarantee a rise in welfare:

$$\hat{Q}_i = g(\lambda + (1 - \lambda)\omega_i) \text{ for } 1 \geq \lambda \geq 0, g > 0, \text{ and all } Q_i.$$

This rule describes a cone of welfare improving quota reforms in Q space. Then we have shown:

THEOREM 2 *Any quota reform which increases the quota in higher transfer categories by more than the average and by less than the rate of transfer is welfare-improving.*

Intuitively, the condition in Theorem 2 is needed because a below (above) average increase in a high (low) transfer category could lead to a rise in the total rent transfer. Of course, the condition is over-sufficient. For the case where the ω_i's are the same the rule collapses to allowing only uniform proportional expansions, but then Theorem 1 applies.

V.2 Practical implications

In this paper an appropriate welfare *measure* is rigorously constructed. It has the intuitively appealing property of being a measure of the efficiency of utilization of the trade opportunity measured in the space of distorted trade. Its rate of change is conceptually identical to the familiar rate of change of total factor productivity. Due to the concavity of the underlying distance function, the useful discrete approximation theorems of that literature are immediately applicable (Caves, Christiansen, and Diewert, 1982). We now show it is readily operational, and contrast it with the typical erroneous tariff equivalent approach.

For implicit separability and uniform rent retention, note from (A.4.10′) that the shadow price

$$\mathbf{r} = (1 - \omega)[\mathbf{P} - \mathbf{P}^*] - \frac{\omega}{\epsilon}\mathbf{P}$$

is fairly simple to calculate in principle. All that is needed is a single import demand elasticity, the calculation of ω, and data on $P - P^*$. For extension to embedded tariffs on Z the shadow value of quotas becomes under implicit separability and uniform rent retention from (A.4.10''):

$$\mathbf{r} = (1 - \omega)[\mathbf{P} - \mathbf{P}^*] - \frac{\omega}{\epsilon}\mathbf{P} - \bar{\tau}\mathbf{P}$$

This again is fairly simple to calculate. When homogeneity of the export aggregate function h(Z) is not plausible, the exact $\bar{\tau}$ requires detailed information on the structure of excess demand, but it can be replaced by $\tilde{\tau}$, the highest tariff in the Z group, to form $\tilde{\mathbf{r}}$. Reforms passing $\tilde{\mathbf{r}}d\mathbf{Q} > 0$ will pass $\mathbf{r}d\mathbf{Q} > 0$.

The most difficult problem is with differential rent retention; and here the analyst must obtain the inverse price derivative matrix $\mathbf{P_Q} = \mathbf{E_{PP}}^{-1}$, discussed in appendix 4.1. But this is no worse than the usual case of welfare analysis, requiring elasticity estimates. We conclude that (4.16) is operational, and should provide useful guidance for trade negotiations.

In practice of course, observation of the unit rents $\mathbf{P} - \mathbf{P}^*$ is far from routine, and differential rents over detailed categories are important and defy easy finessing by aggregation. The analytic foundation of (4.16) emphasizes that such differentials are of the essence in measuring inefficiency, and thus future evaluations of trade reform should spend much effort on gathering such information. In contrast the good news is that the usual effort spent on obtaining appropriate import demand elasticities is not needed for pure import quotas and may not be needed if the rent transfer term is small.[14] We emphasize that the very simple and "partial equilibrium" appearing formula in (4.16) is in fact a rigorously based general equilibrium construct.

It is also straightforward to use the coefficient of trade utilization to evaluate tariff changes. This can be done either in the space of quota-ridden quantities, or in an augmented space which includes the "quota equivalents" of tariffs. The former is straightforward and carried out in our companion paper. The latter can always be used *ex post*, which is frequently the concern of analysts interpreting the past.

We conclude by contrasting the coefficient of trade utilization approach with a typical erroneous "tariff equivalent" approach to evaluation of reform in a single quota. In figure 4.5 the quota is raised from Q^0 to Q^1, keeping other quotas constant. The tariff equivalent to Q^0 is t^0 and to Q^1 is t^1.

The "usual" measure (e.g., see Cline et al., 1978) would be a gain in efficiency of triangle ABE, interpreted as the compensating variation in income required to maintain utility U^0, net of the loss of "revenue" t^0AEt^1. That is, integrate the derivative of the expenditure function with respect to P from $P^* + t^0(Q^0)$ to $P^* + t^1(Q^1)$, and deduct the rent change $Q^0[t^0 - t^1]$. The correct measure is trapezoid ABQ^1Q^0 if the quota rent is 100 percent

Price of quotas

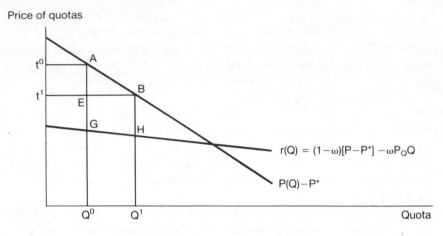

Figure 4.5   Correct versus standard methods of quota reform

retained. This involves integrating the derivative of the coefficient of trade utilization from Q^0 to Q^1. A careful investigator using standard methods realizes that the added tariff equivalent revenue must be incorporated and so also obtains ABQ^1Q^0. Notice however that this involves two separate calculations, hence is arguably more complex. The coefficient of trade utilization evaluates ABQ^1Q^0 relative to initial trade revenue. It is of course possible to obtain ABQ^1Q^0 and interpret it as a compensating variation in income, thus achieving a correct expenditure function measure. But note that the correct measure inevitably must use the coefficient of trade utilization function in the process. Thinking in terms of Δ is more direct and thus it does not invite the conceptual error of figure 4.5 by working directly with quotas. Note also that an accurate value of the slope P_Q is less important to the correct measure. ABE is proportional to P_Q, but ABQ^1Q^0 is not, and the influence of it is very small as t^1 is large.

The potential for error is even more dramatic if the rent is shared. The correct analysis evaluates by integrating under the shadow price of quotas function

$$r(Q) = (1 - \omega)[P(Q) - P^*] - \omega P_Q Q,$$

with measure GHQ^1Q^0 in figure 4.6. For a pure VER, $r(Q) = -P_Q Q$, positively sloped through the origin. This assumes ω is constant with respect to Q for simplicity. (In fact ω will change unless the tax instrument is a domestic base constant *ad valorem* tariff, or the licenses are shared with ω percent going to foreigners). A correct expenditure function approach involves, instead of a single measure, calculating the consumer's surplus t^0ABt^1, working out that all of ABE is gain, and apportioning correctly the revenue loss t^0AEt^1 and the revenue gain EBQ^1Q^0. Evidently the relative simplicity of the direct approach grows with the complexity of the underlying structure.

VI Conclusion

Robert Baldwin's envelope taught us to view the trade opportunity as a technology, with the corollary that inefficient trade is similar to inefficient production. Debreu and Deaton taught us to measure inefficiency in quantity space. This essay marries Baldwin's notion of efficiency in production and trade to the measurement technique of Debreu and Deaton. We define a trade-space concept pointing us back to the Baldwin envelope in two senses of the phrase.

The coefficient of trade utilization provides the basis for a natural accounting system for contemporary trade policy, which is substantially in the form of quotas. Operational measures of the welfare effects of quota reform are developed in terms of its rate of change, substantially generalizing earlier work on trade reform. We believe that further development and application of the coefficient of trade utilization is promising.

Appendix 4.1 The Distorted Trade Utility Function

We begin with the trade expenditure function $E(P, U^0)$:

$$E(p, U^0) = \min_{X} \{pX \mid U(X) = U^0\}. \qquad (A.4.1)$$

where U is a Meade trade utility function in the vector of trades X and p is the price vector.

For the usual trade distortions case, only some products are restricted. Let Q be the amount of trade in the restricted product group, with foreign price P^* and domestic price P. For the unrestricted group, Z is the trade quantity, π is its domestic price $= \pi^* + t$ where t is the specific tax and π^* the free trade price. First we must consider the unrestricted product group.

DEFINITION A.1 *The distorted trade expenditure function is:*

$$E(Q, \pi, U^0) = \min_{Z} \{\pi Z \mid U(Q, Z) = U^0\} \qquad (A.4.2)$$

Alternatively,

$$\tilde{E}(Q, \pi, U^0) = \max_{P} E(P, \pi, U^0) - pQ \qquad (A.4.3)$$

(A.4.3) is a well behaved maximization problem, since E is concave in P, as is well known. Mechanically, the first order conditions solve for the price $\tilde{P}$

which equates demand $E_P(P, \pi, U^0)$ with Q, the supply. The first derivative properties of $\tilde{E}$ are straightforward from (A.4.3):

$$\tilde{E}_\pi(Q, \pi, U^0) = Z \tag{A.4.4.}$$

$$\tilde{E}_Q(Q, \pi, U^0) = -P \tag{A.4.5}$$

The first property follows from Shepard's lemma. The second is less familiar with the intuition that a relaxation of the quota by one unit reduces expenditure on the market group by πZ_Q, which gives the marginal willingness to pay for quota ridden goods. $\tilde{E}$ is concave in π and convex in Q, by its minimum in Z and maximum in P property. Then the important derivative matrix P_Q is negative semi-definite:

$$y' P_Q y < 0 \text{ for any vector y.}$$

Now consider the internal and external payments constraints facing the small economy. Suppose that the fraction of quota revenue captured by the home country is $1 - \omega$ (consistent with awarding the fraction ω of all quota licenses to foreigners, or with a tariff on quota-controlled imports at specific rate $(1-\omega)P - P^*$). Tariff revenue tZ, if any, is captured at home.[15]

In terms of external prices the budget constraint is:

$$b = \pi^* Z + P^* Q + \omega Q[P - P^*] \leq 0, \tag{A.4.6}$$

where the third term represents the transfer to foreigners via the gift of quota licences, or other revenue transfer. This is alternatively

$$b = (1 - \omega)P^* Q + \omega P Q + \pi Z - tZ \leq 0. \tag{A.4.7}$$

Now we substitute into (A.4.7) $-\tilde{E}_Q(Q, \pi, U^0)Q = PQ$, $tZ = t\tilde{E}_\pi(Q, \pi, U^0)$ and $\tilde{E}(Q, \pi, U^0) = \pi Z$ in equilibrium; i.e. use the equilibrium level of U for U^0. The result is:

$$b = -\omega \tilde{E}_Q(Q, \pi, U^0)Q + (1 - \omega)P^* Q$$
$$+ \tilde{E}(Q, \pi, U^0) - t\tilde{E}_\pi(Q, \pi, U^0) = 0,$$

where $\pi = \pi^* + t$. For the differential rent retention case the first two terms on the right hand side of (A.4.8) become

$$\tilde{E}'_Q(Q, \pi, U^0)\Omega Q + P^{*'}[I - \Omega]Q$$

where Ω is the diagonal matrix with the rent transfer shares ω_i on the diagonal, I is the identity matrix, and ' denotes transpose as needed for clarity.

For welfare analysis we implicitly define the (reduced form) utility as:

DEFINITION *A.2: The distorted trade utility function is:*

$$v(Q, \omega, t; P^*, \pi^*) = \{U^0 | -\omega \tilde{E}_Q(Q, \pi, U^0)Q + (1 - \omega)P^* Q$$
$$+ \tilde{E}(Q, \pi, U^0) - t\tilde{E}^\pi(Q, \pi, U^0) = 0\}$$
$$\text{where } \pi = \pi^* + t. \tag{A.4.8}$$

The implicit function theorem yields the properties of $v(.)$. For the present purpose we note:

$$v_Q = -\frac{-\omega \tilde{E}'_Q Q - \omega E_Q + (1-\omega)P^* + \tilde{E}_Q - tE_{\pi Q}}{-\omega \tilde{E}_{QU}Q + E_U - tZ_U},$$

$$= \frac{(1-\omega)[P - P^*] - \omega P'_Q Q + tZ_Q}{-\omega \tilde{E}_{QU}Q + \tilde{E}_U - tZ_U} \text{ using (A.5)}[16] \quad\quad (A.4.9)$$

The denominator of (A.4.9) is the shadow price of foreign exchange.[17] Then the general equilibrium shadow price of a quota is defined as the numerator, generally:

$$r = [P - P^*]'[I - \Omega]Q - P'_Q\Omega Q + tZ_Q. \quad\quad (A.4.10)$$

The evaluation of quota reform proceeds by imposing special cases for evaluating r. For a pure import quota system $r = P - P^*$, the unit quota rent. Other cases need at least some structure restricting preferences.

An important special case used in the text is implicit separability. See our companion paper for more explicit details.

Under this assumption, we can be sure that $P'_Q Q < 0$. This follows from noting that the expenditure function under weak separability is written

$$E(P, \pi, U^0) = E(\phi(P, U^0), \eta\,(\pi, U^0)\,U^0) \text{ implicit.}$$

The derivative matrix $P_Q = P'_Q$ is $(E_{PP})^{-1}$. The homogeneity properties of E guarantee:

$$P = -(E_{PP})^{-1}E_{P\pi}\pi.$$

Using $E_{P\pi} = E'_{\pi P} = Z'_P$, this is

$$P = -(E_{PP})^{-1}[Z'_P]\pi. \qu\quad (A.4.11)$$

Now note that $Q = E_\phi \phi_P$ and that $Z'_P = \phi_P Z'_\phi > 0$ since the Z's and Q's are substitutes under separability. Substituting into (A.4.11).

$$P = -P'_Q Q \frac{Z'_\phi \pi}{E_\phi}.$$

The critical term is now:

$$P'_Q Q = -P\frac{E_\phi}{Z'_\phi \pi} < 0. \qu\quad (A.4.12)$$

The factor $-E_\phi/Z'_\phi \pi$ in (A.4.12) turns out to be the inverse of the aggregate own price elasticity of demand for the Q group, $1/\epsilon$, necessarily negative. From the envelope theorem for the expenditure function $E(\phi(P, U^0), \eta\,(\pi, U^0), U^0)$, E_ϕ equals $F(\phi, \eta, U^0)$, the import aggregate. Also, the standard homogeneity properties imply $F_\phi \phi + Z'_\phi \pi = 0$. This means $-Z'_\phi \pi = F_\phi \phi$ so $-E_\phi/Z'_\phi \pi = \phi F/F_\phi = 1/\epsilon$.

The shadow price of a quota for uniform rent retention is then:

$$r = (1 - \omega)[P - P^*] - \frac{\omega}{\epsilon} P. \tag{A.4.10$'$}$$

Separability also implies that the tariff term tZ_Q in (A.4.10) is a weighted average tariff times minus P. Note that $Z_Q = Z_P \cdot P_Q = Z_\phi (\phi(P, U^0), \eta(\pi, U^0), U^0) \cdot \phi_P \cdot P_Q$. Then recalling $\pi Z_Q = - P$:

$$tZ_Q = -\Sigma \tau_i \frac{\pi_i Z_{i\phi}}{\Sigma \pi_i Z_{i\phi}} P = -\bar{\tau} P, \tag{A.4.13}$$

where $\tau_i = t_i/P_i$. The weights are positive (since all $Z_{i\phi}$ are negative) so $\bar{\tau}$ is a proper average. With implicit separability, the weights can be shown to be the import values. The shadow price of a quota for uniform rent retention and tariffs is now:

$$r = (1 - \omega)[P - P^*] - \frac{\omega}{\epsilon} P - \bar{\tau} P. \tag{A.4.10$''$}$$

Notes

1   By quota we shall mean any quantitative restriction, with the exact means of division of the rent being an additional feature to be specified.
2   See Anderson (1988) for evidence on the considerable size of such inefficiency.
3   Neary (1988) also derives results for quota reform in the polar cases of zero and 100 percent rent retention.
4   It is easy to develop a "coefficient of trade utilization" approach to the large country case following the methods of this paper. Our companion paper develops partial reform expressions in the large country context.
5   "Back to the Baldwin Envelope" in the other sense of the phrase. For the case of final goods, this is a review of theorems in our companion paper. For imported inputs, the theorems are very similar, but novel in their extension to the case of inputs.
6   In the present context this does not matter, though it will for the coefficient of trade utilization.
7   For nonuniform rent retention, the factor $1 - \omega$ no longer cancels in numerator and denominator, but the definition is the same. See below.
8   Sufficiency places some restrictions on the substitutability of the Q's and Z's.
9   For $\mathbf{Q}' = \mathbf{Q}^*$, Δ is defined, so the difficulty at the free trade level disappears.
10   It is straightforward to incorporate $\omega > 0$, and we do so in the formal development.
11   OA'/OA is the output measure of inefficiency. The productivity literature has a well-developed examination of the distinction between the two. In the case shown they are not the same. The choice of approach is formally arbitrary, but in the trade case it is natural to focus on a measure in the space of the instruments. For evaluating trade reform, for example, the link between the instruments and the measure is direct rather than through the entire factor demand system.
    Diewert (1985) develops a distance-type (he does not use this terminology) output-based measure of productive inefficiency in an open economy. In his

model, the quantities under "control" are the domestic outputs, which is less useful for the purpose of evaluating trade control than a measure focussed on the trade quantities.

12 The compensated excess demand system has positive off-diagonal derivatives.

13 This is not an innocuous assumption, but required for definition of Δ.

14 In our companion paper we explore plausible conditions where it is small.

15 No borrowing or other transfer is permitted for simplicity. If it is introduced, the constraining value becomes A rather than 0.

16 We assume it is positive. $\tilde{E}_U$ is positive, and equals E_U by definition of $\tilde{E}$ in (A.4.3). The term $-tZ_U$ is negative and the term $-\tilde{E}'_{QU}Q = \tilde{E}_{UQ}Q = P_U'Q$ is ordinarily positive, both assuming normality. Thus the two distortion terms offset each other. It is conventional in tariff analysis to assume $-tZ_U$ does not become large enough so that the distortion effects of a gift of foreign exchange leading to added utility produce a greater loss than the transfer. By extension this now covers $P'_QQ - tZ_U$. In this case, that implies the shadow price of foreign exchange is positive.

17 $\tilde{E}_U$ is positive, and equals E_U by definition of $\tilde{E}$ in (A.4.3). The term $-tZ_U$ is negative and the term $-\tilde{E}'_{QU}Q = \tilde{E}_{QU}Q = P_U'Q$ is ordinarily positive, both assuming normality. Thus the two distortion terms offset each other. It is conventional in tariff analysis to assume $-tZ_U$ does not become large enough so that the distortion effects of a gift of foreign exchange leading to added utility produce a greater loss than the transfer. By extension this now covers $P'_QQ - tZ_U$. In this case, that implies the shadow price of foreign exchange is positive.

References

Anderson J. E. 1988: *The Relative Inefficiency of Quotas*, Cambridge, Mass.: MIT Press.

Anderson J. E. and Neary J. P. 1988: "A New Approach to Evaluating Trade Reform," unpublished.

Baldwin R. E. 1948: "Equilibrium in International Trade: A Diagrammatic Analysis," *Quarterly Journal of Economics*, 62, 748–62.

Baldwin R. E. 1971: *Nontariff Distortions of International Trade*, Washington: Brookings Institution.

Caves D., Christiansen L., and Diewert E. 1982: "Multilateral Comparisons of Output, Input, and Productivity Using Superlative Index Numbers," *Economic Journal*, 92, 73–86.

Cline W. R., Kawanabe N, Kronsjo T, and Williams T. 1978: *Trade Negotiations in The Tokyo Round: A Quantitative Assessment*, Washington: The Brookings Institution.

Corden W. M. and Falvey R. E. 1985: "Quotas and the Second Best," *Economics Letters*, 10, 67–70.

Deaton A. 1979: "The Distance Function and Consumer Behavior, with Applications to Index Numbers and Optimal Taxation," *Review of Economic Studies*, 46, 391–405.

Deaton A. and Muellbauer J. 1980: *Economics and Consumer Behavior*, Cambridge: Cambridge University Press.

Debreu G. 1951: "The Coefficient of Resource Utilization," *Econometrica*, 19, 273–92.

Diewert W. E. 1985: "A Dynamic Approach to the Measurement of Waste in an Open Economy," *Journal of International Economics*, 19, 213–40.

Dixit, A. K. and Norman, V. N. 1980: *The Theory of International Trade: A Dual General Equilibrium Approach*, Cambridge: Cambridge University Press.

Hicks J. R. 1944: "The Four Consumer's Surpluses," *Review of Economic Studies*, 11, 31–41.

Neary J. P. 1988: "Tariffs, Quotas, and VERs with and without International Capital Mobility," *Canadian Journal of Economics*, 21, 714–35.

Neary J. P. and Roberts K. W. S. 1980: "The Theory of Household Behavior under Rationing," *European Economic Review*, 13, 25–42.

Part II

Trade Policy Issues

5

Reflections on Uniform Taxation
ARNOLD C. HARBERGER

I Introduction

This paper is addressed both to professional economists and to economic
policy makers, to researchers and practitioners, to those who forge new
theoretical advances and to those who labor with the implementation of
policies. The domain of the paper is thus a sort of no-man's-land – a place
that no one may want to call his home.

Nonetheless, it is an important piece of terrain, containing perhaps
unexpected lessons for each of the groups mentioned above.

I feel motivated to explore this territory because I sense an unfortunate
schism between two groups of my friends and colleagues in the field of
public finance. On the one side you have policy-makers and practitioners,
advisers sent out by the World Bank and other aid agencies, plus some
revered sages who have made notable contributions to economics over
many decades.

On the other side you have a younger, more technical, perhaps in some
dimensions more brilliant group, who have made significant theoretical
contributions in recent times, and have enhanced the rigor of our branch of
economics.

It is perhaps good to set the stage by describing the schism in an extreme
way that some might call even a caricature. On one side of the divide we
have the gray-haired veterans who seem almost to find Nirvana in the idea
of uniformity. If there is any way to make taxation more uniform, so much
the better. In indirect taxation the uniform value added tax is the goal; in
tariff policy it is the uniform duty on all imports. The value added tax is
lauded by this group precisely because of its potential for uniformity; when
they criticize a real-world VAT, it is usually because it somehow falls short
of the uniformity that they seek.

On the other side of the divide we have the technicians, usually younger
and more analytically inclined. In their vision of the Nirvana (or maybe the
[second-best] antechambers of Nirvana), the notion of uniformity is
replaced by the Ramsey Rule. To them, it is easy to prove, mathematically,
that uniform taxation is not typically or generally the best answer. The
Ramsey Rule is a better guide. It will tell us when uniform taxation is the

best we can do, and it will also tell us when a better answer is available, and what that answer is. This group views the proponents of uniformity with a certain amount of incredulity – wondering, as it were, how anybody can think that uniform taxation is best, when the Ramsey Rule answer can be mathematically *proved* to be better.

Tariff policy is another place where a chasm opens between advocates of uniformity and others. Here the opposition to uniformity takes different forms, each relying on a different set of arguments. But the proponents of uniform tariffs are quite unified themselves, basing their arguments mainly on the theory of effective protection. Effective protection is shown to be different, depending on the tariff treatment of tradable inputs and outputs. If all importable inputs enter duty free, then a 30 percent tariff translates into 60 percent effective protection if imported inputs account for half the world price of the product, into 90 percent effective protection if such inputs amount to two-thirds of the world price, and into 120 percent effective protection if the imported inputs account for three-quarters of the world price.

In this context the concept of domestic resource cost is usually brought into play. If the market exchange rate is 10 pesos per dollar, the 30 percent tariff invokes a domestic resource cost of up to 13 pesos in order to save a dollar by producing a protected good with no imported inputs. But that figure goes up to 16 pesos for saving a dollar where input costs amount to half of the world price, and all the way up to 22 pesos for saving a dollar where imported input cost is equal to three-quarters of the world price.

The uniform tariff school argues that it makes no sense to pay 22 pesos to save a dollar in one way, 16 pesos to save it in another, and 13 pesos to save it in a third way – all by means of import substitution. Why not reduce the highest rate of effective protection, and increase the lowest, thus saving resources while leaving unchanged the total "amount" of protection (as represented, say, by the number of dollars worth of import substitute production)? One of the key results of effective protection analysis is that only when we have uniform duties on all imports (including imports of raw materials, component parts, and capital goods) do we guarantee equal effective protection of all import-substitute activities. Only then can we be sure that the domestic resource cost of saving a dollar is the same in all import-substituting activities.

Before going on, I am impelled to confess that I have been and in most cases still am one of those veterans who advocates uniformity. But I believe I have thought about the issues involved more than most economists have, and as a result I feel I have a message to impart: *a pretty good case for uniform taxation can indeed be made, but it is not the one we are accustomed to seeing*. Advocates of uniformity are thus well advised to worry a bit more about how they defend their position, while antagonists should weigh carefully the alternative arguments for uniformity that I am about to present.

II The argument for a broad-based uniform tax

Let us start with the argument that uniform taxation is good because it strikes all activities at equal rates. One therefore cannot escape tax by shifting one's demand or supply from one activity to another. Looked at in this way, a uniform tax is like the proverbial lump-sum tax, that economic agents cannot get away from by any known action available to them, and that therefore does not impinge on any of their decisions at the margin.

The above argument is true, but unrealistic. Very early in the academic discussion of these matters, the issue of *leisure* came up. Even if we were able to tax the consumption (or production) of all the goods and services registered in a country's national product, we could not plausibly bring the value of leisure within the tax net. Thus people can escape taxation by substituting away from standard goods and services, taking additional leisure time (sometimes called non-market time) instead.

Here it was early seen that if one cannot in practice tax leisure, but only standard goods and services, then it is no longer obvious that a uniform tax is best. Indeed, it was early shown that uniform taxation is indeed best only when all goods and services are equally good substitutes for leisure. In the expected case where they are not all equally good substitutes, one should tax more heavily those goods which are complements to leisure, and less heavily those goods which are less than average substitutes for leisure. The reasoning is very easy to see by imagining a good which was strictly complementary to leisure. We would like, on grounds of neutrality, to tax at all equal rate all activities, including leisure. However, we are not able to tax leisure directly. Hence, the argument goes, the best we can do entails trying to tax leisure indirectly. If one or more goods exist that are sharp complements to leisure, we may do better by taxing them higher than the rest. This could be viewed as applying to them the standard (uniform) tax, plus a surtax that was really aimed at their complement, leisure.

The technical literature on this subject proved that such a strategy would in general improve welfare. Not only was this true where there were complements to leisure, but also in any case where the different goods and services were differentially substitutable for leisure. Under these circumstances the best solution – in this case the "second-best optimum" – would be to tax more heavily those goods that were less-than-average substitutes for leisure and less heavily those that were better-than-average substitutes for leisure. This result comes from a direct application of the Ramsey Rule.

In my view, we economists in studying this problem have paid far too much attention to "leisure" as the "left-out" commodity. In reality, as any value-added tax administrator will tell you, a whole list of activities, above and beyond leisure, seem to lie beyond the reach of any practicable value added tax. Here is a challenge: go to any country with a value added tax, preferably, a country that aims at broad coverage with a uniform rate. Then take that VAT rate and apply it to the country's consumption figures from the national accounts. The resulting figure is what VAT receipts would be if the tax were fully general on those items actually measured in national-accounts consumption. Now compare this figure with actual VAT receipts. You will find it is far greater. Vast amounts of consumption escape value added tax even when the country thinks and talks about a fully general tax. Consider the services of domestic servants, the imputed income from owner-occupied housing, the services of teachers, doctors and nurses, the consumption represented by international airline tickets, and so on. The list is long in every single real-world case.

What does this mean? Simply that even our most glorified general taxes are very far from being general. What is left out is not only leisure, but a whole host of other things. This seems if anything to strengthen the case for the Ramsey Rule group. For the classic statement of the Ramsey Problem is to "choose a set of taxes $t_1, t_2, \ldots, t_k$, on a subset $x_1, x_2, \ldots, x_k$ out of a broader set consisting of $x_1, x_2, \ldots, x_k, x_{k+1}, \ldots x_N$ goods and services. Choose these taxes so as to raise a given amount of revenue ($\Sigma_{j=1}^{k} t_j x_j = R$), at a minimum deadweight loss (read welfare or efficiency cost.)" Equivalently, the Ramsey problem can be stated "choose taxes on $x_1, x_2, \ldots x_k$ in such a way as to maximize the revenue R that is raised, while imposing on the economy a given deadweight loss (welfare cost)."

In reality, then, we should think of a "left out" group consisting of a whole package of goods and services – leisure, many personal services, much of housing, etc. These make up the untaxed group, while another set of goods and services make up the taxed group. Ramsey rule taxation of the different goods within the taxed group would in principle require that we know something about their cross elasticities with respect to that grand composite that I am now calling the "left-out" group. But we really know very little about this group. It represents the area of the economy where our data are poorest. Also – a point I will return to later – it represents the activities of more conscious evasion and avoidance of the supposedly general tax. For me, the bottom line here is that we have neither adequate data for concluding, nor an adequate basis for guessing, that one component of the taxed group is a better- or less-than-average substitute for the ill-perceived amalgam we are calling the "left-out" group.

A simple tax scenario

In the midst of our ignorance, however, economics comes to the rescue – at least with some modest consolation. Consider this scenario. We have a large taxed group, covered by something that we were thinking of as a uniform, general tax. For reasons beyond our control, however, the tax is not and in reality cannot ever be completely general. What are our margins of choice? What are the interesting decisions facing us?

To me at least, one key class of decisions concerns whether or not to try to shift some item, or some specific class of goods and services, from the "left-out" group to the covered group. In so doing we will quite surely cause output to increase both in the already-covered sector and in what remains of the "left-out" group. The presumption is that any very large mass of goods is going to be a substitute for some subcategory of goods that we pick at random. So when we shift bicycle repair shops from the "left-out" to the taxed category, we see the output of that particular activity going down, with its resources being shifted both to the other items in the taxed group and to the remaining items in the untaxed group. Welfare goes down by the amount of a triangle whose height is the general tax rate and whose base is the reduction in bicycle repair shop activity. But there is a countervailing gain in welfare equal to the general tax rate times the shift of resources to other components of the taxed group. Is the gain bigger or smaller than the loss? Neither gain nor loss is easy to estimate with precision. But maybe it is easier to say whether one is bigger than the other.

In fact, it is so. The condition for the gain to be bigger than the loss is that at least half of the resource reduction in the newly taxed activity be reflected in an increase in already taxed activities. One should accordingly be wary of shifting bicycle repair shops to the taxed group. If side by side with them we have an untaxed bicycle repair activity flourishing in the so-called informal sector, this would mean that the untaxed sector would get the lion's share of the released resources. We should be wary, then, of shifting to the taxed group any subsector that has strong substitutes still being left in the untaxed group. A corollary is that, to the extent possible, when we add one activity to the taxed group, we should try to bring it in, linked in a package with all of its close substitutes that were previously untaxed. On the other hand, a prime candidate for shifting to the taxed group would be anything that we might find in the untaxed group that had strong substitutes already under the tax.

We have a more normal situation when neither strong substitutes nor strong complements can be identified for an item we are contemplating adding to the taxed group. Then we would rely on the phenomenon of generalized substitution that we know exists in economic activity. Other things being equal, we would expect that the resources expelled from the newly taxed sector would be attracted to the two major groups (taxed and untaxed) in rough proportion to the amount of resources already in each. If the two major groups were of equal size, something like half of the expelled resources would go to the taxed sector, and this would create a situation in which the triangle of costs was just matched by the rectangle of benefits.

As the tax gets more and more general, the presumption becomes greater at each step that the resources expelled from a newly taxed activity will go predominantly to already taxed activities. This obviously augments the benefit of widening the tax net.

This is not the place for me to try to extend the above analysis to other questions. Suffice it to say that in deriving the above I used the same analytical machinery as leads to the Ramsey Rule. The only important distinguishing feature is that I have presumed a *realistic level of ignorance* about detailed facts (and in particular about precise substitution parameters).

The pragmatic lessons that follow from the above are:

1   When choosing the set of items to be covered by a "general" tax (say a value added tax) try to keep "packages" of strong substitute items together (i.e., either all in the taxed group or all in the "left-out" group).

2   If a package of close substitutes has some important items that by their nature are difficult to tax, then the course of prudence may be to leave the whole package in the untaxed sector rather than cause sharp tax-induced substitutions by introducing a tax only on part of the group.

3   Once a "general" tax reaches a size worthy of the name, there is a reasonable presumption that shifting additional items from the "left-out" group to the taxed group will be beneficial in terms of economic welfare. This becomes of greater interest once it is realized that the addition of such items brings revenue increases as well.

4   Once a point of plausible generality is reached, the grounds for making the tax even more general are quite strong (see 3). Hence beyond this point the only strong technical arguments against further extending the scope of the tax are administrative in nature. Taxes that are easy to evade will no doubt be evaded. This may determine that whole packages of substitute items be left in the untaxed sector (see 2).

The preceding scenario has derived operating rules for a uniform, reasonably general tax like the VAT, and has done so under what I consider reasonable assumptions concerning the amount and generality of information available to us (whether as technicians or policymakers). I certainly don't want to claim that the resulting general tax would be an "optimum" tax in the technical sense. But it surely would be a good tax, raising a lot of revenue at a relatively low efficiency or welfare cost.

For now I want to leave the technical side at that. We have outlined a good tax, with low deadweight loss per peso of revenue. This comes from the technical side.

Now I want to add some items that are perhaps more philosophical than technical. *First*, do we want our tax system to depend very strongly on people's tastes? Ramsey Rule taxation impinges heavily on those items that people prize most (in the sense of having a relatively inelastic demand for them), and least heavily on those items about which people are relatively indifferent vis-à-vis alternatives (as revealed in a relatively high elasticity of demand for them). On the supply side, likewise, Ramsey Rule taxation looks like a "search and destroy" mission aimed against economic rents. It would be, in principle, the job of a Ramsey Rule tax manager, to find out what were the conditions of supply and demand in the economy, and to set tax rates accordingly, imposing high rates where demand was less elastic, low rates where it was more elastic. (This statement holds where the taxed sectors are independent in demand. The correct technical condition is for taxes to be higher on goods that are poorer substitutes for the "left-out" group.)

One can argue that we should not base tax policy on supply and demand parameters because we do not know enough about them, nor can we hope to in any foreseeable future. But that is not the line I am taking here as my *second* point. What I am doing here is questioning whether we want our policy to be significantly dependent on changes in tastes and technology. I do not intend to answer the question. Rather, I simply note that a broad, general uniform tax of the type developed in the preceding scenario would not be seriously influenced by plausible changes in taste or technology. Thus a question that might prove troublesome to a Ramsey Rule advocate might be of little import to one who worked and thought within the framework of our tax scenario.

My *third* point is value-loaded in comparison to the others. Here we ask the question, do we, in our own vision of the good society, think that the government *should* care about changes in tastes among its citizens? Should it want to change its tax laws because demand has become more elastic for one good, supply less elastic for another, or because a new product has been introduced or an old one improved? Ramsey Rule advocates should in principle say yes to these questions. But there are many thoughtful citizens who would say no. Such citizens would feel more calm and secure in the world described by our tax scenario than in one governed by the Ramsey Rule.

My *fourth* point concerns the fact that the Ramsey exercise contemplates a world of well defined commodities, technologies, and tastes. When a tax is put on x_4, certain substitution occurs between x_4 and other commodities – say x_1, x_2, x_3. The whole framework is known; what is a commodity is known, what are the tastes of people for that commodity and the different ways of producing it are known. Given all this, the Ramsey Rule says, raise the tax on x_4 to 60 percent, while the others are, say, at 30 percent.

Say x_4 is automobiles, and that automobiles are imported. A higher tax causes people to look for substitutes. Some buy trucks and use them as cars. Some buy motorcycles and use them instead of cars. Some ride buses instead of owning a car. All this fits within the framework of known commodities, known technologies, known tastes, from which we derive the Ramsey Rule. But now consider that some people will import trucks and build up a new activity that virtually converts trucks into cars. Others will import motorcycles and convert them into multi-passenger vehicles. Others will take such vehicles and create a new industry competing with existing taxis and buses. All this is in a way standard (and presumably legal) tax avoidance. But it also brings into question the definition of the commodity itself. After some four decades as a professional economist, much of it devoted to public finance problems, my considered judgement is that a commodity is what the tax law and administrative practice say it is. The law and its administration could, in the above case, have defined the commodity such that nobody would have the incentives to create new vehicle types by converting trucks and motorcycles into things that look and function more like cars. In Ramsey Rule taxation, the definition of each commodity is quite critical. But it becomes almost irrelevant when one deals with a broad-based uniform levy.

III   The case for a uniform tariff

Economists quite naturally gravitate to free trade, if only from the point of view that it tends to maximize the welfare of the world as a whole. The only argument for tariffs that can be thought of as a first-best argument deals with the case where a country (or a group of countries like the EEC) possesses monopsony power in the market for one or more internationally traded products. In that case, the imposition of a tariff on that good can help the country to exploit its monopsony position in the world market. But obviously, such a tariff does not augment world welfare. Though technically correct, the argument is distinctly parochial, definitely self-serving from one nation's (or group's) point of view.

(Parenthetically, one of the more curious facts of life in this topsy-turvy world is that hardly any case can be found of a serious attempt to impose a tariff for monopsony purposes. If one asks, who *has* monopsony power in world markets, the answer is undoubtedly the United States and the European Economic Community, with Japan as the most likely potential third case. Over what commodities does such monopsony power prevail? Quite clearly, goods in relatively inelastic overall supply – goods like tin, copper, other non-ferrous metals, agricultural products like coffee, tea, cocoa, and bananas. The mental experiment is easy to make. Suppose the US or the EEC were to place, say, a 50 percent tariff on its imports of any of these items. What would happen to its world price? Without a doubt the world price would go down, benefiting the tariff-imposing country (together with all other net importers of the good), and hurting suppliers of the commodity wherever they might be located (except in the tariff-imposing country itself). Now the odd fact is that the range of products that are the most likely candidates for monopsony-motivated tariffs are precisely those in which free trade has tended to prevail. In most of these products there is no serious domestic production to protect in either the US or Europe. As a result there is no political pressure for tariffs.

There are a few cases in which the policies of the US and the EEC have indeed affected world prices – notably the US sugar policy and the EEC policy on wheat and other grains, as well as meat. But in none of these cases can we ascribe to the policy an intent to exploit monopsony power in world markets. Straight, old fashioned protection of domestic argicultural interests is the self-evident motive in these cases, much more visible than any fear of retaliation from one or more primary-producing countries.

Tariffs are no more than second-best policies under any argument other than that of national monopsony. Hence we must recognize that even a uniform tariff is second-best. If the market exchange rate is 10 pesos per dollar, and a 30 percent uniform tariff is in place, then the domestic resource cost of producing all sorts of import substitutes will be 13 pesos per dollar's worth, while the domestic resource cost of producing export goods will be ten pesos per dollar's worth. Obviously, a distortion exists here, which can be rectified by bringing the 30 percent general tariff down to zero – which leaves us at free trade – or by introducing a uniform 30 percent export subsidy, which by the famous Lerner theorem brings us to free trade in another guise. (Together, a 30 percent general import tax and a 30 percent general export subsidy operate in just the same way, as far as trade items are concerned, as a 30 percent devaluation of the currency.)

We thus cannot realistically deal with real-world tariffs without recognizing that they are distortionary policies. My own thumbnail interpretation is that on the whole these tariffs are imposed out of protectionist pressures, though the revenue motive may have ruled in a few of the poorest countries, while a belief in import-substituting "modernization" may have come into play in getting protection established in some of the middle-income countries. Once in place, of course, protected operations generate their own pressures to perpetuate the policy. Protectionist pressure also explains why tariffs tend to be concentrated on finished goods. They typically leave primary inputs alone, except when there is a domestic primary-producing industry to protect. The protectionist motive thus also explains the pattern that rates of tariff (where they exist) tend to be highest on finished goods and lowest on primary inputs.

I believe that the standard case for a uniform tariff relies on the protectionist motive. Indeed, one needs the protectionist motive in order to sanction the idea that one should accept a domestic resource cost of 13 pesos for producing a dollar's worth of import substitutes while at the same time the domestic resource cost of generating a dollar via the export route is only ten pesos.

In my view, the uniform tariff argument says, "let us accept that the virus of protectionism is rampant throughout the world, and that we cannot stamp it out. But let us try to contain the disease that the virus causes. Let us try to limit the damage it can do."

By accepting the idea that the virus of protectionism is with us to stay, the uniform tariff argument "justifies," or at least explains, why one "should" be content to have a higher domestic resource cost for import substitutes than for exports. But then the uniform tariff argument goes on to point out the absurdity (from an economic point of view) of paying a DRC of 22 pesos per dollar in one place, of 16 pesos per dollar in another, and of 10 pesos per dollar in a third place – all being cases of import substitution, with the last one being (typically) that of raw materials which enter duty-free.

There can be no doubt that, in the absence of monopsony power, a country gains by moving toward equalization of the domestic resource costs of different import substitute activities. In advocating this, the economists who developed the theory of effective protection and who extracted its principal implications were acting as responsible representatives of the economist's traditional role in policy-making.

I would characterize that traditional role as follows: economists favor efficiency, fight ignorance, and strive to represent the general interest. In the case of the uniform tariff, the efficiency goal is served (in a second-best sense) by equalizing effective protection while keeping the total amount of imports (or of domestic production of import substitutes) constant. A uniform tariff fights ignorance in the sense that many citizens and legislators may think (wrongly) that a 30 percent tariff on each of a number of final products represents fair and equal treatment for each industry that is so protected. But effective protection analysis shows how these industries can be favored in dramatically different degrees, simply depending on how much they use imported inputs and on the level of tariffs applying to those inputs. The uniform tariff is thus precisely what is needed to give "fair and equal treatment" in the sense of equal effective protection and an equal willingness by citizens to bear an extra domestic resource cost for import-substituting activities.

The traditional role of economists in representing the general interest makes economists the "natural enemies" of special interest groups. This has indeed been their traditional role. I do not think it has been modified by modern efforts by a small subset of our profession to "explain" why some interest groups have more power than others, and therefore why some tariffs are high and some tariffs are low. Industries with more political "clout" can inflict more damage on the average consumer than industries with smaller influence on governments and legislatures. That may explain, but does not justify the exploitation of consumers and taxpayers, nor does it free economists from what I would consider a moral duty to oppose such exploitation.

Just as in the case of efficiency, some compromise of the general interest is involved in a uniform tariff, but the costs are widely shared and limited in amount. In particular, they do not favor powerful political interests in any obvious way. Indeed, the move from a differentiated tariff to a uniform one might be considered as a way to equalize the political "clout" of all domestic producers of import substitutes. The critical step in bringing about equal effective protection goes beyond raising tariffs on the products whose domestic producers are politically weak and ill-organized. The critical step is that in which the uniform tariff is extended to goods – like some minerals perhaps, and tropical fibers – that are not now, and probably never will be produced in the country. The same goes for complicated capital goods in developing countries. Who is there who will fight for tariffs on such goods? Only the domestic consumers and taxpayers have their interests at stake. The producer groups that exist will be on the other side, fighting for zero or very low tariffs, for these are goods that are inputs into their production processes. To the degree that they succeed, they will get greater effective protection, imposing greater costs on consumers and taxpayers. Economists have a very big task here, in defending the general interest. One of the great virtues of the idea of a uniform tariff is that it gives economists a general principle to appeal to as they wage this struggle. The idea that a uniform tariff gives equal effective protection to everybody is a potential mobilizing force that can be brought to bear on the difficult political task of raising tariffs where no domestic producer group will benefit and indeed where producer groups from the input-using industries are fighting on the other side.

IV Tariffs on inputs revisited

Most expositions of the theory of effective protection start out, as we did in the introduction, with a given tariff on some final products. They then show how the same final-product tariff can lead to very different rates of effective protection, depending on the fraction that the cost of imported inputs (assumed to enter free of duty) bears to the world price of each final product. As a final step they show that if the inputs are subjected to the same tariff rate as the final products, then effective protection on all the products converges to that same rate.

Most economists are aware of the above line of analysis; indeed, they probably have worked through it themselves. What many are not aware of is the fact that it typically would benefit the country to raise the level of input tariffs *above* that applying to the final products. The reason for this is that by raising input tariffs one has the potential to *annul* the so-called production cost of a tariff on a final product.

First, let me review the standard line of argument on the production cost and the consumption cost of a tariff. A tariff of 30 percent is equivalent to its effects to a subsidy of 30 percent on the domestic production of the tariffed good, plus a consumption tax of 30 percent on its domestic use. The producer cost of the tariff is the excess cost of producing at home versus importing from the world market. The consumer cost is the excess burden borne by consumers because the domestic price is higher than the world price.

Suppose now we have a commodity – say bicycles – that uses steel as in input. A 30 percent tariff on bicycles will cause the domestic price to be 30 percent higher than the world price. Consumption will be artificially restrained and production artificially stimulated. But if the price of steel is simultaneously raised, the artificial stimulus to production can be blunted.

Suppose the world price of a bicycle is 100 dollars, which translates into 1,000 pesos at the market exchange rate of 10 pesos per dollar. The 30 percent tariff thus "invites" 300 pesos of extra domestic resource cost. A tariff of 30 percent on steel – assumed to account for one-fifth of the cost of a bicycle at world prices – reduces the extra domestic resource cost to 240 pesos. Producing a bicycle now is profitable at a domestic resource cost of up to 1,040 pesos, instead of 800 under free trade. Since this operation saves 80 dollars of foreign exchange the domestic resource cost per dollar saved is now 13 pesos. But suppose the tariff on steel were set at 70 percent. Now the final product would cost 1,300 pesos, and steel inputs would have a cost to producers of 340 pesos. Only 960 would remain to attract domestic resources to the activity of bicycle-making, and the resource cost per dollar saved would be $960 \div 80 = 12$ pesos. Effective protection would now be only 20 percent. By the same token a 110 percent tariff on steel would reduce the DRC to 11 pesos and the rate of effective protection to 10 percent. Obviously, by raising the tariff on steel high enough, one could bring the domestic resource cost down to 10 pesos per dollar and the rate of effective protection to zero. The critical rate in this case is 150 percent. With this tariff rate, steel inputs cost the producer 500 pesos per bicycle he makes. DRC will be $1,300 - 500 = 800$ pesos for a bicycle whose domestic production saves 80 dollars of foreign exchange. Effective protection is zero.

Consider the general formula for the rate of effective protection t_{ex} on product x. This formula is $t_{ex} = (t_{nx} - \Sigma_j a_{jx} t_{nj})/(1 - \Sigma_j a_{jx})$, where $t_{nx} =$ nominal tariff on output x, $t_{nj} =$ nominal tariff on input j, and $a_{jx} =$ fraction of the world price of x accounted for by input j. If we have a tariff on only one input r, we can render t_{ex} equal to zero by setting t_{nr} equal to t_{nx}/a_{rx}. With tariffs on two inputs there are many ways to get t_{ex} equal to zero. One of these is with a single tariff t_{n*} applying to both inputs, r and s. In this case setting t_{n*} equal to $t_{nx}/(a_{rx} + a_{sx})$ would do the trick.

The general insight to be drawn from the above analysis is that one can annul the production cost of any tariff t_{nx} by imposing on all its imported inputs a tariff equal to t_{nx} times the ratio that the world price of the output bears to the aggregate cost of imported inputs. Note that this ratio will always be greater than one. Hence the production-cost-annulling tariff on inputs is always *greater than* the tariff on final products.

What can we do with this arcane result? I certainly would never argue in favor of input tariffs being made systematically greater than output tariffs. Among other things many inputs are also final products at the same time. Imported inputs also enter different outputs in different proportions.

To me the most relevant use of the above theorem is to reinforce the case in favor of uniform tariffs, if one is in a situation where on other grounds a uniform tariff (as distinct from free trade) seems to make sense.

We saw earlier how real-world tariffs on inputs tend to be fixed at low or even zero rates, and how there is very little political pressure to raise them in the case where domestic production does not (perhaps cannot) exist. It is mainly economists who can make the case for raising such tariffs. For myself as an economist, I find my zeal for raising tariffs on inputs is greatly strengthened by the argument just presented. I feel less content with a situation where input tariffs are below the final product rate, given my knowledge that a second-best optimum rate for input tariffs would be greater – and usually very substantially greater – than the common rate on final products.

I should add, too, that bringing inputs up to the rate on final products is fully compatible with the idea of uniform effective protection. Carrying any one input tariff (or any subset of them) beyond the uniform rate on final products would reduce the DRC for the affected final products to something less than what the uniform final product tariff rate implies.

Thus I feel reasonably content in extracting from the analysis just presented a considerable reinforcement of my zeal in fighting to raise input tariffs to the common level, and at the same time not at all reluctant to stop there, not pressing input tariffs beyond the common final-product rate.

V Summary and conclusions

In this paper we have taken a route different from that of most tax analysis. Here we diverge from the common practice of looking at individual tax changes in a vacuum, as it were, and pretending that they are the only distortions in the picture. At the same time we also diverge from the less common practice of finding a second-best "optimum" package of tax rates, taking certain constraints as given. Instead we have taken as "our world" one in which some effort has already been expended to achieve a uniform rate of tax (or tariff), at least on some commodities.

In the case of value added taxation, we recognize from the outset that a fully general coverage will never be achieved. Instead we explore guidelines that will help the policymaker to decide where to draw the line between a "covered" group of activities and a "left-out" group. The broad conclusion is that there is a presumption for adding additional activities to the covered group, so long as (a) the costs of administration of such a move are not excessively high and (b) we are not shifting one commodity into the covered group, while leaving important close substitutes in the "left-out" group. Thus there is a presumption that, if some activities are themselves hard to bring into the tax net, it may be wise to leave their close substitutes outside the net as well.

In the case of import tariffs, we explore the arguments for equalizing the domestic resource costs of saving a dollar through different activities of import substitution. They have a degree of merit once it is taken for granted that import substitution has some positive value. (Otherwise, there is no basis for having different DRCs for import substitutes than for export goods.) In a real world setting the implementation of a uniform tariff almost invariably means increasing the rates applying to imported inputs and (possibly) capital goods. A political resistance to such tariffs on the part of the input-using industries is recognized to exist. Uniformity of effective protection is suggested as being possibly the best concept or slogan on which to base a campaign for increasing tariff rates on inputs.

The issue of increasing tariff rates on inputs is further explored in section IV. There it is shown that on the whole gains in welfare are still positive when one raises the rates of input tariffs quite a distance beyond the rate applying to final products. This result is not taken as something to be implemented in actual policy, but rather as a reinforcement of the argument for making sure that the coverage of a uniform tariff rate extends to the point of including imported inputs.

The analysis taken as a whole leads me to conclude that one cannot treat uniform value-added taxation or uniform tariffs as desirable and unquestioned goals on which all economists should in principle agree. Their justification is far more subtle and judgmental than that. Supporters of uniform taxation are therefore well-advised to recognize that their conclusion requires a well-reasoned defense. By the same token, it behooves those who argue against uniform taxation to go beyond simple Ramsey Rule mathematics in defending their position, and to cope with some of the subtler arguments (philosophical as well as strictly technical) that comprise the best case for uniform taxation.

Selected References

Auerbach, Alan 1985: "The Theory of Excess Burden and Optimal Taxation," in Auerbach and Feldstein 1985, vol. 1, 61–127.

Auerbach, Alan J. and Feldstein, Martin S. (eds) 1985: *Handbook of Public Economics*, Amsterdam and New York: North Holland.

Atkinson, Anthony 1985: "The Theory of Tax Design for Developing Countries," in Auerbach and Feldstein 1985, chapter 14.

Atkinson, Anthony B. and Stiglitz, Joseph E. 1976: "The Design of Tax Structure; Direct versus Indirect Taxation," *Journal of Public Economics*, 6(1), 55–76.

Atkinson, Anthony B. and Stiglitz, Joseph E. 1980: *Lectures on Public Economics*, New York: McGraw-Hill, chapters 12, 13, and 14.

Bos, Dieter 1985: "Public Sector Pricing," in Auerbach and Feldstein, 1985, chapter 3.

Bos, Dieter 1986: *Public Enterprise Economics: Theory and Application*, Amsterdam and New York: North Holland, chapter 8.

Diamond, Peter A. 1975: "A Many-Person Ramsey Tax Rule," *Journal of Public Economics*, 4, 335–42.

Mirrlees, James A. 1975: "Optimal Commodity Taxation in a Two-Class Economy," *Journal of Public Economics*, 4(1), 27–33.

Musgrave, Richard A. 1985: "A Brief History of Fiscal Doctrine," in Auerbach and Feldstein, 1985, chapter 1.

Newberry, David and Stern, Nicholas (eds) 1988: *The Theory of Taxation in Developing Countries*, Washington DC: The World Bank.

Ramsey, Frank P. 1927: "A Contribution to the Theory of Taxation," *Economic Journal*, 37, 47-61.

Sandmo, A. 1976: "Optimal Taxation - an Introduction to the Literature," *Journal of Public Economics*, 6(1), 37-54.

Stern, Nicholas: "The Theory of Optimal Commodity and Income Taxation."

6

Intellectual Property Rights and North–South Trade

JUDITH C. CHIN AND GENE M. GROSSMAN

I Introduction

The issue of intellectual property rights has become a contentious one indeed in recent trade relations between North and South. In the North, producers of new knowledge and ideas rely on protection in the forms of patents, copyrights and trademarks to enable them to appropriate some of the benefits from investment in research and development. The Northern governments have responded to pleas for assistance from their corporate sectors in the face of billions of dollars of lost revenue and profits from piracy and counterfeiting[1] by applying pressure on the South to provide greater enforcement of property rights and by pushing for new codes of international behavior.[2] At the urging of the United States, for example, the parties to the GATT established as one of the 14 negotiating groups of the Uruguay Round one charged "to clarify GATT provisions and elaborate as appropriate new rules and disciplines regarding international enforcement of intellectual property rights" (Baldwin, 1988, p. 65). The South, for its part, manifests almost total dependency on the North for the technologies needed for growth and development. These countries fear exploitation at the hands of innovative firms in the North in view of their weak bargaining position. They have been quite reluctant to accede to Northern demands for strengthening of standards on protection of intellectual property (GAO, 1987).

The welfare economics of intellectual property rights in a closed-economy setting are reasonably well understood. A fundamental tension exists between the social desirability of widespread dissemination of available know-how and the need for society to provide adequate rewards to purveyors of new information. The tension stems from the public-good nature of most forms of knowledge; once generated, knowledge can be used simultaneously by many parties besides the original creator at zero or minimal additional cost. This consideration argues against protection of intellectual property, since the granting of property rights can only diminish the efficiency of use of a given knowledge base. But in the absence of some form of protection, private agents will have little reason to invest their resources to generate new information and technologies. The socially optimal degree of protection of intellectual property requires a balancing of these fundamentally opposing objectives (see Nordhaus, 1969). Most governments have chosen to award *limited* market power (in the form of narrowly prescribed patents, copyrights and trademarks) to innovators as a compromise solution in which some static misallocation is accepted as the cost of preserving dynamic incentives.

In a world economy inhabited by sovereign governments, the issue of protection of intellectual property becomes all the more complex. The globally efficient degree of protection need not serve the separate interests of the individual governments that must enforce property rights. In particular, one would suspect that national well-being is maximized by a higher degree of protection of intellectual property in countries that develop new technologies and stand to earn monopoly rents from their application than in countries that only consume the goods and services that are produced using new ideas. But conflict of interest between governments is by no means inevitable. As an extreme example, suppose no product development would take place in an industry in the absence of adequate protection against piracy and infringement. Then a country with no capability to conduct R&D would nonetheless benefit from enforcement of patent and copyright laws insofar as its consumers stand to capture some surplus from any new products marketed within its borders. Indeed the US government, in its discussions with trade partner governments in the South, has sought to emphasize the stake that the latter have in the intellectual property rights system (see GAO, 1987, pp. 43–4).

In this paper, we study the welfare economics of patent protection in a North–South trading environment.[3] We suppose that initially a Northern firm and a Southern firm have access to an "old" technology to produce a good that is demanded in both countries. The Northern firm alone also has the ability to devote resources to an R&D project in order to improve the production technology. If foreign intellectual property rights are protected by the government in the South, then the Northern firm will gain via its R&D efforts a competitive advantage over its Southern rival. It can exploit this advantage in the ensuing international oligopolistic competition by capturing an increased share of the market, or, in some circumstances, by licensing its superior technology to its rival. If, alternatively, the government in the South fails to enforce patent protection over the new production process, then the Southern firm will be able to pirate the innovative technology and can once again become an equal competitor in the international marketplace. This prospect, we assume, is well understood by the Nothern firm, which then sets its R&D outlays accordingly.

We investigate the extent to which patent protection by the government of the South adds to social welfare in each country separately, and in the world as a whole. In our model, global patent protection serves to stimulate innovation, so that production costs are lower (for at least the Northern firm) in the sales-stage equilibrium. This effect alone acts to the benefit of both countries. Against this is the fact that enforcement of patent protection mitigates, and in some cases eliminates, oligopolistic competition, to the detriment of welfare in both countries. Finally, the presence or absence of protection of intellectual property in the South has implications for the international distribution of income, as the Northern firm captures a greater share of extra-normal industry profits when rights are protected than it does when infringement takes place.

The remainder of our paper is organized as follows. In the next section we develop the model described above, and compare levels of welfare in each country with and without Southern protection for Northern intellectual property. We maintain the assumption, in this section, that international licensing arrangements between horizontal competitors are infeasible. In section III, we introduce the possibility of licensing, ask when it will take place, and then re-examine the welfare comparisons of the protection and no-protection regimes. We discuss some implications of our analysis for current international economic relations in the concluding section.

II Patent protection when licensing is infeasible

We consider a linear-quadratic Cournot duopoly in an integrated world economy. Initially, one firm in the North and one firm in the South can produce some homogenous good at constant marginal cost, α. The Northern firm now faces an opportunity to devote resources to a deterministic R&D project in order to improve upon the existing production technology. The firm can achieve a *cost reduction* of amount Δ by spending Δ^2/γ on process innovation. Letting R denote its research outlay, its post-innovation marginal cost of production will be[4]

$$C(R) = \alpha - (\gamma R)^{1/2}, \qquad R \le \alpha^2/\gamma. \tag{6.1}$$

Final marginal cost in the South will depend upon whether or not the Northern firm's patent rights to its innovative production process are protected by the government of the South, and on whether or not the Southern firm is able and willing to negotiate a licensing agreement with its Northern rival. We assume throughout this section that the complexity of the technology and the attendant difficulties in writing an enforceable contract preclude any licensing agreements. Then, if property rights are protected, the Southern firm's cost of production remains $c = \alpha$. If, alternatively, the government of the South fails to enforce the Northern firm's patent rights, the Southern firm will be able to imitate the innovative technology. To make our arguments as sharp as possible, we suppose that the cost of reverse engineering is negligible.[5] Then in the absence of protection for intellectual property marginal production costs in the South are equal to those in the North.

After the Northern firm completes its R&D project and the Southern firm imitates if possible, the two firms engage in Cournot (quantity-setting) competition. We adopt a linear form for (inverse) demand in the integrated world market, and choose units so that this curve has a slope of one. Then

$$P = \beta - (y + Y), \qquad \beta > \alpha, \tag{6.2}$$

where P is the market-clearing price of the good and y and Y are the quantities sold by the Southern and Northern firms, respectively. We assume as well that at every price a constant fraction $1/\theta$ of demand originates in the marketplace of the South. This implies an inverse demand function in the South of $p(q) = \beta - \theta q$, where q is the quantity sold there, and also that the South will enjoy a fraction $1/\theta$ of total world consumer surplus at any equilibrium price.

A Property rights violated

We begin by solving the model under the assumption that the government of the South fails to protect the intellectual property rights of the Northern firm. Then the ultimate market structure is one of *symmetric duopoly* with common costs $C = c$. These of course depend on the prior R&D decision of the Northern firm. As is well known, the Cournot equilibrium levels of output in this instance are $y = Y = (\beta - C)/3$ and the equilibrium price is $P = (\beta + 2C)/3$.

We assume that, at the R&D phase, the Northern firm correctly foresees the implications of its actions for the subsequent product-market competition. That is, we seek a dynamic equilibrium that satisfies the sub-game-perfection constraint. The problem facing the Northern firm in the first stage of the game is to choose R to maximize total profits

$$Z(R) = \frac{[\beta - \alpha + (\gamma R)^{1/2}]^2}{9} - R, \tag{6.3}$$

where the expression for operating profits in (6.3) represents the product of price and per-unit profit. The first-order condition for a profit maximum implies[6]

$$R = \frac{\gamma(\beta - \alpha)^2}{(9 - \gamma)^2} \tag{6.4}$$

from whence we derive profits for each firm:

$$Z = \frac{(\beta - \alpha)^2}{9 - \gamma}; \tag{6.5n}$$

$$z = \frac{9(\beta - \alpha)^2}{(9 - \gamma)^2}. \tag{6.5s}$$

Consumer surplus, S and s, in each country is the area between the inverse demand curve and the equilibrium price line. Straightforward calculations reveal

$$S = 18 \frac{\theta - 1}{\theta} \frac{(\beta - \alpha)^2}{(9 - \gamma)^2},$$

(6.6n)

$$s = \frac{18}{\theta} \frac{(\beta - \alpha)^2}{(9 - \gamma)^2}.$$

(6.6s)

Finally total surplus in each country, W and w, is the sum of consumer surplus and producer surplus, or

$$W = \left(9 - \gamma + 18 \frac{\theta - 1}{\theta}\right) \frac{(\beta - \alpha)^2}{(9 - \gamma)^2}$$

(6.7n)

$$w = 9 \left(\frac{\theta + 2}{\theta}\right) \frac{(\beta - \alpha)^2}{(9 - \gamma)^2}.$$

(6.7s)

B Property rights protected

If the government of the South does indeed prevent its local firm from infringing the patent rights of the Northern innovator, then the duopolists bear different marginal costs at the time that they meet in the product market. In this case, three types of equilibria may arise, depending upon the size of the parameter γ describing the effectiveness of R&D in reducing production costs. For small values of γ the R&D efforts of the Northern firm will be modest, and *asymmetric duopoly* will characterize the final stage of competition. For large values of γ the Northern firm will find it optimal to reduce its cost substantially, so much so that it will enjoy an unfettered *monopoly* position in the product market. Finally, when γ takes on intermediate values, the Northern firm will act strategically to induce exit by its rival (see Dixit, 1980). Then its final position in the product market will be one of monopoly, but the firm will find itself constrained to choose a level of R&D spending sufficiently large to guarantee non-positive profits for its rival. We shall refer to this last market structure as one of *strategic predation*. We proceed now to find optimal levels of R&D, and equilibrium profits, consumer surplus, and total welfare for each of these scenarios, and to delimit the values of γ for which each applies.

Consider first the output stage of an asymmetric duopoly with costs C and c. The two first-order conditions equating perceived marginal revenues to marginal costs imply a Cournot equilibrium with $Y = (\beta - 2C + c)/3$ and $y = (\beta - 2c + C)/3$, and an associated equilibrium price $P = (\beta + C + c)/3$. Anticipating these outcomes, the Northern firm chooses R to maximize

$$Z(R) = \frac{1}{9} [\beta - \alpha + 2\gamma^{1/2} R^{1/2}]^2 - R$$

(6.8)

The optimal choice of R when duopolistic competition is foreseen satisfies

$$R = \frac{4\gamma(\beta - \alpha)^2}{(9 - 4\gamma)^2}. \tag{6.9}$$

But, with this level of R&D, output by the Southern firm remains positive if and only if $\gamma < 3/2$. So, $\gamma < 3/2$ is necessary for the duopoly outcome to obtain.

If duopoly does obtain, the expressions for equilibrium outputs and price imply

$$Z = \frac{(\beta - \alpha)^2}{9 - 4\gamma} \tag{6.10n}$$

and

$$z = \frac{(3 - 2\gamma)^2(\beta - \alpha)^2}{(9 - 4\gamma)^2}. \tag{6.10s}$$

We can also calculate levels of consumer surplus, whence we find

$$S = \frac{2(\theta - 1)}{\theta} \frac{(\beta - \alpha)^2(3 - \gamma)^2}{(9 - 4\gamma)^2}; \tag{6.11n}$$

$$s = \frac{2}{\theta} \frac{(\beta - \alpha)^2(3 - \gamma)^2}{(9 - 4\gamma)^2}. \tag{6.11s}$$

Summing the respective consumer and producer surpluses for each country gives

$$W = \frac{(\beta - \alpha)^2}{(9 - 4\gamma)^2}\left[9 - 4\gamma + \frac{2(\theta - 1)}{\theta}(3 - \gamma)^2\right]; \tag{6.12n}$$

$$w = \frac{(\beta - \alpha)^2}{\theta(9 - 4\gamma)^2}[\theta(3 - 2\gamma)^2 + 2(3 - \gamma)^2]. \tag{6.12s}$$

Now suppose, for the moment, that the Northern firm were to face no competition whatsoever. Then its jointly optimal choices of output and research would be $Y = 2(\beta - \alpha)/(4 - \gamma)$ and $R = \gamma(\beta - \alpha)^2/(4 - \gamma)^2$. When would these choices represent an equilibrium despite potential competition from the firm in the South? If, at the implied monopoly price $P = [\beta(2 - \gamma) + 2\alpha]/(4 - \gamma)$ the Southern firm could not cover its production cost α, then the rival would choose to exit the industry. From this, we see that unconstrained monopoly results whenever $\gamma > 2$.[7] In this case,

$$Z = \frac{(\beta - \alpha)^2}{4 - \gamma}, \tag{6.13n}$$

$$S = \frac{2(\theta - 1)}{\theta} \frac{(\beta - \alpha)^2}{(4 - \gamma)^2}, \tag{6.14n}$$

$$W = \frac{(\beta - \alpha)^2}{\theta(4 - \gamma)^2} (6\theta - \gamma\theta - 2), \tag{6.15n}$$

while $z = 0$ and

$$w = s = \frac{2(\beta - \alpha)^2}{\theta(4 - \gamma)^2}. \tag{6.14s}$$

Finally, for values of $\gamma \in [3/2, 2]$, the monopoly choice of research spending invites competition from the Southern rival, whereas the optimal choice of R&D from (6.9) more than suffices to guarantee the rival's exit from the market. For these intermediate values of γ the Northern firm conducts just enough R&D to guarantee $y = 0$; i.e., it drives its own cost to $2\alpha - \beta$ and the price to α. This requires a research outlay of $R = (\beta - \alpha)^2/\gamma$ and yields profits equal to

$$Z = \frac{(\gamma - 1)}{\gamma} (\beta - \alpha)^2. \tag{6.16n}$$

Then consumer surplus and total welfare in the North are given by

$$S = \frac{\theta - 1}{2\theta} (\beta - \alpha)^2; \tag{6.17n}$$

$$W = (\beta - \alpha)^2 \left(\frac{\gamma - 1}{\gamma} + \frac{\theta - 1}{2\theta} \right). \tag{6.18n}$$

In the South, we have, in this case, $z = 0$ and

$$w = s = \frac{(\beta - \alpha)^2}{2\theta}. \tag{6.17s}$$

It is a simple matter to check that, for all $\gamma < 3/2$, Northern profits from (6.10n) exceed those from (6.16n), so that $\gamma < 3/2$ is both necessary and sufficient for the duopoly outcome to obtain. Strategic predation occurs only for values of $\gamma \in [3/2, 2]$.

C Welfare comparisons

We are now prepared to compare levels of welfare in each country and for the world as a whole across regimes when the government of the South does not protect the intellectual property rights of the Northern firm. We begin with the South. For $\gamma < 3/2$, the relevant welfare expressions are those in (6.7s) and (6.12s). Subtracting one from the other, we find

$$\begin{aligned} \text{sgn} \{w^{NP} - w^P\} = \text{sgn} \{ &+ 486\theta - 405\theta\gamma - 108\gamma + 840\gamma^2 + 48\gamma^2 \\ &- 40\theta\gamma^3 - 2\gamma^3\}, \gamma \in (0, 3/2), \end{aligned} \tag{6.19s}$$

where superscripts "NP" and "P" have been used to indicate the regimes without protection of property rights and with protection, respectively. In general, the expression in (6.19s) is of ambiguous sign. But the right-hand side of (19s) is positive when $\theta = 9/8$ for all $\gamma \in (0,3/2)$ and $w^{NP} - w^P$ is increasing in θ for all γ in this range. From this we conclude that the South achieves higher national welfare when it neglects to protect intellectual property rights if a duopoly outcome will result under protection and if its share in world consumption does not exceed 88 percent.

Next consider the range of parameter values for which strategic predation is the outcome under patent protection. We subtract (6.17s) from (6.7s) to find

$$\text{sgn}\{w^{NP} - w^P\} = \text{sgn}\{18(\theta + 2) - (9 - \gamma)^2\}, \quad \gamma \in [3/2, 2]. \quad (6.20s)$$

The expression on the right-hand side of (6.20s) also is positive for all $\theta > 9/8$ and also increases with θ. Hence, when strategic predation will occur under protection, a Southern consumption share of less than 88 percent is sufficient for the South to prefer non-protection.

Finally, we consider the range of parameter values for which the North would capture a monopoly position if its property rights were respected. Recall that this case arises when R&D productivity is especially high. The relevant welfare expressions are (6.7s) and (6.14s), and we find

$$\text{sgn}\{w^{NP} - w^P\} = \text{sgn}\{9\theta(\gamma - 4)^2 + 2(8\gamma^2 - 54\gamma + 63)\},$$
$$\gamma \in [2, 4].$$

$$(6.21s)$$

For γ near 2, this expression remains positive unless the consumption share of the South is very high. But for γ large (near 4), the expression is *negative* for all $\theta > 1$. Thus, we find that protection of foreign intellectual property can benefit the South, but only when R&D is highly productive and the country stands to gain much on the consumption side from the fruits of the Northern firm's research efforts.

In figure 6.1, we have plotted the full range of permissible parameter values for γ and $1/\theta$. In the figure, we show the combinations of parameter values for which protection and non-protection best serve the selfish interests of the South. We see from the figure that the South will generally prefer to "look the other way" when patent infringement occurs, except in cases where its consumers absorb much of the world's output of the good subject to cost reduction or when the cost savings to be reaped from innovation are quite dramatic.

What then are the interests of the North? When we compare Northern welfare levels under protection and no-protection we find that, no matter what the value of γ and hence the market structure that would prevail with protection, the North *always* benefits from having its firm's property rights respected in the South.[8] Evidently, the consumption gain from increased competition can never outweigh the profit-distribution effect and the R&D-incentive effect. We conclude that conflict of interest between the North and the South in regard to the system of intellectual property rights is the rule rather than the exception in our model.

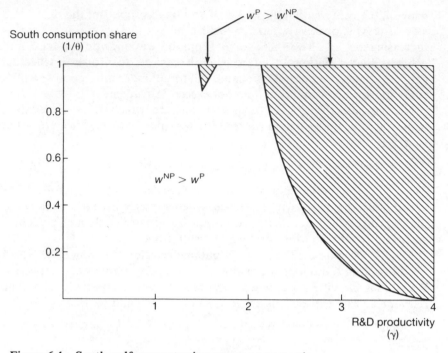

South consumption share
(1/θ)

Figure 6.1   South welfare: protection versus no-protection

When international conflict exists, it is natural to ask whether there are potential gains from cooperation. In the present context we might wonder whether the North could bribe the South to enforce patent protection in cases where protection was not in the narrowly defined self-interest of the latter. A world system of protected intellectual property rights would result from *efficient bargaining with compensation*, for example, if the North's gains from enforcement exceeded the South's losses. To investigate this issue, we define world welfare, $\Omega = W + w$, and compare levels of Ω across regimes.

Suppose first that available productivity gains from R&D are modest; i.e., $\gamma < 3/2$. We have in this case

$$\text{sgn}\,\{\Omega^{NP} - \Omega^{P}\} = \text{sgn}\,\{81 - 126\gamma + 40\gamma^2 - 2\gamma^3\}, \quad \gamma \in (0, 3/2)$$

(6.19w)

The expression on the right-hand side of (6.19w) is positive in the relevant range for all $\gamma \leq 0.875$ and is negative for all $\gamma \geq 0.876$. Thus, protection of foreign intellectual property rights in the South indeed advances global efficiency if the prospects for productivity gain through R&D are sufficiently bright, but for modest potential advances in knowledge world welfare actually is higher when the South *fails* to enforce patent protection.

Evidently, for small innovations, the benefit from the increased competition that results when diffusion takes place outweighs the cost in terms of dampened incentives for R&D investment.

For larger values of γ such that the Southern firm would exit the market in the absence of the ability to infringe upon the Northern firm's patent, protection by the South of intellectual property rights always enhances global efficiency. Straightforward computation reveals that $\Omega^P > \Omega^{NP}$ for $\gamma > 3/2$. Our analysis suggests, therefore, that intellectual property rights ought to be strongly protected in highly innovative industries, but that the argument for protection is less compelling when technological advances are likely to be small.

III Patent protection with potential licensing

Until this point, we have excluded the possibility that, after the conclusion of its R&D project, the Northern firm might elect to license its superior technology to its rival in the South. We justified this exclusion with reference to the costliness of writing enforceable contracts in some situations. But obviously there are circumstances where contracting considerations do not rule out licensing. Katz and Shapiro (1985) have studied the incentives for the sharing of technologies among horizontal competitors in such circumstances. We now adopt their approach to introduce the potential for licensing into our model, and then re-examine the international issues at hand.

A Licensing equilibria

As in Katz and Shapiro (1985), we suppose that licensing contracts can only be signed after research and development has been completed. It seems likely that if, instead, contracts were to be negotiated at some prior stage, and if they called for the sharing of (some amount of) information which at the time was not yet available to either party, then the resulting contracts would be extremely difficult to enforce. We add a third (licensing) stage to our game, one that takes place before the sales competition but subsequent to the commitment of R by the Northern firm. We also rule out, with reference to the antitrust laws applicable in most countries, any contracts that limit competition at the sales stage. We limit attention to contracts calling for a fixed licensing fee.[9]

When licensing agreements must be reached after R&D has been completed and imitation is costless, no agreements are possible in the absence of patent protection in the South. The Southern firm would never be willing to pay a positive fee to use the Northern firm's technology if it were possible for the firm to copy that technology at no cost. So, in this subsection, we limit attention to situations where the South provides protection for intellectual property. We re-introduce the alternative possibility of no protection only when we are ready to perform the regime comparisons.

The licensing of technology between horizontal competitors requires: (1) the existence of joint gains from sharing; and (2) the resolution of a bilateral bargaining problem. Given the existence of potential gains, licensing might not take place if the two parties to the negotiation had asymmetric information about their separate interests and attributes. Since we have nothing to add to the voluminous literature on bargaining, we choose the simplest possible specification of this aspect of the model. We suppose that licensing will take place under patent protection whenever the joint profits of the two firms with licensing exceed joint profits in the absence of licensing. We assume, moreover, that the Northern firm captures a fraction σ of the gains from trade, and treat σ as an exogenous parameter throughout our analysis.

More formally, let $\bar{Z}(R)$ and $\bar{z}(R)$ be the levels of profits that the Northern and Southern firms would obtain in the absence of any licensing agreement, and let $Z(R)$ and $z(R)$ be profit levels (not including any licensing fee) if technology sharing takes place. Then we assume that licensing will occur subsequent to a research effort at intensity R if and only if $Z(R) + z(R) \geq \bar{Z}(R) + \bar{z}(R)$, and that in such cases the Southern firm pays a fee

$$F(R) = \bar{Z}(R) - Z(R) + \sigma[Z(R) + z(R) - \bar{Z}(R) - \bar{z}(R)] \qquad (6.22)$$

for the right to use the Northern firm's superior technology. With this fee, the Northern firm's total profits, $Z(R) + F(R)$, are the sum of hypothetical profits in the absence of an agreement, $\bar{Z}(R)$, and that firm's share σ of the gains from trade.

Katz and Shapiro (1985) have proven that, in models such as this one, licensing will not take place if the potential licensor would enjoy a monopoly position in the product market were it to exclude its rival from the superior technology. For this reason, we restrict our search for licensing equilibria to values of R such that asymmetric duopoly would be the outcome in the absence of any agreement. For these values of R, the relevant expressions for $\bar{Z}(R)$ and $\bar{z}(R)$ are those that would arise in an asymmetric Cournot equilibrium with respective costs $C = \alpha - (\gamma R)^{1/2}$ and $c = \alpha$, while $Z(R)$ and $z(R)$ are those that arise in a symmetric Cournot equilibrium with costs $C = c = \alpha - (\gamma R)^{1/2}$. Inserting the appropriate terms in (6.22), we derive

$$F(R) = \frac{(2+2\sigma)(\beta - \alpha)\gamma^{1/2}R^{1/2} + (3-3\sigma)\gamma R}{9}. \qquad (6.23)$$

Assuming that licensing will take place, the optimal choice of R for the Northern firm is the one that maximizes $Z(R) + F(R)$. The first-order condition for this problem yields

$$R = \frac{\gamma(2+\sigma)^2(\beta - \alpha)^2}{[9+(3\sigma-4)\gamma]^2}, \tag{6.24}$$

with maximal cum-licensing profits (including the fee) equal to

$$Z + F = \frac{(\beta - \alpha)^2}{9[9+(3\sigma-4)\gamma]^2} \times [81 + 9\gamma(\sigma^2+10\sigma-4) + \gamma^2(3\sigma^3+17\sigma^2-28\sigma)]. \tag{6.25n}$$

There remains the question of whether the Northern firm will select a value of R that yields licensing in the post-R&D licensing equilibrium as part of its globally optimal strategy. The firm could instead choose a higher level of R&D such that no licensing agreement would be reached once the research phase had been completed. The profits it could earn by doing so never exceed those given in (6.10n), corresponding to maximal profits in an asymmetric duopoly situation without licensing. In making its choice of R, the Northern firm compares the right-hand sides of (6.10n) and (6.25n). This comparison yields a critical value of γ as a function of σ, $\gamma^* = G(\sigma)$ with $G' > 0$, such that licensing takes place in equilibrium if and only if $\gamma < \gamma^*$. Examining this function, we find that when $\gamma > 1.406$ licensing never takes place (i.e., no matter what the value of σ), whereas if $\gamma < 1.285$ licensing will always occur with protection. For values of γ between 1.285 and 1.406, licensing is more likely to result the larger is σ.[10]

For values of γ such that licensing would not take place in the sub-game perfect equilibrium, the analysis of intellectual property rights is exactly as in section III. So we restrict our attention here to those cases where, in the presence of patent protection, a licensing agreement would be reached. These cases are of special interest, because they imply that international technology transfer takes place in any event, either by commercial arrangement if patent protection is provided by the government of the South, or by piracy if not.

Using (6.24) and our formulae for Cournot equilibrium outputs and prices, we can calculate profits for the Southern firm and consumer surplus levels in each country in a licensing equilibrium. We find:

$$z - F = \frac{(\beta - \alpha)^2}{9(9-(4-3\sigma)\gamma)^2} \times [81 - 18\gamma(\sigma^2-\sigma+4) - \gamma^2(3\sigma^3-15\sigma^2+4\sigma-8)]; \tag{6.25s}$$

$$S = \frac{(\beta - \alpha)^2(\theta - 1)}{9\theta(9-(4-3\sigma)\gamma)^2} [162 - 72\gamma(2\sigma-1) + 8\gamma^2(4\sigma^2-4\sigma+1)]; \tag{6.26n}$$

$$s = \frac{(\beta - \alpha)^2}{9\theta(9-(4-3\sigma)\gamma)^2} [162 - 72\gamma(2\sigma-1) + 8\gamma^2(4\sigma^2-4\sigma+1)]. \tag{6.26s}$$

We calculate total welfare in each country, as before, by summing the consumer and producer surplus measures in (6.25) and (6.26).

B Welfare comparisons

We now are prepared to compare levels of welfare achieved under protection of foreign intellectual property in the South with those that arise when no protection is provided, in situations where protection gives rise to an equilibrium with international licensing of the new technology. This analysis involves comparison of (6.7i) with the sum of (6.25i) and (6.26i), for $i = s, n$. Since the general expressions are quite complicated and provide limited intuition, we proceed by focusing on several special cases.

The first case that we consider arises when $\sigma = 1$. In this case, the Northern firm enjoys all the bargaining power in the licensing negotiations and extracts all the surplus from any agreement. We find

$$\mathrm{sgn}\,\{w^{NP} - w^{P}\} = \mathrm{sgn}\,\{\theta(2\gamma - 9) + \gamma + 9\}. \tag{6.27s}$$

In figure 6.2, we show the combinations of γ and $1/\theta$ for which the right-hand side of (6.27s) is positive, and those for which it is negative. We see that the South may benefit from protection of Northern intellectual property rights, but only if its share in world consumption of the good is quite high. A sufficient condition for non-protection to be the optimal strategy when $\sigma = 1$ is $1/\theta < 0.59$.

From the point of view of the North, we have

$$\mathrm{sgn}\,\{W^{NP} - W^{P}\} = \mathrm{sgn}\,\{\gamma + 9 - 16\theta\} \tag{6.27n}$$

South consumption share
(1/θ)

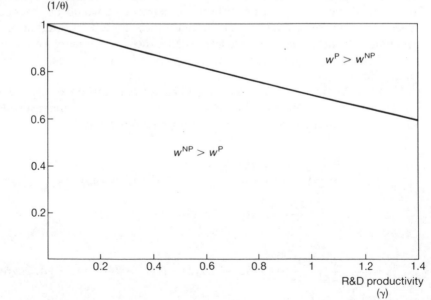

Figure 6.2   South welfare with licensing ($\sigma = 1$)

For $\gamma < 1.406$ (the largest value of γ for which licensing takes place when $\sigma = 1$), the right-hand side of (6.27n) is always negative. So we find again that the North benefits from having its intellectual property rights protected in the South.

Next we consider the opposite extreme case where bargaining power resides entirely with the firm in the South; i.e., $\sigma = 0$. When $\sigma = 0$ the South is more likely to benefit from protecting Northern property rights than it is when $\sigma = 1$, and does so whenever its consumption share exceeds one-half (see figure 6.3). However, when the consumption share of the South is not large (e.g., less than 0.4), the South still prefers to pirate Northern technology than to enter into a licensing agreement in which its firm will capture all of the surplus. This somewhat surprising result stems from the fact that the licensing fee remains strictly positive even when $\sigma = 0$, and also from the differing incentives that the Northern firm has to carry out R&D in the two situations.

Comparing welfare levels for the North, for the case when its firm's bargaining power in the licensing negotiation is nil, we find that, for all permissible values of σ (≤ 1) and γ ($\in (0, 9/7)$), $W^P > W^{NP}$. Even if the Northern firm captures *none* of the surplus from any licensing agreement that materializes between itself and its Southern rival, nonetheless the North enjoys greater welfare when its intellectual property rights are protected by the South.

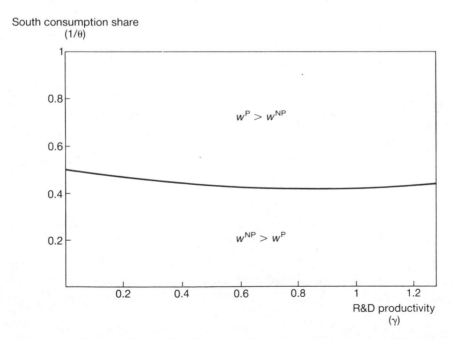

Figure 6.3   South welfare with licensing ($\sigma = 0$)

Lastly, we consider an intermediate case where the gains from trade in knowledge are shared equally between the two rivals; i.e., $\sigma = 0.5$. Figure 6.4 depicts the parameter values for which the South prefers protection. The figure provides the same general message as for the more extreme cases, inasmuch as the South benefits from protection only when its residents absorb a large share of world output of the good. The critical values for $1/\theta$ at which protection becomes preferable lie between those of the earlier cases with $\sigma = 0$ and $\sigma = 1$. Also, we find as before that the North can only be harmed by a failure of the government of the South to protect its patent rights.

Our last inquiry concerns the implications of intellectual property rights for world welfare when protection induces a licensing agreement. Allowing once again for an arbitrary value of σ, we obtain

$$\text{sgn }\{\Omega^{NP} - \Omega^{P}\} = \text{sgn }\{-729(5-\sigma)(1+\sigma) + 486\gamma(1-\sigma)(2+5\sigma) + 108\gamma^{2}(1-2\sigma)(3-5\sigma) - 16\gamma^{3}(1-2\sigma)^{2}\} \quad (6.29)$$

The expression on the right-hand side of (6.29) is always negative for $\sigma \in [0, 1]$ and γ in the range where licensing obtains. Thus, contrary to our findings in section II where licensing was considered to be infeasible, we find now that protection of intellectual property rights *always* enhances global efficiency when trade in technology can take place. Patent protection with licensing allows the world to enjoy both widespread dissemination of knowledge and the benefits of more intense product-market competition,

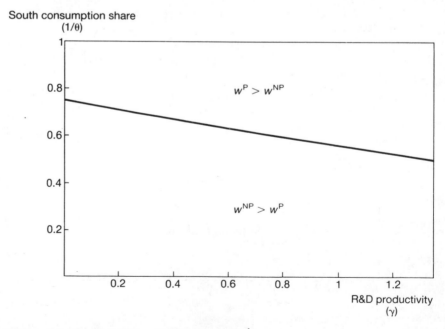

South consumption share
$(1/\theta)$

$w^{P} > w^{NP}$

$w^{NP} > w^{P}$

R&D productivity
(γ)

Figure 6.4   South welfare with licensing $(\sigma = \frac{1}{2})$

while avoiding the disincentive effects that plague a weak system of intellectual property-rights where infringement on patents is pervasive.

IV Conclusions

In this paper we have studied the incentive that a government in the South has to protect the intellectual property rights of Northern firms, and the consequences of the decision taken by the South for welfare in the North and for efficiency of the world equilibrium. We have conducted our partial equilibrium analysis in the context of a competition between a single Northern producer and a single Southern producer selling some good to an integrated world market. In this competition, only the Northern firm has the ability to conduct R&D in order to lower its production costs, but the Southern firm can imitate costlessly if patent protection for process innovations is not enforced by the government of the South.

We found that, contrary to the commonly-voiced polemic of the US government, the interests of the North and South generally conflict in this matter of international economic relations. Unless the South constitutes a majority share of the market for the good whose technology is subject to improvement or the prospects for cost-savings through R&D are quite substantial, social welfare in the South will be higher when its eschews protection of foreign intellectual property than when it succumbs to pressure from the North. The North, on the other hand, always benefits from having the patents of its firm respected outside its borders. Surprisingly, perhaps, the global comparison can go either way; protection of intellectual property rights enhances world efficiency when productivity in R&D is great, but not when innovations are likely to be small. What is at stake here is the familiar conflict between the benefits of widespread diffusion of technology and the increased competition that such diffusion entails, and the costs of dampened incentives to generate technological breakthroughs.

Needless to say, our results hinge on the special assumptions we have introduced. Most important, we feel, are our restriction to situations of duopoly and our exclusion of any possibility of innovation in the South. With more Southern firms and some scope for technological improvement there (including improvements that only serve to move the country closer to the world technological frontier), a strong system of protection for intellectual property may be necessary to prevent the Southern firms from appropriating technologies from each other. Yet some countries have been known to afford unequal treatment to foreigners in patent enforcement procedures (see ITC, 1988, p. 3.7). So protection of domestic and foreign property need not always go hand in hand, the provisions of the Paris Convention for the Protection of Industrial Property notwithstanding.

Our findings may contain an important lesson for negotiators in the

Uruguay Round. Until now, the industrial countries have maintained the posture that governments in the South ought to respect Northern claims for property rights over knowledge and technology partly as a matter of moral principle and partly in their own self-interest. If, as our analysis suggests, the South benefits by "borrowing" freely from the technologies produced in the North, then it may be more productive for the Northern governments to abandon this high moral position and treat the issue of intellectual property as they would any other one of conflicting national interests. In particular, if protection of intellectual property does indeed enhance *global* efficiency, as our analysis shows to be the case at least for substantial innovations, then the North ought to be willing and able to compensate the South for any losses that it would incur in the course of providing such protection. The format of the GATT negotiations presumably presents on ideal opportunity for effecting such compensation, as Southern concessions on this issue might readily be exchanged for Northern concessions on some others (greater market access for Southern exports?).

Notes

The authors are grateful to Avinash Dixit, Ron Jones, Isaac Li, and Anne Krueger for comments on an earlier draft. Grossman thanks the National Science Foundation and the World Bank for partial financial support. Neither of these organizations is responsible for any of the views expressed herein.

1   Responding to a survey conducted by the International Trade Commission (1988), 101 US corporations cited lost export sales in 1986 due to inadequate foreign protection of intellectual property of $6.16 billion. Sixty-four respondents claimed lost sales in the United States totaling $1.80 billion. An additional $3.11 billion of lost royalty payments was noted by 104 respondents to the ITC survey. The ITC estimates that, for the companies in its sample, sales of infringing goods may have represented an average profit reduction of 10 percent in 1986. The International Anti-Counterfeiting Coalition estimates total annual losses of domestic and foreign sales by US firms due to inadequate protection of intellectual property of approximately $20 billion (see Benko, 1987).

2   Further to its survey of US corporations, the ITC (1988) reports that 122 companies cited 54 countries as having inadequate protection of patent rights for foreigners, while 84 respondents cited 52 countries as providing insufficient protection for copyrights. The countries most commonly cited in this regard are Mexico, Taiwan, Brazil and Korea. For discussion of the alleged inadequacies of foreign protection of US intellectual property, see ITC (1988, ch. 3).

3   For an analysis of issues arising from foreign counterfeiting of domestic trademarks, see Grossman and Shapiro (1988a, b).

4   We use an uppercase letter to denote a variable relating to the North and the corresponding lowercase letter for the analogous variable for the South. Greek letters are reserved for parameters.

5   For an analysis of a (closed-economy) R&D game with costly imitation, see Katz and Shapiro (1987).
6   We assume in all cases that α is sufficiently large so that the non-negativity constraint on c does not bind.
7   We restrict attention to $\gamma < 4$, so that R&D remains finite at the monopoly optimum.
8   We compare (6.7n) with (6.12n), (6.17n), and (6.15n), for values of γ that give rise to duopoly, strategic predation and monopoly, respectively. In each case it is possible to show that $W^P - W^{NP} > 0$ at $\theta = 1$, and that the derivative of this difference with respect to θ is positive for all γ in the relevant range.
9   As Katz and Shapiro discuss, the firms will prefer to negotiate contracts calling for royalties on a per-unit output basis, because such provisions can be used to enforce collusive arrangements in the product market. However, these types of contracts might be difficult to monitor and enforce, and might also bring the firms into conflict with the antitrust authorities.
10 These findings accord with the more general results reported in Katz and Shapiro (1985). They show for general demand functions and an arbitrary form of static, oligopolistic competition (satisfying certain intuitive conditions) a small innovation always is licensed if the two firms initially share common costs, and that the set of parameters for which licensing obtains is strictly smaller than the set that gives rise to monopoly in the absence of licensing.

References

Baldwin, Robert E. 1988: "Other Issues: North–South Trade, Intellectual Property Rights and Subsidies," in R. E. Baldwin and J. D. Richardson (eds), *Issues in the Uruguay Round*, Cambridge: National Bureau of Economic Research.

Benko, Robert P. 1987: *Protecting Intellectual Property Rights*, Washington, DC: American Enterprise Institute.

Dixit, Avinash K. 1980: "The Role of Investment in Entry Deterrence," *Economic Journal* 90, 95–106.

General Accounting Office 1987: *Strengthening Worldwide Protection of Intellectual Property Rights*, Washington, DC: United States General Accounting Office.

Grossman, Gene M., and Shapiro, Carl 1988a: "Counterfeit-Product Trade," *American Economic Review* 78, 59–75.

Grossman, Gene M., and Shapiro, Carl 1988b: "Foreign Counterfeiting of Status Goods," *Quarterly Journal of Economics* 103, 79–100.

International Trade Commission 1988: *Foreign Protection of Intellectual Property Rights and the Effect on US Industry and Trade*, Washington, DC: United States International Trade Commission Publication No. 2065.

Katz, Michael L., and Shapiro, Carl 1985: "On the Licensing of Innovations," *Rand Journal of Economics* 16, 504–20.

Katz, Michael L., and Shapiro, Carl 1987: "R&D Rivalry with Licensing or Imitation," *American Economic Review* 77, 402–20.

Nordhaus, William D. 1969: *Invention, Growth and Welfare: A Theoretical Treatment of Technological Change*, Cambridge, MA: MIT Press.

7

Optimal Tariff Retaliation Rules

RICHARD E. BALDWIN

Tariff retaliation has long been employed by countries involved in international trade. Given this prevalence of retaliation policies, it is important to think carefully about what might constitute an optimal retaliation policy. This paper attempts to highlight some of the issues involved in forming an optimal tariff retaliation rule. In the complicated world of international politics, there are many reasons for tariff retaliation ranging from national welfare to pure spite. Here we are concerned only with retaliation rules aimed at strategically deterring undesirable foreign trade policies at a minimum cost to the domestic economy. Given this goal, the considerations addressed by the public finance literature on optimal taxation are clearly relevant. However this is not enough.

Robert Baldwin, through both empirical and theoretical work, has emphasized that trade policy is the outcome of a political economy process. Obviously then the nature of the policy mechanism in the *foreign* country should play a role in shaping *domestic* retaliation rules. For example, suppose that a foreign industry lobbies for an export subsidy and the domestic country attempts to deter the subsidy with a tit-for-tat tariff retaliation rule on the industry's exports. If the rule is credible, then (in addition to the usual public finance effects) it will have the effect of reducing the foreign industry's marginal benefit of lobbying for the export subsidy – thereby reducing the amount of lobbying and the equilibrium export subsidy. An alternative rule, say, retaliate tit-for-tat in some other industry, might well be less effective since it would not directly impact on the benefits of foreign lobbying.

The existing literature on retaliation has two branches. The first extends the standard analysis of Baldwin-envelope tariffs by allowing for foreign retaliation. Johnson (1953), Mayer (1981) and Riezman (1982) show that a tariff might raise national welfare even if the foreign country retaliated. The other branch has focused on the strategic deterrence role of retaliation. A first step in this direction was made by Thursby and Jensen (1983, 1984). Richardson (1986) summarizes the results of this literature; "Retaliation, that is, defensive non-cooperation, is a powerful instrument for encouraging cooperation from trading partners . . . But to be maximally effective, it must be utterly transparent and predictable and also temporary, measured and not unduly punitive. These requirements buttress the case for rules-based retaliation and suggest unsatisfactory consequences from discretionary retaliation.'' However these authors do not investigate the form of an optimal retaliation rule. In particular they do not address the issue of against which foreign industries should retaliation be pursued.

The Thursby and Jensen, and Richardson studies assume that the foreign tariffs are chosen to maximize foreign national welfare. As such, the role of the tariff retaliation is to punish or threaten to punish the foreign country if it imposes a tariff. In this set-up the key to the effectiveness of a retaliation policy must be its ability to inflict "pain" upon the foreign country. None of these studies focuses on the issue of which industries to retaliate against. Presumably the key to an optimal retaliation rule would be its ability to inflict the requisite pain at a minimum cost to the domestic economy. Since a tariff is like a subsidy-cum-tax, the principles of optimal taxation would appear to be a reasonable way to characterize the optimal retaliation rule in the Thursby–Jensen–Richardson set up.

In his agenda for research, Dixit (1986) points out that the problem of international negotiation should not ignore the politico-economic aspects of countries' trade policy. He states, "the countries' internal political mechanisms now have a bearing on the way the intercountry game is played and on its outcome. Such considerations have been found to be of critical importance in many instance of political negotiations. The same must be true of trade policy, but economists have hardly begun to confront these issues in their research."

This paper, like the Brander and Richardson papers, deals with the effects of retaliation on equilibrium tariffs. In particular we attempt to characterize the nature of optimal, linear retaliation rules. The most general result is that, as Dixit conjectured, the structure of an optimal retaliation policy depends crucially upon the process by which the foreign and domestic tariffs are chosen. We elaborate on this general result by using the tools of simple game theory together with the well-established literature on the political economy of tariffs in order to characterize optimal tariff retaliation rules. The extensive theoretical and empirical literature on the political economy of tariffs has stressed that a country's trade policy is heavily influenced by lobbying efforts. Thus we show that a crucial characteristic of an optimal retaliation rule is its ability to reduce the foreign and domestic lobbyists' incentives to lobby for tariffs.

In addition to these very general results we derive two more specific results in the context of a simple political economy model. The first is that in general the optimal retaliation rule will involve retaliation against all foreign industries. The second concerns a rule of thumb for retaliation policies. For a variety of reasons it may be advantageous for a country to commit to a very simple retaliation rule. In this case we find that a reasonable rule of thumb is that, *ceteris paribus*, the retaliation should be against the foreign industry which benefited from offending tariff. Clearly this result applies only to industries with intra-industry trade.

The plane of the paper is as follows. In the first section we describe the general model and show that the optimal retaliation policy depends upon the foreign and domestic tariff processes. The second section examines retaliation rules in the context of a general lobbying model of the tariff process. The last section presents a specific lobbying model and derives several specific results.

I Retaliation policy and the tariff formation process

As Brander and Richardson both point out, retaliation is an inherently difficult concern. The first difficulty is what Brander calls the identification problem. That is, given the multitude of actual and possible policies, it is not easy to identify which domestic policy is a retaliation for which foreign policy, or vice versa. We do not propose a solution to this caveat. Instead we restrict our attention to linear tariff retaliation rules. That is, we consider the class of retaliation rules of the form, $T_i = \sum_{j=1}^{n} \theta_{ij} T_j^{0*}$, where T_i is the retaliatory tariff, T_j^{0*} is the foreign tariff in industry j chosen by the foreign political process, and n is the number of industries in the domestic economy. In terms of this class of rules, we define θ_{ij} as domestic retaliation against the ith industry in response to a foreign tariff in the jth industry. The foreign country is assumed to have a similar retaliation rule.

A more serious problem is that of credibility. Again, we simply dodge the issue. We assume that the countries can credibly commit to any set of non-negative θ_{ij}'s. This approach has many drawbacks, perhaps the principal one being that it ignores all the important considerations of credibility and perfectness. However by restricting our attention only to tariff retaliation, we avoid one of the most serious technical difficulties encountered in problems with commitment, perfect information and no uncertainty. Since the only retaliatory instruments we consider are tariffs, the greatest possible retaliation is a prohibitive tariff. Such a policy clearly does not constitute an infinite threat. The problem of infinite off-equilibrium threats is thereby avoided.

The next problem is how to fit the choice of a retaliation policy into a political economy model. The main lesson of the extensive political economy literature on trade policy is that trade policy is not chosen to maximize national welfare. Rather it is chosen by policy-makers who are interested in getting into and staying in power. In the light of these models, we are faced with the additional question of who chooses the retaliation policy and with what objective in mind. Moreover, there is the question of how the framers of retaliation policy interact with the makers of tariff policy.

The approach taken in this paper is similar to that of Feenstra and

Bhagwati (1982). In that paper, the government is assumed to consist of two parts. One part (the "left-brain") responds to protectionist pressure, while the other (the "right-brain") tries to arrange domestic subsidies in order to maximize welfare knowing how the left-brain and the lobbyist will respond. Feenstra and Bhagwati suggest that this model of a schizophrenic government reflects the confrontation in the US between the pro-trade executive branch and the lobbying-dominated legislative branch.

This framework has a natural interpretation in the context of the class of retaliation rules considered. The left-brain is the politically influenced tariff agency, and the right-brain is the national welfare-maximizing retaliation agency. The total tariff level in a country is the sum of the retaliatory tariff and the politically chosen T_j^0. Thus the θ_{ij}'s and θ_{ij}^*'s are chosen by the domestic and foreign retaliation agencies respectively, while the T_j^0's and the T_j^{0*} are chosen by the domestic and foreign tariff agencies respectively. The objective function of each retaliation agency is to maximize national welfare. The objective of each tariff agency is to get reelected.

What remains is to specify how the four agencies interact. In the exercise we undertake, we assume that the θ_{ij}'s are chosen in order to maximize national welfare, taking full account of the political economy process by which the T_j^0's and T_j^{0*}'s are determined. Moreover, we assume that the T_j^0's are chosen taking the θ_{ij}'s, θ_{ij}^*'s and T_j^{0*}'s as given. The T_j^{0*}'s are chosen taking the θ_{ij}'s, θ_{ij}^*'s and T_j^0's as given. The θ_{ij}'s are chosen taking the θ_{ij}^*'s as given, and the θ_{ij}^*'s are chosen taking the θ_{ij}'s as given. That is to say, each retaliation agency takes as given the retaliation *rule* of the other country, but plays Stackleberg against both the domestic and foreign tariff agencies. The processes by which the T_j^0's and T_j^{0*}'s are chosen are common knowledge to the retaliation agencies in both countries, but are unknown to the two tariff agencies. Again these assumptions are in the spirit of Feenstra and Bhagwati (1982).

The justification for this setup lies in the timing of the retaliation and tariff choices. The setting up of laws and institutions committing a country to a retaliation policy is presumably an event which occurs infrequently. For instance, while the US is not currently committed to retaliation against tariffs, the countervailing duty law imposes a mandatory tariff in the same industry in retaliation against foreign export subsidies. This law has been on the books since the 1890s. In passing this law, Congress undoubtedly realized that the law would affect the foreign choice of subsidies. In contrast, the granting of import protection is an event that occurs constantly. We model this timing by assuming that retaliation agencies play Nash in θ's against each other; tariff agencies play Nash in T^0's against each other; and each retaliation agency plays Stackleberg leader against both tariff agencies.

Formally suppose we can express domestic welfare, W, as a function of the domestic and foreign tariffs. That is $W(\tau, \tau^*)$ where τ and τ^* are the vectors of total domestic and foreign tariffs respectively. Plainly τ and τ^*

are functions of the domestic and foreign retaliation rules. We summarize these rules by the matrices ϕ and ϕ^*. The total domestic tariff in the jth industry is $\tau_j = T_j^0 + \sum_{i-1} \theta_{ij} T_i^{0*}$. The jth row of the ϕ is therefore $(\theta_{j1}, \theta_{j2}, \ldots, \theta_{jn})$. In general there will be a retaliation rule in each domestic industry so that ϕ is an n by n matrix. Clearly, $\theta_{ij} = 0, (j = 1, \ldots, n)$ for all domestic industries, i, that face no import competition.

The problem of the domestic retaliation agency is to choose ϕ, taking ϕ^* as given in order to maximize $W(\tau(\phi, \phi^*), \tau^*(\phi, \phi^*))$. The first order conditions of the domestic retaliation agency's problem are:

$$\sum_{j=1}^{n} \left[\frac{\partial W}{\partial \tau_j} \frac{d\tau_j}{d\phi_{ik}} + \frac{\partial W}{\partial \tau_j^*} \frac{d\tau_j^*}{d\phi_{ik}} \right] \leqq 0 \tag{7.1a}$$

for all $\phi_{ik}, i = 1, \ldots, n, k = 1, \ldots, n$. The foreign retaliation agency has an isomorphic set of first order conditions.

$$\sum_{j=1}^{n} \left[\frac{\partial W^*}{\partial \tau_j} \frac{d\tau_j}{d\phi_{ik}^*} + \frac{\partial W^*}{\partial \tau_j^*} \frac{d\tau_j^*}{d\phi_{ik}^*} \right] \leqq 0 \tag{7.1b}$$

for all $\phi_{ik}^*, i = 1, \ldots, n, k = 1, \ldots, n$. The behavior of the domestic and foreign tariff agencies is implicit in the functions $\tau(\phi, \phi^*)$ and $\tau^*(\phi, \phi^*)$. Assuming there exists a unique and stable Nash equilibrium in ϕ and ϕ^*, (7.1a) and (7.1b) together with the functions $\tau(\phi, \phi^*)$ and $\tau^*(\phi, \phi^*)$ determine the n times n ϕ's in each country as well as the equilibrium τ and τ^*.

The equilibrium in most models is described by a vector of prices. Since we are concentrating on retaliation we do not explicitly calculate the equilibrium price vector. Assuming only that such a price vector exists and is unique and stable for any equilibrium (ϕ, ϕ^*), we can describe the enitre equilibrium by the domestic and foreign retaliation rules.

Equations (7.1a) and (7.1b) give us a very general result. As Dixit (1986) conjectured, the optimal retaliation rules depend critically on the tariff process in the foreign country. The derivatives $(d\tau_j^*/d\theta_{ik})$ summarize the effect of θ_{ik} on the foreign tariff process in the jth industry. We refer to those derivatives as the deterrent effect that domestic retaliation has on the equilibrium foreign tariff. The partial $(\partial W/\partial \tau_j^*)$ weights the deterrent effects by their welfare importance.

Equation (7.1a), however, gives us an additional result. What (7.1a) suggests is that retaliation affects the equilibrium tariff vectors τ and τ^* through its impact on the *domestic* tariff formation process as well as through its impact on foreign trade policy. This secondary effect of the retaliation is summarized by $(d\tau_j/d\theta_{ik})$. For instance, if we adopt the lobbying model of the tariff process, a retaliatory tariff is in effect a free tariff from the point of view of the domestic lobbyists. Thus depending upon the magnitude of the deterrent effect, a retaliation policy might actually lead to higher equilibrium domestic tariffs.

The thrust of this point is that since a retaliation rule might (through its effect on the domestic political tariff process) lead to higher domestic tariffs, retaliation might be undesirable despite its strategic deterrence effects. On the other hand, a retaliation rule might be advantageous even if it had a negligible deterrent effect. The partial $(\partial W/\partial \tau_j)$ reflects the optimal taxation considerations discussed in the introduction. That is to say it reflects the marginal cost of retaliating in the jth industry.

II Optimal retaliation in a lobbying model

The previous section made the simple but important point that the form of an optimal retaliation policy depends crucially on the exact nature of foreign and domestic tariff formation processes. To get a more specific and applicable characterization of an optimal tariff retaliation policy, we must be more specific about the tariff determination process in foreign and domestic countries. There is no generally accepted positive model of the tariff formation process. Much of the trade literature assumes that tariffs are chosen by an deus ex machina government. Another branch focuses on the politico-economic determinants of trade policy. In this paper we pursue the latter approach.

This section extends the section I model by including a fairly general political economy model of the tariff formation process in the home and foreign countries. This model is not intended to incorporate any novel elements. As such it draws heavily on the contributions of Findlay and Wellisz (1982), Feenstra and Bhagwati (1982), Mayer (1984) and Brock and Magee (1979). Baldwin (1986) provides a useful summary of the positive theory of tariff determination.

The basic premise of all political economy models is that policy-makers want to be and stay elected. That is, policy-makers choose policy in order to obtain a certain number of votes. As Baldwin (1982) points out, "Pareto-efficient policies will be implemented under majority rule provided that such conditions prevail as perfect information, no voting costs and the absence of any costs of redistributing income." Since such conditions do not actually prevail, votes depend upon lobbying expenditures as well as the welfare impact of the policies chosen.

In political economy models, policy-makers choose tariffs to stay elected. Lobbying groups lobby to influence the tariff rates in order to maximize profits. In choosing the tariff, policy-makers weigh the loss of votes due to the negative welfare impact of tariffs against the votes gained through lobbying expenditures. Clearly a complete model of the tariff process would require consideration of the timing and strategic assumptions governing the lobbyist–policy maker interaction. Indeed the most sophisticated political economy models explicitly model this game between policy-makers and lobbyists. For simplicity's sake, however, we adopt the black box or reduced form approach of Findlay and Wellisz (1982).

That is to say we do not directly model the process by which the tariff agencies trade off lobbying expenditures against the welfare cost of the tariff. Rather we posit that in both the domestic and foreign countries, the politically chosen domestic tariff vector, T^0, is a function of the matrix of lobbing expenditures, R, and the domestic and foreign retaliation matrices, ϕ and ϕ^*. The lobbying expenditures, R, are a matrix since we allow each industry to lobbying for or against each tariff. Namely, T^0 and T^{*0} are given by:

$$T^0 = T^0(R, \phi^*) \tag{7.2a}$$

$$T^{0*} = T^{0*}(R^*, \phi) \tag{7.2b}$$

We refer to (7.2a) and (7.2b) as the domestic and foreign political tariff processes.

The other key component of a political economy model is the behavior of lobbyists. There is an extensive and important branch of the political economy literature which focuses on the determinants of lobbying efforts. This paper abstracts from these considerations. We assume that industries choose their lobbying expenditures in order to maximize their aggregate indirect utility functions. Since members of an industry lobbying group in general consume some of their own product, a complete analysis of their lobbying choice would take account of this own-consumption price effect. However, it seems reasonable that this effect has a negligible impact on the actual lobbying decision of industries. We therefore ignore it by assuming that industries choose to lobby at the level that maximizes their profits net of their lobbying costs.

The domestic lobbyist's problem in the jth industry is therefore to choose R_{ij}, $i = 1, \ldots, n$, in order to:

$$\max \ \pi_j[\tau, \tau^*] - \sum_{i=1}^{n} R_{ij}, \text{ subject to (7.2a).} \tag{7.3a}$$

Here n is the number of elements in τ, and R_{ij} is the lobbying expenditures by the jth industry for or against the tariff in the ith industry. This setup follows Findlay and Wellisz (1982) in assuming that each lobbying group takes as given the lobbying expenditures of the other groups. The typical jth industry lobbyist in the foreign country faces a similar problem:

$$\max \ \pi_j^*[\tau, \tau^*] - \sum_{i=1}^{n} R_{ij}^*, \text{ subject to (7.2b).} \tag{7.3b}$$

The equilibrium domestic lobbying expenditures are the solution to the set of first order conditions for (7.3a). Namely,

$$\sum_{k=1}^{n} (\partial\pi/\partial\tau_k)(\partial\tau_k/\partial\mathbf{R}_{ij}) - 1 = 0, \text{ for all } \mathbf{R}_{ij} \quad (7.4a)$$

The equilibrium foreign lobbying expenditure matrix is the solution to the n^2 equations:

$$\sum_{k=1}^{n} (\partial\pi^*/\partial\tau_k)(\partial\tau_k/\partial\mathbf{R}_{ij}^*) - 1 = 0, \text{ for all } \mathbf{R}_{ij}^* \quad (7.4b)$$

The Nash equilibrium in lobbying expenditures in each country determines the equilibrium $\mathbf{T}^0$ and $\mathbf{T}^{*0}$ via (7.2a) and (7.2b). These politically chosen tariffs are added to the retaliatory tariffs to give the equilibrium total tariffs τ and τ^*.

With this model of the tariff determination processes in hand, we can now re-examine the problem of the retaliation agencies. The new first order condition for the domestic retaliation agency is:

$$0 = \sum_{j-1}^{n} \{(\partial W/\partial\tau_j)(\mathrm{d}\tau_j/\mathrm{d}\phi_{ik}) + (\partial W/\partial\tau_j^*)(\mathrm{d}\tau_j^*/\mathrm{d}\phi_{ik})\}, \text{ for all } \phi_{ik} \quad (7.5)$$

where,

$$\frac{\mathrm{d}\tau_j}{\mathrm{d}\phi_{ik}} = \left[\sum_{g=1}^{n} \frac{\partial\mathbf{T}_j}{\partial\mathbf{R}_{jg}} \frac{\mathrm{d}\mathbf{R}_{jg}}{\mathrm{d}\phi_{ik}} \right] + \left[\sum_{g=1}^{n} \phi_{jg} \left(\sum_{h=1}^{n} \frac{\partial\mathbf{T}_g^*}{\partial\mathbf{R}_{gh}^*} \frac{\mathrm{d}\mathbf{R}_{gh}^*}{\mathrm{d}\phi_{ik}} \right) \right],$$
$$\text{for } j \neq i \quad (7.6)$$

$$\frac{\mathrm{d}\tau_j}{\mathrm{d}\phi_{ik}} = \left[\sum_{g=1}^{n} \frac{\partial\mathbf{T}_j}{\partial\mathbf{R}_{jg}} \frac{\mathrm{d}\mathbf{R}_{jg}}{\mathrm{d}\phi_{ik}} \right] + \left[\sum_{g=1}^{n} \phi_{jg} \left(\sum_{h=1}^{n} \frac{\partial\mathbf{T}_g^*}{\partial\mathbf{R}_{gh}^*} \frac{\mathrm{d}\mathbf{R}_{gh}^*}{\mathrm{d}\phi_{ik}} \right) \right] + \mathbf{T}_k^*,$$
$$\text{for } j = i \quad (7.7)$$

$$\frac{\mathrm{d}\tau_j^*}{\mathrm{d}\phi_{ik}} = \left[\sum_{g=1}^{n} \frac{\partial\mathbf{T}_j^*}{\partial\mathbf{R}_{jg}} \frac{\mathrm{d}\mathbf{R}_{jg}^*}{\mathrm{d}\phi_{ik}} \right] + \left[\frac{\partial\mathbf{T}_j^*}{\partial\phi_{ik}} \right] +$$

$$\left[\sum_{h=1}^{n} \phi_{jh}^* \left(\sum_{g=1}^{n} \frac{\partial\mathbf{T}_h}{\partial\mathbf{R}_{hg}} \frac{\mathrm{d}\mathbf{R}_{hg}}{\mathrm{d}\phi_{ik}} \right) \right], \qquad \text{for all } j. \quad (7.8)$$

The foreign retaliation agency has an isomorphic set of first order conditions. Again we assume that there is a unique and stable Nash equilibrium in ϕ and ϕ^*. If we had assumed specific functional forms it would in principle be possible to solve for the equilibrium optimal retaliation rules ϕ and ϕ^*. In the absence of explicit functional forms, we can still characterize the optimal retaliation rule by studying (7.5)–(7.8).

Focusing on the domestic retaliation rule, ϕ, the set of equations given by (7.5)–(7.8) provide the second main result of this paper. From these equations it is clear that an essential consideration in the choice of an optimal tariff retaliation rule is the effect of retaliation on foreign and domestic lobbying. This is a straightforward result since, the ultimate source of both the domestic and foreign tariffs is lobbying. The aim of the domestic retaliation is to reduce both τ^* and τ. Thus in analysing the implications of (7.5), we look first at the impact of ϕ on τ^* (which is defined by (7.8)) and then at its impact on τ (which is defined by (7.6) and (7.7)).

Recall that the total foreign tariff τ^* is the sum of the politically chosen T^{*0} and the foreign retaliatory tariff $\Sigma\phi_{ij}^*T_j^0$. An increase in the domestic retaliation parameter ϕ_{ik} therefore affects τ^* through two channels. First is the deterrent effect of ϕ_{ik} on foreign lobbying. This effect is reflected in the derivatives $(dR_{ij}^*/d\phi_{ik})$. To determine the tariff-reducing impact of this lobbying deterrence the partials must be weighted by marginal effectiveness of lobbying by the appropriate industry. This is given by the partial $(\partial T^*/\partial R_{ij}^*)$. The foreign political tariff process (7.2b) defines this partial.

The derivative $(dR_{ij}^*/d\phi_{ik})$ is given implicitly by the set of first order conditions (7.4a) and (7.4b). The retaliation parameter ϕ_{ik} alters the maximization problem of foreign lobbying groups. The parameter will therefore in general alter the lobbying groups' choice of lobbying expenditures. For instance, if there is intra-industry trade in industry i then $\phi_{ii} > 0$ implies that when the foreign industry i lobbies for T^{*0}, it is also lobbying for a retaliatory tariff against its exports to the domestic country. In the next section we study an example which imposes enough structure to allow us to say something about the size and sign of these partials.

The last part of the deterrent channel is the direct impact of retaliation on the foreign political tariff process. Recall that in choosing T^{*0}, the foreign tariff agency balances the lobbying efforts of industries against the general welfare impact of T^{*0}. The retaliation by the home country increases the cost of granting T^{*0} and so will tend to alter the balance towards lower T^{*0}.

The second channel depends of the foreign retaliatory tariff, $\Sigma\phi_{ij}T_j^0$. Changes in the domestic retaliation parameter ϕ_{ik} can in general affect the level of the domestic lobbying expenditures and thereby affect the politically chosen tariffs, T^0. This would in turn affect the level of the total foreign tariff via retaliation. The expression $\phi_{jh}^*(\partial T_h^0/\partial R_{hg})(dR_{hg}/d\phi_{ik})$ reflects these considerations. The size of this product is given by (7.2a), (7.4a), and (7.4b).

Next we turn to the impact of ϕ on τ. τ like τ^* is composed of a politically chosen component and a retaliatory component. Thus retaliation also affects τ through two channels. In equations (7.6), where $j \neq i$, the first channel is summarized by the term $(\partial T_h/\partial R_{ih})(dR_{ih}/d\phi_{ik})$. The second can be seen in the partials $\phi_{jh}(\partial T_h^*/\partial R_{hg}^*)(dR_{hg}/d\phi_{ik})$. In the case where $i = j$, then there is the additional direct effect of changing ϕ_{ik}, which is given by the size of T_k^*.

III An example

In this section we consider an example of simple political economy model which enables us to focus more closely on the relationships between retaliation rules, lobbying expenditures and the equilibrium foreign tariff. In this example there are two industries (industries 1 and 2) in each of the two countries (Home and Foreign). Both Foreign industries export, but only Foreign industry 1 faces import competition. In other words, there is intra-industry trade in industry 1 and inter-industry trade in industry 2. Thus there is only one Foreign tariff, τ^*, but two Home tariffs τ_1 and τ_2.

Since we are interested in focusing on domestic retaliation policy we abstract from issues involved in the domestic political economy of tariffs. That is we suppose that there is no Home tariff agency. The Home tariff levels depend solely upon the Home retaliation rule. That is to say, $\tau_1 = \phi_1 T^*$ and $\tau_2 = \phi_2 T^*$. Moreover we assume that the Foreign country has no retaliation agency. The Foreign tariff level is determined entirely by the politically motivated Foreign tariff agency. These simplifications highlight the effect that the domestic retaliation rule has on the equilibrium lobbying efforts of the foreign lobbyists. Namely, the Home tariff policy is aimed entirely at deterring the Foreign tariff. The Foreign tariff depends only on Foreign lobbying efforts and the Home retaliation rule. The Foreign political tariff process in a simplified version of equation (7.2b). Namely,

$$\tau^* = \tau^*(R^1, R^2, \phi^1, \phi^2) \tag{7.5}$$

where R^1 and R^2 are the lobbying expenditures of Foreign industries 1 and 2, and ϕ^1 and ϕ^2 are the Home retaliation parameters against Foreign industries 1 and 2.

Assuming that Foreign firms perceive themselves as facing constant marginal costs the profits of each industry is the sum of the profits earned in the Home and Foreign markets. Each Foreign industry chooses its lobbying expenditure to maximize profits taking as given the Foreign tariff process. In general the profitability of each industry would depend upon all tariff levels. Thus in general we would expect both Foreign industries to undertake either pro-protection or anti-protection lobbying. In this two-industry, two-country example it would be a simple matter to find conditions under which industry 1 would lobby for τ^*, while industry 2 would be lobbying against it. By contrast, if we considered the more realistic case of n countries, m industries and h factors, it is not at all clear, theoretically, what the attitudes of each industry would be toward the tariff level in any given industry.

Appealing to casual empiricism, however, can give us an indication of what might be reasonable assumptions. At least in the US, pro-protection lobbying is often not actively opposed. Of course major trade legislation typically draws attention from both pro- and anti-protection groups, but in most cases protection is granted only to a single industry. In such cases lobbying is usually undertaken only by the industry directly concerned. The policy-makers choose a tariff by weighing the industry's gain against the general loss of welfare. We refer to such instances as non-competitive lobbying cases. To account for this stylized fact in our simple model we assume that the Foreign industries perceive their profits as depending only on the Foreign and Home tariffs in their own industry. Thus the profits of the Foreign industry 1 are:

$$\pi^{*1} = \pi^{*1H}(\tau_1) + \pi^{*1F}(\tau^*) - \mathbf{R}^1 \tag{7.6}$$

where π^{*1H} and π^{*1F} are the Foreign industry 1 profits earned in the Home and Foreign countries respectively. The Foreign industry 2 profits are:

$$\pi^{*2} = \pi^{*2H}(\tau^2) + \pi^{*2F} - \mathbf{R}^2 \tag{7.7}$$

As before we assume that the Foreign industries 1 and 2 choose $\mathbf{R}^1$ and $\mathbf{R}^2$ respectively to maximize profits. Following Findlay and Wellisz (1982) we assume the two Foreign industries play Nash in lobbying expenditures. Since we abstract from Home lobbying, the maximization problems of the Home industries 1 and 2 are tangential.

The first order conditions of (7.6) is:

$$\left[\left(\frac{d\pi^{*1H}}{d\tau^1} \right) \phi^1 + \frac{d\pi^{*1F}}{d\tau^*} \right] \frac{\partial \tau^*}{\partial \mathbf{R}^1} - 1 = 0 \tag{7.8}$$

The first term constitutes the retaliatory cost of a marginal increase in τ^*. This effect is composed of the sensitivity of industry 1's profits in the Home market to τ^1 and the size of the retaliation parameter. The second term represents the marginal benefit of a higher τ^*. Both terms are multiplied by the marginal effectiveness of industry 1 lobbying expenditures, $(\partial\tau^*/\partial\mathbf{R}^1)$. The third term is the direct cost of marginal lobbying expenditure itself.

Inspection of (7.8) shows that the Home retaliation agency can alter the maximization problem of the Foreign pro-protection lobby in two ways. The first is reflected in the first term in (7.7). If the Home country commits to ϕ^1, then the Foreign industry 2 knows that by lobbying for protection of their domestic market, they are also lobbying for retaliation against their overseas sales. The second is in altering the marginal effectiveness of lobbying, $\partial\tau^*/\partial\mathbf{R}^1$. The Foreign tariff process summarizes the Foreign policy-makers' trade-off between the lobbying expenditures and the general national welfare. Since the profits of industry 1 and 2 enter into the national welfare calculation, the Home commitment to retaliation shifts the trade-off in favor of less protection. That is to say that retaliation reduces the marginal effectiveness of pro-protection lobbying.

The first order condition for (7.7) is:

$$\left(\frac{d\pi^{*2H}}{d\tau^2} \right) \phi^2 \left(\frac{\partial \tau^*}{\partial \mathbf{R}^2} \right) - 1 = 0 \tag{7.9}$$

By assumption τ^* does not affect the profitability of industry 2. The only motive industry 2 has to lobby against τ^* is to prevent retaliation against its sales to the Home country. Obviously if $\phi^2 = 0$ then $\mathbf{R}^2 = 0$.

The Home retaliation agency's problem is to choose ϕ^1, ϕ^2 to:

$$\max \mathbf{W}(\tau^*, \tau^1, \tau^2). \tag{7.10}$$

The first order conditions of (7.10) are:

$$\left(\frac{d\tau^*}{d\phi^1} \right) \left[\frac{\partial \mathbf{W}}{\partial \tau^*} + \frac{\partial \mathbf{W}}{\partial \tau^1} \phi^1 + \frac{\partial \mathbf{W}}{\partial \tau^2} \phi^2 \right] + \left(\frac{\partial \mathbf{W}}{\partial \tau^1} \right) \tau^* \leqq 0 \tag{7.11}$$

$$\left(\frac{d\tau^*}{d\phi^2} \right) \left[\frac{\partial \mathbf{W}}{\partial \tau^*} + \frac{\partial \mathbf{W}}{\partial \tau^1} \phi^1 + \frac{\partial \mathbf{W}}{\partial \tau^2} \phi^2 \right] + \left(\frac{\partial \mathbf{W}}{\partial \tau^2} \right) \tau^* \leqq 0 \tag{7.12}$$

The equilibrium in ϕ^1, ϕ^2, $\mathbf{R}^1$, $\mathbf{R}^2$ and τ^* is described by (7.8), (7.9), (7.11), and (7.12), together with (7.5). The first result in this section is that in general the optimal Home retaliation rule entails retaliation against the pro-protection Foreign industry 1 as well as the anti-protection Foreign industry 2. To see this we show that $(d\mathbf{W}/d\phi^1)$ and $(d\mathbf{W}/d\phi^2)$ are positive evaluated at the point $\phi^1 = \phi^2 = 0$.

To this end we first determine the expressions for $d\tau^*/d\phi_j$ ($j = 1, 2$). By inspection of (7.9), if $\phi^1 = \phi^2 = 0$ then $\mathbf{R}^2$ will be zero. Plainly then $d\mathbf{R}^2/d\phi^i$ ($i = 1, 2$) equals zero. From (7.5) together with the fact that $\mathbf{R}^2 = 0$:

$$d\tau^*/d\phi^1 = (\partial\tau^*/\partial\mathbf{R}^1)(d\mathbf{R}^1/d\phi^1) + \partial\tau^*/\partial\phi^1 \tag{7.13}$$

$$d\tau^*/d\phi^2 = (\partial\tau^*/\partial\mathbf{R}^1)(d\mathbf{R}^1/d\phi^2) + \partial\tau^*/\partial\phi^2 \tag{7.14}$$

In order to evaluate these expressions, we must first examine the partials, $d\mathbf{R}^j/d\phi^i$ ($i = 1, 2, j = 1, 2$). It is easy to show that $d\mathbf{R}^1/d\phi^1 = B/A$, where $B = (\partial\tau^*/\partial\mathbf{R}^1)[(d\pi^{*1H}/d\tau^1) + (d^2\pi^{*1F}/d\tau^{*2})(d\tau^*/d\phi^1)] + (d\pi^{*1F}/d\tau^*)(\partial^2\tau^*/\partial\mathbf{R}^1\partial\phi^1)$ and A is the second derivative of (7.6) with respect to $\mathbf{R}^1$. The quantity A is negative by the second order condition. The term B is negative assuming that π^{*1F} is convex in τ^* (i.e., $d^2\pi^{*1F}/d\tau^{*2} > 0$), and that the marginal effectiveness of industry 1 lobbying is reduced by higher levels of retaliation (i.e., $d^2\tau^*/d\mathbf{R}^1d\phi^1 < 0$)). Likewise $d\mathbf{R}^1/d\phi^2 = -C/A$, where $C = (d\tau^*/d\mathbf{R}^1)(d^2\pi^{*1F}/d\tau^{*2})(d\tau^*/d\phi^2)] + (d\pi^{*1F}/d\tau^*)(d^2\tau^*/d\mathbf{R}^1d\phi^2)$. This partial is negative, given the above conditions together with the assumption that increases in ϕ^2 decrease the marginal effectiveness of $\mathbf{R}^1$. Since $d\tau^*/d\phi^1$ and $d\tau^*/d\phi^2$ are negative it is clear that the first terms in (7.11) and (7.12) are positive when $\phi^1 = \phi^2 = 0$. As long as the marginal costs of retaliation, $(d\mathbf{W}/d\tau^1)\tau^*$ and $(d\mathbf{W}/d\tau^2)\tau^*$, are small (7.11) and (7.12) will be positive. This of course implies that the optimal ϕ^1 and ϕ^2 cannot be zero.

For a variety of reasons a very simple retaliation rule may be desirable. Most of these reasons involve factors that are outside the model. For instance it may be politically difficult to agree on the exact form of a complicated rule. Moreover a simple rule will be more transparent and therefore perhaps more credible to Foreign lobbyists. In any event, a natural question is: if retaliation must be restricted to one industry, should Home retaliate in the same industry ($\phi^1 > 0$) or in another industry ($\phi^2 > 0$)?

In general this is a difficult question to address without resorting to explicit functional forms and parameter values. Nonetheless we show that, other things equal, retaliation against the pro-tariff industry is more effective than retaliation in the anti-protection industry, at least for small ϕ^1 and ϕ^2.

The demonstration of this result boils down to showing that $dW/d\phi^1 > dW/d\phi^2$ when both are evaluated at $\phi^1 = \phi^2 = 0$. At the point $\phi^1 = \phi^2 = 0$, the partials of W with respect to ϕ^1 and ϕ^2 are:

$$dW/d\phi^1 = (\partial W/\partial \tau^*)[(\partial \tau^*/\partial R^1)(dR^1/d\phi^1) + \partial \tau^*/\partial \phi^1] - \gamma^1 \qquad (7.15)$$

$$dW/d\phi^2 = (\partial W/\partial \tau^*)[(\partial \tau^*/\partial R^1)(dR^1/d\phi^1) + \partial \tau^*/\partial \phi^2] - \gamma^2 \qquad (7.17)$$

where $\gamma^1 = \dfrac{\partial W}{\partial \tau^1} T^*$ and $\gamma^2 = \dfrac{\partial W}{\partial \tau^2} T^*$.

Assuming that the direct impact of ϕ^1 and ϕ^2 on τ^* are equivalent and the marginal costs of the two forms of retaliation are the same (i.e., $(\partial \tau^*/\partial \phi^1) = (\partial \tau^*/\partial \phi^2)$ and $\gamma^1 = \gamma^2$), then the only difference between (7.15) and (7.16) is $(dR^1/d\phi^1)$ and (dR^1/ϕ^2). Above we saw that the former is equal to $-B/A$ and the latter is equal to $-C/A$. Since $(d\pi^{1b}/d\tau^1)(\partial \tau^*/\partial R^1)$ is negative, $dR^1/d\phi^1$ is more negative than dR^1/ϕ^2. Clearly then retaliation via ϕ^1 is more effective than ϕ^2, at least for arbitrally small ϕ^1 and ϕ^2.

Conclusions

This paper is intended to show that political economy considerations are important in the formation of optimal retaliation rules. In particular a crucial characteristic of an optimal retaliation rule is its ability to reduce lobbyists' incentives to lobby for tariffs. Additionally in the context of a highly stylized political economy model, we show that the optimal retaliation rule would in general involve some retaliation against all foreign industries. However if, for some reason, the rule must be limited to retaliation against a single industry, then a reasonable rule of thumb is that the retaliation should be against the foreign industry which received the offending tariff.

In a sense this paper argues that the lessons taught us by the political economy work of Robert Baldwin and others, should be used to fashion "politically savvy" retaliation rules.

Note

The author gratefully acknowledges the comments of Harry Foster, Robert Baldwin, Gene Grossman, Paul Krugman, Ron Findlay, Stan Wellisz and Mike Gavin. This research was supported in part by a grant from Columbia Graduate Business School.

References

Baldwin, Robert 1976: "The Political Economy of Postwar US Trade Policy," *Bulletin 1976-4* New York Graduate School of Business Administration, Center for the Study of Financial Institutions.

Baldwin, Robert 1982: "The Political Economy of Protectionism," in J. Bhagwati (ed.), *Import Competition and Response*, Chicago: University of Chicago Press.

Baldwin, Robert 1986: *The Political Economy of US Import Policy*, Cambridge, MA: MIT Press.

Brander J. 1986: "Rationales for Strategic Trade and Industrial Policy," in P. Krugman (ed.), *Strategic Industrial Policy and the New International Economics*, Cambridge, MA: MIT Press.

Brock W. and Magee S. 1978: "The Economics of Special Interest Politics: The Case of Tariffs," *American Economic Review*, 68(2), 246–50.

Dixit A. 1986: "Trade Policy: An Agenda for Research," in P. Krugman (ed.), *Strategic Industrial Policy and the New International Economics*, Cambridge, MA: MIT Press.

Feenstra R. and Bhagwati J. 1982: "Tariff Seeking and the Efficient Tariff," in J. Bhagwati (ed.), *Import Competition and Response*, Chicago: University of Chicago Press.

Findlay R. and Wellisz S. 1982: "Endogenous Tariffs, the Political Economy of Trade Restrictions and Welfare," in J. Bhagwati (ed.), *Import Competition and Response*, Chicago: University of Chicago Press.

Johnson H. 1953: "Optimin tariffs and Retaliation," *Review of Economic Studies*, 21(2).

Mayer W. 1981: "Theoretical Considerations on Negotiated Tariff Settlements," *Oxford Economic Papers*, 33.

Mayer W. 1984: "Endogenous Tariff Foundation," *American Economic Review*, 74(5), 970–85.

Richardson D. 1986: "The New Political Economy of Trade Policy," in P. Krugman (ed.), *Strategic Industrial Policy and the New International Economics*, Cambridge, MA: MIT Press.

Riezman R. 1982: "Tariff Retaliation from a Strategic Viewpoint," *Southern Economic Journal*, 48, 583–93.

8

Services as Intermediate Goods: The Issue of Trade Liberalization

DAVID F. BURGESS

1 Introduction

Rather than satisfying the demands of consumers directly, many services are purchased by firms as intermediate inputs in the production process for final goods. Indeed, the fastest growing component of international trade in services – and the component of greatest interest to the United States in its effort to reduce (or at least avert the growth of) barriers to trade in services – is in so-called business or producer services like banking and finance, insurance, telecommunications, consulting and other professional services, computer software and data processing.[1] Until fairly recently most of these activities were predominantly non-traded; in standard trade models they have been subsumed as part of the infrastructure or technology whereby primary inputs (capital and labor) are transformed into consumable final output. Modern advancements in communication, the removal of certain regulatory barriers, and improved opportunities for specialized inputs in one country to offer their services in other countries has caused some degree of disintegration in production processes. It is now possible – and indeed efficient – for the production of consumable final output to involve stages of processing in several countries.

The purpose of this paper is to examine some of the implications of trade liberalization in services when services perform the role of intermediate inputs in production.[2] Making fairly mild alterations to the standard Heckscher–Ohlin–Samuelson model of international trade we are able to show how international differences in the technology for the provision of services contributes to comparative advantage and the pattern of trade in goods, and how trade liberalization in services impinges on a country's welfare, industrial structure, and the international competitiveness of its goods and service industries.

As several authors (e.g., Hill, 1977; Bhagwati, 1984b) have noted, what constitutes a service transaction – and indeed the size of the service sector itself – is somewhat arbitrary in the sense that many activities performed within the goods-producing firm are service activities which could be contracted out to specialist firms in the service sector. At the margin it is presumably just as costly to devote primary input to in-house servicing as it would be to have the servicing done outside the firm. The model of this paper makes this tradeoff explicit by showing how the demand for servicing by specialist firms is derived as a function of the vector of final output, the price of services and the technology for goods production.

Services may be inherently less tradeable than goods because the fact that they cannot be stored means that production and consumption must occur simultaneously. Nonetheless, modern advances in communications technology have made trans-border trade in many services less costly than it is for goods. The removal of technical or regulatory barriers to trade in services may either strengthen or weaken a country's comparative advantage in goods, and as a consequence trade liberalization in services need not yield benefits to both countries even though it results in global efficiency gains. This point is developed in some detail in the paper.

International trade in services may be conducted in a variety of ways. In certain circumstances a firm producing data processing, research, engineering design, or consulting services in one country may be able to transmit them to another if efficient communications links are available. In other circumstances it may be necessary for a firm to establish a permanent presence in the foreign country in order to provide the service there (e.g., banking and finance). In still other circumstances it may be optimal for certain factors that are crucial to the provision of the service to be deployed temporarily to the task of providing the service in the foreign country (e.g., management, or construction engineering services). In section 4 of the paper we focus on trade in services of the latter type and consider whether such trade is complementary to or substitutable for trade in goods, whether barriers to trade in goods are likely to induce or deter trade in services, and what are the welfare and distributive effects of trade liberalization in services. While there is a presumption that liberalized trade in services results in a Pareto improvement, this need not be the case if it takes place in the presence of barriers to trade in goods.

In addition to the assumption that the output of the service sector is used exclusively as an input in the production of final goods there are several other common features of the analytical framework used throughout the paper. Goods and services are assumed to be produced non-jointly, i.e., there is no reason why the producers of the goods need also be engaged in the servicing of these goods. The service industry is also assumed to be perfectly competitive like the goods industry; there is a uniform price for services of given quality so questions of product differentiation are set aside. Finally, in sections 2 and 3 of the paper we assume that the production of services requires only primary input (capital and labor) that is freely mobile between sectors but the technology for producing services differs between countries. However, in section 4 we assume that the production of services requires certain highly specialized inputs (managers, engineers, etc.) that have no economic value in goods-producing industries but may seek employment opportunities in the service sector abroad and thereby become the vehicle for international trade in services.

2 Some welfare implications of trade liberalization in services

Consider an economy producing two types of final output and one type of service non-jointly under competitive conditions and constant returns to scale using two primary inputs (capital and labor). The technology can be summarized by the following three unit cost equals price equations:

$$\phi^1(w, r, p_s) = p_1 \tag{8.1}$$

$$\phi^2(w, r, p_s) = p_2 \tag{8.2}$$

$$\phi^3(w, r) = p_s \tag{8.3}$$

where $\phi^i(\cdot)$ is the minimum cost of producing a unit of the ith commodity, w and r are the competitive wage and rental rate respectively, p_i $(i = 1, 2)$ are the competitive prices of the two tradable goods, and p_s is the competitive price of services.

Equations (8.1)–(8.3) describe the "structural form" of the technology, i.e., the unit cost functions dual to the linear homogeneous production functions for each industry. If equation (8.3) is substituted into equations (8.1) and (8.2) we have a "reduced form" model in which two final outputs are produced using just two primary inputs. Since the reduced form is identical to the standard Heckscher–Ohlin–Samuelson model, the model of this section merely makes explicit the existence of a domestic service sector within the traditional H–O–S framework. Of course, numerous individual service industries could be introduced without loss of generality; the key point is that the output of the service sector enters as an intermediate input into the production of final goods and all factors used in the service sector have alternative uses in the goods-producing industries.

Making use of Shephard's Lemma (that the first partial derivative of the unit cost function with respect to the price of a factor gives the cost-minimizing per unit demand for that factor) we have the following factor market equilibrium conditions for the two primary inputs, labor and capital:

$$y_1 \phi_w^1(\cdot) + y_2 \phi_w^2(\cdot) + y_s \phi_w^3(\cdot) = \bar{L} \tag{8.4}$$

$$y_1 \phi_r^1(\cdot) + y_2 \phi_r^2(\cdot) + y_s \phi_r^3(\cdot) = \bar{K} \tag{8.5}$$

where y_i $(i = 1, 2, s)$ represents the level of output of the two goods sectors and the service sector respectively. Finally, if technical or regulatory barriers prevent the output of the service sector from being traded internationally, the supply of services must equal the sum of sectoral demands so that:

$$y_1 \phi_{p_s}^1(\cdot) + y_2 \phi_{p_s}^2(\cdot) = y_s \tag{8.6}$$

Equations (8.1)–(8.3) alone will determine the competitive factor prices and the domestic price of services for any combination of world prices for traded goods provided that the economy is not driven to specialize in one of the goods. With factor prices determined by goods prices, the cost-minimizing per unit demands for each primary factor and for services in each sector will be determined, and equations (8.4)–(8.6) then constitute a system of three linear equations in three unknowns which can be solved for the unique set of sectoral outputs as a function of the primary factor endowments. Given the vector of goods prices any change in factor endowments will just change sectoral outputs leaving factor prices and the domestic price of services unaffected provided that the economy remains diversified. Moreover, if two countries with the same technology are permitted to trade freely in goods, differences in factor prices and service prices between countries will be reduced (eliminated if there are no transportation costs) even though neither factor of production is internationally mobile and services themselves cannot be traded. As in the case where services enter the utility functions of consumers rather than the production functions of firms, a reduction in barriers to trade in goods will reduce the incentive to engage in trade in services.

According to the model, the extent to which goods-producing firms "contract out" rather than do their own servicing depends upon the market price of services relative to the prices of the primary inputs (capital and labor). The higher the price of services relative to the wage and rental rates the less will goods-producing firms rely upon the service sector, but the expenditure share for services could go up or down depending upon the degree of interfactor substitution.

International differences in the technology for the provision of services can be an important determinant of comparative advantage in goods if technical or regulatory barriers prevent services from being traded. However, the relationship is not as simple as might first appear. Space limitations preclude a complete analysis here, but it can be shown that if countries differ only in terms of their services technology, the country with the technological superiority in services will have relatively expensive rather than relatively cheap services if the factor intensity ranking of the two industries is opposite to the factor intensity ranking of the two final outputs taking into account the primary factor requirements for the services used as an intermediate input in each sector. A technological superiority in services will be reflected in higher returns to primary factors and these higher input costs could more than compensate for the technological superiority. Even if services are relatively cheap in the advanced country they may or may not confer comparative advantage upon industries that use services relatively intensively. Cheaper services could mean that industries that use services intensively will expand relative to other industries, but it could also mean that industries that make intensive use of the factor used intensively in the service sector will expand. These need not be the same industries. For example, if services use only labor and the technology is Leontief so that input-output coefficients are independent of input prices then a neutral technological improvement in the service sector will cause the labor-intensive good to expand and the capital-intensive good to contract, no matter which good uses services intensively. However, if the technology is Cobb–Douglas so that factor shares in each sector are independent of input prices the good that uses services intensively will expand relative to the other good.

It follows from the above that the international diffusion of services technology can have an important impact on income distribution and the terms of trade even if the output of the service sector cannot be traded. The question arises whether a country will undermine its comparative advantage if it permits its technological superiority in services to be transferred abroad either through licensing arrangements or free of charge. The answer is in the affirmative if the technological superiority in services is the only source of comparative advantage or if it reinforces other determinants of comparative advantage such as difference in relative factor endowment. However, if a country's technological superiority in services tends to offset other more important determinants of comparative advantage the transferring country can capture some of the benefits of the transfer through an improvement in its terms of trade even if the technology itself is made available free of charge.[3]

Suppose, for example, that the country which the technological superiority in services is also capital-abundant. Capital abundance alone contributes to comparative advantage in capital-intensive goods but if the service sector is labor-intensive and if services are used intensively in the production of labor-intensive goods the technological superiority in services will contribute to comparative advantage in labor-intensive goods. Suppose that the difference in relative factor endowment is the overriding determinant of comparative advantage and trade. If the technological superiority in services is transferred abroad free of charge it will expand the output of labor-intensive goods abroad and contract the output of capital-intensive goods. Assuming that Samuelson's strong factor intensity condition holds (thereby ruling out factor intensity reversals), the terms of trade will improve for the transferring country.

Thus, while the free transfer of services technology makes countries more alike by removing one source of difference between them it does not necessarily follow that it will hurt the service-exporting country by undermining its comparative advantage. On the contrary, when services are intermediate inputs in production trade liberalization in services (whether it involves the removal of barriers to the transfer of services technology or the removal of barriers to trans-border trade in the output of the service sector) may well hurt the service-importing country.

Suppose that under free trade in goods but prior to trade liberalization in services the home country is specialized in good 1 and the foreign country in specialized in good 2. Such specialization could result from differences in primary factor endowment or it could result from differences in the technology of goods production. Each country now contains just two industries: its goods-producing industry which produces final output for domestic consumption or export and its service industry which satisfies the intermediate demand for services by the goods industry. The initial equilibrium under free trade in goods only is shown in figure 8.1 at A where for simplicity we have assumed that the home country and the foreign country exchange their respective outputs y_1^0 and y_2^0 for the preferred consumption bundle C.

Competitive conditions and free mobility of primary factors between the two industries within each country will ensure that efficient production techniques are used but the existence of prohibitive barriers to trade in services prevents service prices from being equalized. The locus TT represents combinations of final output that can be produced by the two countries if the output of the service sector in one country could be used as an input by firms in the other country. The slope of the frontier at A

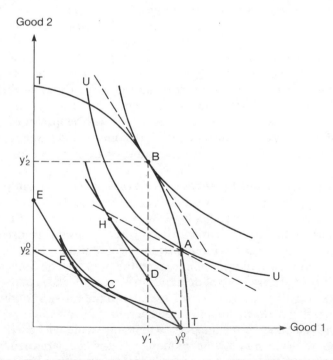

Figure 8.1   Trade liberalization in services can hurt the service-importing country

represents the ratio of the marginal product of services in production of good 2 in the foreign country to the marginal product of services in production of good 1 at home. Suppose now that all barriers to trans-border trade in the output of the service sector are removed. Since the slope of TT at A exceeds the slope of UU the home country will export services and the new free trade equilibrium will move to B. The output of good 1 in the home country contracts because primary factors are drawn out of the production of good 1 directly and indirectly in order to produce services for export; the output of good 2 abroad expands because more primary factors are employed directly and indirectly in the production of good 2 than the foreign country's endowment. Thus, the change in the composition of world output that results from trade liberalization in services implies a deterioration in the terms of trade for the service-importing country. This deterioration in the relative price of the good produced by the service-importing country is a cost of trade liberalization that must be weighed against the benefit from access to cheaper services from abroad. There are global efficiency gains from trade liberalization in services which are represented by the move from A to B, but there is no guarantee that these gains will be shared between the countries.

Figure 8.1 illustrates the case where the service-importing country is hurt by trade liberalization in services. Since the exporter of services receives the marginal product of his services abroad in return for the marginal product of his services at home, and since the slope of the tangent at B represents the ratio of the marginal product of services abroad versus at home in the new equilibrium, the home country's endowment point moves from y_1^0 to D. By exporting services the home country gives up $y_1^0 - y_1^1$ units of good 1 in return for Dy_1^0 units of good 2. Meanwhile, by importing services the foreign country obtains Ey_2^0 additional units of good 2 (Ey_2^0 is the difference between $y_2^1 - y_2^0$ and Dy_1^1). The budget lines for the home and foreign countries pass through D and E respectively with slopes equal to the new equilibrium ratio of goods prices. The home country moves from C to H and is better off but the foreign country moves from C to F and is worse off.

So far we have assumed that trade in services takes the form of trans-border flows in the output of the service sector but it could take the form of a transfer of service sector technology. In the present context if the home country has technological superiority in services and transfers this superiority free of charge the foreign country could still be made worse off but the conditions are those familiar from the literature on immeserizing growth – low price elasticities of demand for imports in each country and a high income elasticity of demand for imports in the foreign country. The basic point is that to the extent that trade liberalization in services reinforces pre-existing comparative advantages it will involve a hidden benefit for the service-exporting country and a hidden cost for the service importing country and there is no a priori reason why these distributive effects may not dominate the efficiency gains from improved global resource allocation so as to leave the importing country worse off.

3 Trade liberalization in services and international competitiveness

In this section we analyze the implications of trade liberalization in services for the pattern of trade in goods and for the long-run viability of the goods and service industries in each country. We begin with a situation of free trade in the outputs of the two goods-producing industries but no trade in the output of the service sector. For simplicity, the technology for producing goods using services as an input is assumed to be identical across countries. However, the technology for producing services differs between countries – the result of international differences in a third primary factor such as infrastructure, climate, knowledge, etc. This third factor is of the "creation of atmosphere" type which means that its return is fully appropriated by capital and labor. Thus, an international difference in the technology for producing services conspires with an international difference in the ratio of primary factor endowments to determine a country's comparative advantage and pattern of trade in goods as discussed in the previous section.

If the international difference in the service sector technology is significant but not paramount, the pattern of trade in goods prior to trade liberalization in services will reflect standard Heckscher–Ohlin theory; the capital-abundant country will export the capital-intensive good. However, free trade in goods will fail to equalize the prices of primary factors because of the underlying difference in the service technology. There will be an international price differential for services, but because of technical or regulatory barriers to trade in services this international price differential will fail to produce trade in services. The country with the superior services technology will enjoy a higher overall standard of living, but as discussed earlier it does not necessarily follow that services will be relatively cheap nor that the real wage and the real return to capital will both be higher in the technologically advanced country.

Suppose that free trade in services is now possible in the usual sense that it becomes feasible to produce services in one country and transmit them to the other country for consumption there. If the services technology were identical in the two countries, free trade in both goods and services would equalize factor prices, and the pattern of trade in goods and services would be indeterminate for reasons discussed in Melvin (1968). All that can be said in this case is that the capital-abundant country would export a bundle of output that is more capital-intensive than its import bundle, and vice versa for the labor-abundant country.

However, we assume that there is a difference in the technology for producing services between the two countries and the question is whether and under what conditions free trade in goods and services together will eliminate the service industry in the country with the inferior services technology. The answer, as we shall see, is that the service sector in the country with the inferior technology may well survive. Free trade in both goods and services must induce some specialization in at least one country since a completely diversified industrial structure cannot persist in both countries at common output prices when there is a technology difference between the countries. However, the specialization may result in the elimination of one of the goods-producing industries in one of the countries rather than the elimination of the service industry in one of the countries. Even if the service industry is eliminated in one of the countries it does not follow that the country with the inferior technology for producing services losses its service industry. Finally, only if international specialization results in the elimination of the service industry in the country with the inferior technology will trade liberalization in services equalize factor prices between the two countries.

Prior to trade liberalization in services the capital-abundant home country is assumed to export the capital-intensive good 1 and import the labor-intensive good 2. The reverse pattern occurs in the labor-abundant foreign country. Comparative advantage is based upon differences in the K/L endowment ratio and differences in the technology caused solely by the technological disparity in the service sector.

When services trade is liberalized several patterns of specialization can occur. There are two sets of circumstances that it is useful to distinguish; they depend upon whether the service sector uses a capital-labor ratio intermediate between the two goods-producing industries or whether it uses a lower (or higher) capital-labor ratio than either goods-producing industry.

The first set of circumstances is summarized graphically in figure 8.2. Under free trade in both goods and services a common set of output prices must prevail in both countries and at these prices there will be three unit value isoquants which describe the capital and labor requirements for a dollar's worth of each output in each country. Because the technology for producing each good is identical between countries, the unit value isoquants for the goods-producing industries 1 and 2 will be identical in the two countries. However, the unit value isoquant for the service industry in the home country will be everywhere inside the unit value isoquant for the service industry in the foreign country.

Note that at least one country must lose one of its industries when trade in services is liberalized. This follows because the unit value isoquants for the three industries cannot all be tangent to a single isocost locus within each country at the same time. The immediate consequence of this is that (unlike the analysis of Melvin, 1968) the pattern of production and trade will be uniquely determined.

Suppose that the *home* country remains completely diversified under

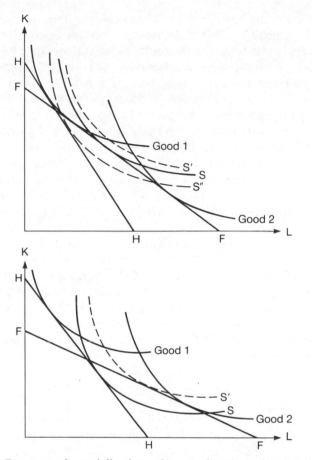

Figure 8.2   Patterns of specialization when services have intermediate factor intensity

trade liberalization in services. Then in the top panel of figure 8.2 the isocost locus must be FF which is tangent to unit value isoquants for goods 1, 2, and S. The unit value isoquants for goods 1 and 2 in the foreign country are identical, but the unit value isoquant for the service sector is S′. It follows that the service sector is not competitive in the foreign country and it will produce a mixture of good 1 and good 2 depending upon its K/L endowment ratio. It also follows that factor prices will be equalized between the two countries. Therefore, despite the fact that the foreign country loses its service industry it clearly benefits because its standard of living is brought up to the level prevailing in the home country.

Suppose instead that the *foreign* country remains completely diversified. We must then interpret the unit value isoquant S in the top panel of figure 8.2 as referring to the foreign country, and S″ as the corresponding unit value isoquant in the home country. In this case the home country loses its labor-intensive good 2 industry. Moreover, since the isocost locus for the home country is HH while the isocost locus for the foreign country is FF, factor prices will not be equalized. Not only does the service sector survive in the foreign country but it may become a net exporter of services. However, since the price of the foreign country's export good (good 2) has fallen relative to its import good (good 1) it may well be worse off.

The third possibility illustrated in the bottom panel of figure 8.2 has the home country losing its good 2 industry and the foreign country losing its good 1 industry. Interestingly enough, it is the service industry that survives in *both* countries despite the fact that the only source of technological difference between the two countries is in the service sector. Here, trade liberalization in services results in some degree of "de-industrialization" in both countries.

Figure 8.3 summarizes the case in which services are more labor-intensive than either goods-producing industry. Suppose that the home country remains completely diversified under trade liberalization in services. HH is the isocost locus in the home country, simultaneously tangent to the isoquants for goods 1, 2, and S. The foreign country's unit value isoquant for the service sector is S'. Two outcomes are now possible: either the foreign country loses its service industry and specializes in goods 1 and 2 resulting in factor price equalization, or the foreign country loses its good 1 industry and specializes in good 2 and S with the isocost locus given by FF. The second case seems more plausible than the first if the K/L endowment ratios differ significantly between the two countries.

Suppose instead that the foreign country remains completely diversified after trade in services is liberalized. We must then interpret HH as the isocost locus for the foreign country and S as the relevant unit value isoquant. The home country's unit value isoquant for services is now S″ and its corresponding isocost locus is H′H′. Therefore, the home country loses its labor-intensive good 2 industry.

Finally, both countries could be driven to specialize. The outcome is shown in the bottom panel of figure 8.3 where the home country loses its service industry and the foreign country loses its good 1 industry. The interesting point about this case is that the home country loses its service industry even though it has the technological superiority in services.

The important conclusion that emerges from this discussion is that if the services produced in each country are perceived to be perfect substitutes for each other trade liberalization in services will induce greater specialization than would otherwise occur, but the specialization need not take place in the service sector even if the only difference between the technologies in the two countries occurs in the service sector. This conclusion is just a statement that the pattern of trade is determined by comparative rather than absolute advantage.

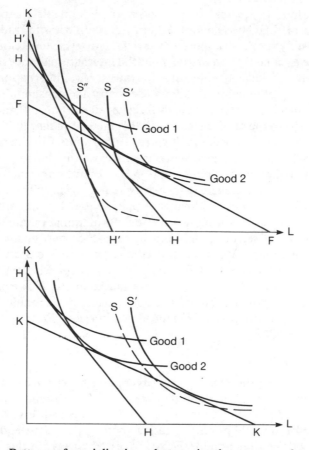

Figure 8.3 Patterns of specialization when services have extreme factor intensity

4 National treatment of services inputs in the presence of barriers to trade in goods

As Caves (1971) and others have noted, if all factors are freely mobile between sectors and perfectly competitive conditions prevail there is no way to explain the process of foreign direct investment. Yet the predominant mode of international trade in many service industries involves the establishment of a facility in the foreign country to provide the service there, or at least the redeployment of factors specific to the service sector in the production of services abroad. The purpose of this section is to incorporate the foreign direct investment option into the model and to examine how barriers to trade in goods impact on the decision to engage in foreign direct investment in services.

We continue to assume that services are intermediate inputs in the production of final goods and that there are no barriers to trade in goods except possibly for those imposed by tariffs. However, unlike the previous sections we assume that no matter what the international price differential in services it is technically impossible to trade services internationally in the sense of having production occur in one country and consumption occur in the other. Instead, international differences in the rate of return to the factor specific to the service sector (call this factor "managers") will cause some of this factor to seek employment opportunities in the high return country. Whether managers actually move to the foreign country in response to higher rates of remuneration is not important; the key point is that international differences in the return to managers will induce some of them to seek and accept employment opportunities abroad rather than at home, and this has important implications for national economic welfare.

As in previous sections, the model consists of two goods-producing industries operating under competitive conditions and constant returns to scale and requiring capital, labor and "management services" as inputs. Therefore equations (8.1) and (8.2) continue to apply. However, we now introduce a third primary factor, managers, in addition to capital and labor as an input in the production of management services. Equation (8.3) must now be replaced by:

$$\phi^3(w, r, s) = p_s \qquad\qquad (8.3')$$

where s represents the return to managers and p_s represents the price of management services. Equations (8.1), (8.2), and (8.3') contain three factor prices w, r, and s in addition to the price of management services p_s so that for any vector of world prices for traded goods (p_1, p_2) these equations will no longer suffice to determine factor prices. However, in this section we assume that capital is freely mobile between countries so that for any vector of world prices for traded goods and the world rental rate for capital equations (8.1), (8.2), and (8.3') determine the wage rate, the return to managers and the price of management services. Thus, if two countries with identical technologies are permitted to trade freely with each other and there are no barriers to the international mobility of capital, the wage rate, the return to managers and the price of management services will all be equalized across countries despite international differences in the endowment ratio of laborers to managers.

To complete the model we must specify factor market equilibrium conditions for those factors in less than perfectly elastic supply to the economy as a whole as well as a market clearing condition for management services. Equations (8.4) and (8.6) continue to apply as the conditions for equilibrium in the markets for labor and management services respectively, but equation (8.5) must be dropped because capital is now assumed to be perfectly mobile internationally. Since the only other domestic primary factor is managers, and since we assume that managers are less than perfectly mobile internationally, we have:

$$y_s \phi_s^3(\cdot) = T(s - s^*) \tag{8.5'}$$

where $T(\cdot)$ represents the supply of managers available to the domestic economy given the differential rate of payment for managers between the home and foreign country. (A variable with an asterisk represents its value in the foreign country.) We assume that managers continue to consume in their home country even though they may derive part or all of their income from employment in the foreign country.

The complete model consists of equations (8.1), (8.2), (8.3'), (8.4), (8.5'), and (8.6), and it contains six endogenous variables w, s, p_s, y_1, y_2 and y_s. In response to any given vector of prices for traded goods and rental price of capital ($\mathbf{p}_1$, $\mathbf{p}_2$, $\mathbf{r}$) the model can be solved for the endogenous variables. We can then determine the welfare, distributive, and allocative effects of various policy changes.

While the structure of this model appears to be somewhat novel and unfamiliar, its reduced form is fundamentally no different from a standard H–O–S model since it contains just two primary factors (labor and managers) and two types of final output. To see this, substitute equation (8.3') into equations (8.1) and (8.2) and recall that the rental rate on capital, like the prices of traded goods, is determined internationally so that we can rewrite the unit cost equals price equations in the form:

$$\Phi^1(w, s; r^*) = p_1^* \tag{8.7}$$

$$\Phi^2(w, s; r^*) = p_2^* \tag{8.8}$$

where an asterisk above a variable indicates its value in the foreign country. (In the case of a small open economy the variables with an asterisk would be determined exogenously.) From equations (8.7) and (8.8) it is clear that while managers are specific to the service sector they are indirectly employed in the production of both types of final output because management services enter each goods industry as an input. The first partial derivatives of the $\Phi^i(\cdot)$ functions in (8.7) and (8.8) with respect to the factor prices give the cost-minimizing direct plus indirect per unit demands for each primary input in the production of each type of final output.

Next, substitute equation (8.1) into equations (8.4) and (8.5') and rearrange terms to obtain:

$$y_1[\phi_w^1 + \phi_w^3(\cdot)\phi_{ps}^1(\cdot)] + y_2[\phi_w^2 + \phi_w^3\phi_{ps}^2(\cdot)] = \bar{L} \tag{8.9}$$

$$y_1[\phi_{ps}^1(\cdot)\phi_s^3(\cdot)] + y_2[\phi_{ps}^2(\cdot)\phi_s^3(\cdot)] = T(s - s^*) \tag{8.10}$$

The expressions in squared brackets can be interpreted as the direct plus indirect primary input requirements per unit of each type of final output. We have already noted that these input requirements are given by the first partial derivatives of the $\Phi^i(\cdot)$ in (8.7) and (8.8). Equations (8.9) and (8.10) constitute two linear equations in two unknowns once the international price vector $(\mathbf{p}_1, \mathbf{p}_2, \mathbf{r})$ is given and they can be rewritten in the following form:

$$y_1 \Phi^1_w(\cdot) + y_2 \Phi^2_w(\cdot) = \overline{L} \tag{8.11}$$

$$y_1 \Phi^1_s(\cdot) + y_2 \Phi^2_s(\cdot) = T(s - s^*) \tag{8.12}$$

The system of reduced form equations (8.7), (8.8), (8.11), and (8.12) has the same structure as the standard H–O–S model.

Given the 2×2 structure of the model certain familiar properties follow. Thus, consider the effect of the home country imposing a tariff at percentage rate τ on imports of its labor-intensive good. If we restrict attention to the small country case for simplicity we know from Jones (1971) that the competitive wage rate will rise by a greater percentage than the tariff, and the return to managers will fall so that $dw/w > \tau > 0 > ds/s$.

If there were prohibitive barriers to international trade in services – which in the present context means that domestic managers cannot accept employment opportunities abroad – then the home country would experience the familiar welfare loss from its protection policy.[4] (A welfare loss is guaranteed because the home country is assumed to be small.) Real wages would be higher, but the benefits to labor would be more than offset by the reduced incomes of domestic managers. However, suppose that international trade in services is now liberalized in the sense that national treatment is accorded to foreign managers by either country. Then the home country's tariff will cause some managers to seek and accept employment opportunities abroad and according to the magnification effect of the standard H–O–S model the loss of managers will result in a further expansion of the protected industry and a further contraction of the export industry with an associated social welfare loss equal to the tariff revenue foregone. We conclude that the home country will be made worse off if it agrees to liberalize trade in services when trade in goods is distorted by tariffs.

A similar argument can be developed to prove that if the foreign country imposes a tariff on its management-intensive good, and thereby raises the real incomes of managers abroad, the influx of managers from the home country will entail a net welfare loss for the foreign country. Therefore, the model of this section predicts that trade liberalization in services in the presence of tariffs on trade in goods will not be mutually beneficial for both countries.[5] Even if there is free trade in goods and free mobility of capital if technology differences between the two countries cause the return to managers to differ trade liberalization in services may hurt one country through adverse terms of trade effects despite the fact that it raises world real income.

5 Conclusion

Economists have a strong a priori belief that trade liberalization – whether in goods or in services – is on balance desirable for all countries. This belief does not depend upon whether a country is a net exporter or a net importer of the goods or services being liberalized and it is reinforced rather than weakened by the knowledge that the country in question is small. My tactic in this paper has been to keep an eye out for situations in which trade liberalization in services in one form or another might have adverse effects on a country, in the belief that knowing when these situations are likely to occur is valuable in devising an appropriate policy response.

Throughout the paper the focus has been on the role of services as inter-mediate inputs in the production of final goods. Of course, this does not include all services, but it seems to include many of the important services that countries have in mind in present discussions about trade liberaliza-tion. There is a strong presumption that access to more efficient services on account of trade liberalization will improve the production process for final output and have beneficial effects throughout the economy – benefits that are widely shared because services are part of the infrastructure of the economy. We corroborate this presumption but also note situations when not all agents benefit.

The analysis of this paper suggests that with relatively mild altera-tions standard models of international trade in the Heckscher–Ohlin–Samuelson–Ricardo–Viner tradition can be usefully applied to the trade in services question. We have shown that the service sector can influence a country's comparative advantage in goods in ways that are subtle and complex and that the liberalization of trade in services can have important and quite dramatic implications for national economic welfare and for the international competitiveness of goods and service industries. While we have identified several instances in which trade liberalization in services may not yield a Pareto improvement for a country, these situations represent the workings of pre-existing distortions such as unexploited market power in trade or tariffs and taxes on capital movements. In situations where trade is not distorted and the country is small we confirm the fundamental proposition that there is a net welfare gain from trade liberalization in services. The existence of a net gain is, of course, not often the decisive issue; distributive effects are usually critical and we have found that a wide range of distributive effects is possible depending upon the particular model of trade in services.

Notes

The author wishes to thank Ron Jones for helpful comments on a previous draft and the Institute for Research on Public Policy for financial support.

1   See Office of the United States Trade Representative (1984) for a comprehensive and insightful discussion of the role of services in international trade and for evidence on the growing importance of international trade in producer services.
2   Much of the early analytical work on international trade in services tends to focus on services as a final output which cannot be traded. International trade in services occurs when certain inputs crucial to the provision of services in one country make themselves available for employment abroad. See e.g. Bhagwati (1984a), Deardoff (1985), and Melvin (1987).
3   For useful discussions of the issues raised by technology transfer in general equilibrium trade models see McCulloch and Yellin (1982) and Grossman and Shapiro (1985).
4   The tariff may cause either an inflow or an outflow of capital depending upon whether the protected industry has a higher or lower direct plus indirect capital requirement than the unprotected industry. Our demonstration of additional welfare loss from protection in the presence of internationally mobile factors is analogous to the results of Brecher and Díaz-Alejandro (1977) in the standard H–O–S model.
5   If the foreign country has no tariff on its import-competing industry but faces a tariff on its exports then it will be better off if it accords national treatment to foreign managers since their influx would yield positive net benefits. There would be no tariff revenue loss to the country because it has imposed no tariffs and although it faces tariff-distorted prices for its exports they represent the relevant social opportunity costs. However, the usual situation is that each country has imposed a tariff to protect its import-competing industry and is engaged in a bargaining process which precludes the unilateral removal of its own tariff without reciprocal action from abroad. In such a context trade liberalization of services will result in a net welfare loss for both countries.

References

Bhagwati J. N. 1984a: "Why are Services Cheaper in the Poor Countries?" *Economic Journal*, 94 (June), 279–86.
Bhagwati J. N. 1984b: "Splintering and Disembodiment of Services and Developing Nations," *The World Economy*, 7 (June), 133–43.
Brecher, Richard, and Díaz-Alejandro Carlos 1977: "Tariffs, Foreign Capital, and Immiserizing Growth," *Journal of International Economics*, 7, 317–22.
Caves R. E. 1971: "International Corporations: The Industrial Economics of Foreign Investment," *Economica*, 38 (February), 1–27.
Deardorff A. V. 1985: "Comparative Advantage and International Trade and Investment in Services," in R. M. Stern (ed.), *Trade and Investment in Services: Canada/US Perspectives*, Toronto: Ontario Economic Council.
Grossman G. and Shapiro C. 1985: "Normative Issues Raised by International Trade in Technology Services," in R. M. Stern (ed.), *Trade and Investment in Services: Canada/US Perspectives*, Toronto: Ontario Economic Council.
Hill T. P. 1977: "On Goods and Services," *Review of Income and Wealth*, 23, 315–38.
Hindley B. and Smith A.: "Comparative Advantage and Trade in Services," *The World Economy*, 7, 369–90.

Jones R. W. 1971: "A Three Factor Model in Theory, Trade and History," in J. N. Bhagwati et al. (eds), *Trade, Balance of Payments and Growth*, Amsterdam: North Holland.

McCulloch R. and Yellin J. 1982: "Technology Transfer and the National Interest," *International Economic Review*, 23, 421–8.

Melvin J. R. 1968: "Production and Trade with Two Factors and Three Goods," *American Economic Review*, 58, 1248–68.

Melvin J. R. 1987: "Trade in Services: A Heckscher–Ohlin Approach," IRPP Discussion Paper, January.

Office of the United States Trade Representative, 1984: *US National Study on Trade in Services*, a submission by the US Government to the GATT, Executive Office of the President, Washington, DC, December.

9

International Trade in Capital and Capital Goods

RACHEL MCCULLOCH AND J. DAVID RICHARDSON

Among Robert Baldwin's many pathbreaking contributions to the analysis of international trade is his prescient 1966 discussion of capital accumulation, capital-goods trade, and financial flows in a two-sector model of economic growth (Baldwin 1966). The paper is not one that has been widely cited. Indeed, it rates no mention in the two fine Handbook surveys of that literature by Findlay (1984) and Smith (1984), although the introductory chapter by Jones and Neary (1984, p. 39) refers to it in passing.

Yet there is Bob Baldwin at his best: rich and complex graphical analysis that is concise but still highly accessible;[1] relevant and informative discussion of observable patterns and trends that makes no sacrifice of logical rigor; early recognition of a phenomenon that will grow to central importance in the years ahead. In the light of all this, subsequent scholarly neglect[2] of the 1966 paper is surprising, especially given the considerable number of Baldwin articles that remain staple items on graduate reading lists around the world. However, Bob perhaps anticipated that in this particular case his own contribution might be eclipsed by other contemporaneous work. The first footnote, with Bob's usual self-effacing grace, reports:

> since this paper was written, H. Oniki and H. Uzawa have published an elegant mathematical analysis of trade in capital goods. In contrast to the comparative statics approach here, Oniki and Uzawa frame their analysis in dynamic terms. The main difference in basic assumptions is that they postulate a constant average propensity to save throughout the accumulation process, whereas savings is made a function both of the interest rate and the level of income in the model used here.

In this paper, we seek to honor the distinctive qualities of analysis and insight that Bob Baldwin has brought to a wide range of important questions of international trade theory and policy over the years. Accordingly, we have attempted to emulate the master by employing Baldwinesque graphics on a Baldwinesque theme, with Baldwinesque references to salient trends and patterns.[3] We hope that readers and critics will take such imitation as the sincere expression of our admiration for an esteemed colleague and our gratitude for many years of fruitful bilateral and multilateral contact.

Part I of our paper introduces a simple graphical analysis similar to that of Baldwin (1966), and then demonstrates the consistency of its predictions with recent trends in trade and capital flows between the United States and Japan. Part II of the paper discusses in more detail some aspects of these trends that cannot be captured in the simple graphics, especially distinctions among the motivations for and effects of different types of investment flows. Part III concludes the paper with a retrospective consideration of Baldwin (1966).

One of Bob's great ongoing achievements is the ability to gain the ear of those concerned with detailed decision-making and policy implementation without losing the attention or the respect of abstract modellers, and we have tried once more to imitate. We discuss how policy changes influence the fundamental economic determinants of trade patterns and payments balances. We also describe the potential impact of some important determinants beyond those fundamentals – risk, regulation, control. In analyzing policy change and realistic response to it in a careful, consistent way, we hope that we reveal our debt to a grandmaster of practical political economy.

I A simple model of intertemporal optimization

Recent trends in US trade and external borrowing have stimulated a profusion of novel and often complex theoretical approaches. Yet much of the emerging pattern can be explained by a simple and familiar graphical analysis, which relates these trends to liberalization of trade and financial flows, shifts in national fiscal policies, and changes in the climate for investment.

We begin with a two-sector model of capital accumulation similar to that of Baldwin (1966). In figure 9.1, $Q_K Q_C$ represents an economy's production-possibility curve between capital goods and (current-period) consumption goods.[4] Consumption goods must be consumed in the current period; capital goods last forever, with each unit generating output worth r (measured in consumption goods) each period. For an economy closed to international transactions, the vertical axis can also be considered to measure the economy's real stock of claims on future goods – its real wealth. In a closed economy, current production of capital goods is the only means of increasing real wealth (or of maintaining real wealth, if depreciation of capital is taken into account). Production of capital goods is investment, which must be equal in the closed economy to savings, the share of current income not allocated to current consumption.

National preferences are assumed homothetic, but with respect to the

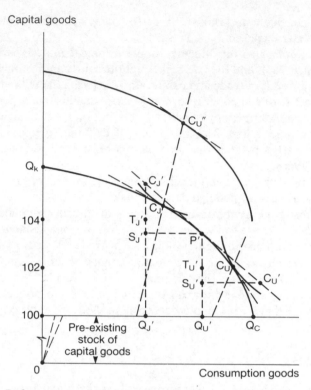

Figure 9.1   Reference case and alternatives for inter-temporal trade

origin marked 0 rather than the one marked 100; that is, at given prices and interest rates, consumption is kept proportional to wealth. The former origin can be considered to index households' choice between wealth and current consumption, a stock-flow decision. The latter origin can be considered to index firms' choice of sectoral production mix, a flow-flow decision. The slope of a straight line such as $C'_J C'_U$, expressed as a positive number, measures the price of current consumption goods relative both to capital goods (exchange within a period) and future consumption goods (intertemporal exchange). Steeper slopes denote cheaper capital goods and higher interest rates.[5]

To analyze the effects of recent changes in underlying economic conditions, we choose an easily visualized reference case: let $Q_K Q_C$ represent identical production possibilities for Japan and the United States, with the rest of the world to enter the analysis later. More realistic reference cases, with Japan economically smaller or differing in relative factor endowment, would leave unaffected our particular conclusions about the effects of recent *changes*.[6] We further assume, for purposes of the reference case, that Japan's national savings rate is high by world and US standards,[7] and that the two economies are closed not only to capital movements but to trade in commodities as well.

In the reference case, then, Japan's equilibrium could be described by point C_J, with the highest attainable preference contour tangent to Q_KQ_C at that point. The real interest rate, reflected in the slope of the tangent line, would be low. Equilibrium for the United States, with a lower savings rate but otherwise identical to Japan, could be described by point C_U. The real interest rate would be higher in the United States than in Japan.

We are now able to consider the effects on Japan and the United States of changes that capture in stylized form some significant economic developments of the 1970s and 1980s.

1 Trade liberalization

Once notorious for closing its markets to foreign products, in recent decades Japan has dramatically reduced formal barriers to trade. In our very simplified model, liberalization of commodity trade between the two economies has striking effects. In the extreme, both economies would produce at P'. However, Japan would now consumer at C'_J, importing $C'_JS'_J$ of capital goods and exporting S'_JP' of consumer goods. The United States would consume at C'_U, with a mirror-image trade pattern. With no international capital flows permitted, trade would necessarily be balanced. Nonetheless, trade liberalization does affect real interest rates, which are now equalized across countries. The real interest rate is thus higher in Japan and lower in the United States than in the absence of commodity trade.

As a consequence of these interest rate movements, Japan's relative spending on capital goods would increase, as would the savings rate.[8] These changes would in turn produce an increased growth rate of Japan's capital stock and gross national product (GNP). US effects would be opposite: the current consumption share would rise, the savings rate would fall, and investment and growth would decline (although US welfare would rise[9]).

There are several interesting consequences of simple trade liberalization in this scenario, each with a suggestive correspondence to recent trends. First, trade liberalization accentuates national differences in savings rates.[10] A second is that trade liberalization alters relative growth rates of GNP, not merely current purchasing power. By allowing national savings rates to become more different, trade liberalization speeds up the divergence of growth trajectories that would have occurred even in the absence of trade. (As a consequence of Japan's higher savings rate, its production-possibility curve would shift outward more rapidly than that of the United States.)

A third consequence is the further expansion of trade over time; the altered growth pattern induced by liberalization is trade-biased. Japan's higher rate of capital formation, via the Rybczynski effect, enhances especially its ability to produce its own exportable, consumption goods, which are by assumption capital-intensive. Likewise, the lower rate of capital formation in the United States encourages production and export of labor-intensive capital goods.[11]

2 Financial liberalization

Japan first moved to reduce tariffs and quotas, and only later, in the 1970s, began to dismantle barriers to inward and outward foreign investments. In our simplified model, the removal of capital controls (liberalization of international financial trade) has interesting consequences for savings and growth. The principal change is that the allocation among nations of the world's capital stock and of its wealth are now independently determined.

A simple way to describe the change analytically is that in addition to commodity trade, there is also free international trade in certificates of ownership to the stock of productive capital, i.e., in pieces of paper that entitle the holder to the stream of income generated by a machine, whether that machine is located in the holder's backyard or halfway around the world. Savers are assumed indifferent between acquiring physical capital and these ownership certificates.

Under these conditions, some of Japan's excess demand for claims on future goods can be satisfied by Japanese purchases of ownership certificates, rather than by physical shipment of the capital goods themselves.[12] US exports of capital goods may in fact decline as a result of the opening of trade in financial substitutes. While we have not explicitly considered transport costs in the model, it is obviously cheaper to transport pieces of paper than machines.

With the opening of trade in financial assets, a US deficit on commodity trade with Japan can develop, necessarily offset by a US surplus on exchanges of financial assets. In fact, a recurrent Japanese demand for US financial assets would cause US commodity trade to move into a position of sustained deficit. This would make the United States appear "uncompetitive" relative to Japan even though the underlying technologies, production relationships, factors, and commodities themselves were identical in the two countries.

The requisite exchanges of goods for paper could continue indefinitely between growing economies like those pictured in figure 9.1. To see this, it is helpful to discuss one of the (infinitely many) possible equilibria,[13] one that serves also as a second useful reference equilibrium. Each economy produces at P'. Japan would consume at C_j', importing $S_j'C_j'$ of ownership claims to US capital (not the machines themselves) and exporting $S_j'P'$ of consumer goods. The United States would consume at C_U', with the mirror-image trade pattern. Commodity trade would no longer be balanced, as it was before financial liberalization. Japan would run a current-account surplus equal to $S_j'P'$ (or $S_j'C_j'$ valued in capital goods) and a capital-account deficit of the same size. The United States would have mirror-image imbalances.

The Japanese-owned capital stock would grow by $Q'_jC'_j$, just as it did before financial liberalization. But the Japanese-domiciled share of this increment would grow only by $Q'_jS'_j$; $S'_jC'_j$ would represent "net foreign investment" in the United States by Japan. The growth rate of the capital stock physically located in Japan would be lower than previously, as would the growth rate of Japanese output (gross domestic product, GDP). In fact, the rate of growth of Japanese output would be identical to that of the (geographical) United States in this equilibrium, because $Q'_jS'_j$ is equal to Q'_UP'.

The geographical economies would remain identical in periods subsequent to the one depicted. But Japanese residents would own a larger and larger share of the growing US capital stock as time went on, with corresponding claims over a larger and larger share of US GNP. Although US residents' ownership *shares* of its capital stock would fall, their claims over future goods would still be rising. In the period illustrated in figure 9.1, the United States adds $Q'_US'_U$ to the US-owned portion of the nation's capital stock.

For the illustrative numbers given on the vertical axis of figure 9.1, each of the geographical economies might grow at slightly over 3 percent (GDP).[14] However, Japanese real income (GNP), including net income from foreign investments, would grow at slightly over 5 percent, while US real income (GNP) would grow at slightly over 1 percent. The Japanese ownership share of the US capital stock would rise from zero to roughly 18 percent over a decade of such equilibria, but this increase in foreign ownership would not necessarily entail any absolute US sacrifice in the form of decline in living standard.[15]

This outcome, though dramatic, should not be viewed as necessary cause for alarm. No particular incentive exists in this reference equilibrium for Japan to begin repatriating earnings on its US-domiciled capital. Correspondingly, the United States is not in any inexorable danger of becoming a "problem debtor" merely because it is becoming more and more "indebted" to Japan (and at a rather rapid rate, too, with US borrowing to finance domestic capital formation at just less than 2 percent of its capital stock per year).

If, however, Japan does begin repatriating earnings (or selling the claims themselves) for any reason, there is still no necessary problem or cause for alarm. In fact, the equilibrium simply shifts from the reference equilibrium with financial liberalization towards that without. A simple way to see this in the diagram is to assume that $S'_jT'_j$ of repatriation is carried out in machines, Japan's importable. This repatriation causes a decline in the Japanese trade surplus (US trade deficit) and other adjustments in international balances. It may also cause the two geographical economies to begin growing apart again, losing their identical character on the production side, with Japan's investment and GDP growth exceeding that of the geographical United States.[16]

This account highlights several interesting consequences of international financial liberalization. First, such liberalization has the potential to shrink trade in capital goods that serves as a substitute for trade in financial instruments. Second, it can alter trade balances and measures of international competitiveness in ways that might appear unprecedented by historical norms (without financial liberalization), and in ways that trade liberalization alone does not.

Third, financial liberalization creates a distinction between geographical and "national" measures of economic performance, and can cause the former to converge even as the latter diverge.[17] Fourth, it can create trends in national balances of international indebtedness that are not necessarily causes for either jubilation or hand-wringing, however large they may turn out to be.

3 Fiscal counter-trends

In the 1980s, US fiscal policy has produced budget deficits of an unprecedented size at the same time as Japan and some European nations reduced their own deficits. Recent conventional wisdom has linked fiscal policy, and especially the rapid growth of the US budget deficit, to the accompanying and equally spectacular growth of the US merchandise trade deficit.

From our simple framework, we can identify the assumptions necessary for that linkage. We introduce a further difference across the two economies by allowing the US government to run a budget deficit financed by issues of new Treasury securities every period. The government uses the proceeds of security sales to make transfer payments.

If the United States were a completely closed economy, it is possible that nothing would change as a result of introducing this feature. The Treasury securities might be considered "inside" rather than "outside" assets, with some US residents (future taxpayers) in effect owing their value to other US residents (holders of Treasury securities). In this extreme case – Ricardian equivalence – there would be no change in the US production-possibility curve in figure 9.1 nor in US savings behavior. Nor, of course, would there be any (aggregate) burden of the public debt.[18]

In the open-economy setting, matters are more complex, whatever one believes about Ricardian equivalence. From Japan's point of view, US Treasury securities are clearly "outside" assets, purchases of which represent an increase in Japan's *aggregate* capability to consume future goods; we assume that Japanese investors regard these securities as perfect substitutes for ownership certificates to the US capital stock. Viewed by a representative Japanese decision-maker, the US government budget deficits, and the issue of new Treasury securities every period, shift the US production-possibility curve *vertically* by exactly the increased deficit/issue. From the Japanese point of view, the United States produces wonderful Treasury securities every year and equally wonderful capital goods! There is of course no real shift, but that is irrelevant for what concerns us here.

What is crucial is the potential change in intertemporal transformation opportunities facing heterogeneous agents. Like the ownership certificates, the Treasury securities provide a mechanism for transferring current purchasing power from high savers in Japan to low savers in the United States, in return for the promise of reverse transfers in the future. However, the amount of such transfers is no longer necessarily limited by the ability of the United States to produce additions to its capital stock.

Under these conditions, the perceived shift in Japan's ability to use external trade to transform present goods into claims on future goods can influence trade patterns and growth rates. To isolate the motive for such trade, we assume now that US and Japanese intertemporal preferences are identical after all, and depicted by the preference contours through point C_J. Then, because from a Japanese perspective US Treasury securities are outside assets, and because the perceived US production-possibility frontier has been shifted vertically, Japan will also perceive higher potential real interest rates at C_U'' than at C_J, as reflected in the steeper tangent price line. Japanese residents (unlike US residents) will be prepared to bid for assets at prices between those implied by the two tangents.

Putting this in another way, an expanded supply of claims on future goods (with supply of current goods unchanged) will tend to depress the price of those claims. The result will be increased Japanese exports of consumer goods to the United States, in return now for Treasury securities as well as certificates and/or capital goods that are perfect substitutes for the Treasury securities. The United States will incur a corresponding trade deficit (thus, the twin deficits of conventional wisdom – trade and budget) and debt-service obligations, offset by a capital account surplus.

However, central to this argument is at least *some* expanded excess supply of claims on future goods to international capital markets. To the extent that US residents anticipate future tax liabilities associated with the new Treasury issues, that supply will be diminished; US taxpayers will be induced to acquire (demand) a larger share of claims than previously in order to meet those future obligations. In the extreme, the open-economy equivalent of Ricardian equivalence obtains, with no change from the case considered in section 2.[19]

In this account, with the two countries identical except for fiscal policy, trade effects can arise only from the incomplete anticipation by US residents of their future tax liability,[20] i.e., from the failure of private savings to completely offset public dissavings. Thus, the real effect of a US budget deficit arises in an open economy for precisely the same reason that it would arise in a closed economy, namely redistribution between two groups of agents that differ in the degree to which they consider government securities to be net outside wealth.[21]

The most important consequence of this account of fiscal counter-trends is that divergent fiscal policies can reinforce the impulses caused by financial liberalization. Except in the extreme case of Ricardian equivalence, US fiscal expansion relative to the rest of the world can discourage US exports of capital goods and make the United States appear less competitive in global markets.

4 Third-country influences

So far we have ignored the existence of other regions. However, developments elsewhere are likely to have a significant impact on bilateral trade and capital flows between the United States and Japan. The reference cases above can be modified to analyze the consequences of changes in other countries. The simplest way to do so is to focus on Japan and the United States, examining the effect of global changes on the terms and volume of trade between them and the rest of the world. For simplicity, we examine such changes from an initial equilibrium in which the (equalized) world relative price of future consumption is given by the convenient reference line $C_J'C_U'$ in figure 9.1. In this reference equilibrium, there is no net trade in goods or assets between the rest of the world and either Japan or the United States.

By an argument similar to that of section 3, fiscal policy changes in a third region will alter the equilibrium only to the extent that the region's excess supply of claims on future consumption rises or falls, either through less-than-complete anticipation of resulting changes in future taxes or through induced redistribution between groups with different savings behavior.

Consider a reduction in the budget deficit of, say, West Germany. If German taxpayers fail to anticipate fully the resulting reduction in their future tax burden, private demand for claims on future consumption goods will fall by less than the supply of German government securities. The result will be a fall in Germany's excess supply of claims to world financial markets; at the old terms of trade, there will now be an excess demand for claims and an excess supply of current consumption goods.

Reestablishment of equilibrium will therefore require a movement toward larger capital outflow and trade surplus for Germany. The United States will experience a still-larger capital inflow and trade deficit, while Japan's capital outflow and trade surplus are reduced. In the new equilibrium, the world price line will be flatter (future goods have risen in value; the world interest rate is lower than previously).

The perception of increased risk of claims issued by less-developed countries (LDCs) is more difficult to treat within our framework, which has so far taken all claims on future consumption to be perfect substitutes, but even a very simple experiment yields some suggestive conclusions.

Assume now that LDC capital and claims begin to be viewed as risky in comparison to otherwise similar assets.[22] Again a world excess demand for claims will arise at the initial terms of trade. In this case, however, the excess demand is for (riskless) claims issued outside the LDCs, while (risky) LDC claims are in excess supply. From an initial situation with rates equalized, the less attractive investment climate induces asset holders to demand some premium on investments in that region. Reestablishment of equilibrium will require a change in the relative price of the two types of assets (which is unity as long as they are viewed as perfect substitutes). The new relative price measures the risk premium required to make the marginal investor indifferent between holding developing-country issues and other claims.

The risk premium required by LDC claims also influences ongoing trade in goods and claims. Developing-country capital goods, and claims on them, are now less attractive relative to current consumption goods and thus command a lower price, which discourages both LDC production of capital goods and issue of new claims. The reverse is true elsewhere. Beginning in a situation with no net capital flows between the LDCs and the integrated US–Japan capital market, reestablishment of equilibrium will entail some net flow of LDC investment toward the US–Japan market.[23] This flow will raise (expected) returns on newly-produced capital in LDCs, while lowering returns in the United States and Japan, until the differential is sufficient to offset the increased perceived riskiness of LDC assets.

While by assumption the initial situation offered no motive for trade between the regions, the developed countries now enjoy comparative advantage in producing (riskless) claims on future consumption. Once again, the effect is to make the United States appear less competitive, by (further) increasing its deficit on trade. But as in the case of restrictive fiscal policy in a third region, Japan's trade surplus is also reduced, so that the weight of bilateral US–Japan transactions in explaining trends in the overall balances of the two countries must fall.[24]

Such conclusions have an air of applicability to them; but the more interesting general consequence of this discussion is to show how bilateral payments balances can be shaped by events in third countries.

II Other motives for international capital transactions

The simple model of part I focuses attention primarily on productive capital and financial claims as alternative vehicles for optimization of consumption between present and future periods. The central message from the experiments is that "real" effects, specifically persistent trade deficits, can be rooted entirely in differences of individual or collective preferences. Trade deficits can, and do, emerge from national choices of present versus future consumption, rather than being issues of technology, productivity, quality, reliability, style, capital costs, labor-management relations, or any of the many other "problem" areas for US industry that have been singled out in recent years by those concerned with US international competitiveness.[25]

However, while our very simple model can be useful in explaining the size and direction of net international capital flows, it provides little guidance for analyzing other significant developments in international capital markets, specifically those in which the composition as well as the net volume of asset transactions is important. Examples are the greatly increased extent of international financial intermediation (as evidenced by the rapidly increasing size of gross relative to net flows) and of direct investments by European, Canadian, and Japanese firms in the United States. It is obviously beyond the scope of this paper to treat these subjects. Here we merely seek to identify some of the critical elements in such transactions that are missing from our simplified framework. These are risk, tax and regulatory issues, market imperfections, and control.

1 Risk

In part I we have focused on intertemporal substitution in a world of certainty, bringing in risk only in considering the potential impact of less-developed countries on US–Japan bilateral flows. Moreover, since we deal entirely in real rather than nominal claims, there is no way to incorporate discussion of exchange risk into our framework. In contrast, real-world financial markets provide means of reallocating consumption not just inter-temporally but between states of nature, with the preponderance of risk-driven transactions occurring among the developed countries and with exchange-rate movements accounting for a major part of the risk confronting investors.

A framework similar to that of part I could be used to analyze trade in contingent claims or in real assets subject to risks that are not perfectly correlated (see, for example, Helpman and Razin (1978)). Such trade offers expanded opportunities for diversification and is likely to produce two-way trade in claims, something that will not occur in the riskless world of our simple model.

If the return on an asset is decomposed into systematic (non-diversifiable) and nonsystematic (diversifiable) risk, the decomposition depends on the set of alternative assets available to the holder. By expanding the set of alternative assets, international securities trade in effect reduces the relative importance of systematic risk and thus allows the same assets to be rearranged into more desirable portfolios. Alternatively, if the asset price is decomposed into several "factors," the prices of the individual factors are likely to differ across separated national markets; like other differences in autarky prices, these provide the opportunity for mutually beneficial trade.

Although risk characteristics are important foremost in explaining composition of investment portfolios (and thus accounting for two-way trade in similar assets), risk may also interact with other real-world features such as capital-market imperfections. In some cases, investors may be unable to achieve optimal portfolio diversification directly, and the direct investments of multinational corporations, discussed below, may serve as a second-best vehicle for diversification.[26]

2 Tax and regulatory issues

Our simple framework incorporates no taxes on returns from real or financial assets. In real-world securities markets, tax treatment and statutory limitations on portfolio choices help to shape asset transactions both within and between countries. During the 1980s, several major changes in US tax law have altered the relative returns on particular classes of real and financial assets, leading to one-time readjustments of portfolios and changed proportions in ongoing allocations between alternative assets.

Specifically, any change in the tax status of a given class of assets will alter its relative valuation by domestic and foreign investors. For example, the Tax Reform Act of 1986 lowered overall tax rates while eliminating the generous tax treatment of many types of US assets. As a consequence, the value to US residents of these previously tax-advantaged assets fell. But for foreign investors, taxes paid to the US government are credited against tax liability at home. Tax-advantaged assets are therefore *less* attractive to foreign holders. The 1986 tax changes thus made sales of such assets by US holders to foreign investors mutually beneficial.[27]

Likewise, national or local regulation of financial intermediaries may play an important role in determining the extent and composition of international capital flows. For example, elimination of certain restrictions on the portfolios managed by Japanese insurance companies and pension funds was an essential precondition for the massive acquisitions of US long-term government bonds and other US fixed-income securities by these institutions during the early 1980s.

3 Market imperfections

The model of part I assumes markets for both goods and securities are atomistic and frictionless and commodities are homogeneous. That real-world markets are often oligopolistic and real-world commodities are often differentiated gave rise to older theories of the multinational firm (e.g., Hymer, 1960; Kindleberger, 1969) as well to the "new" theories of intra-industry trade and direct foreign investment (e.g., Helpman and Krugman, 1985). These theories emphasize strategic behavior, entry considerations, scale economies, and other features that play no role in our simple analysis.

Of real-world market imperfections, probably the most important are those affecting transactions in knowledge. Our framework assumes that each country has access to the same technology and thus ignores the role of knowledge in international capital transactions. The global expansion of multinational corporations is intimately linked to the production and international transmission of proprietary knowledge; the appropriability of returns from creation of such knowledge depends critically on the investment channels available to innovating firms (e.g., Magee, 1977).

According to the conventional wisdom, protection of the domestic market from imports may also create incentives for direct investment from abroad. Our simple model cannot be used to explore this issue, since with only one imported good, increased protection necessarily means less rather than more capital inflow. Moreover, the assumptions of the model rule out any potential advantage of a foreign firm over an indigenous one in serving the protected market.

4 Control

In our discussion of Japanese acquisition of an increasing share of the US capital stock in part I, no mention was made of concerns, whether economic or noneconomic, that in practice have accompanied the rapid increase in foreign holdings of US real and financial assets. The real-world concern is that inward investments allow foreign firms (and perhaps, governments) to gain control over critical elements of the US economy. The underlying assumption is that the decisions of foreign-based managers will differ systematically from those made by their indigenous counterparts under similar circumstances, to the detriment of national welfare.

The simple model of part I ignores the issue of managerial control over business operations. Thus, the output of Japanese-owned capital in the United States is, by assumption, no different from what would be obtained if the same capital were owned by US residents. However, direct foreign investment is precisely investment that conveys control over operations in one country to a firm based elsewhere. Because real-life direct foreign investors typically face higher operating costs than their domestic rivals, the benefits from the actual or potential exercise of this control must be sufficient to outweigh these higher costs. In the language of industrial organization, there must be an *internalization* advantage – an advantage to substituting internal modes of resource coordination within a single firm for an external market-based arrangement between independent firms. In other words, there must be an advantage of integrated global management.

As noted above, these advantages may be rooted in the firm's need to optimize with respect to market imperfections or risk. A global production and distribution network permits the firm to diversify risk and, more generally, increases its options when conditions are volatile (e.g., Kogut, 1983). The risk-handling motive may be relevant in explaining investments in the post-Bretton-Woods era of volatile exchange rates but also the classic direct foreign investments in extractive industries. Enhanced opportunities for tax avoidance are another widely cited benefit of global management.

III Baldwin (1966) in retrospect

Our discussion in this paper owes much to Baldwin (1966), especially in its interpretative graphics. Yet the exogenous changes discussed, the key assumptions made, and the flavor of our conclusions are all quite different.

Baldwin emphasized international differences in endowments and down-played differences in preferences, as has always been the fashion in Heckscher–Ohlin–Samuelson analysis. It is indeed a persuasive fashion when considering preferences across commodities at a point in time. It is less persuasive when considering intertemporal preferences, for both abstract and empirical reasons. In the abstract, well-accepted theories support all of the following accounts of why national preference maps between current and future consumption differ: different demographic make-ups of a population, different attitudes toward bequests for succeeding generations, different tastes for economic security because of differences in socio-political stability. Empirically, there remain wide differences in national saving patterns even in the face of narrowing international differences in rates of return on comparable savings instruments.

In this paper, unlike Baldwin (1966), few of our observations depend on international differences in factor endowments. Most depend on different preferences for current and future consumption, although for simplicity we have not embodied either the analytic reasons or empirical evidence for such. We think that our simple analytic framework goes some distance toward explaining recent trends, for example, divergent growth rates and rising trade shares of world output. In our framework, importers of capital and capital goods accelerate their growth because of such imports, and exporters decelerate. Such changes in growth rates are pro-trade-biased. The flavor of Baldwin's conclusions, by contrast, is that capital-poor importers of capital goods and capital-rich exporters converge ultimately to the same capital-labor ratios, with convergent growth rates and a dying away of trade.

Many of our observations, especially in part II, depend on institutional changes no one foresaw in the mid-1960s: the dramatic global integration of financial markets, the growing importance of multinational corporations from all countries, not just the United States, the international pressure for tax reform and deregulation since the late 1970s, the sharp division of less-developed countries into those that are newly industrializing and those that are not. These institutional changes have increased the role played by fiscal policies, diversification, options value, and corporate struggles for control in explaining international capital movements and payments imbalances. They have also caused most of the parts in the play to be assigned to relatively prosperous countries, not to the less-developed countries as Bob anticipated.

Yet these are all minor distinctions. On the central issue in his 1966 paper,

Bob was – as usual – right on target. It seems appropriate to quote him as the last word in a paper that began with him as the first:

> [The] traditional approach [to explaining trade patterns] is completely inadequate in these times, when economic growth is such an important goal, especially for the less-developed nations . . . The production of capital goods must be introduced into trade models, and the entire analysis integrated with domestic capital accumulation theory.

Economic growth of course remains an important goal and often an elusive one, although as much for the developed "rich" countries as for the less-developed. And it is a pleasing turn of fate that Gene Grossman, Bob's own son-in-law, is among those who have recently responded to Bob's challenge to trade theorists (Grossman and Helpman, 1988a, b).

Notes

The authors are indebted to Ronald Jones, Anne Krueger, and Robert Stern for extensive comments on an earlier version of the paper, and to the Ford Foundation for research support.

1 Anyone who thinks algebra is necessarily a more efficient shorthand than graphics needs to attend Bob's apocryphal introductory course, "Graphics for Economists," meant to be taught side by side in every graduate program with "Mathematics for Economists." Bob's treatment of the same material as the famed Oniki–Uzawa (1965) paper is seven pages long, while theirs requires 23 pages.

2 After the exchange with Ramaswami (Ramaswami, 1968; Baldwin, 1968), there seems little reference.

3 And, on request, the authors will speedily send reprints in a Baldwinesque envelope.

4 The diagram and some of the results discussed below are adapted from Arndt and Richardson (1987).

5 The intertemporal interpretation of the slope of the price line comes from seeing that a machine worth p of consumption goods pays a percentage rate of return $(r/p) \times 100$ in each period, which is the real interest rate by definition. If r is fixed, varies less than p, or varies inversely to p, then the interest rate varies inversely with the price of capital. This inverse covariation is assured along a given production-possibility curve by the conventional assumption (Findlay, 1984, pp. 206–7; Smith, 1984, p. 300) that capital goods are produced *labor*-intensively relative to consumption goods. The root of the convention in the theoretical literature is the need to assure existence of a stable equilibrium in a closed two-sector model (Shinkai, 1960; Uzawa, 1961), although it turns out to be unnecessary in an open-economy model (Fischer and Frenkel, 1972, pp. 212–13). However strange the convention first seems as an empirical proposition, it is not demonstrably wrong in light of Leamer's (1984, pp. 66–73) reaggregation of Hufbauer's (1970) estimates of primary

input–output coefficients, and it has the same persuasiveness as the argument that production of human capital (education, training) and technological capital (patents, blueprints, research laboratories) is labor-intensive. Having said all this, it is interesting that Baldwin (1966, p. 844) makes precisely the opposite assumption, that the production of capital goods is relatively capital-intensive.

6 As a simple illustration, only quantitative calculations would be altered if Japan's production-possibility curve were "telescoped in" to a position roughly halfway between the origin marked 0 and the US curve $Q_K Q_C$. This would certainly be more "realistic" as a reference case, given the different sizes of the two economies, but while the graphical analysis would become more congested, the qualitative conclusions would be unaffected.

7 Hayashi (1986) reviews a wide variety of proposed explanations of Japanese savings behavior. He concludes that a "dynastic" view seems to explain the evidence most parsimoniously. However, he offers no direct test of the hypothesis.

8 In this model, purchase of capital goods is the only form of saving.

9 For the reference case, we assume a set of infinitely lived households, which as a result of expanded opportunities for exchange are able to choose a welfare-improving intertemporal consumption pattern. Under less restrictive assumptions, current consumers do not necessarily take into account the effects of their own decisions on opportunities faced by future generations; a more detailed analysis is then required to determine welfare changes for the latter.

10 In general, trade based on differences in production possibilities increases differences in actual production patterns (relative to autarky or more restricted trade), while trade based on differences in tastes increases differences in actual consumption patterns. The reference case illustrates the latter.

11 With the opposite and less conventional configuration of factor intensities, Baldwin's (1966) model generates a secular decline in trade (in the extreme, cessation of trade), so that, somewhat paradoxically, trade is self-extinguishing.

12 For reference, we assume that newly produced machines do not differ from existing machines. Capital vintages would not affect the qualitative conclusions.

13 The multiplicity is due to our assumption that ownership certificates and physical machines are perfect substitutes in trade. Fischer and Frenkel (1972, p. 232) view this multiplicity as a "difficulty" because they want to explain a region's physical capital formation. Thus, they introduce imperfect substitutability via installation costs. Our goal here is to explain a region's response to policy changes, and we believe our answers are invariant to which of the infinitely many possible equilibria in the perfect-substitutes case is the starting point.

14 For reference, we assume that any other factors (or their productivity) grow exogenously at the same rate as the capital stock.

15 Three percent annual growth compounded over a decade leaves the capital stock at 134.4, given an initial value of 100. One percent annual growth in the US-owned part of that capital stock leaves the United States owning 110.4 at the end of the decade, or roughly 82 percent, with the Japanese owning the other 18 percent. As before, welfare effects depend on whether US residents can be

viewed as infinitely lived households or successive generations. With a growing population, US per capita income could be stagnant or declining if the national savings rate is low enough.

16   This might occur, for example, if increased repatriation and reduced net inflows were the result of new Japanese or US regulations toward foreign investments.

17   Baldwin (1966, p. 846) and others anticipated this observation, but probably few understood in the mid-1960s how quantitatively important the distinction would become, principally because of growing factor mobility. Lipsey and Kravis (1985, 1986) document and discuss a closely related observation for the US corporate sector.

18   However, this outcome requires strong assumptions. If, more realistically, the proceeds and the future tax liability are distributed unequally over different generations, the consequence might be a change in aggregate savings behavior and a corresponding change in the autarky equilibrium. In general, redistribution from younger to older generations tends to reduce the aggregate savings rate. See Kotlikoff (1988).

19   New terminology is needed here. In the international version of Ricardian equivalence, Treasury securities held by Japanese investors are outside liabilities of the United States.

20   Of course, most non-economists regard the notion that future taxpayers fully anticipate such tax liabilities as unrealistic. Casual empiricism reveals that many *current* taxpayers are blissfully unaware of their *current* marginal tax rate.

21   A second possible vehicle for translating a US budget deficit into a trade deficit with Japan is through induced effects on savings behavior. As noted in section 2, a lower savings rate is enough to move the United States into persistent trade deficit. Even if individual preferences are identical in the two countries, and even if all individuals correctly anticipate future tax liabilities, US fiscal policy could reduce the current aggregate savings rate if on net it redistributes income from younger to older generations.

22   Such risk might arise from possible expropriation of assets. We assume that the risk is inherent in the assets and, in particular, that holders both within and outside the LDCs perceive the same risk in holding such assets.

23   Also, because investors will choose to hold positive amounts of both risky and riskless assets, there can now be two-way trade in securities.

24   The share of the overall US trade deficit due to its deficit with Japan indeed fell from over 50 percent in 1981 to roughly 37 percent in the mid-1980s. The share of the overall Japanese trade surplus due its surplus with the United States fell from roughly 80 to 60 percent over the same period.

25   We hasten to add that any, or possibly all, of these may indeed be problem areas for US industries. Our point is that it is quite possible to have large and persistent trade deficits even without any of these microeconomic failings.

26   Agmon and Lessard (1977) concluded that shareholders were willing to pay a premium for stocks of internationally diversified companies, although further liberalization of international capital transactions in the subsequent years is likely to have eroded that premium. However, the rapid growth enjoyed since the mid-1970s by financial intermediaries specializing in the provision of inter-

nationally diversified portfolios suggests that many investors still face significant market imperfections.

27 Scholes and Wolfson (1988) claim that the 1986 tax changes, while increasing corporate taxes, actually made the United States a "tax haven" for foreign investment, because the before-tax return on US assets must rise to compensate for the elimination of tax credits and the reduction in the acceleration of depreciation.

References

Agmon, Tamir and Lessard, Donald 1977: "Investor Recognition of Corporate International Diversification," *Journal of Finance*, 32, 1049–56.

Arndt, Sven W., and Richardson, J. David 1987: "Real-Financial Linkages Among Open Economies: An Overview," in Arndt and Richardson (eds), *Real-Financial Linkages Among Open Economies*, Cambridge, MA: MIT Press.

Baldwin, Robert E. 1966: "The Role of Capital-Goods Trade in the Theory of International Trade," *American Economic Review*, 56, 841–8.

Baldwin, Robert E. 1968: "The Role of Capital-Goods Trade in the Theory of International Trade: Reply," *American Economic Review*, 58, 943–4.

Bhagwati, Jagdish N. (ed.), 1987: *International Trade: Selected Readings*, Cambridge, MA: MIT Press.

Findlay, Ronald 1984: "Growth and Development in Trade Models," in Jones and Kenen (1984).

Fischer, Stanley and Frenkel, Jacob A. 1972: "Investment, the Two-Sector Model, and Trade in Debt and Capital Goods," *Journal of International Economics*, 2, 211–33, reprinted in Bhagwati (1987).

Grossman, Gene M., and Helpman, Elhanan 1988a: "Product Development and International Trade," National Bureau of Economic Research Working Paper No. 2540 (May).

Grossman, Gene M., and Helpman, Elhanan 1988b: "Comparative Advantage and Long-Run Growth," manuscript (August).

Hayashi, Fumio 1986: "Why is Japan's Saving Rate so Apparently High?" *NBER Macroeconomics Annual 1986*, 147–210.

Helpman, Elhanan, and Krugman, Paul R. 1985: *Market Structure and Foreign Trade*, Cambridge, MA: MIT Press.

Helpman, Elhanan, and Razin, Assaf 1978: *A Theory of International Trade Under Uncertainty*, New York: Academic Press.

Hufbauer, Gary C. 1970: "The Impact of National Characteristics and Technology on the Commodity Composition of Trade in Manufactured Goods," in Raymond Vernon (ed.), *Technology Factor in International Trade*, New York: Columbia University Press.

Hymer, S. Y. 1960: *The International Operations of National Firms*, unpublished Ph.D. dissertation, Cambridge, MA: MIT Press.

Jones, Ronald W., and Kenen, Peter B. (eds) 1984: *Handbook of International Economics*, Volume I, Amsterdam: North Holland.

Jones, Ronald W., and Neary, J. Peter 1984: "The Positive Theory of International Trade," in Jones and Kenen (1984).

Kindleberger, C. P. 1969: *American Business Abroad*, New Haven: Yale University Press.

Kogut, Bruce 1983: "Foreign Direct Investment as a Sequential Process," in Charles P. Kindleberger and David B. Audretsch (eds), *The Multinational Corporation in the 1980s*, Cambridge, MA: MIT Press, pp. 38–56.

Kotlikoff, Laurence J. 1988: "The Deficit Is Not a Well-Defined Measure of Fiscal Policy," *Science*, 241, 791–5.

Leamer, Edward E. 1984: *Sources of International Comparative Advantage: Theory and Evidence*, Cambridge, MA: MIT Press.

Lipsey, Robert E., and Kravis, Irving B. 1985: "The Competitive Position of US Manufacturing Firms," *Banca Nazionale del Lavoro Quarterly Review*, 153, 127–54.

Lipsey, Robert E., and Kravis, Irving B. 1986: "The Competitiveness and Comparative Advantage of US Multinationals, 1957–1983," National Bureau of Economic Research Working Paper No. 2051 (October).

Magee, Stephen P. 1977: "Information and the Multinational Corporation: An Appropriability Theory of Direct Foreign Investment," in J. N. Bhagwati (ed.), *The New International Economic Order*, Cambridge, MA: MIT Press.

Oniki, H., and Uzawa, H. 1965: "Patterns of Trade and Investment in a Dynamic Model of International Trade," *Review of Economic Studies*, 32, 15–38.

Ramaswami V. K. 1968: "The Role of Capital-Goods Trade in the Theory of International Trade: Comment," *American Economic Review*, 58, 940–2.

Scholes, Myron S., and Wolfson, Mark A. 1988: "The Effects of Changes in Tax Laws on Corporate Reorganization Activity," Stanford University Graduate School of Business (May).

Shinkai, Yoichi 1960: "On Equilibrium Growth of Capital and Labor," *International Economic Review*, 1, 107–11.

Smith, Alasdair 1984: "Capital Theory and Trade Theory," in Jones and Kenen (1984).

Uzawa, Hirofumi 1961: "On a Two-Sector Model of Economic Growth," *Review of Economic Studies*, 29, 40–7.

Part III

Political Economy of Trade Policy

10

Asymmetries in Policy between Exportables and Import-competing Goods

ANNE O. KRUEGER

One of the most widely agreed-upon policy prescriptions among economists, both historically and currently, is the optimality of equating the domestic and international marginal rates of transformation. In most circumstances, this implies that existing structures of protection through tariff and nontariff barriers are demonstrably Pareto inferior to free trade.[1]

Until recently, however, there has been a strong tendency to assume that protective structures were therefore decided upon by persons who were ignorant of economic principles.[2] For the most part, there was little attempt to understand why the political process continued to make these decisions when it was readily demonstrable that alternative policies could yield a net benefit for the community. Income distributional considerations, such as those suggested by the Stolper–Samuelson theorem, and other factors were sometimes cited as causative in leading to protection, but these were usually fairly casual statements, with little or no empirical testing of the validity of the assertion.

More recently, however, there has been increasing discomfort with this assumption. A field of political economy of protection has developed. Economists are attempting to understand the political determinants of trade barriers, and indeed suggesting that tariff structures themselves may be at least in part endogenous, as political decisions may be made in responsive to economic phenomena and vice versa. Robert Baldwin has been a pioneer in this endeavor. He was among the first to call attention to the tension between economists' proofs that trade interventions were seldom optimal policy and the real world's apparent intransigence in continuing to use instruments and policies that are, even when viewed in the most favorable possible light, second or third, or nth best (see Baldwin, 1982, 1985).

To date, a number of models of the political economy of protection have been developed. A great deal of progress has been made in understanding some of the determinants of levels of protection. In this essay, I seek to make a contribution to that literature by extending the analysis in one particular, but important, direction. That is, as an empirical proposition, there is an asymmetry in the treatment of exportable and import-competing industries that does not, at first glance, appear to be accounted for in existing models of political determinants of protection. Yet, to date, political-economy explanations of protection have taken as given that protection would be accorded only to import-competing industries. I attempt to broaden the discussion by asking why import-competing industries should receive preference in the political process over exportable industries.[3]

To develop the argument, the next section briefly reviews some of the chief insights arising from the literature on the political economy of protection. Section 2 sets forth the argument that examining only protection to import-competing goods may be misleading. Then, in section 3, reasons why the policy-formulation process itself may initially be biased against exportables are examined. Section 4 considers imperfections in the political market that encourage decisions in favor of perpetuation, or even increases in, protection, once in place. It will be argued that "identity bias" profoundly disadvantages efforts to reduce protection. A final section provides conclusions and suggestions for further research.

1 The political economy of protection

Baldwin's recent volume (1985) provides an excellent statement of the modern approach to the political economy of protection. The underlying assumption is that individuals are rational in seeking their self-interest in the political market, as well as in the economic market. On that assumption, the circumstances under which the political process would generate a regime of free trade can be set forth. Analysis then shifts to consideration of what happens when these assumptions are removed – and this provides guidance as to the circumstances under which the political process would generate protection.

The starting point[4] is to assume that voters directly determine policy outcomes by majority vote; that voting is costless; that all voters have full and perfect knowledge of the economic consequences[5] to themselves of free trade or protection (which is assumed to be the only policy issue under consideration); that there is perfect competition (under constant returns to scale) with fixed supplies of labor and capital, both of which are perfectly mobile throughout the economy; and that all individuals have identical preferences for goods and services.

The questions, as posed by Baldwin and others, are: (1) whether voters in a small country, unable to influence their terms of trade, will decide on free trade or protection of import-competing industries;[6] and (2) how removal of each assumption affects the decision-making process when all voters know and act on their self-interest. Several insights follow immediately: (1) in a Heckscher–Ohlin framework, those relatively well endowed with the country's abundant factor (used intensively in the export industry) will favor free trade while those relatively well endowed with the country's scarce factor will presumably favor protection; and (2) the gainers from free trade could compensate the losers in such a way that even those who would lose directly through free trade (contrasted with protection) would vote in favor of it (with compensation).

As Baldwin (1985, pp. 7–8) notes,

> Under the voting framework assumed up to this point, these results mean that free trade will always be selected over a policy of tariffs. If the productive factors who gain under free trade represent a majority of voters, it is not necessary for them to compensate the losers under free trade in order to achieve the policy they favor. But if capitalists are the gainers under free trade and they are in the minority, they will have to tie a particular income redistribution scheme to the free trade vote that will overcompensate enough losers to secure a majority vote for the free trade policy.

Although the conditions set forth to generate a free trade political decision are something of a straw man, they serve as a convenient framework within which to analyze why the political process might generate a decision in favor of protection. Baldwin focused in particular on costs of voting, lack of information and the likelihood that information may be costly to acquire, and the possibility of a gap between the decisions of elected officials and the voters they represent.

The presence of any one of these factors leads to a situation in which smaller, more concentrated, groups of voters (or their representatives[7]) in the import-competing sector find it in their self-interest to spend resources on obtaining information, lobbying, and/or voting. By contrast, if benefits from free trade are diffused, a free rider problem can result as individuals count on others to bear the costs of lobbying, etc., while still standing to gain by the benefits. This can result in an "imperfect political market" and protection, even when it goes against the self-interest of the majority of voters.

Two broad classes of models of this type have been developed. One class models the behavior of pressure groups.[8] In these models, capitalists may stand to incur short-run capital losses (because of the reduced value of their investment in fixed capital) under free trade, or capital stands to gain with protection. The ability to organize and lobby for protection is assumed to depend on their geographic and economic concentration, as the free rider problem prevents organization of diffuse groups. Thus, these models suggest that the level of protection will be greater the more concentrated the industry. The other model, developed by Caves, is generally referred to as the "adding-machine" model. In this model, representatives attempt to please their voters in the legislative process, but they cannot possibly satisfy all voters on all issues; they are therefore assumed to decide their votes with regard to the issues that their voters feel most strongly about. With regard to the issue of protection relative to free trade, it is assumed that workers in import-competing industries will "care the most" and thus be heavily represented in votes on trade matters. Moreover, Caves notes that elected officials are likely to be more sympathetic to the claims of import-competing industries in which there are a large number of voters.[9]

All of the political-economy models of protection share the view that decisions in the political arena are made by individuals (or their representatives) whose preferences reflect the economic self-interest of the voters (insofar as voters know them and subject to the free rider bias) who count on the issue in question. They have attempted to incorporate economic rationality into political decision-making models, endogenizing political decisions.[10]

2 Asymmetry between exportables and import-competing industries

Despite this effort to come to grips with rationality, however, none of the models of protection has thus far addressed one of the most fundamental theorems of international trade and, indeed, of economics in general: protection of one group is discrimination against another. If the relative price of import-competing goods rises through protection, the relative price of exportables must, by definition, fall.[11]

Even as analysts have posed the question of the determinants of protection, they have assumed either explicitly or implicitly that if exporting interests are able to capture the majority vote (whether by pressure groups or through greater numbers) the result will be free trade. A natural question is why export interests, when in the majority, should not vote themselves positive rewards in the form of export subsidies or other benefits commensurate with those received by import-competing interests when they are in the majority. Why should free trade, as contrasted with export "protection" be the logical alternative to tariff protection? Indeed, why should not free trade happen to be the outcome only when exportable and import-competing interests are exactly balanced, in the relevant political sense?

Even causal observation suggests that there are important asymmetries in the political market that lead to differences in political decisions with regard to exportable and import-competing industries. Although it is true that countries do adopt measures to promote exports, the magnitude of protection afforded to exportable industries is in almost all cases vastly smaller than that accorded to import-competing industries, and can often be regarded as little more than a partial offset to the disincentives created by protective mechanisms.[12]

In addition to explaining whether there will be protection, and what the determinants of levels of protection among import-competing interests are, then, a complete political economy explanation of trade policy should also inquire as to the origins of the asymmetries between the treatment of exportables and import-competing commodities. An important question, neglected by those concentrating on barriers to imports, is that, if any, the characteristics of import-competing industries are that make them more likely to receive special treatment, or to receive quantitatively larger special treatment, through the political process, than exportable industries with comparable political power are likely to obtain.

As Baldwin initially posed the question, voters were to decide between free trade and import-competing industries. A more general approach might be to inquire as to the characteristics of industries that voters or their representatives would tend to favor: if posed in that way, the factors tending to favor special treatment for particular industries might equally well result in, e.g., export subsidies. Indeed, one would have thought that, if special interests are politically represented, export industries would on average be larger and more concentrated than import-competing industries[13] and hence, by the logic of the political economy of protection, have more voice in the political process. Yet, empirically, tariffs, quotas, and other trade barriers against imports are far more protective than are the special and differential treatments of exportable industries.

The challenge for this essay is to consider factors conducing to asymmetry in the treatment of (otherwise apparently similar) exportable and import-competing industries. The argument proceeds in two stages: a first stage must consider what, if any, reasons there are for believing that preferential treatment for import-competing industries is more likely to be instituted than preferential treatment for exports. The second stage then examines reasons why, once protection of import-competing industries is in place, there will be biases in the political process that tend to perpetuate or possible even intensify protection.

3 Why initially favor import-competing industries?

In the remainder of this paper, it will be argued that there are a number of factors inherent in the political process that tend to lead to choices in favor of those whose identities are known, contrasted with choices which would provide equal favor to the same number of unknown persons. That "identity bias" in the political system tends to favor continued protection of import-competing goods once that protection is in place. A prior question, however, is why there should be an initial bias in favor of protection of import-competing industries at all.

In this section, focus is on how and why protection to imports initially comes about. In section 4, the question of why there are biases in favor of its perpetuation is considered.

A number of factors probably conduce to initial favoring of import-competing industries. Number one, long-since recognized, is the revenue motive of governments. A second is that tariffs and quotas lack transparency contrasted with export subsidies. Third, to the degree that foreigners are harmed by the imposition of protection against imports (due, presumably, to a deterioration in the terms of trade), they are not represented in the political process. Fourth, there is the rent-seeking explanation for the breakdown of mercantilism. Finally, it may be argued that there has been an asymmetry of worldwide events, which have been more conducive to the imposition of protection to import-competing interests than to assistance to exporters.[14] I shall term this class of factors "historical accident."

3.1 The revenue motive

It has long been recognized that the revenue motive is both an explanation for governments' initial preferences for protecting imports over promoting exports and for the perpetuation of protection. Tariffs have historically been an important source of governmental revenue. In the United States, for example, 84 percent of federal government revenue originated from customs duties in 1800, and even in 1900, 41 percent of federal revenues was from import duties.[15] The revenue argument represents an obvious, and well-known, asymmetry: any significant export protection can occur only through mechanisms which have a substantial budgetary cost, as they would have to take the form of export subsidies.[16] Stated in another way, if the Ministry of Industry wants protection of 10 percent for import-competing steel producers and a subsidy of 10 percent for producers of exportable chemicals, the Ministry of Finance is likely to fight harder against the latter than the former. Likewise, other ministries anxious to obtain budgetary resources for their own goals are likely to be more opposed to the subsidy than to the tariff. Moreover, even if the subsidy becomes effective, it will probably be subject to scrutiny during annual budget discussions; a tariff, once on the books, is likely to be scrutinized much less frequently.

To be sure, if consumers' votes were as negatively affected by higher prices for import-competing goods as they were by direct taxes, the asymmetry would disappear. The diffusion of costs and concentration of benefits, as set forth by Olson (1965) and used in the political economy of protection, is certainly important as an underpinning for understanding the initial asymmetry of treatment between industries that produce exportables and those that produce import-competing goods.

One indication that the diffusion of costs is important in diminishing political opposition is the escalation of tariffs that typically occurs in tariff structures. When an imported commodity is an intermediate good in production, the import duty is perceived as an increase in costs by producers using the input, who then oppose tariffs on their imported and import-competing inputs. The fact that producers are affected by increases in their input costs makes them much more sensitive to tariffs on raw materials and intermediate goods than are consumers of imported and import-competing final products.[17] Thus, protection would be expected to be lower on inter-mediate goods relative to final commodities, due to the opposition of the consuming industries.[18]

The fact that tariffs raise revenue may or may not represent a positive benefit from the viewpoint of those deciding on tariffs, but it certainly makes the imposition of tariffs on imports relatively easier than a commensurate production subsidy on exports.[19]

3.2 Transparency

It has long been recognized that policies whose costs are immediately evident are politically more difficult to impose than those whose costs are obscured. Several factors serve to make tariffs and quotas – the main instruments of import protection – less transparent than export subsidies. First, a tariff schedule, once determined, is not normally subject to automatic legislative or administrative review. By contrast, any measure requiring expenditure from the budget is typically subject to annual appropriations. The absence of explicit review in itself reduces transparency. Second and probably more important, however, is the fact that import duties, being levied at the point of a commodity's entry, are not typically seen by consumers as a "tax" – the higher price of the import or import-competing commodity is simply a fact of life to the consumer.[20]

3.3 Lack of foreign representation

Although the imposition of a tariff on net has welfare costs, there are producer gains which offset a part of consumer losses. An export subsidy, by contrast, imposes domestic costs and to the extent that there is a terms of trade loss, the gains are obtained by foreigners. To that extent, if all interests are heard in the political decision-making process, that process is likely to reflect more opposition to export subsidies than to import duties.

3.4 Breakdown of mercantilism

Mercantilism was, historically, a system in which favors were conferred or domestic producers in the form of grants of monopoly rights in the domestic market, formation of cartels for the purposes of exporting, and provision of protection against imports. For a variety of reasons, the system of domestic controls broke down, and with the emergence of an increasing number of nation-states, the possibility of obtaining any monopoly power on the international market was greatly reduced. This left considerable protection against imports in place while the traditional technique for fostering exports, i.e. provision of monopoly privileges, became ineffective.[21]

3.5 **Historical accident**

If one inquires as to how protectionist measures were put in place, a significant number were a response to international events. In the Great Depression, a number of countries erected or increased trade barriers; while some also attempted export subsidies, the budgetary cost of the latter (the revenue motive, discussed above) led governments effectively to protect their domestic markets to a significantly greater degree than they could subsidize sales internationally.

Similarly, the First and Second World Wars served as heightened natural protectionist barriers, behind which new industries grew up in a large number of countries. At the end of these wars, these industries were threatened by the reestablishment of normal trading channels, and clamored for, and in many instances received, protection.[22]

Related to this line of argument, Ronald Jones[23] has argued that voters are naturally sympathetic to "underdogs," and that they identify losers with those competing with imports and winners with their export industries. A tariff would, with the usual results, increase the domestic price of import-competing commodities, and decrease the relative price of exportables, with a change in the relative price of nontradable goods lying in between. If the voters knew this, and identified exporters as being economically strongest and import-competing industries being economically weakest, with non-tradable producers in between, a tariff could have desirable income distribution implications.

It might also be argued that industries which experience difficulty are natural candidates for protection, and that an exportable industry encountering trouble might even be an import-competing industry, due presumably to lags in political response, by the time protection was granted. It is difficult, however, to think of cases of this sort.

In sum, the reasons why tariffs were initially imposed may vary from country to country, but the result has been that tariffs were used far more frequently than export subsidies, at least since mercantilist times. The next question is why, once protection is in place, there are asymmetric pressures to perpetuate it.

4 Factors perpetuating protection: identity bias

Some of the factors conducive to protection discussed above are also important in its perpetuation. For example, the fact that raising a tariff may lead to increased revenue[24] whereas lowering it might be expected to reduce revenue would lead to more resistance to lowering than to raising tariffs.[25]

In addition to the asymmetry inherent in likely government behavior because of the budget constraint and related issues, there is another source of systematic bias in the treatment of exportable and import-competing industries once protection is initially granted. It is a phenomenon widely recognized in other contexts but has so far not been explicitly dealt with in considering the political economy of protection. I shall call the phenomenon "identity bias" in decision-making.

Its essential characteristic is that the political process will tend to favor groups about whom more characteristics are known over "people in general," or groups about whom less is known. Schelling has aptly discussed the phenomenon in another context:

> There is a distinction between individual life and a statistical life. Let a six-year-old girl with brown hair need thousands of dollars for an operation that will prolong her life until Christmas, and the post office will be swamped with nickels and dimes to save her. But let it be reported that without a sales tax the hospital facilities of Massachusetts will deteriorate and cause a barely perceptible increase in preventable deaths – not many will drop a tear or reach for their checkbooks.
>
> Amelia Earhart lost in the Pacific, a score of Illinois coal miners in a collapsed shaft, an astronaut on the tip of a rocket, or the little boy with pneumonia awaiting serum sent by dogsled – even the heretofore anonymous victims of a Yugoslavian earthquake – are part of ourselves . . . not a priceless part but a private part that we value in a different way, not just quantitatively but qualitatively, from the way we measure the incidence of death among a mass of unknown human beings, whether that population includes ourselves or not. If we know the people, we are. Half the entertainment industry and most great literature is built on this principle.[26]

While Schelling's discussion was directed at societal estimates of the value of life, the same considerations apply to a variety of other phenomena: hostages, appeals for charitable giving in which write-ups of families constitute the core of the appeal, and so on.

They are also pertinent to societal assessments of the importance of economic gains and losses as well. The emotive appeal of an "unemployed person" is much less than that of the more specific description of a married head of household with two small children. If, in addition, it is known that the person lives in a particular city, and had been employed by the same firm for eight years, sympathy, and political interest rise further still.

Identity bias is highly relevant to the political economy of protection: if protection is to be increased, workers and employers whose industries will gain in the first instance are identified; the losers, who might have opened or expanded businesses for export but also who will not find it profitable to do so, are unidentified.

To formalize the concept, consider a law that might be proposed which will benefit citizens $1, \ldots, k$, which I shall call the k group, in the amount of x per member of k. Assume further that the provisions of the law would cost y per person to citizens $k + 1, \ldots, n$, whom I shall call the n group.

Finally, assume there is also a group r, consisting of all remaining citizens who will neither benefit nor be harmed by the passage of the proposal.[27]

Now assume that all persons, both voters and their representatives, know what the overall effects of the law will be and agree on the distributional consequences as set forth. There are four possible situations: (1) it is known with certainty which group each person belongs to; (2) it is known who the beneficiaries would be but the identities of those in the n and r groups are not known: (3) it is known which citizens fall into the n group, but the identities of those belonging to the k and r groups are not known; and (4) no one knows which group he will belong to.

Identity bias will be said to exist if the likelihood of passing the law is greatest in case (2) and least in case (3). As an empirical proposition, it seems to be reasonably important on a number of issues; as will be argued below, it is probably a potent force in affecting the relative pressures for and against legislation and regulations surrounding international trade.

Several examples of the pressures likely to arise for different types of policies may illustrate the phenomenon of identity bias, although in reality the political pressures surrounding most policy actions probably contain elements of both identity bias and other phenomena.

It is relatively easy to think of cases which come fairly close to case (1). Instances would include proposals for a revenue-constant change in the tax structure, or an increase in current social security benefits financed by an increase in current payroll taxes. Indeed, almost any welfare-expenditure proposal which was accompanied by revenue measures to finance it might be expected to be close to the first class of cases.[28]

The second case might correspond to a proposal to increase highway speed limits: truckers and others whose time cost of road transport was significant would benefit while those who would be maimed or killed under the higher speed limit and not under the lower (group n members) would not know who they were. If the identities of the victims were known ex ante,[29] it is arguable that not only would the victims themselves fight hard and/or more effectively against increased speed limits but that others in the r and n groups would be more strongly opposed to, or less in favor of the increased speed limit than they would be in the case of unknown identities.[30] To express it otherwise, it would be harder for truckers and other beneficiaries of a higher speed limit to support the proposal as effectively if it were known that Mrs Jones, mother of four, and eight-year-old Johnny, would be among the victims, and opposition to the measure would surely arise from persons in the r group who might be expected to remain neutral when identities of those in the k group were unknown.

Many other pieces of safety and environmental legislation undoubtedly have elements of identity bias affecting the support for and opposition to them. However, once there have been identified victims of particular phenomena, identity bias may work to favor passage of remedial policies, thus possibly representing case (3) where the victim but not the beneficiaries are known, rather than case (2). Clearly, whenever case (2) identity bias exists for proposals to increase something, case (3) will be present if the proposal is to lower it, and vice versa.

It is hardest to think of examples of the fourth case (which is somewhat reminiscent of the Rawlesian (1971) decision-making criterion for social justice): it might arise, at least within the eligible group, when it was proposed to conduct a military draft by lottery.[31]

In reality, cases may merge into each other: truckers will probably recognize their potential benefit (and perhaps even overestimate it, failing to recognize the effects of competition and new entry), insurance companies may represent in part the interests of potential victims, and consumer groups may fail to recognize that they may pay lower prices if transport costs are lower. How powerful each of these pressures is will be a factor in determining the political equilibrium speed limit, but identity bias will surely influence the outcome.

To argue that identity bias is a factor influencing protectionist structures is not to deny that other factors may play a role as well. Indeed, there may be interactions between them. Identity bias is not the same as the concentration arguments of Olson and others. They have argued, convincingly, that when either of costs or benefits is concentrated, while the other is not, the costs of organizing for effective lobbying, and especially the free rider problem, will swing the political balance more in favor of the concentrated group than it would be if those harmed and those benefiting from a prospective political decision were equally concentrated. While there is no doubt that costs of collective action and the free rider problem bias decisions in favor of concentrated groups, the existence of identity bias can work either way. In the speed limit example given above, the concentration of victims (arguably about 1,000 per year per mile of speed limit) probably exceeds the concentration of truckers and others benefiting from higher speed laws, but identity bias nonetheless exists.[32]

Identity bias is probably especially powerful when it comes to protection against imports and when there are proposals to reduce protection against imports. Capitalists and workers already employed in protected industries know their identities and believe they know how they would fare. Thus, the identities of the losers are reasonably well known. When it is thought that shoeworkers or garment workers would suffer, the identity bias phenomenon results in strengthened opposition and weakened support for reduction in protection. If protection were lowered, by contrast, some export industries would expand (possibly through the action of the exchange rate) and some capitalists and workers would achieve intramarginal gains as output and employment in export-oriented industries expanded, but those persons are less likely to know who they are. Insofar as new factories might open, it is in principle unknowable who would obtain employment (or receive higher wages) in those industries.

The existence of identity bias may help explain why "employment" arguments for protection are apparently so appealing to the body politic. Economists have for years argued that protection is inherently no more than a second-best instrument for employment policy: overall macroeconomic policy measures clearly dominate. Nonetheless, the effectiveness of the "loss of jobs" appeal for protection cannot be denied and has been noted for years.[33]

Thus, those in import-competing industries will not only lobby for maintaining protection, but they will be able to convince[34] others that they too will lose and thereby make it more difficult to advocate reduced protection. There is no counterpart for the worker who would potentially find employment in the expanded export sector. It is in this sense that identity bias results in an asymmetry in the political market for protection, once there is already a tariff structure in place.[35]

One can, of course, turn the argument around. Once protectionist measures are enacted, voters and their representatives can see the expanded (and/or more profitable) import-competing industries.[36] They cannot see the jobs that were not created, or the firms that did not enter (or expand) their exportable activity because of the legislation. It is in principle unknowable who would have been hired had exportable industries expanded, and equally so which new firms would have been successfully established.[37] With adequate econometric techniques, however, the aggregate orders of magnitude of these phenomena can be known. To the extent that identity bias exists in the political decision-making process, it surely works asymmetrically in support of continuing or raising protection.

It remains to ask how identity bias is related to other phenomena that have been suggested as important in literature on the political economy of protection. Three phenomena must be considered: lack of knowledge, diffusion of costs or benefits, and the conservative social welfare function.

Lack of knowledge can clearly be a contributing element to support protection, especially when coupled with the fact that the consumer costs of protection are normally widely spread. However, it is not a priori evident why a particular proposal to lower protection will affect fewer workers (or capitalists or landowners) than one to increase it: what is different is that the identity of those workers is known.[38]

The second phenomenon, diffusion of costs and benefits, is more difficult. One might ask whether the phenomenon of identity bias is anything more than societal willingness to bear risk. After all, if the likelihood of gaining a job in an export industry is one in a million, votes may dismiss the probability as being too small to be worth supporting. By contrast, the probability of difficulty for shoeworkers is sufficiently high so that the identified group finds it in its interest to lobby against reduced protection. In a sense, the question is whether the outcome would be unaffected if the identity of those persons who would gain employment or income from lowered protection were known. Devising empirical tests to ascertain which of the two phenomena drives political-decision making is beyond the scope of this paper, but the answer is clearly of practical importance.

An interesting question is the relationship between identity bias and the conservative social welfare function, enunciated by Corden (1974) Corden asserted that society as a group demonstrates a preference for protecting people's income streams, and that protection normally is a consequence of this preference. In part, his argument was directed to the origins of protection; in part, however, he addressed the question of why protection is perpetuated. Insofar as identity bias is a key factor in perpetuating protection, the existence of identity bias might explain the observed social choice and be the underpinning to the conservative social welfare function: resistance to lowering protection comes about precisely because the identity of those likely to lose is known. In Corden's formulation, the conservative social welfare function was set forth as itself an indicator of social preference. If identity bias were the underpinning from which a conservative social welfare function were observed, however, it is an interesting question as to whether one should regard the revealed preferences as an unbiased indicator of social welfare.

5 Conclusions and suggestions for further work

In this essay, I have suggested, first, that examining the structure of protection across protected industries, while important, leaves unanswered an important question from the viewpoints both of political economy and of economic policy formulation. That is, why is there apparent asymmetry in the treatment of industries based upon their trade classification? Why do not countries with voter characteristics such that exportable industries would be favored provide subsidies and incentives to exportable industries comparable to those that are provided to import-competing industries in countries where voter characteristics lead to protection? Indeed, why are industries with apparently similar characteristics likely to be more favorably treated if they produce import-competing goods than if they produce exportable commodities?

In addition to factors earlier adduced in the literature, such as ignorance of voters, I have suggested that the government budget constraint biases decisions in favor of protection, as does the interest of the state in maintaining a sizeable bureaucracy. Similarly, the phenomenon of "identity bias" may, when present, result in decisions more favorable to producers of import-competing goods than of exportables than would be taken were beneficiaries as well as victims equally known or unknown. In a sense, it occurs because of the general equilibrium consequences of protection: however, it is the result of those general equilibrium consequences that impact on particular individuals, as distinct from the diffuse general equilibrium consequences of higher consumer prices, and changes in factor rewards that may also result from changing protective structures.

Important questions remain. One is how great the asymmetry in treatment between exportables and import-competing goods is, both between goods within countries, and among countries. A second, equally important question, is how important identity bias is. If, as seems plausible, it is a major factor in political decisions, it could represent a sizable imperfection in the political market, in addition to whatever consequences follow from the free rider problem and the absence of appropriate information on the part of decision-makers. An important question would then be the welfare consequences of such a bias.

Notes

The author is greatly indebted to Ronald W. Jones, Richard Snape, Edward Tower, and participants in the Sloan International Economics Workshop at Duke for stimulating discussions and helpful comments on the first draft of this paper.

1   The only clear exception would be monopoly power in trade and, even then, the degree of monopoly power and the likelihood of retaliation would need to be taken into account. Even the infant-industry case, which is recognized as a basis for a departure from free trade, is a case for a production subsidy to the infant industry as first-best policy. Baldwin (1969), in one of his major contributions, adroitly questioned whether even a production subsidy would help in the presence of the sorts of infant-industry considerations usually adduced.
2   See Bhagwati (1988) for a recent statement of the view that ideas and ideology remain significant causal factors underlying both free trade and protectionist sentiment and measures.
3   There are other important questions that are not addressed here, although some of the considerations pertaining to protection may also be relevant for these issues. They include the determinants of the levels of protection to individual industries, and also the determinants of the forms of protection. If it is difficult to explain asymmetries in the treatment of import-competing and exportable industries, it is even more difficult to explain the political process which selects between tariffs and import quotas. There is also a broader question as to why tradables may receive protection relative to nontradables.
4   This discussion follows Baldwin (1985, pp. 6ff.)
5   It is assumed that there are no non-economic consequences of alternative trade policies.
6   Note that this formulation of the question *assumes* asymmetry of treatment of export and import-competing industries. If positive protection of import-competing industries is negative protection to exportables, why should the free trade point be considered the origin? When, in the Baldwin–Mayer setup, the majority of votes favor export industries, why should these not receive one form or another of protection?
7   It is widely recognized that representatives of the voters, and government officials carrying out the decisions of those representatives, may have interests of their own. Indeed, the Brock–Magee model portrays representatives as needing money to win votes, and losing votes by representing special interests.

An equilibrium exists for a particular representative when the votes gained through the monies received from an additional special-interest contribution equal the votes lost from supporting that special interest.

8 This literature has its origins in Olson's (1965) seminal work. Perhaps the best-known pressure-group model is that of Brock and Magee (1978). See also Bhagwati's (1988) treatment.

9 Caves believes that elected officials will further be more sympathetic to industries in which there are a large number of smaller firms than they will to highly concentrated industries. See Baldwin's empirical tests of these hypotheses (1985, ch. 4).

10 For a recent example, see Mayer (1984).

11 It has been argued that one might "protect" both import-competing and exportable industries relative to home goods through a policy of export subsidies and import duties. In practice, however, tariffs are more frequently observed and they are on average considerably higher than export subsidies and subsidy equivalents.

12 As a stylized fact, it seems almost self-evident that asymmetries exist. Efforts at formal empirical documentation have not, to this author's knowledge, been made. Almost all estimates of effective protection based on input–output tables show positive means and are higher for import-competing sectors than for export sectors, although the link to trade classification is seldom made explicitly. See, for example, Balassa (1965). For some empirical evidence of asymmetry in developing countries within a class of commodities, see Krueger, Schiff, and Valdes (1988) where it is shown that despite all rhetoric about the importance of foodgrains in budgets of low-income consumers, foodgrains seem to be protected in countries where they are import-competing and taxed in countries where they are exportables. See also Garcia Garcia (1988), who shows that, in Colombia, commodities that were protected when they were import-competing became taxed once they were exportables. In instances similar to this, trade is taxed in both cases, although the income distributional consequences are entirely different (and levels of export taxation are typically well below earlier levels of protection).

13 To make this assertion empirically testable would require the definition of an industry, which is a very difficult problem. In this statement, the only intention is to convey a much more naive, equal-ignorance, proposition: if all industries were of equal size in consumption, then those that produced for the export market as well would be larger than those where part of domestic demand was met by imports. That export industries might be more concentrated might follow from the need for distribution networks and start-up costs in overseas markets.

14 This is not to deny that "ignorance" and failure to understand the consequences of protection may not also be a factor leading both to protection and to its perpetuation. Certainly, this ignorance, or possibly even ideological motives (see Bhagwati, 1988) may have been very important, especially for developing countries, in erecting their structures of protection.

15 Data are from *Historical Statistics of the United States*. C3.134/2: H62/1789–1970/part 2, p. 1106.

16 There are mechanisms, such as provision of cheap credit under credit rationing and of subsidized inputs, which can constitute off-budget export subsidy

equivalents. The degree to which exports can be encouraged by these measures, however, is limited. Countries which have met with any degree of success in exporting through use of these measures, such as Israel, have found them to be inflationary as the magnitude of subsidization grew.

17   This is probably a partial political-economy explanation for the escalation in tariff structures observed in virtually all industrial countries. The fact that using industries oppose protection for their inputs represents a counter-balancing political pressure and thus results in a lower, "equilibrium" level of protection.

18   To be sure, it could be argued that consumers might object to tariffs on other imports that are directly consumed by them. The tariff-escalation story is only compatible with a logic-of-collective-action argument as to why industrial users, and not individual users, of imported commodities, oppose protection.

19   This proposition, simple though it is, probably is the explanation for the political preference for import duties rather than production subsidies to importers or exporters. It is well known that a production subsidy can provide the same benefits to producers of either import-competing or importable goods as a tariff (or its quota-equivalent) or export subsidy, but that instrument is rarely used. The revenue motive surely is a major part of the explanation.

20   See Krueger (1989) for a discussion of the importance of transparency.

21   See Ekelund and Tollison (1981) for an elaboration of this argument.

22   In this case, "identity bias," to be defined and discussed below, was clearly already at work in initiating protection: had potential exporters known who they were and recognized the extent to which their interests would be negatively affected by protection, protectionist measures would, at a minimum, have been significantly dampened.

23   In correspondence commenting on an earlier draft of this paper.

24   It is well known that there is a maximum revenue tariff, and that raising tariffs beyond that level will reduce government revenue. Some tariffs are clearly above maximum-revenue tariffs; whether their levels were determined because of other considerations or because policy-makers failed to recognize the revenue consequences is an open question. As long as decision-makers believe that raising tariffs will raise revenue, the bias in favor of proposals to increase protection, as contrasted with proposals to lower protection, will exist.

25   Indeed, even in proposals for policy reform programs in developing countries in the 1980s, a frequent dilemma, and source of conflict even among tech-nocrats, has been the positive resource allocation effects of tariff reductions contrasted with their perceived negative fiscal implications.

26   Schelling (1984, p. 115). This paper was revised just after very large resources were devoted to the rescue of two whales in Alaskan waters. See the *Economist*, October 29, 1988, p. 31.

27   The argument centers crucially on there being one group knowledgeable as to the benefits or costs to itself and another one ignorant. This logically implies the existence of a third group (because otherwise everyone who did not know he was a beneficiary/victim would know he fell into the opposite group), although the argument would not be significantly altered if group r members received small benefits relative to the k group or incurred small costs relative to the y group. See below for further discussion of the relationship between identity

bias, uncertainty, ignorance, and the diffusion of benefits/concentration of costs arguments.

28 To be sure, resource misallocation costs might differ from measure to measure. They might be subject to identity bias and other political pressures as well, but the point here is that the impact effect on individuals of the proposal would be reasonably well known.

29 Highway speed limits are an interesting case in part because, even ex post, there is no way of distinguishing clearly the group which would in any event have incurred accidents (or less severe accidents) under a lower speed limit from the victims who would have been accident-free or less seriously injured at a lower speed limit, yet it is statistically provable that there are a reasonable number of such persons. Deaths from highway accidents fell approximately 10,000 persons per year (and even more proportionately per passenger mile) after the speed limit was lowered in 1973, and the absolute number of deaths has not yet reattained the 1973 level. See *Statistical Abstract of the United States*.

30 Insurance companies, of course, would (and did) lobby against such legislation, illustrating the proposition that there is no such thing as a pure case.

31 When a group of individuals decide that something must be done, and that who will do it is to be subsequently determined by drawing straws is another example, although usually not one found in law.

32 As Robert Bates pointed out to me in conversation, the fact that the losers in exportable industries from increased protection have unknown identities is a built-in barrier to their effective organization for political purposes. One of the mechanisms that may give rise to identity bias in decision-making is that one group can identify its constituents with lower cost and greater ease than can another.

33 See Grossman (1988) for a recent effort to evaluate the employment argument for nine American industries.

34 This is not to say that all arguments made by those advocating continuation of protection are correct. Ignorance may be a factor as well. Nonetheless, those urging lower tariffs are frequently asked "what would the new industries be?" – an inherently unanswerable question and an illustration of the existence of identity bias.

35 An interesting question is why some costly phenomena, such as the selective service draft, are done by lottery. Any other selection principle (such as, for example, alphabetical order) would presumably do equally well. Yet it is clearly unthinkable. The identity bias inherent in the latter procedure seems a reasonable and plausible explanation for this preference.

36 For expositional purposes, I ignore the possibility that protection may not even benefit the intended workers or firms, a distinct possibility in reality.

37 In the same sense, one could statistically estimate the causative factors resulting in factory closing, and perhaps conclude that a decline in the real exchange rate was x percent of the problem while incompetent management was 100 minus x percent of the problem. However, there is no way of ascertaining, even in principle, which x percent of workers lost their jobs because of the exchange rate and which 100 minus x percent of the workers became unemployed because of poor management. Identity is simply not knowable.

38 It has for years been argued that ignorance was based in part on the "fallacy of

misplaced concreteness'': when people see a Volkswagen on the street, they identify that automobile with the "loss of jobs" to American automobile workers, without recognizing the "gain in jobs" in export industries, and in auto service and repair industries. Failure to recognize these aspects of the situation may intensify identity bias.

References

Balassa, Bela 1965: "Tariff Protection in Industrial Countries: An Evaluation," *Journal of Political Economy*, 73, 573–94.

Baldwin, Robert E. 1969: "The Case against Infant Industry Tariff Protection," *Journal of Political Economy*, 77(3), 295–305.

Baldwin, Robert E. 1982: "The Political Economy of Protection," in J. N. Bhagwati and T. N. Srinivasan (eds), *Import Competition and Response*, Chicago: University of Chicago Press, 263–86.

Baldwin, Robert E. 1985: *The Political Economy of Postwar US Import Policy*, Cambridge, MA: MIT Press.

Bhagwati, Jagdish N. 1988: *Protectionism*, Cambridge, MA: MIT Press.

Brock, William A. and Magee, Stephen P. 1978: "The Economics of Special Interest Politics: The Case of the Tariff," *American Economic Review Proceedings*, 68, 246–50.

Caves, Richard E. 1976: "Economic Models of Political Choice: Canada's Tariff Structure," *Canadian Journal of Economics*, 9, 278–300.

Corden, W. M. 1974: *Trade Policy and Economic Welfare*, Oxford: Clarendon Press.

Ekelund, Robert B., Jr and Tollison, Robert D. 1981: *Mercantilism as a Rent-Seeking Society*, College Station: Texas A & M University Press.

Garcia Garcia, Jorge 1988: *The Political Economy of Agricultural Price Policy: Colombia*, Final Report, World Bank.

Grossman, Gene 1988: "The Employment and Wage Effects of Import Competition in the United States," *Journal of International Economic Integration*, 2(1), 1–23.

Krueger, Anne O. 1989: "The Political Economy of Controls: The Case of American Sugar," in D. Lal and M. Scott (eds), *Public Policy and Economic Development*, Oxford: Oxford University Press.

Krueger, Anne O., Schiff, Maurice and Valdes, Alberto 1988: "Agricultural Incentives in Developing Countries: Measuring the Effect of Sectoral and Economy-Wide Policies," *World Bank Economic Review*, 2 (3), 255–71.

Mayer, Wolfgang 1984: "Endogenous Tariff Formation," *American Economic Review*, 74(5), 970–85.

Olson, Mancur 1965: *The Logic of Collective Action: Public Goods and the Theory of Groups*, Cambridge, MA: Harvard University Press.

Rawls, John 1971: *A Theory of Justice*, Cambridge, MA: Harvard University Press.

Schelling, Thomas C. 1984: *Choice and Consequence*, Cambridge, MA: Harvard University Press.

11

Trade Policy, Development, and the New Political Economy

GERALD M. MEIER

This paper considers some political economy aspects of trade policy in the less developed countries – more than 30 years on. A more literary little might be "Ideas, Ideology, and Interests." Writing in the 1950s Meier and Baldwin (1957), as still recent graduate students, were concerned with ideas. In recent years Baldwin, after much practice in actual trade negotiations and experience with the role of ideology and interest groups in the corridors of power, has written about the political economy of trade policy. But his focus has been mainly on the more developed countries. It may therefore be of interest to relate Baldwin's early interest in development to trade policy, especially as now viewed from the perspective of the new political economy.

Section 1 recalls Meier and Baldwin's reactions to the ideas of the 1950s on trade policy and development. Section 2 considers how economists' thought on the subject has changed in response to the policy lessons from development experience over the past three decades. The third section turns to the new political economy and examines both its usefulness and limitations in illuminating the role of ideology and interests in the practice of trade policy by the LDCs. The final section draws on both the old and new political economy to explain the adoption of import substitution policies and the turning from import substitution to export promotion.

1 Early thought

Considering the relation between commercial policy and development, Meier and Baldwin (1957, ch. 19) examined the various arguments for trade interventions in order to accelerate a country's development. A critical assessment was made of the following arguments: the alleged "inferiority of agriculture" thesis, infant industry, infant economy, diversification, terms of trade, attracting direct foreign investment, increasing the amount of compulsory saving, and promoting balance of payments equilibrium. Although the validity of some of these arguments was recognized under certain narrowly defined conditions,[1] the conclusion was that:

The costs of departure from a liberal trade policy must always be recognized. There are strong advantages to free trade and to an expansion in trade for poor countries as well as for the more developed countries. Each departure from free trade must therefore be carefully examined, and the merits of the exception must be established. Unless the exceptions are kept to a minimum, the poor country may only be perpetuating its poverty by denying itself the gains that are possible from international trade. A poor country cannot afford the luxury of forgoing international trade: it must take advantage of world markets as an indispensable means of accelerating its own development. (p. 409)

In the 1950s, much attention was also given to the Myrdal–Singer–Prebisch contentions that the export sector in an LDC did not contribute to the advance of the rest of the economy and that international trade operated as a mechanism of international inequality.[2] In contrast, Meier and Baldwin concluded that all these arguments suffer from misplaced emphasis. Instead of questioning the worth of international trade, one should recognize that the lack of carry-over of export production to the rest of the economy is basically an internal problem involving the obstacles of market imperfections and vicious circles.

Instead of protection, it is better to focus on removing the market imperfections and allowing foreign trade to help break the vicious circles. Instead of attempting to solve the problem of a dual economy by restricting trade, it would be more appropriate to pursue domestic policies designed to create alternative forms of social and economic organization,[3] increase the knowledge of market conditions, expand credit facilities, widen the capital market, create greater opportunities for technical substitutability of factors, and reduce monopolistic practices. If the internal limitations to development were removed or reduced, then adjustments could more readily be made to changing conditions in international trade, advances in the export sector could have more repercussions throughout the economy, and the export sector could even be the leading propulsive sector in the economy. To lose the potential for development that can come from expanding export markets would be to run the risks of distorting development and losing the gains from trade. (p. 403)

From the standpoint of the remainder of this paper, however, there were two major deficiencies in Meier and Baldwin's analysis. The contribution of trade to development was analyzed essentially in terms only of the static neoclassical gains from trade: the dynamic gains from trade were given insufficient attention. Although the neoclassical gains from trade indicate that a higher level of per capita income can be attained, additional analysis is required to indicate how trade can contribute to a permanently faster rate of growth in income. Section 2 indicates how the case for development through trade can actually be expressed in stronger terms than its neoclassical version.

Sections 3 and 4 attempt to overcome the second weakness – viz. the neglect of the State and endogenous policymakers. Along with many others, Findlay and Wellisz (1986, pp. 221–2) note that

> economists have traditionally approached the subject of trade policy from a Benthamite perspective, i.e., they have tended to look at the issues from the standpoint of what is in the "best interest" of the community at large rather than in terms of the competing interests of the factions involved. While modern economists would be embarrassed to say that they are concerned with "the greatest good of the greatest number," most of them would probably subscribe to the view that trade policy ought to be considered in terms of how to maximize a "social welfare function," of some Bergson–Samuelson "individualistic" type, which is to say Bentham purged of overtones of interpersonally comparable cardinal utility.

The analysis in Meier and Baldwin is subject to that criticism. Later, however, Baldwin (1984) contributed significantly to the emerging theory of "endogenous trade policy," itself a branch of the new political economy. As indicated in the last two sections of this paper, more must now be done to extend the insights of the new political economy to the practice of policy-making in less developed countries.

2 Policy lessons

Since Meier and Baldwin wrote in 1957, three decades of experience with trade policy in developing countries have yielded a number of policy lessons. Mainstream development economists now clearly recognize the superiority of a trade strategy of export promotion (EP) over that of import substitution industrialization (ISI).

The early postwar period of development economics, however, was dominated by export pessimism and widespread support for ISI. The potential for export substitution – the promotion of non-traditional exports – was not recognized. A major turning point came with the arguments and evidence presented by Little, Scitovsky, and Scott (1970) who concluded that export demand and domestic supply are both elastic.[4] Since then the adverse effects of ISI have been documented in detail for numerous countries (Bhagwati, 1978; Krueger, 1978; Balassa, 1982; Lal and Rajapatirana, 1987).

From these studies it is evident that in most countries a strategy of ISI was not pursued according to systematic economic criteria but instead was adopted in a chaotic, inefficient manner and for too long a time. At the micro level, too many plants produced too small an output; quality was inferior; capital was underutilized; and the industrial structure became increasingly monopolistic or oligopolistic. Few if any firms were able to realize the object of Krugman's "protection as export promotion": the scale advantage of greater production that might be provided by protection did not succeed in moving oligopolistic firms down the learning curve to lower marginal costs, and hence to the eventual realization of higher profits by establishing a competitive position in export markets (Krugman, 1984).

Although the sheltered firm's profits in local currency could be high, the domestic resource cost was excessive, and the cost increased per unit of foreign exchange saved. Given high effective rates of protection, the domestic value added in some cases was actually negative at world prices. Moreover, economic resources were diverted to rent-seeking activities (Krueger, 1974) and directly unproductive profit-seeking activities (Bhagwati, Brecher, and Srinivasan, 1984).

In general equilibrium terms, the bias in resource allocation to the domestic production of importables caused agriculture to suffer as the rural-urban terms of trade deteriorated for agriculture. Moreover, exports also suffered as the ratio of the effective exchange rate for the country's exports to the effective exchange rate for imports became less than unity (by a Bhagwati–Krueger type of calculation) (Bhagwati, 1978, pp. 207–9; Krueger, 1978; Bhagwati, 1988, pp. 32–3).

Not only did the protecting countries fail to develop their exports of manufactures, but their exports of primary products also lagged. The handicap on exports, together with the import intensity of the ISI strategy itself, tightened the foreign exchange constraint. There was an increasingly stringent exchange control regime and a growing dependence on foreign capital.

Further, policy-induced price distortions – negative real rates of interest, excessively high wages for unskilled labor, and undervalued foreign exchange – were pervasive. As the import-substitution process continued from the easy first stage of replacing non-durable consumer goods, it entailed production that was increasingly high cost and less economic; the incremental capital-output ratio increased; the rate of growth in aggregate output slowed down; and employment lagged as further import substitution became more difficult. In short, the ISI syndrome of policies imposed dynamic losses on the entire economy that were far greater than simply the loss of neoclassical static allocative efficiency.

In contrast to the dismal performance of those countries that overdid the ISI strategy, the developing countries that adopted an export-promoting strategy realized higher rates of increase in per capita income. They also demonstrated superior performance in terms of increases in saving ratios, investment ratios, total factor productivity, employment, real wages, a declining incremental capital-output ratio, a more equitable distribution of income, and better adjustment to external shocks.[5]

Why has export promotion had such a strong favorable impact on development?[6] As for the effect on the balance of payments one might think that there is little difference between earning a unit of foreign exchange through exports or saving a unit of foreign exchange through import substitution. But the domestic resource cost of earning foreign exchange has been shown to be less than the domestic resource cost of saving foreign exchange at the margin. Moreover, export-promoting countries have become more creditworthy and their foreign exchange constraint has been relaxed.

Especially significant is the fact that an export-oriented industrialization strategy has resulted in not simply a once for all improvement in resource allocation according to the country's comparative advantage in international trade, but more importantly in the realization of dynamic benefits. While a reallocation of resources in conformity with comparative advantage can raise the level of income, the dynamic gains have been most important in increasing the rate of growth in income.

There has been increased capacity utilization of plant, realization of economies of scale, the creation of employment through export of labor-intensive products, a multiplier effect that gives rise to increased demand for intermediate inputs and increased demand by consumers, and an increase in total factor productivity. Export expansion has been shown to be positively, and import substitution negatively, correlated with changes in total factor productivity (Nishimizu and Robinson, 1984, table 5). Econometric analysis also indicates that marginal factor productivities in export-oriented industries are significantly higher than in the non-export-oriented industries (Feder, 1982). The difference seems to derive, in part, from intersectoral beneficial externalities generated by the export sector.

Most important has been a realization of dynamic efficiency in the sense of a fall in the incremental capital-output ratio, the realization of "X efficiency," the extension of informational efficiency, enjoyment of external economies, and realization of Verdoon effects. Considering the latter, there is evidence that the faster export output grows, the faster is the growth in productivity. This is because of economies of scale, higher investment embodying capital of a more productive vintage, and a faster pace of innovation in products and processes (Amsden, 1985).

More generally, dynamic efficiency may be interpreted as a reduction in what Myint terms "organizational dualism" (1987). Myint observes that even if one could remove all the policy-induced distortions in an LDC, a substratum of "natural" dualism would still exist in factor markets, goods markets, and in the administration and fiscal system because of institutional features and the costs of transactions, transportation, information, and administration. This keeps the country on a lower curve within its production possibility – namely, its production-feasibility curve. Moreover, the gap between the production-possibility curve and the production-feasibility curve is not uniform, but is skewed against an increase in output of the traditional sector.

The incompletely developed organizational framework that confines a country within its production-possibility frontier can be improved or repressed by appropriate or inappropriate trade policies. By overcoming indivisibilities and filling in the gaps in the organizational framework of the traditional sector, the expansion of exports may be able to shift the production-feasibility curve upward. In moving from a position on the production-feasibility curve to the production-possibility curve, a developing country therefore gains much more than simply a once-over change to comparative advantage. Organizational dualism is reduced in the sense of a reduction in the costs of transactions, transportation, information, and administration.

The improved effectiveness of the domestic economic organization allows the developing country to take advantage of available external economic opportunities in the form of international trade, foreign investment, technological adaptation, and adoption of ideas from abroad. There is institutional adaptation to realize the potential comparative advantage in trade. The mutual interaction between economic policies and economic institutions results in improvement of the organization of production, more effective incentives, and a strengthening of markets. Dynamic efficiency is achieved as the diseconomies of a small economy are overcome, the transformation capacity of the economy widens, and the learning rate of the economy accelerates. The superior development performance of countries that follow export-oriented industrialization can be attributed to these indirect dynamic benefits from trade that extend far beyond simply the direct static gains from a removal of distortions (Myint, 1987).

The essential conclusion is that whereas proponents of the old export pessimism could criticize neoclassical trade theory and assert that the dynamic gains from ISI would outweigh the possible static costs of protection, it is now realized that the dynamic gains are actually far superior for export promotion. The case for development through trade can now be expressed in stronger terms than its neoclassical version.

Among the list of policy lessons for developing countries prominence is given to export promotion.[7] Harberger (1984, pp. 430-1) urges countries to "take advantage of international trade," warns that "some types and patterns of trade restrictions are far worse than others," and advises that "if import restrictions become excessive, and reducing them directly is politically impossible, mount an indirect attack on the problem by increasing incentives to export." Krueger (1985, pp. 107-8) lists first among eight prerequisites for a successful outward-oriented strategy the following:

(1) The government's policy cannot be half-oriented toward import substitution and half-oriented toward export promotion. Either the economy is outward-oriented, and the rewards and incentives are for performance in the international market, or the economy is inward-oriented, and firms are sheltered and find the domestic market rewarding. The bias on average must not be toward the internal market. (2) There must be a clearcut commitment on the part of the government that it is undertaking an export-oriented strategy, will continue to do so, and will make exporting profitable.

The normative theory of trade policy and empirical evidence support these policy prescriptions. And yet – while economists advocate export promotion – their advice is commonly ignored by government policy-makers. It is therefore now important to ask: Why are the economists' policy prescriptions not adopted? Why do governments do what they do?

For an attempted explanation, we outline in the next section some of the insights of the "new political economy." In section 4, we shall then relate considerations of political economy directly to trade policy.

3 The new political economy

The term "new political economy" refers to the recent use of neoclassical economic methodology to explain the determinants of policymaking.[8] Such a positive theory of political behavior does not assume that government is an exogenous force but is instead endogenous; political rationality is postulated; and the policies that government undertakes can be explained by neoclassical concepts of marginalism, optimization, equilibrium. The analysis attempts to disaggregate and operationalize the "State," utilizing theories of public choice, collective choice, transaction costs and property rights, rent-seeking and directly unproductive activities.

In this analysis the government cannot be viewed as a Platonic Guardian nor a benevolent dictator achieving Pareto efficiency or maximizing a social welfare function. No longer can the development economist refer to a Pigou–Meade or Bergson–Samuelson type of planner.

Denying that governments are the agencies of public interest, the new political economy has gone on to designate a typology of government that focuses on the state as a Leviathan or predatory state, or as factional, or as bureaucratic.[9]

The Leviathan model interprets government as seeking profits and rents from the activities in which it engages. Such an objective explains the imposition of quantitative restrictions, tariffs, bulk buying, controls over wholesale and retail trade. Another objective of Leviathan is likely to be net revenue maximization. In this predatory view of the nature of government, the state preys on its citizens, with an insatiable appetite for revenue that it consumes for its own sake (Findlay and Wilson, 1987 p. 290).

Findlay and Wilson view the state as a "natural monopoly," and the "surplus" that the state maximizes is a sort of monopoly "rent" that the sovereign can enjoy. But they then postulate that the surplus originally enjoyed purely by the sovereign attracts a horde of office seekers anxious to get their hands on some of it. A monarchical-type Leviathan may thus be transformed into a bureaucratic Leviathan. A budget-maximizing hypothesis is then attributed to the behavior of the bureaucratic Leviathan.

At the other extreme from a Leviathan acting in an autonomous fashion is the interpretation of the State as a passive reflection of interest groups. Viewed in principal–agent terms, citizens are the principals and politicians the agents who are to conform to the objectives of the principals. The principals are especially interested in transfers – in policy issues of who gets what. Where elections matter, the politicians undertake transfer so as to maximize the possibility of re-election. Where the politicians worry about a take-over, they may try to avoid contestability and deter entrants by courting their support through favorable measures of distribution.

We should also analyze the activities of the public bureaucracy in order to illuminate the behavior of governments. The new economics of organization can help do this by allowing us to incorporate a contractual perspective on organizational relationships, a focus on hierarchical control, and formal analysis via principal–agent models.[10] To minimize problems of adverse selection and moral hazard it is rational for a government to internalize contracting relationships by extending its own bureaucracy instead of engaging in marketlike transactions with private contractors.

The administration of government regulations acquires particular importance when markets do not clear and there are disequilibrium prices. For then bureaucratic allocation can grant favors, premia, and rents to particular individuals or groups. Through these administratively conferred benefits or through the threat of sanctions, bureaucratic controls can be used to organize political support and maintain the regime in power.

The foregoing interpretations of the role of the State have the merit of departing from the economist's usual notion of a benevolent well-informed State acting in the public interest – a notion for which Meier and Baldwin can be criticized. The actual behavior of a government is far from the economist's technocratic view of a government maximizing a social welfare function subject to resource and technological constraints. The political economy perspective suggests that a more realistic interpretation of why governments do what they do can be based on the concepts of a political market, government preferences, political resources, political costs, political constraints, political risk aversion, political loss aversion, and the demand for and supply of policy outputs. These considerations were ignored by Meier and Baldwin, and they still remain to be incorporated in a development text.

Thus, although the new political economy has opened one or two windows in the black box of the State, much more research must be undertaken to extend its relevance for developing countries. The neoclassical dimensions of the new political economy are too narrow once we go outside the liberal democratic state and beyond game theoretic or rational choice models. Its major contributions so far have been for the more developed countries in which political participation is high, voters play a major role, legislative bodies are also major actors, and elections have importance.[11]

Much of the new political economy is based on a pluralist model in which public policy is the result of the pressures upon decision makers from large numbers of competing groups in society. The State provides a more or less neutral institutional and procedural framework in which conflicting groups form coalitions, and policy change occurs because different coalitions of interests manage to gain power and impose their preferred solution on society.

This model, however, has limited transferability to most of the developing countries where

> interest aggregating structures tend to be weak. Political parties, for example, may be more important as mechanisms by which elites control mass followings than as means by which interests are articulated from below to government leadership. This is particularly true in regimes in which single or dominant parties direct the political state. Elsewhere, parties may be vehicles for the personal ambitions of individual politicians who are divorced from any real commitment to achieving goals beyond the acquisition of government jobs and their distribution to loyal followers. In other countries, technocratic military regimes have abolished parties.
>
> Interest groups may be similarly ineffective as structures for presenting collective demands to political leadership. Interest associations frequently are captive organizations of ruling parties, exist only at the sufferance of the government, or, like parties, are formed for the single purpose of protecting the political interests of their leadership . . . [F]requently there are few organizations in existence that are capable of representing the interests of broad categories of citizens and formulating policies responsive to their particular needs. Those few that are effective in this role tend to be the creatures of wealthy and powerful groups such as bankers, industrialists, and landowners. (Grindle, 1980, p. 16)

Moreover, the pluralist model tells us little about the actual process of decision-making and does not recognize any independence for political leaders or policy-makers to shape alternatives.

Another difficulty with the formal models of the new political economy lies in the formulation of an appropriate utility function. To say that the State maximizes its own utility is vacuous without further specification, but the possible variety of utility functions is extensive, and many cannot be predicted but only identified ex post. Nor in view of external pressures from overseas donors and international agencies can it be said that the government always acts according to its own interests and preferences.

Although different maximands may be considered, the new political economy always views government as being a rational maximizer. In contrast, however, conditions of bounded rationality may prevail, (Bendor, 1988, p. 381–3), social-psychological elements in decision-making should be considered, and the government may be "satisficing" instead of optimizing – in accord with Hirschman's "coping state" (Hirschman, 1963, p. 18).

As opposed to the rationality hypothesis, it is often illuminating to adopt a behavioral perspective and incorporate concepts and hypotheses from the older political economy. We might then better explain policy choices by understanding the role and consequences of ideology, nationalism, classes, elites, power, status, patron–client relations, political culture, the structure of the state itself – its rules and institutions. Beyond neoclassical political economy, we should recognize the cultural, social and psychological determinants of political change.

Moreover, the models should be extended beyond their focus only on decision-making with respect to policy choice. For, as a condition precedent to that decision, we should first analyze the problem of agenda formation. In this connection, Hirschman has usefully distinguished between "pressing" and "chosen" problems. Pressing problems are those "that are foced on the policymakers through pressure from injured or interested outside parties." Chosen problems are those that decision-makers "have picked out of thin air" as a result of their own perceptions and preferences. Pressing problems are generally those in which a perception of crisis is apparent (Hirschman, 1963).

After the policy-making decision is made, there must be implementation of the policy. In the models of the new political economy political activity is focused on the input stage of the policy process when interest groups influence the policy-making decision. In contrast, we should recognize that in developing countries it is at the output stage – at the stage of implementation and enforcement – that a large portion of individual and collective demand-making occurs, interests are represented, and there is a resolution of conflict (Grindle, 1980, pp. 15–18).

Many of the most important policies established by political elites involve distributive and redistributive measures.

> In the context of very scarce resources, who gets what and how much is of central concern to the populace. In order to have any impact on decision-making, many in a developing country have found the implementation phase of the policy process to be particularly suited to their needs. In attempts to acquire government goods and services, individuals and groups find it especially rewarding to focus their demand-making efforts on officials and agencies empowered to distribute benefits, or on politicians who may have influence over individual allocations. The factions, patron–client linkages, ethnic ties, and personal coalitions that are often the basis of political activity are well suited to making individualized demands on the bureaucratic apparatus for the allocation of goods and services. This means that the implementation process may be the major arena in which individuals and groups are able to pursue conflicting interests and compete for access to scarce resources. It may even be the principal nexus of the interaction between the government and the citizenry, between officials and their constituents. (Grindle, 1980, pp. 18–19).

Furthermore, the credibility and sustainability of a policy – attributes that are essential for policy reform – are determined during the implementation phase. If policy reform is to succeed, it is then that conflict, resistance, and reversibility must be avoided. Given the concentration of political activity on the implementation process, it is much more difficult to predict the efficacy of policies than would be indicated by the new political economy's confinement to decision-making with respect to merely the policy choice.

Given these limitations, instead of relying on only the new political economy, we must seek a more eclectic approach that combines the old and new political economy. As an illustration of this broader but necessarily more informal analysis, let us now consider the behavior of a developing country's government with respect to trade policy – in particular its attraction to import-substituting industrialization (ISI).

4 Political economy of ISI and EP

As noted for the early period of the 1950s, development economists could certainly present a number of logically valid arguments for protection of import-substitution industries. Rarely, however, was protection actually instituted because of these arguments, let alone applied by a government in a technically correct fashion. In contrast, protection in practice has been adopted for reasons best explained through a political economy perspective.

Trade policy in a developing country is put on the agenda as a pressing problem. Balance of payments crises and the foreign exchange constraint require the State to take some action. As Hirschman expresses it,

> the state loses its august character of sovereign pursuing its own objectives and initiating politics to this end; rather, it is seen as coping, as best it can, with a variety of emergencies, as constantly plugging holes, and stopping a wheel from creaking by applying a bit of grease in a hurry. Note that this conception of the coping state goes farther than the interest-group or bureaucratic-politics approaches; these are still concerned with improving our understanding of the state's action, rather than with affirming that most of the time the state does not act, but reacts. (1975, p. 389)

This pressing problem of the balance of payments also becomes a privileged problem, in the sense of gaining the attention of the policymaker, because it is reinforced by the ideology of nationalism and the appeal of economic independence. In a newly emergent country the economics of development may initially be an economics of discontent as the politically independent government seeks to overcome its colonial legacy, is attracted to the values of modernization, and the correlative policy of "industrialization from the top downward."

Another interpretation would have governments respond to political demands of various interest groups. In some countries ISI has been promoted by a development coalition composed of industrialists, urban wage earners, bureaucrats, and intellectuals. In others, there is what Peter Evans calls a "triple alliance" of multinational corporations, elite local capital, and the "state bourgeoisie" (1979).

Formal models of lobbying by interest groups have been presented by Findlay and Wellisz (1983), Wellisz and Findlay (1984), and Wellisz and Findlay (1988). A trade regime involving a tariff is determined by the government, which has a "tariff-formation function" reflecting its own preferences – that is, its ideology, the self-interests of the governing group, public support considerations, international obligations, etc. Lobbying expenditures by pro- and anti-tariff factions then enter the tariff-formation function as arguments and link the political with the economic system. The political system is viewed as an institutionalized market in conflict resolution, and the endogenous tariffs that emerge are the terms of trade reflecting the lower organizational costs of the particularized (protectionist) interests relative to the generalized (free trade) interest (Magee, 1984, p. 46).

In these models of lobbying, economic resources are used to obtain politically created rents. The restriction of manufacturing imports raises the marginal product of labor in manufacturing, leading to an increase in rent on capital. The strength of a lobby's pressures may be measured by how much it spends. To promote the aims of its faction rationally, each lobby spends resources on the basis of its perception of the actions of its opponent. The political struggle to determine the tariff level can be thought of as a Cournot–Nash process in which each faction, taking the actions of the other side as given, calculates the optimal level of its own spending in the light of the tariff–formation function and the structure of the economy. At the equilibrium point for each faction, the marginal cost of political expenditure equals marginal revenue, which is the benefit that would be derived from the change in the tariff resulting from the marginal increase in political spending (Wellisz and Findlay, 1988, pp. 69–70). For the government, a large or even the major part of its revenues is derived from tariffs. An alliance between a revenue-maximizing or surplus-maximizing Leviathan and protection-seeking manufacturers would then lead to a tariff that is higher than one maximizing revenue but that falls short of outright prohibition. Tariffs can be interpreted as "prices" that clear political markets. In the presence of uncertainty, however, the risk-avoiding manufacturers will prefer a quota to a tariff.[12] The government could then gain revenue through the sale of import licences. Rarely, however, is this done. Instead the government uses the import-licensing regime to dispense patronage within the ruling bureaucratic and political elite (Findlay and Wellisz, 1986, pp. 225–6).

In these models, the government tends to be soft – that is, vulnerable to group pressures, and the trade systems tend to be highly distorted. Under these circumstances, "favor-seeking" flourishes. To the extent that real resources are used in lobbying for trade restrictions or in revenue or rent-seeking, such activities may redistribute income within the economy, imposing costs on some sectors and bringing benefits to others. The general conclusion is that high levels of protection in LDCs, which are totally irrational in terms of the conventional theory of trade and welfare, are perfectly explicable in terms of the rational self-interest of the relevant pressure groups in the economy (Wellisz and Findlay, 1984, pp. 148-9, 151).

Although protectionist policies may coincide with the interests of dominant groups in society, this need not be the result of a weak state being in fact dominated by group interests. In terms of the old political economy, this may be the result of the conviction on the part of state elites that these policies are the most feasible for achieving national development, or it may be a result of interactions of bargaining, conflict, and compromise between state elites and social classes. Instead of clear domination of the state by specific interests, policies may be influenced by the development ideologies adopted by state elites, or by the leadership ("political entrepreneurship") of specific individuals, or by the political accommodations and bargains that are struck between state elites and various social groupings (Grindle, 1986, pp. 18-19). In societies with strong states, the government may impose policy over the objections of particularistic interests.

For a variety of reasons, therefore, a host of policies have been adopted in an ad hoc and indiscriminate fashion in a number of developing countries – resulting in a restrictive trade regime that is quite different from an economically rational system of protection. For a Leviathan that seeks revenue, tariffs appeal. But while high tariffs or quantitative restrictions are also imposed on imports of the final commodity, the intermediate inputs have low or no tariffs, thereby giving high effective rates of protection on the domestic value added. The final assembly of imported components may also be subsidized by low rates of interest, easy access to credit, foreign exchange allowances, provision of industrial estates, low public utility rates, and favorable tax allowances. At the same time, the subsidization of the import-competing industries tends to be embedded in a general environment of inflation and the maintenance of an overvalued exchange rate that becomes a covert way to tax the agricultural sector.

Whether weak or strong, governments have not adopted the first best policies in the neoclassical policy hierarchy. As a result of the syndrome of policies associated with ISI, profits in local currency and rents have been high even though the domestic resource cost is excessive and domestic value added may even be negative at world prices. At the same time, inequalities in income distribution have been aggravated, and employment creation in the urban import-replacement industrial sector has not kept pace with the rural–urban migration. Overvalued exchange rates have encouraged capital flight, and foreign borrowing by governments has often gone to finance the private sector's accumulation of foreign assets, rather than to an increase in export capacity: the foreign exchange constraint has thus not been relaxed.

For some countries a turnaround from ISI to export promotion (EP) has occurred after the first easy stage of import substitution. For purposes of policy appraisal it is important to consider why this turnaround occurs. It is not because of laissez-faire on the part of the government. On the contrary, export-led development has generally been State-led: government has consulted with and cooperated with business in establishing incentives, and government policies have made use of the market in a selective and sophisticated way.

True, economists have certainly emphasized the deficiencies and adverse effects of ISI. Their advice has been effective at some times in some countries, but to bear fruit their ideas have had to fall on fertile ground. There were other reasons for the turnaround in policy-making.

Actual experience may itself be more telling than neoclassical prescriptions. As Bhagwati observes, "Many developing countries learned (the policy lessons) the hard way; by following ISI policies too long and seeing the fortunate few pursuing the EP strategy do much better. Perhaps learning by other's doing and one's own undoing is the most common form of education!" (Bhagwati, 1988, p. 41).

There is indeed an international demonstration effect in government policies, and some countries may simply import and imitate the policies practiced in other countries. Under international leverage through the elites of the World Bank, IMF, or OECD there may also be some suasion to import the EP policies.

In a formal sense, we can of course say that a government adopts EP policies when the costs to the government of not doing so become excessive. In this connection, a major reason for the shift to EP lies in the perception by the Leviathan state that its organic interest in autonomy is better served by the outward-orientation policy (Findlay, 1986, p. 21). The ISI policy eventually founders on the shortage of foreign exchange as requirements for intermediate imports and capital goods rise more rapidly than domestic production can replace imports of final goods. Foreign aid and more external borrowing become necessary to relax the foreign exchange constraint. Thus, instead of continuing along the ever-more difficult path of ISI, why not turn to EP and capitalize on the unprecedented world trade boom of the 1960s and early 1970s? Diversification of export markets and supply sources could actually ensure that increased participation in the world economy, as measured by higher trade ratios, would result in less dependency and more autonomy, contrary to dependency ideology (Findlay, 1986, p. 22).

A switch to EP involves not only a change in trade policies but also exchange rate adjustment and stabilization measures. The differing exchange and trade regimes in Latin America and Asia bring out another force contributing to the more effective EP policies in Asia – namely, long-term differences in the balance of power between urban and rural interests. Latin American governments have found their most important constituencies among urban workers and capitalists. Trade restrictions tend to shift income from the agricultural and mineral producing sectors toward the industrial and service sectors. The relative power of the agricultural sector has declined since the Great Depression of the 1930s, and the agricultural sector has been relatively weak, with peasants only loosely organized. Moreover, political unrest is most dangerous in the cities.

In contrast, governments in Asia have felt the pressing need to win support of, or at least to appease, the stronger rural sector (Korea, Taiwan, Malaysia, Indonesia, Thailand).[13] The link between rural influence and export promotion is the first step in instituting an export program. But once export-promoting policies get under way, urban-industrial exporters become their own lobbyists and eventually become the dominant political force in favor of an undervalued exchange rate, with rural interests losing their relative influence.

The switch to EP does not appear, however, to be a function of any particular type of political regime. The switch has occurred in regimes as different as those South Korea, Thailand, or Brazil (in the 1960s). The policy shift from ISI to EP has also taken place within countries with essentially unchanged political regimes, such as South Korea. On the other hand, ISI has continually been pursued in some countries despite radical differences and changes in their political regimes – for example, for more than half a century, in Egypt and Turkey (until 1980).

To conclude: having now analyzed for more than 30 years the effects of trade policy in developing countries, many economists have come to advocate EP policies. Export pessimism has been abandoned, the case for ISI has been dismissed, and policy lessons from development experience support EP. But the economists' prescriptions frequently remain ignored. If there is to be policy reform, it is therefore first essential to undertake positive analysis of why government policy-makers undertake trade policies that are contrary to economic rationality.

We have attempted a start in this direction by considering the political economy of trade policy in developing countries. But neither the old political economy, nor the new political economy, nor a synthesis of the old and the new is yet fully satisfactory. The models of the new political economy need to be made more relevant for the developing countries, and more application to empirical case studies is required. The subject is still in only a rudimentary stage. But we may look forward to a subsequent Festschrift for someone among the next generation of development economists who will make the needed advances.

Notes

See for instance, Robert E. Baldwin, "The Political Economy of Protection," in J. N. Bhagwati and T. N. Srinivasan (eds), *Import Competition and Response*, Chicago: University of Chicago Press, 1982, pp. 263–86. Also see references elsewhere in this volume.

1   The infant industry argument, however, was not evaluated sufficiently critically. Baldwin (1969) later demonstrated that tariff protection may not represent a welfare improvement compared with *laissez-faire* because it does not induce behavior to capture the externality and thus imposes costs without correcting at all the source of the distortion.

    Moreover, advances in international trade theory since the 1950s and more extensive empirical evidence now allow a more extensive critique of measures of protection and their effects in developing countries. See, for example, Anne O. Krueger, "Trade Policies in Developing Countries," *Handbook of International Economics*, vol. I, edited by Ronald W. Jones and Peter B. Kenen (Amsterdam: Elsevier Science Publishers BV, 1984), ch. 11.

2   These arguments are summarized in Meier and Baldwin 1957 pp. 324–33.

3   See the later analysis by Hla Myint (1987) of "organizational dualism" and the contribution that trade can make to its removal. Cf. section 2, below.

4   For more extensive discussion of the "rout of export pessimism," see C. Díaz Alejandro, in *International Trade and Finance*, edited by P. B. Kenen, Cambridge: Cambridge University Press, 1975, pp. 116–22; Ian M. D. Little, *Economic Development*, New York: Basic Books, Inc., 1982, pp. 136–46.

5   See various empirical studies by Little, Scitovsky, Scott (1970), Balassa (1971), Donges (1976), Bhagwati (1978), Krueger (1978), Feder (1982), Lal and Rajapatirana (1987). A good summary of these statistical results is in Bela Balassa, "The Importance of Trade for Developing Countries," *World Bank DRD Discussion Paper*, Report No. DRD248, February 1987, section III.

6   The following paragraphs are adapted from Meier (1989).

7   See, for example, the list of policy prescriptions presented by Balassa (1982, 1985), Harberger (1984), Hughes (1985), Krueger (1985).

8   This section is adopted from Gerald M. Meier, "Do Development Economists Matter?", Fourth Dudley Seers Memorial Lecture, presented at the Institute of Development Studies, University of Sussex, May 4, 1988.

9   See, for example, D. C. Colander (ed), *Neo-Classical Political Economy*, Cambridge, MA: Ballinger Publishing Co., 1984; Findlay, 1986; Deepak Lal, "The Political Economy of the Predatory State," World Bank Development Research Department Discussion Paper 105, Washington DC, processed; T. N. Srinivasan, "Neo-Classical Political Economy, The State and Economic Development," *Asian Development Review* 3(2) (1985), 35–58.

10   See Jonathan Bendor, "Formal Models of Bureaucracies," *British Journal of Political Science*, 18, 353–95; with extensive bibliography.

11   Robert Bates also observes that "outside of offering an interpretative heuristic or a set of tools for understanding relatively restricted phenomena, this major stream of political investigation [democratic theory] proves a disappointing source of theory for the study of governmental behavior in the developing countries. For the basic conditions which support positive political analysis –

electoral accountability and the existence of well defined institutions – prevail but ephemerally in the less developed societies, by comparison with the advanced industrial nations." "Macro-Political Economy in the Field of Development," Duke University Program in International Political Economy, Working Paper No. 40, June 1988, pp. 40–1.

12 For a more detailed analysis of why different forms of protection are adopted, see Findlay and Wellisz (1986).
13 This paragraph presents the argument of Jeffrey Sachs, "External Debt and Macroeconomic Performance in Latin America and East Asia," *Brookings Papers on Economic Activity*, 1985, pp. 350ff.

References

Amsden, Alice H. 1985: "The Division of Labor is Limited by the Rate of Growth of the Market: The Taiwan Machine Tool Industry in the 1970s," *Cambridge Journal of Economics*, 9, 271–84.

Balassa, Bela 1971: *The Structure of Protection in Developing Countries*, Baltimore: Johns Hopkins University Press.

Balassa, Bela 1982: *Development Strategies in Semi-Industrial Economies*, Baltimore: Johns Hopkins University Press.

Balassa, Bela 1985: *Change and Challenge in the World Economy*, Basingstoke: Macmillan Press.

Baldwin, R. E. 1969: "The Case Against Infant-Industry Protection," *Journal of Political Economy*, 77, 295–305.

Baldwin, R. E. 1984. "Trade Policies in Developed Countries," *Handbook of International Economics*, vol. I, edited by R. W. Jones and P. B. Kenen, Amsterdam: Elsevier Science Publishers BV.

Bendor, Jonathan 1988: "Formal Models of Bureaucracies," *British Journal of Political Science*, 18, 353–95.

Bhagwati, Jagdish N. 1978: *Anatomy and Consequences of Exchange Control Regimes*, Cambridge, MA: Ballinger Publishing Co.

Bhagwati, Jagdish N. 1988. "Export-Promoting Trade Strategy: Issues and Evidence," *World Bank Research Observer*, 3(1).

Bhagwati, J. N. Brecher, Richard A. and Srinivasan, T. N. 1984: "DUP Activities and Economic Theory," in D.C. Colander (ed), *Neo-Classical Political Economy*, Cambridge, MA: Ballinger Publishing Co., ch. 1.

Donges, J. 1976: "A Comparative Study of Industrialisation Policies in Fifteen Semi-Industrial Countries," *Weltwirtschaftliches Archiv*, 112(4), 626–59.

Evans, Peter 1979: *Dependent Development*, Princeton, NJ: Princeton University Press.

Feder, G. 1982: "On Exports and Economic Growth." *Journal of Development Economics*, 12(1/2), 59–73.

Findlay, Ronald 1986: "Trade, Development, and the State," Economic Growth Center, Yale University, April, processed.

Findlay, Ronald and Wellisz, Stanislaw 1983: "Some Aspects of the Political Economy of Trade Restrictions," *Kyklos*, 36(3), 469–81.

Findlay, Ronald and Wellisz, Stanislaw 1986: "Tariffs, Quotas and Domestic-Content Protection: Some Political Economy Considerations," *Public Choice*, 50, 221–42.

Findlay, Ronald and Wilson, John D. 1987: "The Political Economy of

Leviathan," in Asaf Razin and Efraim Sadka (eds), *Economic Policy in Theory and Practice*, London: Macmillan, ch. 8.

Grindle, Merilee S. 1980: *Politics and Policy Implementation in the Third World*, Princeton, NJ: Princeton University Press, pp. 15–18.

Grindle, Merilee S. 1986. *State and Countryside*, Baltimore: Johns Hopkins University Press.

Harberger, Arnold C. 1984: *World Economic Growth*, San Francisco: Institute of Contemporary Studies Press.

Hirschman, Albert O. 1963: *Journeys Toward Progress*, New York: The Twentieth Century Fund.

Hirschman, Albert O. 1975. "Policymaking and Policy Analysis in Latin America – A Return Journey," *Policy Sciences*, 6, 389.

Hughes, Helen 1985: *Policy Lessons of the Development Experience*, New York: The Group of Thirty.

Krueger, Anne O. 1974: "The Political Economy of the Rent-Seeking Society," *American Economic Review*, 64(3), 291–303.

Krueger, Anne O. 1978: *Liberalization Attempts and Consequences*, Cambridge, MA: Ballinger Publishing Co.

Krueger, Anne O. 1985. "The Experience and Lessons of Asia's Super Exporters," in *Export-Oriented Development Strategies*, edited by Vittorio Corbo, Anne O. Krueger, and Fernando Ossa, Boulder and London: Westview Press, pp. 187–212.

Krugman, Paul 1984: "Import Protection as Export Promotion," in H. Kierzkowski (ed.), *Monopolistic Competition and International Trade*, Oxford: Clarendon Press, pp. 180–93.

Lal, Deepak, and Rajapatirana, Sarath 1987: "Foreign Trade Regimes and Economic Growth in Developing Countries," *World Bank Research Observer*, 2(2), 189–216.

Little, I. M. D., Scitovsky, T. and Scott, M. F. G. 1970: *Industry and Trade in Some Developing Countries*, London: Oxford University Press.

Magee, Stephen P. 1984: "Endogenous Tariff Theory," in D. Colander (ed.), *Neoclassical Political Economy*, Cambridge, MA: Ballinger Publishing Co.

Meier, G. M. 1989: "Trade Policy and Development" in *Public Policy and Economic Development*, edited by M. F. G. Scott and Deepak Lal, Oxford: Oxford University Press.

Meier, Gerald M. and Baldwin, Robert E. 1957: *Economic Development: Theory, History, Policy*, New York: John Wiley and Sons.

Myint, Hla 1987: "The Neoclassical Resurgence in Development Economics: Its Strength and Limitations," in *Pioneers in Development*, Second Series, edited by Gerald M. Meier, New York: Oxford University Press, pp. 123–30.

Nishimizu, Mieko and Robinson, Sherman 1984: "Trade Policies and Productivity Change in Semi-Industrialized Countries," *Journal of Development Economics*, 16, 177–206.

Wellisz, Stanislaw and Findlay, Ronald 1984: "Protection and Rent-seeking in Developing Countries," in D. C. Colander (ed.), *Neoclassical Political Economy*, Cambridge, MA: Ballinger Publishing Co., pp. 141–53.

Wellisz, Stanislaw and Findlay, Ronald 1988: "The State and the Invisible Hand," *World Bank Research Observer*, 3(1), 59–80.

12

Does 1992 come before or after 1990? On Regional versus Multilateral Integration

ANDRÉ SAPIR

Introduction

The creation of a large unified market plays a central role in the process of European integration. Since the Treaty of Rome established the European Economic Community (EC) in 1957, the development of the internal market has undergone three phases. The first was the removal of customs duties and quantitative restrictions on trade between the original six member states. During the second, starting in 1973, the Community went through three enlargements, extending the earlier achievements to twelve member states. At the same time, however, rising structural problems and unemployment increasingly led Community governments to reinforce existing nontariff barriers (NTBs) and introduce new ones, thereby severely impeding or even reversing European integration. This situation prompted the European Commission to prepare a White Paper listing remaining barriers to intra-EC trade and a timetable for their removal. The adoption, in December 1985, of the Single European Act embodying the White Paper directives paved the way toward the final phase in the completion of the internal market by the end of 1992.

Much has been written recently on the likely impact of 1992 on European economies. On the other hand, relatively little attention has been devoted to the external impact of the internal market. Yet, given the importance of the Community in world trade, the completion of Europe's domestic market could exert a profound influence on nonmember countries, depending upon the common external trade policy. In particular, trade partners for whom the Community represents an important market are increasingly concerned about the impact of 1992. As the *Economist* recently put it:

> How should outsiders react to the plans for a single European market – with glee, because there will be great opportunities for all-comers, or with alarm, for the fear the result will be a protectionist "Fortress Europe"?

The purpose of this paper is to examine the external impact of 1992. In particular, it seeks to analyze the relationship between 1992 and the Uruguay Round of GATT negotiations which are scheduled to conclude in

1990, taking into account the political-economic determinants of commercial policy in Europe. The paper is divided into four parts. The first presents the basic tools for analyzing the impact of integration on trade and welfare. The second briefly reviews the experience of the first 30 years of European integration. The third attempts to assess the external impact of 1992 in the light of theory and past experience. The fourth looks at the interaction between 1992 and the Uruguay Round.

1 The analytics of integration

The purpose of this section is to examine the effects of integration on trade and welfare. The analysis is partial-equilibrium, focusing on the market for a single product subject to trade barriers. It assumes three countries, two countries with integrate, and a third country, representing the rest of the world.

We follow the recent work on integration by Krugman (1987, 1988) and distinguish two situations according to whether production is taking place under constant returns to scale and perfect competition or economies of scale and imperfect competition. In the first case, trade is based on comparative advantage resulting from differences between countries in factor endowments or technology. In the second one, trade is driven by scale economies.

A Constant returns to scale and perfect competition

In a world where returns to scale are constant and perfect competition prevails, the removal of trade barriers will lead to further specialization of countries according to their comparative advantage and to gains from trade. Given that European integration involves a reduction of trade protection in the world, one would expect it to produce similar effects. Since Viner's (1950) discussion of customs unions in terms of trade creation and trade diversion, economists know that this expectation may not be valid. The reason is that regional integration, as opposed to world integration, eliminates one kind of distortion but introduces a new one.

In any EC country, integration reduces the price of supplies from other EC members relative to those from domestic producers, thereby creating trade at the expense of domestic production. At the same time, European integration drives a wedge between the price of supplies from member and non-member countries, hence diverting trade from the latter to the former. Altogether, therefore, integration can be expected to increase intra-Community imports at the expense of both domestic production and extra-EC imports. The welfare implication for the importing country is, however, ambiguous. On the one hand, trade creation is always beneficial since it enables a net saving of resources. On the other, trade diversion is detrimental or beneficial depending upon whether it results from the removal of what Pelkmans and Winters (1988) refer to as revenue-generating measures (such as tariffs) or cost-increasing barriers (such as nontariff barriers). If the European barriers are revenue-generating, trade diversion involves a real resource cost. However, if the barriers are cost-increasing, their removal saves real resources.

Nevertheless, contrary to what Pelkmans and Winters imply, removing cost-increasing barriers may be welfare-worsening *if*, as it is likely, *tariff and nontariff barriers are both present*. In this case, the removal of NTBs among EC members may induce a social cost because of the loss of tariff revenue. For a given EC member, figure 12.1 shows domestic demand and supply schedules, DD and SS, and imports available, under free trade, at price p_R from the rest of the world or at price p_E from EC partners. All foreign supplies are subject to a nontariff barrier n. In addition, a tariff t is imposed on imports from the rest of the world. Initially, the domestic price is $p_R + t + n$, domestic consumption and production are T and U, respectively, and imports $M = (T - U)$, entirely from the rest of the world. When the nontariff barrier is removed between EC members, the domestic price falls to p_E, domestic consumption and production becomes R and Q, respectively, and imports $M' = (R - Q)$, now entirely from within the Community. These imports replace some domestic supplies (trade creation) and all previous (cheaper) imports from the rest of the world. The welfare implications are: consumer surplus rises by $(A + B + C + D)$, producer surplus falls by A and government revenue falls by E. This last term is ignored by Pelkmans and Winters (1988, p. 19). Clearly, the net effect, $(B + C + D)$ minus E, can be either positive or negative.

The policy implication of the previous analysis is that trade creation

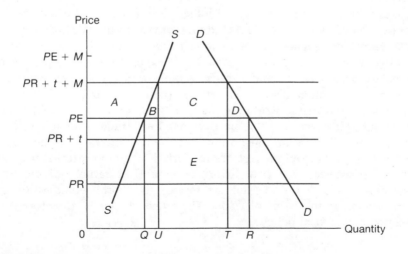

Figure 12.1   The effects of tariff and nontariff barriers on imports

should be enhanced and trade diversion generally opposed. In political terms the distinction between trade creation and trade diversion could, however, lead to a very different conclusion than the one based purely on economic efficiency. In a little-known essay, Hirschman (1981) notes that, politically, integration will be aided by trade diversion and weakened by trade creation:

> The larger the trade-creating effects, . . . the greater will be the resistance to the union among various concentrated and vocal producer interests of the member countries . . . Trade diversion implies, on the contrary, that concentrated producer groups of the member countries will be able to capture business away from their competitors in nonmember countries. These effects will therefore endear the customs union to the interest groups concerned and will provide some badly needed group-support for a union. (p. 271)

The policy conclusion is that it may be desirable to balance off the economically desirable trade creation with some politically vital trade diversion.

When trade is given by comparative advantage, the relative importance of trade creation and trade diversion depends upon three factors: relative factor endowments or technology, the extent of integration and the level of protection against third countries. Trade creation is most likely when integration involves economies that differ in factor endowments or technology. In addition, the more the participating countries already trade with each other, the more trade creation is likely to dominate, because there is only a small volume of extra-EC imports to be diverted. On the other hand, the higher the common level of protection against third countries, the more these countries are discriminated against and likely to suffer from trade diversion.

In conclusion, the main effect of integration on trade is the increase of intra-Community imports. To the extent that returns to scale are constant, integration increases inter-industry trade in line with the EC members' comparative advantage. In principle, one should expect Community producers to replace both domestic and extra-EC suppliers. It is not clear, however, how the effect will be distributed between these two suppliers. If barriers vis-à-vis the rest of the world are high, trade diversion will be relatively important. However, if these barriers are low, trade diversion will be unimportant. European integration could even increase, rather than decrease, imports from the rest of the world if common external barriers were sufficiently lowered. In this case there would be external trade creation instead of trade diversion, and the rest of the world would enjoy an improvement in the terms of trade. The crucial factor is, therefore, the common commercial policy.

B Economies of scale and product differentiation

Integration in the presence of economies of scale also increases specialization and intra-Community trade. Integration is likely to generate the traditional trade creation and trade diversion effects. However, two additional outcomes can be expected in this context: cost reduction and trade suppression (see Corden, 1972). The first effect happens if integration increases the scale of existing domestic production. In this case, specialization results in lower average costs of domestic supplies. Cost reduction is, therefore, welfare-improving for the domestic economy. The second effect, trade suppression, occurs when imports from outside the Community are replaced by newly established domestic supplies which, despite the fall in average costs due to integration, would not survive without protection. Trade suppression is alike to trade diversion: it is detrimental to welfare because a costlier source replaces a cheaper source. Altogether, European integration can be expected to increase domestic production and intra-Community imports at the expense of extra-EC imports. The welfare implication is ambiguous: trade creation and cost reduction generate welfare gains; trade diversion and trade suppression generally induce losses.

When economies of scale are the basis for trade, the relative importance of trade creation and trade diversion or suppression depends on three factors: the size of the members' domestic market, the extent of integration, and trade policy. Trade creation is most likely when integration results in a large unified market replacing domestic markets that are too small to achieve efficient scales of operation. Trade diversion and/or suppression are most probable when the external trade policy is protectionist.

The principal effect of integration on trade in the presence of scale economies is, once again, an increase in intra-Community imports. The nature of the additional trade depends on whether the product concerned is homogeneous or differentiated. If the product is homogeneous, integration will expand output in some locations and eliminate production elsewhere. The result will be an increase in inter-industry trade. If, however, the product is differentiated, integration could expand the production in all locations, each specializing in distinct varieties of the product. The outcome will be an increase in intra-industry trade. The impact of all this on extra-EC suppliers is as in the previous section; it rests, crucially, on the common commercial policy.

2 The first thirty years of European integration

To what extent has the Community's commercial policy accelerated or slowed down the process of world integration in the past 30 years? Has European integration proceeded in the spirit of freer world trade embodied in the General Agreement on Tariffs and Trade (GATT)?

The cornerstone of the GATT is the principle of unconditional most favored nation (MFN), or equal treatment of all contracting parties. The principle requires that any concession granted, within the framework of the Agreement, between GATT members must be extended to all other contracting parties "immediately and unconditionally." The GATT provides, however, for certain exemptions to the rule of non-discrimination. The most significant one is Article XXIV which permits customs unions and free trade areas, provided their aim is to facilitate trade among the member countries rather than raise barriers against third countries. The concern of the GATT's founding fathers was that preferential arrangements should b e a step toward, rather than away from, freer world trade. Essentially, the requirements set out in Article XXIV are that such arrangements should be trade-creating rather than trade-diverting (see, for instance, Hine (1985) and Pomfret (1988)).

Mindful of the Community's obligations and interests in world trade, Article 110 of the Treaty of Rome specified that:

> By establishing a customs union between themselves Member States aim to contribute, in the common interest, to the harmonious development of world trade, the progressive abolition of restrictions on international trade and the lowering of customs barriers.

This general declaration of principle, along with specific measures setting out the common external tariff, established a fair degree of conformity of the EC customs union to the spirit and rules of the GATT (see Pelkmans, 1984).

During the first phase of the EC (1958–72), the compatibility of European integration with world integration was reinforced, for manufactured products, by the reduction of the common external tariff during the Dillon and Kennedy Rounds of GATT negotiations. As a result, the rapid expansion of intra-Community trade in manufactures resulted mainly from trade creation; trade diversion was a relatively unimportant phenomenon. There was also a great deal of external trade creation. By contrast, there was considerable trade diversion for agricultural products, an area not covered by the GATT (see Balassa, 1975). The importance of trade diversion in the field of agriculture is a perfect illustration of Hirschman's argument on the political economy of integration.

During the second phase of integration (1973–85), the earlier trends continued (see Jacquemin and Sapir, 1988a). The first enlargement of the EC was followed by MFN tariff cuts on manufactured goods during the Tokyo Round, thereby producing more external trade creation. On the other hand, the trade-diverting effect of the Common Agricultural Policy progressively increased. After the second enlargement, the staggering costs of trade diversion provoked a rising opposition both within and outside the Community. The outcome was the inclusion of agriculture in the Uruguay

Round and the agreement to bring, for the first time, the GATT discipline to this area of international trade.

Nevertheless, the second phase of integration differed from the first one in a significant way. Whereas, initially, intra-Community imports of manufactured goods had increased faster than extra-EC imports, the opposite occurred from 1973 on (see Jacquemin and Sapir, 1988a). The relative slowdown of intra-Community trade can, probably, be ascribed to three factors.

The first one is the progressive dismantling of the common external tariff. This process has not been confined, however, to multilateral actions for the benefit of all GATT members. Over the years, the Community has increasingly transgressed the principle of non-discrimination by constructing a complex hierarchical system of preferential arrangements. Since the late seventies, the so-called "pyramid of privilege" consists of three layers. At the top are the countries granted duty-free access for all their manufactured exports: the six current countries of the European Free Trade Association (EFTA), the twelve Mediterranean countries and the 66 African, Caribbean and Pacific (ACP) states of the Lomé Convention. The middle layer includes all the other developing countries, with the exception of Taiwan, which are beneficiaries of the EC's Generalized System of Preferences (GSP). At the bottom, there is a handful of countries subject to the full common external tariff, namely Australia, Canada, Japan, New Zealand, South Africa, Taiwan, and the United States. (As in the Indian caste system, below these three layers lie the outcasts: Eastern Europe and other Comecon countries which are not granted MFN treatment.) These preferential arrangements have, to some extent, increased the Community's total imports. More importantly, however, they have undermined the GATT discipline and diverted EC imports from less- to more-preferred sources.

The second factor is the rapid growth of Japan and the newly industrializing countries (NICs) as exporters of manufactures. In the EC market for manufactured products (excluding intra-Community trade), this is reflected by a steady increase of the combined share of Japan and the four Asian NICs (Hong Kong, Korea, Singapore, and Taiwan) from 8 percent in 1965 to 28 percent in 1986 (see figure 12.2).

The last factor in the relative slowdown of intra-Community trade is the failure to complete the internal market. During the period 1973–85, member states have increasingly resorted to protectionist barriers hampering intra-Community trade. This rise of intra-EC protectionism has coincided with the increased use of nontariff barriers against imports from non-member states documented by several economists at the World Bank and elsewhere (see, for instance, Nogues, Olechowski, and Winters (1986) and Klepper, Weiss, and Witteler (1987)). In fact, the desire of member states to protect their industries from the competition of third countries has reinforced the ascent of intra-Community barriers. For example, Owen

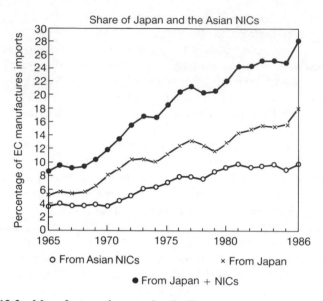

Figure 12.2   Manufactures imports by the European Community

(1983) notes that the harmonization of technical regulations for cars in the Community has blocked "on fears that it will facilitate unrestricted Japanese entry to Community markets" (p. 161).

The root of EC protectionism lies in the prolonged slow growth and high unemployment in the EC stemming from market rigidities that make it difficult to adjust to shifts in comparative advantage (see, for instance, Lawrence, and Schultze (1987)). There is apprehension that Europe may be caught between competitors at both ends of the "technological spectrum:" the NICs, which pose a challenge in mature sectors using relatively standardized production technologies; and the United States and Japan, whose strength lies in high-tech sectors dominated by oligopolistic corporations that can take advantage of scale economies, learning by doing and barriers to entry against rivals, all of which are fostered by large domestic markets and promoted by government policies. As a result, there has been an increased tendency in Europe to grant protection to both ends of the spectrum: in low-tech (such as textiles, clothing, and footwear) as well as in high-tech sectors (such as aircraft, computers, and telecommunications equipment).

The concern in Europe is especially vivid at the upper technological end because it encompasses sectors which are viewed as vital: "Locating them behind one's own borders is often seen as a matter of securing broader political and economic benefits" (Bhagwati, 1988, p. 108). To the extent that these sectors are subject to scale economies, the fragmentation of the European market by domestic protectionist measures has undermined the

European industry. (For econometric evidence of the impact of trade barriers and scale economies on European competitiveness, see Jacquemin and Sapir (1988b)). Part of the challenge of 1992 is to remedy this situation.

3 The external impact of 1992

The loss of momentum in Europe has prompted the Community to aim at completing the internal market by 1992. The purpose is to eliminate all physical, technical and fiscal barriers so as to ensure the free circulation of goods, services, and factors of production among the member states. The rationale behind the creation of a single market is that it should improve European specialization and efficiency, intensify competition and, thereby, increase trade and foster economic welfare.

The removal of nontariff barriers within the Community has important implications for international trade policy. Although a central part of the Treaty of Rome was the establishment of a common commercial policy towards third countries, it did not, in fact, provide a definition of commercial policy. Article 113, which confers on the Community its powers over commercial policy, only lists examples: tariff changes, measures of liberalization, export policy and measures against dumping or subsidies. As a result, member states have often taken a great deal of liberty in the application of NTBs against third countries. The outcome has been a long-standing dispute on the division of powers between the Community and the member states in many of the fields covered by the 1992 initiative.

The completion of the internal market requires a parallel expansion of the Community's competence in the field of external trade. The enlargement of the common commercial policy is viewed with apprehension both inside and outside the Community. Inside the Community, some fear that the common barriers against third countries might be too weak. As one of the foremost legal advisers of the Commission has, rightly, noted:

> Member States, especially the "larger" ones are anxious to keep their own powers as much as possible and are reluctant to relinquish them to the Community because they fear that the Community would be unable to act or that the Community policy would be wrong. (Bourgeois, 1983, p. 4)

On the other hand, countries outside the Community worry that the price for internal liberalization will be greater external protection. Among the industrial countries, the concern is the greatest on the part of the EFTA countries who ship about two-thirds of their manufactured exports to the Community – nearly as much as the EC members do (see table 12.1). The Americans and the Japanese also apprehend Europe's new trade policy. With the exception of the NICs, developing countries export relatively little manufactured goods to the Community. But for many of them, especially the 66 ACP countries and the twelve Mediterranean countries, the reliance on the Community market is all-important. State-trading countries, particularly those of Eastern Europe, could also be greatly affected by a more difficult access to the Community market.

Table 12.1   Importance of EC-12 market for selected trading partners, manufacturing products[a], 1980–86 averages ($ billion)

	Import Market		Ratio EC-12:OECD, percentage
Exporter	EC-12	OECD	
Industrial countries			
EC-12	243.8	357.2	68
USA	37.2	99.8	37
Japan	21.7	88.5	25
EFTA	39.8	61.4	65
Developing countries			
ACP countries	1.6	2.6	60
Mediterranean countries	6.4	9.4	69
Latin-America	2.6	15.6	17
Asia	18.8	73.0	26
State-trading Countries			
Comecon	7.0	10.3	68

[a] SITC 5, 6 (minus 68), 7 and 8.

The purpose of this section is to examine in some details the external impact of the 1992 measures. In spite of the importance of the service sector in the plans to create a unified market, the scope of analysis will be limited to trade in goods for lack of space. Nonetheless, some comments on trade in services will be made in the last section of the paper.

The main barriers to intra-Community trade in goods are: border controls, technical barriers and public procurement policies. Each of these barriers will be reviewed in turn, focusing on the implication of their removal on international trade. The analysis will conclude with a sectoral assessment of the potential effect of 1992 on trade flows.

A Abolition of border controls

The achievement of the internal market implies that after 1992 intra-EC trade will no longer be subject to border controls. This will have a direct implication for imports from third countries.

Although quantitative restrictions on intra-EC trade are forbidden by the Treaty of Rome, member states have continued to maintain quotas on imports from third countries which had been introduced prior to either the formation of the EC or the member's accession to the Community. These quantitative restrictions, applied to nearly a thousand industrial and agricultural items, are reported annually in the *Official Journal of the*

European Communities. At the same time, however, the Treaty of Rome guarantees the free circulation of goods within the EC, regardless of whether they originate in member states or come from third countries. National import quotas would, therefore, be largely ineffectual unless trade deflection (i.e. indirect imports of restricted third-country goods via another, unrestricted, member state) could be prevented. In order to preserve the effectiveness of their quantitative restrictions, Article 115 enables member states to request the Commission to suspend the free circulation of goods coming from third countries. Clearly, the safeguard afforded by Article 115 depends on the possibility of border controls between member states. Their elimination implies, *de facto*, the abrogation of Article 115 and the necessity for member states to adopt a common stand on quantitative restrictions.

During the period 1979–87, the Commission has approved a total of 1649 requests for protection under Article 115. As table 12.2 indicates, more than 80 percent of these requests came from only three countries: France (685), Ireland (409) and Italy (236). Among the nine countries that were members of the EC throughout the period, two had almost no requests: Denmark (9 cases) and Germany (15 cases). The numbers for 1986 and 1987 give some credence to the oft-alleged North–South European divide: a protectionist South (with the exception of Greece and Portugal) and a more liberal North (with the exception of Ireland). Care must be taken, however, in interpreting these numbers as other protective devices, besides Article 115, are commonly used. For instance, most member states, including Germany (a country with no Article 115 limitations in recent years), limit their imports from Eastern Europe through export restraint arrangements.

Table 12.2 Article 115 case acceptances, by member-state, 1979–87

	1979	1980	1981	1982	1983	1984	1985	1986	1987	Total
Benelux	44	25	17	19	22	14	4	0	1	146
Denmark	3	4	0	0	0	0	0	0	2	9
France	124	105	80	85	57	39	66	67	62	685
Germany	6	1	2	2	4	0	0	0	0	15
Greece			0	0	0	0	0	0	0	0
Ireland	33	57	32	26	48	59	57	45	52	409
Italy	17	23	23	29	37	34	30	20	23	236
Portugal								0	1	1
Spain								4	13	17
UK	33	7	12	13	20	19	9	5	3	131
EC-12	260	222	166	174	188	165	176	137	143	1,649

Source: *Official Journal of the European Communities*, various issues.

Products covered by the application of Article 115 constitute a small, but hard-core, sub-set of products subject to national import quotas. As table 12.3 shows, by far the most important use of Article 115 is as complement to the Multi-Fibre Arrangement, which sets national import quotas for textiles and clothing. Other sensitive items concerned in the application of Article 115 include: vehicles from Japan (in Italy, Portugal and Spain); footwear (in France, Ireland, and the United Kingdom), electronic equipment (in France, Spain, and the United Kingdom) and toys (in France and Spain) from the Asian NICs and China; and bananas from Latin America (in France, Italy, and the United Kingdom).

Table 12.3   Article 115 case acceptances, by product category, 1979–87

	1979	1980	1981	1982	1983	1984	1985	1986	1987	Total
Textiles	199	164	120	116	131	120	119	102	105	1,176
Other manufactures	59	53	43	52	49	37	45	36	49	423
Agricultural products	2	5	3	6	8	8	12	3	3	50
EC-12	260	222	166	174	188	165	176	137	143	1,649

Source: *Official Journal of the European Communities*, various issues.

The impact of the abolition of border controls on trade depends on the future shape of Community commercial policy. There are two obvious alternatives to the present system of national quotas. One is the simple abolition of quotas, which might be feasible for a few not too sensitive products such as handtools, sewing machines and umbrellas. The result would be, probably, internal and external trade creation, with the division of gains between Community and third-country suppliers depending upon their respective competitive strength. The second alternative is the introduction of Community quotas, which is more likely for sensitive products such as cars, color TVs, and bananas. If the Community quota were equal to the sum of the members' quotas, the only possible trade effect would be internal trade creation resulting from either comparative advantage or scale economies. Winters (1988) shows that the replacement of national quotas by such a single Community quota is desirable for EC consumers, even if there is no trade creation. This is especially the case if foreign producers enjoy some degree of monopoly power and practice discriminatory pricing in national markets segmented with the help of Article 115.

There is a clear danger, however, that national quotas will be replaced by national or Community "voluntary" export restraints (VERs), rather than by Community quotas; or that Community quotas, if judged too liberal by some member states, will be accompanied by national VERs. The risk is particularly strong in view of the fact that many of the sensitive products are already subject to both national quotas and national or Community VERs. For instance, Japanese car exports to the EC are restrained by quotas in Italy, Portugal and Spain and by VERs in several other member states. In

January 1988, the Commission demanded that Japan accept a temporary Community VER in exchange for phasing out national import restraints. The objective of European car manufactures is, reportedly, to freeze Japanese exports at the 1985–6 level of one million cars. In principle, the VER would be lifted after 1992. But based on past experience, there is little hope for such an outcome. The first-ever Community VER was introduced in February 1983 to limit Japanese exports of video recorders. (For a discussion, see Hindley, 1986). It formally lapsed in January 1986 but was renewed soon afterwards along with a VER agreement with Korea. Both VERs were still in place in mid-1988, together with a quota in Spain and a VER in France.

B Elimination of technical barriers

According to the Commission of the European Communities (1988), technical barriers (i.e. technical standards or regulations and certification procedures) constitute the most important obstacle to intra-Community trade. They also cover a wide spectrum of industries ranging from motor vehicles, electrical and electronic equipment to footwear, paper products and man-made fibers (see Nerb (1988) quoted in Buigues and Ilzkovitz (1988), table 1).

Earlier attempts to eliminate technical barriers had focused on international harmonization. In view of the difficulty in bringing together long-standing national rules, the 1992 project is based, instead, on the principle of mutual recognition. This principle derives from the 1978 decision of the European Court of Justice in the *Cassis de Dijon* case, whereby a German requirement resulting in the exclusion from the German market of certain liqueurs from other EC members was found contrary to the Treaty of Rome. Mutual recognition implies that products lawfully marketed in one member state must be admitted to the market of all other member states. The principle does not, however, apply to health and safety regulations, for which Community standards are being established.

The principle of mutual recognition has a direct impact on extra-Community imports. By virtue of the principle of free circulation referred to earlier, mutual recognition means that third-country products which are imported by and marketed in any member state must be granted access to all other member states, regardless of whether they fulfill the regulations of these states. For instance, after 1992, American products which meet Spanish standards and are imported into Spain will have to be admitted to the German market, even though they may not conform to German standards. Hence, suppliers from third countries will, in principle, benefit from the elimination of technical barriers within the Community. The trade effect should be both internal and external trade creation. The Community might, however, adopt discriminatory measures that would result in trade diversion.

There are, essentially, three ways foreign producers might be discriminated against. First, the Community might adopt strict harmonized health and safety standards which would be nearly impossible to meet for developing countries. In 1986, the Commission had to drop a Community standard on chocolate at the request of some member states fearing for the interests of developing country producers. Stringent health standards might also affect industrialized country producers. One such instance is the 1988 Community standard on hormone-treated meat for which the United States has obtained a one-year exemption. If applied in 1989, the EC's ban on hormones would bar about $150 million of US beef from the Community and could result in retaliatory actions. Second, the Community could introduce technical standards for high-tech products (such as computers and telecommunications equipment) designed to exclude, at least temporarily, foreign suppliers. Third, the principle of mutual recognition which applies to indirect imports may not extend to direct imports. In the previous example, this would mean that direct imports from the United States into the German market would still be prohibited; only indirect imports via the Spanish market, adding to the costs of transportation of American exports, would be allowed.

C Opening up public procurement

The importance of purchases by public bodies reportedly varies between 10 and 20 percent of GDP in the twelve member states. The overwhelming majority of public procurement is biased in favor of domestic suppliers (see Commission of the European Communities, 1988). As a result, the import content of public supplies is several times lower than the import content of private supplies for similar product categories (see Pelkmans and Winters, 1988). The completion of the internal market is expected to remove discriminatory public purchasing practices within the Community.

The 1992 project will have an important external impact since importers and subsidiaries from third countries established in the Community will, in principle, enjoy the same access to public markets as EC producers. The opening up of public procurement would, therefore, result in both internal and external trade creation. Nonetheless, the Community might adopt commercial policy measures which would make it difficult for foreign producers to bid for public contracts. The most obvious discriminatory measure would be the adoption of strict Community technical standards designed to protect EC suppliers. The likelihood of such action is particularly strong in high-tech sectors (such as computers and telecommunications equipment) where the fragmentation of the European market by national procurement policies has weakened European firms relative to their American and Japanese competitors. Another possible discriminatory measure would be the exclusion of bids from foreign subsidiaries which do not meet local content requirements. The distinction among third-country subsidiaries according to their level of Community content is already widely used by the Commission in different circumstances, such as antidumping investigations.

D The sectoral impact of 1992

The external impact of the internal market depends on three factors: the removal of nontariff barriers, the relative competitiveness of European producers and the EC's trade policy. The elimination of NTBs inside the Community should lead to an increase of trade as domestic producers lose some of their protection. The winners of the trade expansion could be Community producers or producers from third countries, depending upon their relative strength and the shape of Community commercial policy.

Although these three factors will have an effect on most activities, their precise impact is likely to vary a great deal across sectors. The assessment of the external impact of 1992, therefore, requires a two-step procedure. The first one consists in the identification of the sectors which are currently most affected by nontariff barriers. The second step involves, for these sectors, the detailed analysis of the relative competitiveness of EC producers and of the common commercial policy.

The first step has already been conducted by Buigues and Ilzkovitz (1988) who have classified over 100 three-digit manufacturing sectors according to the extent of market fragmentation in the Community. Their study uses two indicators of fragmentation: nontariff barriers and price dispersion. The authors identify 40 sectors as being particularly sensitive to the completion of the internal market, eleven with high and 29 with moderate nontariff barriers.

These 40 sectors are shown in Table 12.4 where, in addition to the degree of NTB found by Buigues and Ilzkovitz (1988), I present three trade indicators. The first indicator divides (apparent) consumption expenditures in the member states into three shares: the share supplied by domestic producers, the share supplied by Community partners and the share supplied by third-country producers. In 1983, the average shares for the entire manufacturing sector were, respectively, 76, 14, and 10 percent. This indicator sheds light on the extent of competition between domestic and foreign producers and between Community and third-country suppliers. The latter information is also reflected in the other two measures. The second indicator gives the ratio of intra-EC imports to total (intra- and extra-EC) imports. It varies between 0 and 100 percent. The average value for the manufacturing sector as a whole was 60 and 58 percent, respectively, in 1973 and 1983. The third indicator is an index of revealed comparative advantage (RCA) defined as net trade (exports minus imports, adjusted for the country's overall trade imbalance) divided by total trade (exports plus imports). This ratio ranges between -1 and $+1$; a positive value indicates a comparative advantage and a negative one a comparative disadvantage.

Table 12.4 The sectors most sensitive to the completion of the internal market, ranked by the share of domestic suppliers in consumption

NACE Sector description	NTB Level	Share of consumption supplied by			Ratio of Intra-EC to total EC imports (in percent)		Revealed comparative advantage index			Economies of scale level	R&D intensity level
		Domestic suppliers	Intra-EC imports	Extra-EC imports	1973	1983	EC-12	USA	JAPAN		
427 Brewing and malting	H	96.1	3.6	0.3	92	93	0.91	−0.08	−0.88	M	L
428 Soft drinks	H	95.5	4.2	0.3	94	94	0.73	−1.00	0.23	n.a.	L
315 Boilermaking	H	92.9	5.1	2.0	79	72	0.82	0.55	0.93	H	L
362 Railway equipment	H	92.6	5.3	2.1	68	72	0.76	0.11	0.70	H	L
417 Pasta	H	89.6	9.7	0.7	92	93	0.81	−0.71	−0.78	n.a.	L
361 Shipbuilding	H	88.7	3.5	7.8	44	31	0.26	−0.03	0.85	M	L
341 Insulated wires and cables	H	87.5	7.6	4.9	71	61	0.33	0.00	0.72	n.a.	M
425 Champagnes and ciders	H	85.9	13.7	0.4	95	97	0.94	−1.00	−1.00	n.a.	L
421 Chocolate	H	80.1	15.3	4.6	75	77	0.28	−0.67	−0.95	H	L
342 Electrical machinery	H	79.5	11.7	8.8	66	57	0.27	0.12	0.57	H	M
257 Pharmaceuticals	H	78.4	13.4	8.2	66	62	0.43	0.47	−0.78	M	H
481 Rubber products	M	69.6	22.2	8.2	78	73	0.33	−0.42	0.56	L	M
321 Agricultural machinery	M	68.9	24.6	6.5	81	79	0.59	0.25	0.71	M	M
247 Glass and glassware	M	68.5	23.0	8.5	81	73	0.36	−0.08	0.24	M	L
325 Mining equipment	M	67.8	20.9	11.3	72	65	0.53	0.37	0.84	L	M
493 Photo processing equipment	M	66.1	19.0	14.9	56	56	−0.07	0.98	0.45	n.a.	M
248 Ceramics	M	65.1	25.5	9.4	74	73	0.58	−0.50	0.73	M	L
346 Electrical appliances	M	62.9	27.1	10.0	84	73	0.08	−0.44	0.82	M	M
453 Clothing	M	56.2	19.7	24.1	54	45	−0.21	−0.83	−0.62	L	L
351 Motor vehicles	M	53.6	33.4	13.0	86	72	0.43	−0.51	0.91	M	M
324 Machinery for food indust.	M	50.6	34.1	15.3	74	69	0.58	0.28	0.50	L	L
326 Transmission equipment	M	48.5	31.9	19.6	62	62	0.26	−0.02	0.56	M	M
322 Machine tools	M	46.9	28.7	24.4	63	54	0.31	−0.04	0.69	L	M

344 Telecommunications	M	46.3	24.7	29.0	57	46	0.14	0.38	0.37	H	H
431 Wool industry	M	45.3	31.7	23.0	62	58	−0.16	−0.38	−0.55	L	L
451 Footwear	M	40.0	37.8	22.2	71	63	0.30	−0.87	−0.89	L	L
345 Ratio, TV	M	38.1	22.9	39.0	50	37	−0.25	−0.17	0.79	M	H
455 Household textiles	M	37.4	26.3	36.3	56	42	−0.05	−0.34	−0.80	L	L
494 Toys and sports goods	M	35.4	26.5	38.1	48	41	−0.32	−0.59	−0.01	n.a.	M
347 Electrical lamps	M	35.0	46.8	18.2	79	72	0.50	−0.16	0.41	n.a.	M
327 Other machinery	M	34.5	41.9	23.6	74	64	0.53	−0.03	0.33	L	M
432 Cotton industry	M	32.5	42.5	25.0	70	63	0.13	0.10	0.41	L	L
256 Other chemicals	M	29.9	49.8	20.3	68	71	0.43	0.67	−0.28	H	M
438 Carpets	M	29.3	42.4	28.3	65	60	0.09	−0.17	−0.12	H	L
372 Medical equipment	H	28.4	35.1	36.5	56	49	−0.20	0.49	0.05	M	M
364 Aerospace	M	19.1	36.4	44.5	31	45	0.11	0.57	−0.91	H	H
323 Textile machinery	M	13.8	52.6	33.6	65	61	0.54	−0.14	0.73	L	M
330 Office machinery	H	8.0	42.3	49.7	56	46	−0.33	0.40	0.58	M	H
251 Basic chemicals	M	n.a.	n.a.	n.a.	n.a.	n.a.	n.a.	n.a.	n.a.	H	M
491 Jewelry	M	n.a.	n.a.	n.a.	26	34	0.13	−0.39	−0.76	n.a.	M

n.a. = not applicable

Sources: NTB level: Buigues and Ilzkovitz (1988); economies of scale: Nerb (1988) and Pratten (1988); R&D intensity; Jacquemin and Sapir (1988b); other indicators: own computations based on EC data.

The RCA index is computed separately for the EC, the US, and Japan. Clearly, although it is meant to reflect comparative advantages, the index also captures barriers to trade. The last two columns of the table display the degree of scale economies and of research and development (R&D) intensity.

In order to assess the external impact of the internal market, I have ranked the 40 sectors according to the importance of domestic producers in their local market. Three groups of sectors can be distinguished. Group 1 comprises eleven sectors where domestic producers are, so far, practically unrivaled, accounting for at least 78 percent of sales on their local market. Group 2 includes 14 sectors where domestic producers, although they remain the principal suppliers of local markets (with a share of between 45 and 70 percent), are under strong competition from Community or third-country firms. Group 3 contains 13 sectors where domestic suppliers account for no more than 40 percent of local sales and, with the exception of two sectors, the main source of supply is foreign. Two sectors could not be classified due to lack of data.

All the sectors included in *group 1* are characterized by a high level of NTBs in the form of either technical barriers (food-processing activities, pharmaceuticals) or government procurement (boilermaking, railway equipment, shipbuilding, insulated wires and cables, electrical machinery). These barriers have prevented imports from within or outside the Community. In general, the completion of the internal market should result in an increase of intra-EC imports at the expense of domestic production. The external impact, however, is likely to vary across three sub-groups of sectors.

In the first sub-group (food-processing activities and pharmaceuticals), extra-EC imports should remain very low due to the strong competitive position of European producers, which is reinforced by strict standards and (for some food products) high transportation costs. The second sub-group comprises two activities displaying important economies of scale, where EC producers have maintained a strong position vis-à-vis their US and Japanese competitors despite the fragmentation of the European market: boilermaking and railway equipment. Here also extra-EC imports should continue at a low level after 1992. The last sub-group contains three sectors where EC producers are losing or have already lost ground against foreign producers, not only in Japan but also the NICs: shipbuilding, insulated wires and cables, and electrical machinery. In all three sectors, the ratio of intra-EC imports to total EC imports has dropped about 10 percentage points between 1973 and 1983. In addition, the EC's RCA indices were relatively low in 1986, especially compared to those of Japan. The external impact of 1992 in these sectors will depend crucially on the EC's trade policy.

With the exception of telecommunications where public procurement is all-important, *group 2* contains sectors displaying a moderate level of nontariff barriers caused by technical standards. These barriers have not, generally, prevented a fair amount of intra- and extra-EC imports. The external impact of removing these barriers will vary between three sub-groups of sectors.

The first sub-group contains sectors where Community producers, although they have lost some ground against other Community suppliers, remain relatively strong competitors on the EC market: rubber products, agricultural machinery, glass and glassware, mining equipment, ceramics, machinery for food industries, and transmission equipment. In these sectors – with the exception of the last two where the market share of foreign producers is already significant – extra-EC imports should stay quite low. The second sub-group includes low- or medium-tech sectors where EC producers have suffered important setbacks in recent years. This is reflected by a severe decline in the ratio of intra-EC trade between 1973 and 1983 (electrical appliances, motor vehicles, machine tools), a negative RCA index in 1986 (photo processing equipment, wool industry) or both (clothing). In some of these sectors, the share of extra-EC imports in the apparent consumption of the member states rivals or even surpasses that of intra-EC imports. As a result of their loss of competitiveness, European producers in some of these sectors have obtained various forms of protection, including national quotas or VERs. Decisions on the future of quotas and VERs in the Community will be critical for the external impact of 1992. The last sub-group contains only one sector, namely telecommunications, a high-tech sector characterized by important economies of scale. The fragmentation of the EC market has fostered domestic production and extra-EC imports (mainly from the US) at the expense of intra-EC imports. This is one of the few sectors, among those shown in table 12.4, where the RCA index of the EC is smaller than that of both the United States and Japan. The completion of the internal market should help European producers to expand production, lower their costs and, hence, regain some group. The fact that it is regarded as vital means that, besides various subsidies, this sector might receive protection at the Community level. Altogether, the effect of 1992 might well be both cost reduction (i.e. an increase in domestic production) and trade suppression (i.e. a decrease in extra-Community imports).

Like the previous group, *group 3* comprises sectors with generally moderate nontariff barriers resulting from technical standards. Three exceptions are medical equipment, aerospace and office machinery (including computers), which are relatively dependent on public procurement. Despite (or because of) these barriers, foreign producers already dominate the market in the member states. Consequently, the completion of the internal market, in itself, should have only a limited impact on trade in these sectors – as long as trade policy remains unchanged. However, in two sectors 1992 might increase the share of domestic producers and intra-EC imports in consumption at the expense of extra-EC imports. The first one is aerospace, a high-tech sector characterized by important economies of scale and, like telecommunications, suffering from the fragmentation of the European market. The second possible candidate for cost reduction and trade suppression is computers, another high-tech sector where the RCA index of the EC is well below that of both the United States and Japan.

In conclusion, the external impact of 1992 will vary substantially across sectors, with two clearly distinct categories of activities. In the *first category* the completion of the internal market will have relatively little external impact because EC suppliers have either a very strong competitive position (most sectors in group 1) or a very weak one (most sectors in group 3). Yet, some of these industries could be affected by changes in trade policy not directly related to the completion of the internal market. The *second category* comprises sectors, many with a declining competitive position of EC producers, where most of the impact of 1992 on foreign producers can be expected. The nature of this impact will depend upon the underlying determinants of trade. When the loss of competitiveness is due to changing comparative advantages in low or medium R&D-intensive industries characterized by a low or medium level-of-scale economies (many sectors in group 2, but also others such as shipbuilding, footwear, or textiles), foreign producers should benefit from 1992. However, in high-tech sectors featuring relatively important scale economies (such as telecom-munications, aerospace or, to a lesser extent, computers), the removal of barriers fragmenting the EC market could help revitalize European producers at the expense of foreign ones. Equally influential, however, in shaping the external impact will be the Community's trade policy. In low- or medium-tech industries, there is a danger that trade policy may be used instead of much needed (and more effective) structural adjustment measures. At the same time, policy-makers influenced by interest-group pressures may apply neo-infant-industry protection to high-tech oligo-polistic industries when other policies (such as research programmes and increased competition) seem more relevant in the national interest (see, for instance, Geroski and Jacquemin (1985)).

4   1992 and the Uruguay Round

The creation of a large single market is expected to revitalize the European economy by fostering competition and improving resource allocation. Hence, the removal of barriers within the Community should promote structural changes and economic growth. This scenario, if successful, is likely to promote world trade and augment extra-Community imports via a direct (traditional) income effect and an indirect one. The latter is a *political economy effect*: more rapid economic growth would reduce unemployment in the EC and, hence, the demand for protectionism (see Grilli (1988) which documents the link between unemployment and the "new" protectionism of the 1970s and 1980s in Europe). On this account, 1992 can be expected to play an important role in shaping up a more open European commercial policy.

Nonetheless, third countries fear that the completion of the internal market will result in greater discrimination between EC members and non-members. The fact that only EC countries can enjoy improved access to the Community market might, indeed, lead to a reduction of extra-EC imports. The possibility of trade diversion could be avoided if (as it was the case during the Dillon and Kennedy Rounds with customs duties) the elimination of barriers inside the Community were accompanied by a similar lowering of external barriers. The key question for third countries is, therefore, whether they will also be able to improve their access to the Community, and under what conditions. Put it differently: what kind of reciprocity will the Community demand from its trading partners in order to grant them the benefits of the fully liberalized internal market?

Two types of trade policy measures associated with 1992 must be distinguished when it comes to reciprocity: those already covered by GATT and those that are not. For measures covered by the Agreement, a further distinction must be drawn between situations where the Community is bound by the principle of non-discrimination and instances where Article XXIV can be applied. If the MFN principle prevails, the Community must extend the benefits of 1992 to all GATT members without any reciprocal concessions. For matters covered by GATT, the Community can only seek reciprocity if it is able to maintain an element of discrimination between members and non-members (like the common external tariff) by virtue of Article XXIV. In principle, the quest for reciprocity would need to respect the GATT rule of multilateralism. The situation is entirely different for trade measures not covered by GATT, where the Community is free to seek full reciprocal benefits from its partners via either bilateral or multilateral negotiations.

Where *trade in goods* is concerned, the analysis in section 3 has identified some of the commercial policy instruments that will require action by the EC in connection with 1992: quantitative restrictions, safeguards, technical barriers, and government procurement. I will briefly review the treatment of these instruments in GATT.

The Agreement calls for the general elimination of quantitative restrictions to trade subject to a number of qualifications, including an escape clause (Article XIX) intended to safeguard domestic industries seriously injured by imports. Article XIX insists on equal treatment of all imports of specific products and compensation of supplying countries. In reality the article has been largely ignored as countries apply selective discriminatory quotas and VERs in violation of GATT rules. The Tokyo Round attempted to bring safeguard actions back within the boundaries of GATT, but stumbled on the issue of selectivity. The safeguard issue is back on the agenda of the Uruguay Round, with selectivity again the dominant concern for negotiators. Proponents of selectivity, primarily the EC, argue that safeguard actions should apply only to countries causing the injury, therefore reducing the use of protection. On the other hand, many of the smaller (especially developing) countries in GATT stress that selectivity in fact increases protection by lowering the costs of safeguard actions to the importing country. These countries are particularly keen on the non-discriminatory application of Article XIX in order to prevent large countries from abusing their bargaining power in bilateral negotiations (see Sampson, 1987). Unless an agreement limiting selectivity can be reached in the Uruguay Round, small countries may fear that the abolition of border controls and the abrogation of Article 115 will be detrimental to their interests. The transformation of national quotas into Community quotas (or VERs) after 1992 would, then, reduce their retaliatory power against selective measures taken by a block of twelve countries instead of individual member states.

The Tokyo Round was the first comprehensive attempt to bring nontariff barriers within the discipline of GATT. It produced a series of agreements on codes of conduct for NTBs, two of which have direct relevance for the completion of the internal market: the agreement on technical barriers to trade and the agreement on government procurement. Both codes provide rules on national and non-discriminatory treatment of imported products originating from signatory trading partners. There is some legal confusion about the possibility for the Community to invoke the rules on free trade areas in Article XXIV with respect to these two codes (see Steenbergen, 1983). Accordingly, it is not clear whether the Community is able to apply different technical regulations or public purchasing practices to member states and third countries, and therefore to seek reciprocity in GATT negotiations on matters covered by the codes. The coverage of the GATT codes, however, is much more restrictive than the 1992 project. For instance, the standards code does not deal adequately with testing and certification procedures; and the government procurement code does not apply to the key sectors of transport, energy, water supply and telecommunications, nor to all public authorities. That means the Community enjoys large discretionary power in negotiating access to the EC market either bilaterally or multilaterally.

The discretionary power of the EC is even larger for *trade in services*, an area not at all covered by GATT rules where the demands for reciprocity in Europe are loudest. The freedom to provide services within the Community after 1992 will imply that firms from any member state will be granted rights of establishment and national treatment throughout the Community. Since Article 58 of the Treaty of Rome considers foreign-owned subsidiaries as nationals of member states, it means they will have full access to the unified internal market even though their home country might not grant such treatment to EC firms. For instance, Sweden and France might have a bilateral agreement allowing the establishment of banks; after 1992 a

Swedish subsidiary already established in France would be able to provide services to Germany, although German banks might not be allowed to do business in Sweden for lack of bilateral agreement. Similarly, Belgium and the State of New York might have a bilateral understanding granting New York banks established in Belgium access to the entire Community market after 1992, while neither Belgian nor other Community banks might have access to California's market.

All these areas of the internal market project where GATT rules are either inadequate, incomplete or nonexistent are on the agenda of the Uruguay Round. Since the Community does intend to seek reciprocal benefits from its trading partners, this provides an opportunity to choose between bilateral reciprocity and multilateral negotiations. There are several reasons why the Community should favor the latter option. First, full multilateral reciprocity in the GATT sense (i.e., a broad balance of concessions by all parties) offers more opportunities for trade-offs, would permit greater specialization, and hence more gains from trade (see, for instance, Baldwin (1987)). Yet, some degree of bilateral reciprocity might be necessary to prevent free riding and unfairness from generating political opposition to trade liberalization. Second, bilateral reciprocity, especially if it focuses on a particular sector, would heighten trade disputes. Instead, multilateralism would tend to diffuse the confrontational facets of trade negotiations. Finally, bilateral reciprocity would enable the Community to expand its exports (or curtail its imports) at the expense of smaller trading partners. This would run counter to the international responsibility of the Community and the objective of European integration to foster "the harmonious development of world trade."

Conclusion

Liberalization of the European internal market offers the prospect of important economic gains through greater specialization in production. The other side of the coin, however, may be painful adjustment and income redistribution which could lead to greater protection against third countries.

During the early phase of European integration the political costs of trade liberalization were lessened by two factors. The first one was the increase of intra-industry specialization rather than inter-industry specialization. This phenomenon occured not only within the Community but also with third countries as trade expansion focused primarily on industrialized nations with similar production patterns. Agriculture, the one area where trade liberalization among industrialized countries could have led to substantial inter-industry specialization, was excluded from the process of tariff reduction precisely to avoid painful political problems. The second factor which lessened the political costs of trade liberalization was the environment of growing incomes worldwide. The growth of income was such that the decline of market in industries losing to foreign competition was often merely relative rather than absolute, thereby reducing the need for onerous adjustment.

The 1992 programme is likely to require much greater economic adjustment, not least because of the disparities in economic configurations among the present twelve member states. But even among countries with relatively similar economic conditions, the removal of existing nontariff barriers is likely to cause important changes. For instance, the opening up of national public procurement should leave only a few of the present European producers after 1992 in certain industries subject to important economies of scale. At the same time, the present environment of slow growth of the world economy renders adjustment much more painful. The political costs of 1992 could, therefore, be substantial.

These costs, and the risk of greater protection against third countries, can be avoided. One crucial element will be the translation of much-needed political consensus into sufficient resources for structural adjustment so as to ensure that no one loses from the completion of the European internal market. Another factor, already at work in the late 1980s, is the positive climate created by the potential benefits of the single market in terms of higher income and lower unemployment. In fact, one the remarkable achievements of the 1992 programmes has been the transformation of "Euro-pessimism" into "Euro-optimism." This climate is essential for the success not only of European integration but also of the Uruguay Round: 1990 and 1992 in fact do come together!

Note

The author is grateful to Bela Balassa, Pierre Buigues, Nicole Dewandre, Enzo Grilli, Fabienne Ilzkovitz, Alexis Jacquemin, Anne Krueger and Alan Winters for helpful comments on an earlier draft. The findings, interpretations, and conclusions are the author's own. They should not be attributed to any person or organization.

References

Balassa, B. 1975: "Introduction: The Common Market experience," in B. Balassa (ed.), *European Economic Integration*, Amsterdam: North Holland.

Baldwin, R. E. 1987: "Multilateral liberalization," in Finger and Olechowski (1987).

Bhagwati, J. N. 1988: *Protectionism*, Cambridge, MA: MIT Press.

Bourgeois, J. H. J. 1983: "The Common commercial policy – Scope and nature of the powers," in Völker (1983).

Buigues, P. and Ilzkovitz, F. 1988: "The sectoral impact of the internal market," Commission of the European Communities, mimeo.

Commission of the European Communities 1988: "The economics of 1992," *European Economy*, 35, 1–235.

Corden, W. M. 1972: "Economies of scale and customs union theory," *Journal of Political Economy*, 80, 465–75, reprinted by Jacquemin and Sapir (eds) (1989).

Finger, J. M. and A. Olechowski (eds) 1987: *The Uruguay Round: A Handbook on the Multilateral Trade Negotiations*, Washing, DC: The World Bank.

Geroski, P. and Jacquemin, A. 1985: "Corporate competitiveness in Europe," *Economic Policy*, 1, 169–218, reprinted in Jacquemin and Sapir (eds) (1989).

Grilli, E. 1988: "The macroeconomic determinants of trade protectionism in the 1970s and 1980s," *The World Economy*, 11.

Hindley, B. 1986: "European Community imports of VCRs from Japan," *Journal of World Trade Law*, 20, 168–84.

Hine, R. C. 1985: *The Political Economy of European Trade – An Introduction to the Trade Policies of the EEC*, Brighton: Wheatsheaf Books.

Hirschman, A. O. 1981: *Essays in Trespassing – Economics to Politics and Beyond*, Cambridge: Cambridge University Press.

Jacquemin, A. and Sapir, A. 1988b: "European integration or world integration?" *Weltwirtschaftliches Archiv*, 124, 127–39.

Jacquemin, A. and Sapir, A. 1988b: "International trade and integration of the European Community: An econometric analysis," *European Economic Review*, 32, reprinted in Jacquemin and Sapir (eds) (1989).

Jacquemin, A. and Sapir, A. (eds) 1989: *The European Internal Market – Trade and Competition*, Oxford: Oxford University Press.

Klepper, G., Weiss, F. D. and Witteler, D. 1987: "Protection in Germany: Toward industrial selectivity," in H. Giersch (ed.), *Free Trade in the World Economy – Towards an Opening of Markets*, Tübingen: J. C. B. Mohr (Paul Siebeck).

Krugman, P. R. 1987: "Economic integration in Europe: Some conceptual issues," in T. Padoa-Schioppa, *Efficiency, Stability and Equity*, Oxford: Oxford University Press, reprinted in Jacquemin and Sapir (eds) (1989).

Krugman, P. R. 1988: "EFTA and 1992," *Occasional Paper No. 23*, Geneva: European Free Trade Association.

Lawrence, R. Z. and Schultze, C. L. (eds) 1987: *Barriers to European Growth: A Transatlantic View*, Washington, DC: Brookings.

Nerb, G. 1988: "The completion of the internal market: A survey of European industry's perception of the likely effects," *The Costs of Non-Europe*, vol. 1, Brussels: Commission of the European Communities.

Nogues, J., Olechowski, A. and Winters, L. A. 1986: "The extent of non-tariff barriers to imports of industrial countries," *The World Bank Development Review*, 1, 181–99.

Owen, N. 1983: *Economies of Scale, Competitiveness, and Trade Patterns within the European Community*, Oxford: Clarendon Press.

Pelkmans, J. and Winters, L. A. 1988: *Europe's Domestic Market*, Chatham House Papers – 43, London: Routledge, for The Royal Institute of International Affairs.

Pelkmans, J. 1984: *Market Integration in the European Community*, The Hague: Martinus Nijhoff.

Pomfret, R. 1988: *Unequal Trade – The Economics of Discriminatory International Trade Policies*, Oxford: Basil Blackwell.

Pratten, C. 1988: "A survey of the economies of scale," *The Costs of Non-Europe*, vol. 2, Brussels: Commission of the European Communities.

Sampson, G. 1987: "Safeguards," in Finger and Olechowski (1987).

Steenbergen, J. 1983: "Trade regulations after the Tokyo Round," in Völker (1983).

Viner, J. 1950: *The Customs Union Issue*, New York: Carnegie Endowment for International Peace.

Völker, E. L. M. (ed.) 1983: *Protectionism and the European Community*, Deventer: Kluwer.

Winters, L. A. 1988: "Completing the European internal market – Some notes on trade policy," *European Economic Review*, 32.

Part IV

Empirical Studies of Trade Issues

13

The Structure and Effects of Tariff and Nontariff Barriers in 1983

EDWARD E. LEAMER

Tariffs have relatively clear primary effects on product prices and arguable secondary effects on employment, earnings, profits, consumer welfare, etc. Nontariff barriers, on the other hand, have quite unclear effects on product prices, and largely unknown secondary effects. For those who find it desirable to know what their governments are doing, the apparent increase in nontariff barriers is thus a cause for concern. Indeed, it may be conjectured that the primary reason for nontariff barriers is precisely that their effects can only be guessed, and the resultant uncertainty diffuses the political response that would be made to tariffs of equal restrictiveness. Many will therefore welcome quantitative information on the restrictiveness of nontariff barriers.

This paper reports some results on the estimation of the effects of tariff and nontariff barriers using cross-section data collected in 1983. The theory on which the method of estimation rests is presented in section 1. Section 2 describes the sources of the data that are analyzed. Section 3 discusses tables and graphs of the data. Section 4 reports the econometric estimates.

A fundamental problem facing the estimation of the effects of trade barriers is caused by the dimension of the data sets that might be analyzed. These data sets are very thin in terms of number of years of data, fairly thin in terms of the number of countries imposing trade barriers, and very thick in terms of the number of commodities. It is accordingly essential to use the cross-commodity variation to estimate the effects of the barriers. But relying on the cross-commodity experiment can be uncomfortable. This is like estimating a demand equation by comparing demand of different commodities. Suppose, for example, that apples face low barriers and have high imports, but oranges face high trade barriers and have low imports. Is this evidence that barriers deter trade? If you think so, suppose that the commodities were wheat and automobiles.

In other papers, Leamer (1988) and Leamer and Bowen (1981), I have shown that the traditional Heckscher–Ohlin–Vanek theory of trade offers a very insecure footing to these cross-commodity regressions. But in the absence of a longer time series, or more countries, we are forced to rely on what we have: lots of commodities. Accordingly, in this paper estimates of the effects of barriers are based partly on cross-country variability but also on cross-commodity variability of barriers and imports. A justification of this kind of regression is offered in section 1 which presents a general equilibrium model with log-linear production and utility. This model implies that net exports of selected commodities depend on country and commodity scale variables, trade barriers, and interactions between country and commodity characteristics. The statistical models that are used to analyze the data set are loosely based on this general equilibrium model. One kind of model controls for differences in commodity and country with dummy variables. The other kind retains the commodity dummies but includes also interactions between measured country characteristics and commodity characteristics. Models are estimated with an overall measure of nontariff barriers and also barriers disaggregated into quantitative restrictions, price maintenance barriers, quality controls and threats.

The goal here is to estimate the impact that trade barriers have had on trade, and, in effect, to "score" countries according to their degree of "openness." Overall, barriers are estimated using one model to have reduced imports of the 14 importers included in the data base by about 4 percent, 3 percent due to nontariff barriers and 1 percent due to tariff barriers. A surprise is that although the Japanese have very frequent barriers, one estimated model suggests that these barriers have been largely ineffective. Disaggregation of the barriers leads to the conclusion that quality regulations have the greatest impact, which is a finding that offsets the conclusion that the Japanese barriers are relatively ineffective.

These results have to be viewed with some scepticism. The connection between the theory and the estimated model is weak enough to be uncomfortable. No attempt has been made to treat the simultaneous equations problem caused by the fact that barriers may be put in place in response to high import levels. The sensitivity analyses that should be carried out to support these inferences are limited. Nonetheless, the results are of interest, if only in pointing to the ways that data analyses can (and cannot) help us understand the effects of barriers.

1 A general equilibrium model

A theoretical foundation is important for any data analysis, especially one that tries to draw inferences about price elasticities from cross-commodity variation in prices and quantities. A natural starting point is the traditional general equilibrium model which is based on the assumptions: (1) identical homothetic tastes, (2) constant returns to scale and identical technologies, (3) perfect competition in the goods and factor markets, (4) costless international exchange of commodities, (5) internationally immobile factors of production that can move costlessly among industries within a country, (6) equal numbers of goods and factors, and (7) sufficient similarities in factor endowments that countries are all in the same "cone of diversification.'' These assumptions imply that all countries have the same factor prices (factor price equalization), and identical input/output ratios.

The production side of the general equilibrium model can be summarized by the system of equations:

$$Q = A^{-1}V \tag{13.1}$$

$$w = A'^{-1}p \tag{13.2}$$

$$A = A(w, t) \tag{13.3}$$

where Q is the vector of outputs, V is the vector of factor supplies, A is the input-output matrix with elements equal to the amount of a factor used to produce a unit of a good, p is the vector of commodity prices, and w is the vector of factor returns. Equation (13.1), which translates factor supplies V into outputs Q, is the inverted form of the factor market equilibrium conditions equating the supply of factors V to the demand for factors AQ. Equation (13.2), which translates product prices into factor prices, is the inverted form of the zero profit conditions equating product prices p to production costs $A'w$. Equation (13.3) expresses the dependence of input intensities on factor prices w and on the state of technology t, $A(w, t)$ being the cost-minimizing choice of input intensities at time t. The assumption of constant returns to scale implies that A depends on the factor returns w but not on the scale of output Q.

In the absence of barriers to trade, all individuals are assumed to face the same commodity prices, and if they have identical homothetic tastes, then they consume in the same proportions:

$$C = sC_w = sA^{-1}V_w \tag{13.4}$$

where C is the consumption vector, C_w is the world consumption vector, V_w is the vector of world resource supplies, and s is the consumption share. Thus trade is

$$T = Q - C = A^{-1}V - sA^{-1}V_w = A^{-1}(V - sV_w) \tag{13.5}$$

The consumption share s will depend on the level of output and also on the size of the trade balance, $B = \pi'T$, where π is the vector of external prices which in the absence of trade barriers would equal the internal prices p. Premultiplying (13.5) by the vector of prices π and then rearranging produces the consumption share:

$$s = (\pi'A^{-1}V - B)/\pi'A^{-1}V_w = (\text{GNP} - B)/\text{GNP}_w, \tag{13.6}$$

This model without trade barriers is relatively "clean" because prices can be entirely hidden from view and no explicit commitment is necessary to a specific utility function and a specific set of production functions. This follows from the fact that all countries are assumed to face the same prices of traded goods and services. Given a suitable list of assumptions including identical constant-return-to-scale technologies and equal numbers of traded goods and nontraded factors, it can then be shown that all countries have the same prices for the nontraded goods and services as well as for the traded goods and services. Then the input–output intensities $\mathbf{A}$, which are generally price-dependent, are the same for all countries, and for cross-country comparisons at a point in time prices can be suppressed.

When trade barriers are erected, the home prices of commodities must vary from country to country, and the effects of prices can no longer be suppressed. To model the effects of trade barriers it is necessary to make specific assumptions about the elasticities of supply and demand. A convenient way to do that is to use a log-linear (Cobb–Douglas) utility function and log-linear production functions.

Log-linear utility implies that the budget shares are fixed parameters:

$$p_k C_k / Y = \alpha_k \tag{13.7}$$

where C_k is consumption of commodity k, p_k is the internal (tariff inclusive) price, Y is total expenditure and α_k is the fixed expenditure share. Then using the identity that trade is the difference between production and consumption, we can solve for the trade equations as:

$$\mathbf{T} = \mathbf{A}^{-1} \mathbf{V} - \mathbf{P}^{-1} \alpha Y.$$

where $\mathbf{P}$ is a diagonal matrix with internal prices on the diagonal.

The level of a tariff on commodity k will be denoted by t_k and the corresponding external price by π_k. Then the internal price of the commodity is

$$p_k = \pi_k (1 + t_k).$$

Some assumption is necessary concerning the use to which the tariff revenues are put. The most convenient assumption is that these revenues are spent as if they were ordinary income. Expressed differently, we may assume either that tariff revenues are redistributed to consumers in a way that does not distort their consumption choices or alternatively that the government has the same utility function as the "representative consumer." Then we may solve for the expenditure level of the economy by imposing the trade balance condition $B = \pi' T$:

$$Y = (\pi' \mathbf{A}^{-1} \mathbf{V} - B)/(\pi' \mathbf{P}^{-1} \alpha) = (\text{GNP} - B)(1 + t.), \tag{13.8}$$

where GNP is the value of output at world prices $\pi' \mathbf{A}^{-1} \mathbf{V}$, and $t.$ is an index of trade barriers overall:

$$(1 + t.) = (\Sigma \alpha_k / (1 + t_k))^{-1}. \tag{13.9}$$

Incidentally, the summation in this expression extends over all commodities, including export items. For example, if tariffs are uniformly set to t for all import commodities, then $(1 + t.) = (1 + t)/1 + \alpha_x t)$ where α_x is the share of imports and exports in consumption.

Cobb–Douglas (log-linear) production functions and cost minimization imply fixed factor shares: $\theta_{fk} = w_f A_{fk}/p_k$ where θ_{fk} is a technologically fixed parameter, w is the factor return, p is the product price and A is the input-output ratio. In matrix form this becomes

$$\Theta = \mathbf{W}\,\mathbf{A}\,\mathbf{P}^{-1},$$

where Θ is a matrix of technologically fixed factor shares and where notation indicating the dependence of all of the variables on time is suppressed. Substituting this into (13.1) yields the production relationships

$$\Theta\,\mathbf{P}\,\mathbf{Q} = \mathbf{W}\,\mathbf{V}.$$

In words, the product of the input shares Θ matrix times the value of output $\mathbf{PQ}$ is equal to the value of the input $\mathbf{WV}$.

The Stolper–Samuelson mapping of commodity prices into factor prices given this Cobb–Douglas technology can be found by substituting the cost minimization condition for selecting the amount of input f in commodity k, $V_{fk} = \theta_{fk} p_k Q_k / w_f$, into the unit *value* isoquants $1 = p_k Q_k$ which can be written as:

$$0 = \ln(p_k) + \ln(\alpha_k) + \Sigma_f \theta_{kf} \ln(V_{fk}), \quad k = 1, 2, \ldots,$$

After substitution this produces the system:

$$\Theta' \ln(\mathbf{w}) = \ln(\mathbf{p}) + \ln(\mathbf{k}) \tag{13.10}$$

where $\ln(\mathbf{w})$ is a vector of logarithms of factor returns, $\ln(\mathbf{p})$ is a vector of logarithms of prices, and $\ln(\mathbf{k})$ is a vector of constants. Solving this system for factor returns as a function of product prices we obtain:

$$\log(w_f) = c_f + \Sigma \log(p_k)\theta^{kf} = c'_f + \Sigma \log(1 + t_k)\theta^{kf} \tag{13.11}$$

where θ^{kf} is the (k, f) element of the inverse of Θ and where c_f and c'_f are suitably selected constants.

Under these assumptions the trade vector satisfies

$$\mathbf{PT} = \Theta^{-1}\mathbf{W}\mathbf{V} - \alpha Y = \Theta^{-1}\mathbf{W}\mathbf{V} - \alpha\,\mathrm{GNP}\,(1 + t.) \tag{13.12}$$

where the internal factor prices $\mathbf{W}$ are functions of the product prices according to the log-linear relationship (13.10). In words, the net export vector evaluated at internal prices is a function of factor supplies evaluated at internal prices and the product of GNP evaluated at external prices times an index of trade barriers.

Equations (13.11) and (13.12) fully describe the effects of tariffs in this general equilibrium model with logarithmic production functions and logarithmic utility functions. The principle effect of the tariff in the trade system (13.12) is to revalue the factor supplies $\mathbf{V}$ and the trade flows $\mathbf{T}$. The revaluation of the factor supplies is described by the system of equations (13.11).

The equation for commodity k taken from the system (13.12) is

$$\pi_k T_{ik} = \{\Sigma_f[\theta^{kf} w_{if} V_{if}] - \alpha_k\,\mathrm{GNP}_i(1 + t_i)]\}/(1 + t_{ik}) \tag{13.13}$$

where $\pi_k T_{ik}$ is the (f.o.b.) value of net exports of commodity k by country i, t_{ik} is the tariff barrier on commodity k in country i, V_{if} is the supply of factor f in country i, $t_{i.}$ is the tariff average of country i, θ^{kf} is a component of the inverse of the factor share matrix Θ^{-1}, α_k is the consumption share of commodity k, and w_{if} is the internal reward to factor f in country i satisfying (13.11). The model consisting of equations (13.11) and (13.13) presents many puzzles for a data analysis. One of the more difficult problems is that (13.11) involves the elements of the *inverse* of the factor input matrix θ^{kf}. Some input shares are observable, but given the large number of commodities, it is unlikely that there will be a square matrix of shares. Moreover, any attempt to include variables like the elements of an inverse of input intensities is surely taking the n-good n-factor general equilibrium model too seriously.

One "solution" is to note that we can generally write an element of the inverse of the factor share matrix as a function of the corresponding element of the matrix

$$\theta^{kf} = \beta_{kf}/\theta_{kf}$$

where β_{kf} is an unobservable with a value implied by the partitioned inverse rule. If the matrix is arranged so that kf selects a diagonal element, then

$$\theta^{kf} = \det(\Theta_{(fk)})/\det(\Theta)$$
$$= \det(\Theta_{(fk)})/\theta_{fk}\det(\Theta_{(fk)} - \Theta_{(k)}\Theta_{(f)}'/\theta_{fk})$$

where det( ) refers to a determinant, $\Theta_{(fk)}$ is the submatrix of Θ with row f and column k omitted, $\Theta_{(k)}$ is column k with element f omitted and $\Theta_{(f)}$ is column f with element k omitted. Thus

$$\beta_{kf} = \det(\Theta_{(fk)})/\det(\Theta_{(fk)} - \Theta_{(k)}\Theta_{(f)}'/\theta_{fk})$$

which is equal to one if this factor is not used in any other industry, $\Theta_{(f)} = 0$, or if this industry uses only this factor $\Theta_{(k)} = 0$. An empirical approximation to this assumption is that

$$\beta_{kf} = 1 + \epsilon_{kf}$$

where ϵ_{kf} is a random variable with mean zero.

Another approximation is that the structure of barriers has a negligible effect on the earnings of the factors,

$$w_{if} = w_f$$

With these assumptions, (13.13) becomes

$$\pi_k T_{ik} = \{\Sigma_f[(1 + \epsilon_{kf})w_f V_{if}/\theta_{kf}] - \alpha_k \text{ GNP}_i(1 + t_{i.})]\}/(1 + t_{ik})$$
$$= \text{GNP}_i\{\Sigma_f[(1 + \epsilon_{kf})s_{if}/\theta_{kf}] - \alpha_k(1 + t_{i.})]\}/(1 + t_{ik}) \tag{13.14}$$

where s_{if} is the share of earnings of factor f in country i, $s_{if} = w_f V_{if}/\text{GNP}_i$.

Equation (13.14) is the loose justification for running a regression of the logarithm of imports on measures of trade barriers, a country scale variable

(GNP$_i$), a commodity scale variable α_k, and interactions between country factor supplies and industry input intensities s_{if}/θ_{kf}. The first set of regressions do not use any observables but control for differences in countries and commodities with a set of dummy variables only. The second set of estimates use GNP and the interaction variables s_{if}/θ_{kf} but control for commodity scale differences with a set of dummy variables since direct measures of the consumption scale variables α_k are unobservable.

Clearly this offers only a loose justification for the cross-section data analysis. A couple of untreated problems are worth mentioning: (a) This model of *net* exports does not justify treating exports and imports separately, and (b) the data that are analyzed are aggregated at least to some extent. This model of *net exports* can be aggregated easily, but aggregation separately for imports and exports producers an extremely complex model that is unlikely to be amenable to a data analysis. Accordingly, the model offers little foundation for the analysis of the effects of barriers on the gross imports and commodity aggregates.

2   Overview of data set

The main features of the trade data set that is the subject of this analysis are:

Year: 1983.
Importers: Fourteen industrial countries including Finland, Japan, Norway, Switzerland, the USA, and the EEC countries: Belgium–Luxembourg, Denmark, France, West Germany, Greece, Ireland, Italy, Netherlands, and the United Kingdom.
Commodity classification: 4-digit Standard Industrial Trade Classification SITC(R1).

The variables that are included are:

Imports
NTB coverage ratios: four categories of import-weighted NTB coverage ratios.
Tariffs: Import-weighted tariff averages

The data set on nontariff barriers has been compiled by UNCTAD as part of an on-going project measuring the extent of nontariff barriers to trade. The express purpose of the project is to reduce the intransparency of national trade policies and to determine the effects of these policies, especially as they relate to the trade of developing countries. Portions of the data set have been turned over to the World Bank where, presumably, they have been manipulated further. The data sources include both GATT and government publications. GATT data normally cover only those measures brought to the attention of the GATT secretariat either by countries applying them or by countries complaining of their application. Sixty percent of the data records were culled from government publications such as those distributed to customs officers. (*Source*: UNCTAD TD/B/940, Annex III).

The difficulties that arise in the construction of this data base must surely be nearly overwhelming. There are substantial problems of classification of barriers that are known to exist and there are extraordinary problems of uncovering barriers. UNCTAD(1985) reports: "Clearly the compilation, updating and extension of the Data Base is a highly complex and detailed exercise, but its usefulness is highly dependent on the accuracy of the data and its correct classification. Thus, the data has been checked to the extent possible, and to this end, the UNCTAD secretariat has sought the active collaboration of Governments . . . These consultations have enabled the secretariat to obtain clarifications and additional information." This leaves the impression that the presence or absence of a barrier on the data base is the result of a complex negotiation between representatives of the states included in the data set and representatives of UNCTAD.

Coverage of barriers

This data set on nontariff and tariff barriers is incomplete in several respects:

1 Only product-specific barriers are included. General barriers are excluded. Excluded are measures such as national import-substitution policies, global import targets, foreign exchange controls, state monopoly of imports, discriminatory financing charges favoring exporters over importers, tax structures, capital controls etc.
2 Domestic subsidies and export measures are excluded. States which rely less on border measures against imports and relatively more on non-border measures will appear to have relatively low trade barriers.
3 No record of tariff or nontariff barriers exists if imports are zero.

NTB aggregation

The basic data set includes 52 different product-specific nontariff barriers ranging from wildlife prohibitions to Voluntary Export Restraint programs. These 52 different barriers have been arranged hierarchically as reported in table 13.1. The main division of NTBs consists of the following four groups:

1 *Price Maintenance* NTB's that attempt to control the domestic price of the imported goods.
2 *Quantitative Restrictions* that limit the quantity of imports.

Table 13.1 Classification of nontariff barriers

A Price-oriented policies

Tariffs	ad valorem	seasonal 100.11
		charges on declared value 101.1
	non-ad valorem	specific	two-part tariff 100.02
			seasonal tariff 100.12
			charges on declared value 101.2
			(product-) specific taxes 112
		combined	ad valorem tariff with specific minimum 100.2
			seasonal tariff 100.14
		other	ad valorem tariff with quota 100.01
			non-ad valorem from tariff file
	unspecified	supplementary tariff 100.3
		two-part tariff 100.0
		seasonal tariff 100.1
Duties and domestic price maintenance	variable duties	variable lavy 102.11
		variable component 102.12
	fair price duties	countervailing duties 102.21
		anti-dumping duties 102.22
	minimum pricing	minimum pricing 401, 402, 403
		VER, price 405
	CAP	Common Agricultural Policy 595

B Quantity-oriented policies

Prohibitions	total	prohibition 201.1; health & safety 201.2; wildlife 201.3; seasonal 201.5; indirect imports 201.7
	conditional	on basis of origin 202.2; state monop. of imp. 202.31
Quotas	ver	VERs 215
	textile	quota/regime 216, 217
		MFA quota/consultation 590, 590.10, 590.13
	other quotas	quota 211; global quota 212; quotas by country 213; seasonal 214

C Quality-oriented policies

Quality control	health & safety	prohibition 201.2; imp. auth. depending on cert. 301.1; technical requirements 501
	technical standards marketing, packing requirements	imp. auth. depending on cert. 301.2; technical requirements 502 technical requirements 503
Other	import auth.	(non-automatic authorizations to control entry) discretionary: import auth. 300.01; discretionary licence 300.02; licence

300.03; declaration with visa 300.04; imp. auth. restr., slct purchasers 300.05; import permit 300.06;
conditional: auth. dep. on purchase of dom. prod. 300.13
(non-automatic authorizations to control standards)
health & safety 301.1; tech. standards 301.2;

D   Threats

Threats	price monitoring	investigations	anti-dumping 41, 411
			countervailing 41, 412
		surveillance 421	
	quantity	(automatic authorizations)	
	monitoring	311 licence for surveillance	
		312 liberal licensing	
		313 automatic licensing	
		314 declaration without visa	
		315 intra-community surveillance	
		317 monitoring	

The numbers correspond to the UNCTAD classification scheme.
Each UNCTAD category maps into only one of our categories. There are three minor exceptions: 201.2, 301.1, and 301.2 each feed into two of our categories.

3   *Quality Regulations* that assure that imports meet certain quality standards.
4   *Threats* that suggest the possibility of future restrictions of an unspecified nature.

In principle, the health and safety regulations could be regarded to be quantitative restrictions that prohibit the importation of certain products, but this observation seems overly pedantic and the separation of health and safety regulations from quantitative restrictions turns out to be informative.

An ideal classification system for nontariff barriers would distinguish trade measures that have substantially different economic effects and would not distinguish measures that have substantially the same economic effects. Suppose, for example, that there were two types of barriers that were signaled in the data set by dummy variables NTB_1 and NTB_2. If imports as a function of the presence of the barriers could be written as $M = \alpha + \beta_1 NTB_1 + \beta_2 NTB_2$, and if these different barriers had identical effects, $\beta_1 = \beta_2$, then we can aggregate to $M = \alpha + \beta NTB$ where $NTB = NTB_1 + NTB_2$.[1] Thus the separate measures NTB_1 and NTB_2 would ideally be retained only if there were a substantial difference in their effects, $\beta_1 \neq \beta_2$.

This ideal classification system seems virtually impossible to achieve in practice because of the great complexity and subtlety of the measures that are used by governments to deter trade. For example, in some countries "automatic" licences are automatically granted only if the importer is an accepted member of a domestic producer association; in other countries automatic licenses are used as part of a monitoring system or can be used, through administrative procedures, to retard imports (usually at a cost to the importer through warehousing and the opportunity cost of capital which is not at work.) It would be an extraordinary task to attempt a classification scheme for NTBs that was broad enough that it would allow one to distinguish one kind of "automatic" licensing from the other, and would also make all other similar subtle distinctions. Even if such a data base did exist, we couldn't deal econometrically with the morass of NTB variables that it would surely include. Some form of aggregation would surely be required.

An ideal NTB grouping scheme clusters barriers which have similar effects within groups and different effects between groups. Our four-part scheme is intended to have this feature but it is built entirely on simplistic theoretical ideas without reference to this data set. Ideally, this aggregation should have been driven partly by a well-organized theory, partly by the data. But it is probably too much to ask of the data to determine very much about the best aggregation scheme. As a matter of fact, it is even difficult to obtain credible estimates of the different effects of our four different categories of measures.

Concordance problems

Parenthetically, it needs to be understood that there are great problems in putting together this data set because of the number of different commodity classification schemes, five in total: CCCN-based systems, TSUS, SITC(R1), SITC(R2), and SIC. The raw non-USA data is presented in CCCN-based classifications. The raw USA data is in TSUS form. Suffice it to say that this causes extraordinary difficulties; a full account will be provided on request.

3 Preliminary data analysis

The presence or absence of a nontariff barrier is signalled in the data set by a variable NTB_{ijkn} taking on the value one if a nontariff barrier of type n is applied against the imports of commodity k by importer i from exporter j. These NTB indicators are aggregated to form NTB coverage ratios applicable to importer group I, exporter group J, commodity group K and NTB group N:

$$NTB_{IJKN} = \sum_{i \in I, j \in J, k \in K} w_{ijk} \, NTB_{ijkN}$$

$$NTB_{ijkN} = \underset{n \in N}{Max}(NTB_{ijkn})$$

$$w_{ijk} \geq 0,$$

$$\sum_{i \in I, je J, ke K} w_{ijk} = 1$$

The indicator NTB_{ijkN} takes on a value of one if there is an NTB in group N imposed by importer i against the exports of J of commodity K. If the weights are proportional to the level of imports, then these coverage ratios are equal to the percentage of a commodity class covered by an NTB of type N. Note that if NTB group N is disaggregated into subclasses A and B, then the indicator for the aggregate is generally less than the sum of the indicators for the components, $NTB_{IJKN} \leq NTB_{IJKA} + NTB_{IJKB}$, with equality if and only if no import item is subjected to both an NTB of type A and an NTB of type B.

An ideal but unavailable set of weights in these averages would be the level of imports that would have occurred in the absence of barriers. Three alternative sets of weights are commonly used instead of these ideal weights (e.g. Nogues et al., 1986): home imports, world imports and equal weights. Each of these sets of weights is likely to depart substantially from the ideal. Weighting by home imports understates the ideal coverage ratios if barriers are effective in reducing imports. For example, a country that had strict prohibitions against a subset of commodities and no barriers otherwise would have a zero coverage ratio if own imports are used as weights.

Coverage ratios weighted by total world imports can also suffer from downward bias especially if the commodity structure of barriers is similar in most countries since then the world weights are inappropriately low whenever barriers are severe. However, variability of barriers across importers will make the world weighted coverage ratios less subject to this kind of downward bias. On the other hand, world weighted averages do not take any account of the special features of importers that make them relatively dependent on particular products. To put this differently, the world weighted averages ignore the component of variability in the ideal averages that is due to the ideal variability of weights across countries.

Unweighted averages of NTB indicators seem likely to be even worse approximations to the ideal averages since barriers against commodities with negligible trade are treated the same as barriers against the imports of major commodities. In addition, like world weighted averages, unweighted averages ignore differences in countries that would cause differences in their free-trade import levels.

Own-import weighted NTB coverage ratios for each of the 14 importers, for the EEC countries and for the 14 importers as a group are presented in the first column of numbers in table 13.2. Switzerland has the most frequent

Table 13.2 NTB coverage ratios by importing country weighted by own imports

Importer	All NTBs	Price	Quotas	Health	Threats	Tariff	Tariff CR
Switzerland	47	13	3	**22**	**21**	3	85
Japan	38	3	11	**31**	.	3	67
Finland	35	6	1	**28**	3	5	49
EEC	27	**12**	**13**	4	7	4	49
France	26	5	**18**	2	5	2	23
14 Importers	18	5	7	6	3	3	46
Netherlands	17	**8**	3	3	**7**	2	21
Norway	15	.	9	7	.	5	63
USA	13	5	6	.	3	4	79
Belgium & Luxembourg	12	4	2	6	7	1	14
Denmark	11	**8**	4	.	2	3	34
Great Britain	11	7	4	2	3	3	30
West Germany	10	6	5	1	2	3	29
Italy	8	5	4	2	2	2	20
Greece	7	4	5	1	1	1	16
Ireland	5	3	2	.	1	2	23

"Usually high" coverage ratios in boldface. See text.
. indicates less than 0.5%

NTBs with 47 percent of imports affected. Japan is second with a 38 percent coverage ratio. The countries with the lowest NTB coverage ratios are members of the European Economic Community. According to our data set, there are no barriers on intra-EEC trade, and consequently the coverage ratios for the EEC countries are relatively low. These coverage ratios for the EEC members contrast with the relatively high number of 27 percent for the EEC as a whole, this higher figure referring only to external EEC trade.

Columns 2-5 of table 13.2 contain the figures for the disaggregated NTB coverage ratios: price maintenance NTBs, quantity restrictions, health and safety regulations, and threats. Coverage ratios that are "unusual" are indicated in bold face. These "unusual" ratios are those numbers that are both the largest for the importing country and also exceed the coverage ratio for the 14 importers overall.

By this definition, the Swiss have unusually frequent health and safety regulations and threats. The Japanese have unusually frequent health and safety regulations. The EEC has unusually frequent price maintenance NTBs and quotas. France has frequent quotas. The USA has no unusually frequent NTBs since all of its ratios are smaller than the averages for the 14 importers overall.

The coverage ratios of each of the four types of NTBs are displayed in figure 13.1. Many of the facts that are apparent in the table stand out even more in these figures. Health and Safety Regulations, which for the 14 importers are not unusually frequent, are very frequently applied to the imports of Japan, Finland and Switzerland. Threats are also a frequent barrier in Switzerland, but are not used at all by the Japanese. Quantity restrictions are applied frequently by France, but infrequently by Switzerland and by Finland. Price maintenance NTBs are infrequently used by Japan and Norway.

The last column of table 13.2 contains "tariff coverage ratios" which indicate the percentage of imports to which a tariff is applied. Adjacent to this column are the corresponding tariff averages. The tariffs and tariff coverage ratios are displayed in figures 13.2a and 13.2b with importers ordered by overall NTB ratio, as in figure 13.1. If countries with high NTB coverage ratios had also high tariff coverage ratios and high tariffs, then figures 13.2a and 13.2b would look like figure 13.1, with the relatively long bars on the left of the figure. Figure 13.2a does have some similarities with figure 13.1, but the USA and Norway are clear outliers with unusually frequent tariffs. Belgium-Luxembourg is an exception going the other way: relatively infrequent tariffs. The tendency of the numbers to decline as the eye moves to the right is less evident in figure 13.2b, which displays the tariff averages. Thus, although there is some tendency for countries with frequent tariff barriers also to have frequent nontariff barriers, there is less of a relationship between nontariff barriers and tariff averages.

Tables 13.4 and 13.5 contain coverage ratios applicable to the ten commodity groups constructed by Leamer (1984) on the basis of similarity

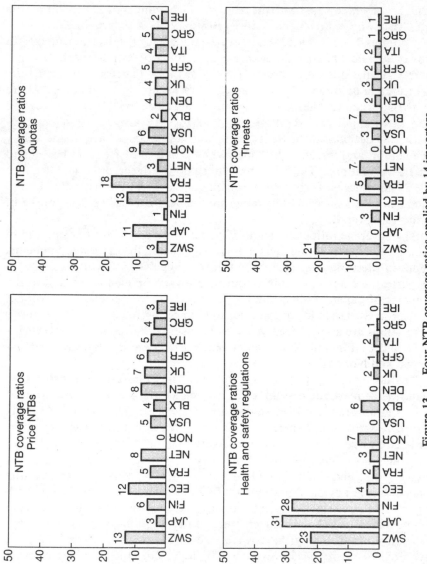

Figure 13.1   Four NTB coverage ratios applied by 14 importers

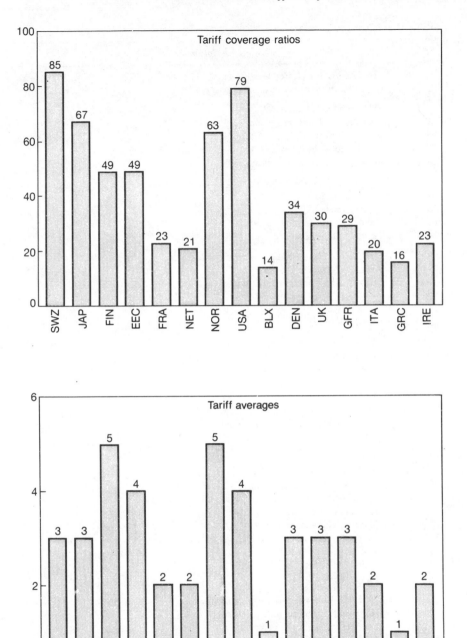

Figure 13.2 Tariff coverage ratios and tariff rates by 14 importers

Table 13.3   Commodity aggregates

SITC	Description
	1 PETRO: Petroleum
33	Petroleum, petroleum products
	2 MAT: Raw materials
27	Crude fertilizers, crude materials
28	Metalliferous ores, metal scrap
32	Coal, coke, briquettes
34	Gas, natural and manufactured
	3 FOR: Forest products
24	Wood, lumber, cork
25	Pulp, waste paper
63	Wood, cork manufactures
64	Paper, paperboard
	4 TROP: Tropical agricultural products
5	Fruit, vegetables
6	Sugar, sugar preparations, honey
7	Coffee, tea, cocoa, spices, etc.
11	Beverages
23	Crude rubber
	5 ANL: Animal products
0	Live animals
1	Meat, meat preparations
2	Dairy products, eggs
3	Fish, fish preparations
21	Hides, skins, furskins, undressed
29	Crude animal, vegetable minerals
43	Animal, vegetable oils, processed
94	Animal, not elsewhere specified
	6 CER: Cereals, etc.
4	Cereals, cereal preparations
8	Feeding stuff for animals
9	Miscellaneous food preparations
12	Tobacco, tobacco manufactures
22	Oil seeds, oil nuts, oil kernels
26	Textile fibers
41	Animal oils, fats
42	Fixed vegetable oils
	7 LAB: Labor-intensive manufactures
66	Nonmetallic mineral manufactures
82	Furniture
83	Travel goods, handbags, etc.
84	Clothing
85	Footwear
89	Miscellaneous manufactured articles, n.e.s.
91	Postal packages not classified according to kind
93	Special transactions not classified according to kind
96	Coin, nongold, noncurrent

8   CAP: Capital-intensive manufactures

61	Leather, dressed furskins
62	Rubber manufactures, n.e.s.
65	Textile yan, fabrics, etc.
67	Iron and steel
69	Manufactures of metal
81	Sanitary, fixtures, fittings

9   MACH: Machinery

71	Machinery, other than electrical
72	Electrical machinery
73	Transport equipment
86	Professional goods, instruments, watches
95	Firearms, ammunition

10   CHEM: Chemicals

51	Chemical elements, compounds
52	Mineral tar and crude chem. from coal, petroleum, natural gas
53	Dying, tanning, coloring materials
55	Essential oils, perfume materials
56	Fertilizers, manufactured
57	Explosives, pyrotechnic products
58	Plastic materials, cellulose, etc.
59	Chemical materials, n.e.s.

n.e.s. = not elsewhere specified

of net export patterns. The full description of these aggregates in terms of the two-digit SITC codes is reported in table 13.3. The first two of these aggregates (PETRO and MAT) are raw materials. The next four (FOR, TROP, ANL, CER) are crops and the last four (LAB, CAP, MACH, CHEM) are manufactures. ALL refers to all commodities. These commodity aggregates are roughly arranged to suggest a ladder of development with the least developed countries concentrating exports on the first products (raw materials) and the most developed concentrating exports on the last (chemicals).

To facilitate the reading of table 13.4, coverage ratios in excess of the overall (ALL) average are printed in boldface. This identifies for each importer or importer-collective the products that are most frequently subjected to a nontariff barrier. For the 14 importers overall, it is the crops and raw materials that are subject to especially frequent barriers. Most of the other unusually large numbers are also the coverage ratios applicable to crops.

Departures from the typical pattern of protection are the unusually high coverage ratios applicable to commodities that are not unusually protected by the 14 importers overall. For example, petroleum overall is relatively unprotected with a coverage ratio of 13 percent, but Switzerland, Finland, Netherlands, Norway and Belgium and Luxembourg have unusually

Table 13.4   NTB coverage ratios applicable to ten commodity groups weighted by own imports

	All	PETRO	MAT	FOR	TROP	ANL	CER	LAB	CAP	MACH	CHEM	MISC
Switzerland	47	**98**	6	5	**75**	**94**	**65**	26	12	46	72	.
Japan	38	3	**57**	**52**	**99**	**99**	**80**	18	28	19	**98**	.
Finland	35	**97**	31	3	**41**	**43**	25	**45**	31	.	8	**99**
EEC	27	24	9	17	**60**	**77**	**81**	**40**	**36**	14	6	4
France	26	**71**	19	18	**40**	26	**40**	12	10	9	4	**54**
14 Importers	18	13	**19**	**20**	**37**	**36**	**51**	14	15	13	15	4
Netherlands	17	**24**	8	10	**46**	17	**58**	13	5	4	1	7
Norway	15	**21**	.	.	**98**	**77**	**78**	**32**	2	.	**21**	.
USA	13	.	1	**27**	**18**	**23**	1	3	**27**	**21**	7	.
Belgium & Luxembourg	12	**15**	1	6	**21**	**14**	**40**	**25**	6	5	1	6
Denmark	11	.	.	**15**	**27**	**38**	**53**	**12**	**12**	5	.	6
Great Britain	11	.	1	11	**41**	**34**	**43**	**20**	10	5	1	3
W. Germany	10	.	3	10	**26**	**19**	**49**	**20**	**14**	4	1	3
Italy	8	.	1	**11**	**21**	**18**	**38**	**16**	**19**	4	4	4
Greece	7	.	2	**16**	**13**	**16**	**23**	7	**11**	**9**	.	**17**
Ireland	5	.	.	**12**	**18**	**14**	**20**	2	5	3	1	**9**

Coverage ratios in excess of the ALL average printed in bold
. indicates less than 0.5%

Table 13.5 NTB coverage ratios and tariff measures applicable to ten commodity groups weighted by own imports

IMP Product (%)	All NTBs	Price	Quotas	Health	Threats	Tariff	Tariff CR
4.3 Cereals, etc.	51	**33**	6	**28**	1	2	15
4.5 Tropical agric.	37	**27**	8	**14**	2	6	51
4.4 Animal products	36	**17**	6	**23**	4	3	31
4.0 Forest products	20	5	1	7	9	2	30
8.6 Raw materials	19	.	7	11	2	1	22
100.0 ALL	18	5	7	6	3	3	46
7.6 Capital-intensive	15	6	9	2	7	4	53
7.3 Chemicals	15	3	3	**10**	1	3	37
10.6 Labor-intensive	14	1	9	3	**8**	7	59
20.4 Petroleum	13	1	7	1	4	1	50
26.0 Machinery	13	3	7	2	1	3	59
2.2 Miscellaneous	4	3	3	.	3	.	2

"Unusually high" coverage ratios in boldface. See text.
. indicates less than 0.5%

frequent barriers applied to petroleum products. Some other "outliers" are the frequent barriers against chemicals by the Swiss, the Japanese and the Norwegians, and the frequent barriers against the labor-intensive manufactures by the US and several of the EEC countries.

Table 13.5 contains the disaggregated coverage ratios, tariffs and tariff coverage ratios for the 14 importers overall. Here the commodities are ordered by the overall NTB coverage ratio. As in table 13.2, numbers are printed in boldface that are both among the largest numbers applicable to the commodity and are also larger than the overall averages. This table indicates that the crops are frequently subjected to price maintenance NTBs and to health and safety regulations. Quotas apply to the labor- and capital intensive manufactures. Threats apply to the labor-intensive manufactures.

The commodity profiles of the NTB coverage ratios are graphed in figure 13.3. Quantitative restrictions seem to be fairly uniformly distributed over these commodity classes, but somewhat infrequent on forest products, which are subject to relatively frequent threats. Price maintenance NTBs and health and safety regulations are concentrated on the crops. Threats are especially frequent against forest products, labor- and capital-intensive manufactures.

Figure 13.4 displays the data on tariff averages and tariff coverage ratios applied to each of the commodity groups by the 14 importers. The tariff coverage ratios are typically higher than the NTB coverage ratios, but the tariff averages are generally rather low. Tariffs are relatively high against the labor- and capital-intensive manufactures, and against tropical agricultural products.

4 Estimates of the effects of barriers on imports

The first set of regressions control for differences in importer and commodity with a set of dummy variables. In the model reported subsequently, differences in importer and commodity are explained by a set of variables such as resource supplies for countries and capital/labor ratios for commodities. The model with explicit variables imposes the restrictions that the country and commodity effects are linear combinations of certain observed variables. If these restrictions are correct, the estimates of the effects of trade barriers will be more efficient, but if the restrictions are incorrect, the estimates will be biased and inconsistent. If the data set were large enough in both the commodity and country dimensions, the coefficients on the dummy variables could be estimated accurately, and any restrictions on their values would be unnecessary and probably unwise. But in samples with the number of importers limited to 14, the sample size is unlikely to be large enough to support the dummy variable model. To express this differently, after controlling for commodity and importer with

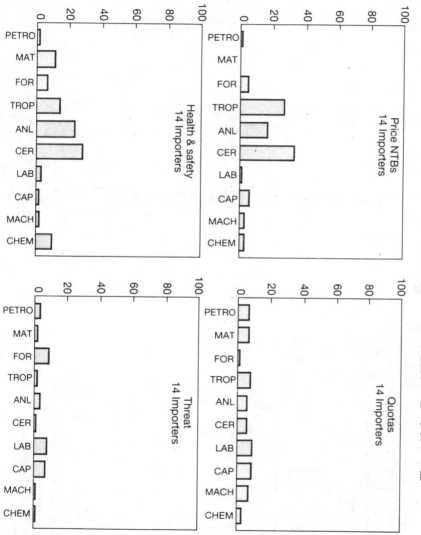

Figure 13.3   Four NTB coverage ratios applicable to major commodity groups

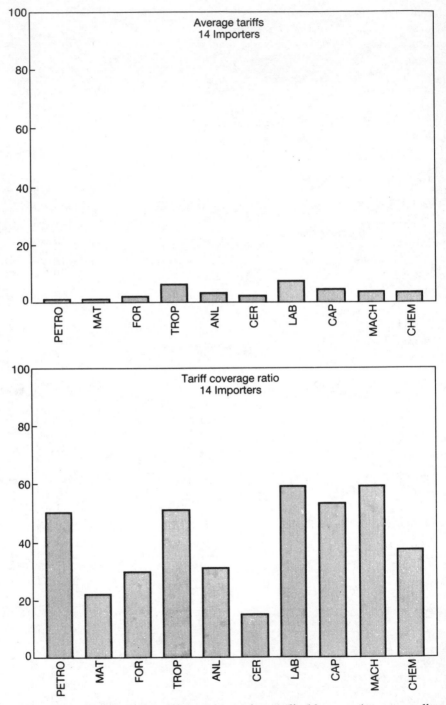

Figure 13.4 Tariffs and tariff coverage ratios applicable to major commodity groups

dummy variables, there may remain very little variation in the variables measuring the barriers, and therefore detecting the effect of the remaining small variation may be impossible. The dummy variable model is none-theless of interest since the estimated effects of trade barriers, though noisy, are nonetheless unbiased.

Formally, the dummy variable models take the general form:

$$\log(M_{ik}) = \alpha_i + \alpha_k + (\beta_i + \beta_k)NTB_{ik} + (\gamma_i + \gamma_k)TAR_{ik}$$
$$+ \beta'' NTB_{i''k} + \gamma'' TAR_{i''k} + \epsilon_{ik} \tag{13.15}$$

i = importer
i'' = importers other than i
k = commodity
M = Imports in thousands of US dollars
NTB = coverage ratio of nontariff barriers, (0.0–1.0)
TAR = import-weighted tariff average (percent, 0–100)

This model allows for both nontariff and tariff barriers to deter trade with effects that vary by importers and commodity. It allows trade to be diverted from other importers(i'') if they have relatively high barriers.

This model can be estimated subject to a number of simplifying assumptions listed in table 13.6. Model 8 is the general unrestricted model. The other models impose one or more restrictions on this general model. The most restrictive model is the first which has the importer, exporter and

Table 13.6   Models with importer and commodity dummy variables
$\log(M_{ik}) = (\alpha_i + \alpha_k) + (\beta_i + \beta_k)\,NTB_{ik} + (\gamma_i + \gamma_k)\,TAR_{ik} + \beta''NTB_{i''k} + \gamma''TAR_{i''k}$

	$(\alpha_i\ \alpha_k)$	$(\beta_i\ \beta_k)$	$(\gamma_i\ \gamma_k)$	(β'')	(γ'')
1	* *	c			
2	* *	c	c		
3	* *	c		*	
4	* *	c	c	*	*
5	* *	* *			
6	* *	* *	c		
7	* *	* *	c	*	*
8	* *	* *	* *	*	*

Cases: * = included, c = constant without the subscript

1: Direct NTB effect
2: Direct NTB and tariff effects
3: Direct NTB and tariff effects and NTB importer diversion
4: All effects of barriers constant
5: Variable direct NTB effect
6: Variable direct NTB effect and constant direct tariff effect
7: Variable direct NTB effect and all other effects
8: Full model

commodity dummies, and the direct NTB effect with a constant coefficient. The second model allows for tariffs as well as NTBs to affect imports. The third and fourth models allow trade diversion through the NTB variable. The fifth includes the tariff effect; the sixth and seventh allow for a variable effect of NTB by importer, exporter and commodity. The eighth includes the diversion variables as well.

The results based on these models are reported in tables 13.7 to 13.11. The full model does better than the smaller models in terms of the adjusted R^2 reported in table 13.8, although the differences are not dramatic. Table 13.7 contains the estimated effect of the trade barriers. This log linear model takes the form $M = \alpha \exp(\beta x)$ where x may refer to a tariff average or an NTB coverage ratio. The ratio of imports at x to imports at $x = 0$ is $\alpha \exp(\beta x)/\alpha \exp(\beta 0) = \exp(\beta x)$. The values of $\exp(\beta x)$ for the NTB coverage ratios, and the tariff averages are reported in table 13.7.

When the NTB and tariff effects vary with commodity and importer, the

Table 13.7   Estimates of effects of barriers: $\exp(\beta)$

Model	NTB_{ik}	TAR_{ik}	$NTB_{i''k}$	$TAR_{i''k}$
1	0.801			
2	0.815	0.635		
3	0.544		0.0043	
4	0.550	0.695	0.0047	0.032
5	1.629[a]			
6	1.623[a]	1.168		
7	1.962[a]	1.196	4.017	3.747
8	20.56[a]	$\exp(320)$[b]	21.501	0.303

[a] $(\Sigma\beta_i)/14 + (\Sigma\beta_k)/163$
[b] $(\Sigma\gamma_i)/14 + (\Sigma\gamma_k)/163$

Table 13.8   Adjusted R^2s and t-values of effects of barriers

Model	R^2	k	NTB_{ik}	TAR_{ik}	$NTB_{i''k}$	$TAR_{i''k}$
1	0.7383	185	-2.24			
2	0.7383	186	-2.01	-0.76		
3	0.7435	186	-5.35		-6.73	
4	0.7433	188	-5.08	-0.49	-6.49	-0.51
5	0.7732	360 nf	3.09[a]			
6	0.7730	361 nf	3.08[a]	0.23		
7	0.7730	363 nf	2.79[a]	0.22	1.34	0.20
8	0.7894	543 nf	1.93[a]	3.00[a]	2.74	-0.12

[a] F statistic for testing if the coefficient is constant across importer, commodity.
number of observations = 2,387
k = number of parameters
nf = deficient rank

number reported in table 13.7 is based on a simple average of the estimated values of β. It would be better to use an import-weighted average since an import-weighted average is an approximate answer to the question: by how much would imports change if NTB coverage ratios increased from zero to 100 percent. Generally, the percentage change in imports can be expressed using the linear approximation

$$\Delta \log(M_{ik}) = (\beta_i + \beta_k) \, \Delta \, NTB_{ik} \text{ as}$$
$$\Delta M/M = \Sigma M_{ik} \, \Delta \log(M_{ik})/\Sigma M_{ik} = \Sigma M_{ik} (\beta_i + \beta_k) \, \Delta \, NTB_{ik}/\Sigma M_{ik}.$$

$$(13.16)$$

The special case, $\Delta NTB_{ijk} = 1$ implies the import-weighted average:

$$\Delta M/M = \Sigma_{ik} M_{ik} (\beta_i + \beta_k)/\Sigma_{ik} M_{ik}$$

(The analogous formula for the case in which the coefficient does not vary uses the linear approximation: $\exp(\beta x) - 1 \simeq \beta x$, which is applicable for small values of βx.) These import-weighted averages are used below for studying several counterfactuals.

The NTB effects in table 13.7 for the first five models do have the right sign as does the tariff. Depending on whether the model controls for NTBs of other importers, the estimated effect of increasing the coverage ratio from zero to 100 percent is to reduce imports to either 80 percent or 55 percent of the original value. When these effects are allowed to differ by importer and commodity, the results are mixed, but the average has the "wrong" sign.

The trade diversion effect should be positive, meaning that an increase of barriers by some country will divert trade elsewhere. The trade diversion effects are the wrong sign for the small models but do take on the right sign for models 7 and 8 in three of four cases. These estimated effects seem very substantial, however.

The t- and F-values for these coefficients are reported in table 13.8. The nontariff barriers generally are statistically significant (the effects are measurable), and the tariff effects generally are not.

The overall averages of the effects of barriers reported in table 13.7 can be broken down by importer using the formula (13.16) indicating the effect of a hypothetical change in the levels of the barriers. The effects of different counterfactuals are reported in tables 13.9, 13.10, and 13.11. The counterfactuals considered are:

1 By how much would imports of country i decrease if its coverage ratio applicable to all exporters and all commodities increased from zero to 100 percent ($\Delta NTB_{ik} = 1$).
2 By how much would imports of country i decrease if its coverage ratios increased from zero to the observed value NTB_{ijk} ($\Delta \, NTB_{ijk} = $ current value of NTB_{ijk}):

Table 13.9   Effects of NTBs by importer: bivariate model

	NTB avg (1)	Overall effect (2)	NTB avg (3)	NTB Elast (4)
Finland	0.351	−0.140	0.347	−0.404
Switzerland	0.467	−0.097	0.463	−0.209
France	0.261	−0.060	0.259	−0.232
Norway	0.150	−0.048	0.147	−0.329
United States	0.111	−0.029	0.111	−0.262
Netherlands	0.166	−0.021	0.156	−0.134
Denmark	0.110	−0.019	0.106	−0.175
West Germany	0.105	−0.018	0.102	−0.174
Great Britain	0.118	−0.017	0.118	−0.144
Belgium & Luxembourg	0.124	−0.017	0.117	−0.142
Greece	0.074	−0.016	0.072	−0.223
Italy	0.087	−0.016	0.086	−0.186
Ireland	0.049	−0.009	0.049	−0.180
Japan	0.385	0.038	0.421	0.091

(1) Import weighted coverage ratio
(2) Counterfactual 1′
(3) (2) divided by (4)
(4) Counterfactual 1
Counterfactual 1: By how much would imports of country i decrease if its coverage ratio applicable to all exporters and all commodities increased from zero to 100 percent ($\Delta NTB_{ik} = 1$):

$$\sum_k M_{ik}(\beta_i + \beta_k)/ \sum_k M_{ik}$$

Counterfactual 1′: By how much would imports of country i decrease if its coverage ratios increased from zero to the observed value $NTB_{ik}(\Delta NTB_{ik} = NTB_{ik})$:

$$\sum_k M_{ik} NTB_{ik}(\beta_i + \beta_k)/ \sum_k M_{ik}$$

Parenthetically, note that the counterfactual of raising barriers to their current level and the counterfactual of raising barriers to 100 percent are related by the formula:

$$\Sigma M_{ik}(\beta_i + \beta_k) NTB_{ik}/\Sigma M_{ik} =$$
$$[\Sigma M_{ik}(\beta_i + \beta_k) NTB_{ik}/\Sigma M_{ik}(\beta_i + \beta_k)] \times [\Sigma M_{ik}(\beta_i + \beta_k)/\Sigma M_{ik}]$$
$$= \text{NTB average} \times \text{Average elasticity}$$

In words, the percentage reduction in imports associated with raising barriers to their current level is equal to an NTB average times an average elasticity. The average elasticity is the answer to the counterfactual: by how much would imports decrease if barriers were raised from zero to 100 percent. The NTB average is weighted by the product of the level of imports and the elasticity.

Estimates of the importer counterfactuals for NTBs and tariffs are reported in tables 13.9 to 13.11. These are based on Bayesian estimates of

Table 13.10   Effects of tariffs by importer

	TAR avg (1)	Overall effect (2)	TAR avg (3)	TAR Elast (4)
Norway	0.053	−0.063	0.051	−1.231
Great Britain	0.029	−0.033	0.029	−1.141
West Germany	0.027	−0.029	0.026	−1.127
Italy	0.016	−0.027	0.015	−1.760
Japan	0.034	−0.026	0.030	−0.864
United States	0.041	−0.024	0.037	−0.640
Netherlands	0.017	−0.019	0.017	−1.157
Greece	0.014	−0.018	0.013	−1.333
Belgium & Luxembourg	0.012	−0.016	0.012	−1.430
France	0.019	−0.016	0.018	−0.852
Switzerland	0.028	−0.012	0.025	−0.499
Ireland	0.018	−0.011	0.018	−0.594
Denmark	0.029	−0.005	0.025	−0.212
Finland	0.048	0.046	0.051	0.893

(1) Import weighted tariff average
(2) Counterfactual 1'
(3) (2) divided by (4)
(4) Counterfactual 1
Counterfactual 1: By how much would imports of country i decrease if its tariff average applicable to all exporters and all commodities increased from zero to 100 percent ($\Delta TAR_{ik} = 1$):

$$\sum_k M_{ik}(\beta_i + \beta_k)/ \sum_k M_{ik}$$

Counterfactual 1': By how much would imports of country i decrease if its tariff averages increased from zero to the observed value $TAR_{ik}(\Delta TAR_{ik} = TAR_{ik})$:

$$\sum_k M_{ik} TAR_{ik}(\beta_i + \beta_k)/ \sum_k M_{ik}$$

the model that shrink the estimated coefficients to a common value. The relatively complex model with the effects of barriers varying with importer and commodity produces many "wrong" signs. The models that do produce "good" results are the simpler models which do not allow the coefficients to vary with importer and commodity, but these models do not yield answers to the interesting questions concerning the importers and commodities that are most affected by nontariff barriers. The solution to this problem is to allow the coefficients some freedom to vary by commodity and importer, but not as much freedom as the ordinary least squares regression with the full model. This can be accomplished by supplementing the data set with a fictitious data set that encapsulates the notion that the coefficients are not very different. This is a Bayesian method with a prior distribution that suggests that the coefficients do not vary much, and that consequently shrinks the importer and commodity effects to a common value. Details are available on request.

The second column of table 13.9 is the estimated effect of trade barriers on the imports of each of the 14 importing countries. The table is ordered by this column. The first column is the overall NTB coverage ratio. In the absence of information about the relative impact of NTBs applied by different importers against different commodities, the restrictiveness of the barriers would be indicated by this first column. The "news" in the statistical procedure is the discrepancy between these two columns, which is pretty clearly signaled by an odd elasticity in column (4). In particular, although Japan has relatively frequent nontariff barriers, the estimated effect of these barriers is actually to increase trade because the estimated elasticity in column (4) is positive. It would be possible to tighten the prior distribution to eliminate this anomalous sign, but in tightening the prior the relative ordering of countries is unlikely to change much.

It is worth pausing briefly to consider the feature of the data set that would lead to the conclusion that the Japanese barriers are relatively ineffective. The model includes both commodity dummy variables and importer dummy variables. One can think of the process of estimation in two steps: first the effects of the importer and commodity dummies are removed; then the NTB effect is estimated from the remaining variability. Thus the conclusion that the Japanese barriers are relatively inconsequential is due to the fact that for those commodities against which the Japanese have unusually frequent barriers, the Japanese do not have unusually low imports, in fact the opposite is true. One possibility is that the Japanese have unusually frequent barriers against many of the crops, but the Japanese level of imports of these crops is not unusual compared with the other 14 importers. The important point is that the comparison is strictly with the other importers, and no adjustment is made for the fact that the Japanese, because of shortage of farmland, would in the absence of barriers be much more dependent on imports of crops than the other importers. Another way to say this is that the model has the feature that in the absence of barriers all countries are predicted to have the same commodity composition of imports. This doubtful assumption is remedied by the next set of models that include variables like farmland that allow for differences in the pattern of barrier-free trade.

For most of the countries, the estimated effect of the NTBs in table 13.9 is not substantial, mostly less than 2 percent of imports. For France the effect is 6 percent, for Switzerland 10 percent and for Finland 14 percent. The large estimate for Finland is partly due to the frequent barriers, but also due to the large elasticity.

The effects of tariffs that are reported in table 13.10 are the same order of magnitude as the effects of nontariff barriers, attaining a maximum trade-suppressing effect for Norway of 6 percent of imports. Again the "news" in this table is the discrepancy in ordering of columns (1) and (2), column (1) indicating the import-weighted tariff average and column (2) indicating the predicted effect of the tariffs on imports. Norway has the highest average tariffs and also the highest predicted trade effect. Finland has relatively high tariffs but the lowest trade effect (the wrong sign, in fact.) As I have mentioned above, the anomaly of a wrong sign could be eliminated by shrinking the coefficients more dramatically to a common value, but further shrinkage may not greatly alter the ordering of importers. One thing that is of interest is that it is mostly the EEC countries that have the high elasticities in column (4). This may seem a little surprising but remember that the EEC tariff is the average of the extra-EEC rate and a zero internal rate. Thus in order to have a selected level of the average tariff the external tariff must be very high and it is not inconceivable that it would have a greater "bite" than the same average rate applied by another country.

The combined effect of tariff and nontariff barriers is reported in table 13.11 which is sorted by size of the combined effect. Norway and Switzerland at the top of the list are both estimated to have barriers that reduce trade by 11 percent. Then come Finland and France. The United States is next with a total effect of barriers equal to 5 percent of imports. Japan is the anomaly with a positive total effect, a consequence of the estimated NTB effect. I repeat again that this anomaly could be eliminated by further shrinkage of the estimates, which is not done for two reasons. First further shrinkage may not alter greatly the ordering of countries. Secondly, by retaining the anomaly, we are reminded of the somewhat arbitrary nature of the estimates. Another way to express this is that standard errors for these numbers would have to be rather large.

Table 13.11   Combined effect of tariff and nontariff barriers

	NTB effect	Tariff effect	Total effect
Norway	− 0.048	− 0.063	− 0.111
Switzerland	− 0.097	− 0.012	− 0.109
Finland	− 0.140	− 0.046	− 0.094
France	− 0.060	− 0.016	− 0.076
United States	− 0.029	− 0.024	− 0.053
Great Britain	− 0.017	− 0.033	− 0.050
West Germany	− 0.018	− 0.029	− 0.047
Italy	− 0.016	− 0.027	− 0.043
Netherlands	− 0.021	− 0.019	− 0.040
Greece	− 0.016	− 0.018	− 0.034
Belgium & Luxembourg	− 0.017	− 0.016	− 0.033
Denmark	− 0.019	− 0.005	− 0.024
Ireland	− 0.009	− 0.011	− 0.020
Japan	0.038	− 0.026	0.012
Average	− 0.027	− 0.009	− 0.036
Average (excluding +)	− 0.029	− 0.012	− 0.037

Models with country structure

These initial regressions impose no special structure on the commodity and importer effects and, because of the number of degrees of freedom that are consumed estimating these dummy coefficients, the remaining evidence about the NTB effects may be slight. In this section a model is presented that imposes some structure on the importer dummy variables by substituting in their place some variables that measure characteristics of countries and commodities. The form of the model used only slightly reduces the number of parameters devoted to estimating the importer effects. It would also be desirable to impose some further structure on the commodity effects but the appropriate variables are not available.

Another important difference in this model is that the predicted commodity composition of imports, in the absence of trade barriers, is not the same for all countries. For example, countries with relatively little land are allowed by the model to have relatively great imports of the land-intensive products.

The model is:

$$\log(M_{ik}) = \alpha_{1k} + \alpha_2\log(S_i) + \eta_{ik} + \beta_{ik}NTB_{ik} + \beta''NTB_{i''k}$$
$$+ \gamma_{ik}TAR_{ik} + \gamma''TAR_{i''jk} + \epsilon_{ijk} \qquad (13.17)$$

where

$$\eta_{ik} = \Sigma_f(\delta_{1f}X_{fi} + \delta_{2f}X_{fi}Z_{fk})$$
$$\beta_{ik} = \beta_0 + \beta_1'X_i + \beta_2'Z_k$$
$$\gamma_{ik} = \gamma_0 + \gamma_1'X_i + \gamma_2'Z_k$$

and

S_i = a measure of the economic size of the country: GNP
X_i = characteristics of the country
    (Population/GNP, Arable land/GNP)
Z_k = corresponding characteristics of the commodity
    (capital per man hour, land per man hour)

A full description of the sources and methods is available on request.

The difference between this model and the dummy variable model (13.15) is that in place of the importer and exporter dummies we have here

$$\alpha_2\log(S_i) + \eta_{ik}$$

This model controls for differences in the scale of trade across countries with a variable measuring the size of the Gross National Product. The ideal variable in this equation would be "potential" GNP: the level of GNP in the absence of trade barriers. This model takes actual GNP of the 14 importers as given and ignores whatever effects the trade barriers may have on GNP. But if the barriers lower GNP of the 14 importers in the sample by approximately the same percentage, the measured value of the logarithm of GNP will be proportional to the logarithm of "potential" GNP, and the use of actual rather than potential GNP increases the GNP coefficient but leaves unchanged the estimated effects of the barriers. Still, for doing a policy analysis, it may be necessary to allow for the effect of barriers on actual GNP.

Differences in the economic importance of the different commodity classes could be measured in a way analogous to "potential" GNP by a variable like "potential" worldwide production of the commodity. Neither this variable nor its counterpart, actual production, is available. One variable that is available is total imports of the commodity by the 14 importers. But the use of total imports seems to be a disguised way of estimating a model with commodity dummy variables and, if so, the loss of degrees of freedom in estimating these dummy coefficients is improperly ignored. Accordingly, we will retain the commodity dummies. Whether total imports or commodity dummies are used in the equation, the effect of barriers on the worldwide composition of trade is ignored just as the effects of the barriers on GNP are ignored. Though it seems possible to argue that the effect on GNP takes a form that leaves the estimated equation relatively unaffected, a similar argument cannot be made in the case of the commodity structure of trade. The commodity structure of trade barriers of these 14 countries has a substantial degree of similarity that is likely to depress relatively the trade in some commodities more than others. There doesn't seem to be much that can be done about this unless we had a variable that came close to measuring the barrier-free level of world-wide production.

The effects η_{ik} account for the comparative advantage of the importer and exporter. After controlling for country and commodity size, there are interactions between country and commodity characteristics that make a country more or less dependent on imports/exports of particular commodities. A country that is abundant in land is less likely to have great amounts of agricultural imports; a country that is very abundant in capital compared with labor is likely not to import capital-intensive products. This coupling of country and commodity characteristics can be justified only in an ad hoc fashion as we have discussed in section 1.

The application reported below has two factors, $f = 2$. The first factor is labor and the second is land. The effect η_{ik} then refers to four variables: (Population$_i$/GNP$_i$, Arable Land/GNP$_i$, (Population$_i$/GNP$_i$ × capital per man in industry k, Arable Land/GNP$_i$ × land per man in industry k)). Note that the country characteristics are allowed to enter individually, but the commodity characteristics cannot because of the commodity dummy variables which are necessarily perfectly collinear with the commodity characteristics.

Eight different varieties of this model are estimated differing in whether the trade diversion variables are included and whether the trade barrier variables differ by country and commodity characteristics. These eight varieties are listed in table 13.12.

Table 13.12   Models with importer comparative advantage variables

	α	η_{ik}	$(\beta_0\ \beta_m)$	$(\gamma_0\ \gamma_m)$	(β'')	(γ'')
1	*	*	*			
2	*	*	*	*		
3	*	*	*	*	*	
4	*	*	*	*	*	*
5	*	*	* *			
6	*	*	* *	*		
7	*	*	* *	* *	*	*
8	*	*	* *	* *	*	*

Cases: * = included

1: Direct NTB effect
2: Direct NTB and tariff effects
3: Direct NTB and tariff effects and NTB importer diversion
4: All effects of barriers constant
5: Variable direct NTB effect
6: Variable direct NTB effect and constant direct tariff effect
7: Variable direct NTB effect and all other effects
8: Full model

The adjusted R^2s for these eight models are listed in table 13.14 together with the t-values of the effects of the trade barriers. There is not a great deal of variability in these measures of fit, but they slightly favor the larger models.

The estimates of the effects of barriers, reported in table 13.13, generally have the expected sign. The tariff effects are much greater than the NTB effects, in fact in this case the tariff effects are enormous. Though the direct barriers have the expected sign, the diversion variables do not.

The t-values for the comparative advantage part of the model are reported in tables 13.15. The country size variables, not surprisingly, are highly significant. Next is the land abundance variable, which has a trade-suppressing effect. The labor abundance variable contributes positively to imports, though the effect is not as statistically significant (i.e. measureable) as the land variable.

The interactive effects reported in table 13.15 for the importer variable take on the correct signs: Land abundance reduces imports of commodities that use a lot of land; labor abundance increases imports of commodities that are capital-intensive. The land interaction is the more statistically significant effect.

To conclude, then, the model which accounts for differences in comparative advantage in terms of measurable characteristics of commodities and countries does a fairly good job of explaining the structure of trade, but leaves the impression that the NTB effects are difficult to detect, whereas the effects of tariffs are more clear and more substantial.

Table 13.13 Estimates of effects of barriers: bivariate model. Models with importer and exporter comparative advantage variables, $\exp(\beta)$

Model	NTB_{ik}	TAR_{ik}	$NTB_{i''k}$	$TAR_{i''k}$
1	0.453			
2	0.535	0.043		
3	0.407	0.047	0.028	
4	0.411	0.034	0.032	0.007
5	0.560^a			
6	0.680^a	0.031		
7	0.555^a	0.024	0.081	0.004
8	0.604^a	0.007^a	0.102	0.016

^{a} = average

Table 13.14 Adjusted R^2s and t-values of effects of barriers: bivariate model. Models with importer and exporter comparative advantage variables

Model	R^2	k	NTB_{ik}	TAR_{ik}	$NTB_{i''k}$	$TAR_{i''k}$
1	0.7084	177	-8.35			
2	0.7119	178	-6.30	-5.29		
3	0.7141	179	-7.63	-5.13	-4.27	
4	0.7140	180	-7.49	-4.51	-4.05	-0.71
5	0.7137	181	11.25^a			
6	0.7178	182	12.47^a	-5.75		
7	0.7188	184	10.40^a	-4.93	-2.93	-0.80
8	0.7222	188	12.88^a	7.73^a	-2.67	-0.60

^{a} F statistic for testing equality of coefficients

Table 13.15 t-values for comparative advantage component of the model

	Country			Industry interaction	
	GNP	POP	Land	POP	Land
1	37.61	2.72	-12.27	0.82	-3.42
2	38.09	1.97	-11.69	1.21	-3.59
3	38.02	1.58	-11.45	1.33	-3.64
4	37.76	1.58	-11.46	1.34	-3.62
5	36.06	1.27	-9.45	1.09	-4.43
6	36.50	0.34	-8.46	1.41	-4.57
7	36.31	0.26	-8.60	1.48	-4.58
8	36.71	2.58	-9.48	0.30	-4.34

Models with disaggregated NTB variables

To this point, all the models have made use of the overall NTB coverage ratio. This overall ratio is now disaggregated into price NTBs, quotas, quality controls and threats. The versions of model (13.15) and (13.17) that are considered are:

MODEL A

$$\log(M_{ik}) = \alpha_i + \alpha_k$$
$$+ \beta_p PRICE_{ik} + \beta_q QUOTA_{ik} + \beta_c CONTR_{ik}$$
$$+ \beta_t THREAT_{ik} + \gamma TAR_{ik}$$
$$+ \beta'' NTB_{i''k} + \gamma'' TAR_{i''k} + \epsilon_{ik}$$

MODEL B

$$\log(M_{ik}) = \alpha_{1k} + \alpha_2 \log(S_i) + \eta_{ik}$$
$$+ \beta_p PRICE_{ik} + \beta_q QUOTA_{ik} + \beta_c CONTR_{ik}$$
$$+ \beta_t THREAT_{ik} + \gamma TAR_{ik}$$
$$+ \beta'' NTB_{i''k} + \gamma'' TAR_{i''k} + \epsilon_{ik}$$

where:

$PRICE$ = coverage ratio of price NTBs
$QUOTA$ = coverage ratio of quotas
$CONTR$ = coverage ratio of quality controls
$THREAT$ = coverage ratio of threats

Note that the dependence of the trade barrier coefficients on importer and commodity have been eliminated in order to focus on the disaggregation of the NTB variable. For the same reason, the models do not include disaggregated trade diversion variables. Only two cases of these models will be considered, the first without the diversion variables ($0 = \beta'' = \gamma''$) and the second with the diversion variables. These are comparable with cases 2 and 4 considered earlier and these numbers will be retained for easy reference: *case 2* without the trade diversion variables, and *case 4* with.

Estimates and t-values, and adjusted R^2s are reported in tables 13.16 and 13.17. The adjusted R^2s in table 13.17 for the more complete models (A4, B4) with the trade diversion variables included are slightly higher than for the smaller models. The dummy variable model A does better than the comparative advantage model B. The adjusted R^2 for model A4 in table 13.17 is slightly less than the adjusted R^2 for model 4 reported in table 13.18, suggesting that disaggregation of the NTB variables is not helpful in the model with the trade diversion variables.

The estimates of the effects of barriers reported in table 13.16 are equal to the predicted value of trade with the barriers divided by the predicted value without the barriers $\exp(\beta)$, and would be less than one if the barriers were estimated to suppress trade. The difference between models 2 and 4 is that model 2 excludes the diversion variables. Exclusion of the diversion variables makes it difficult to measure the effect of quantitative restrictions (*QUANT*) (small *b* and small t-value), but the other NTB variables are "statistically significant." These estimates compare with the estimates for the aggregate model 2 reported in table 13.7 of 0.815 for NTBs and 0.635 for tariffs. The estimates of the tariff effect in table 13.16 is larger, as are all but the *QUOTA* variable for NTBs. In order of magnitude of the predicted effect of barriers, the estimates for model A4 are: threats, quality controls, price maintenance NTBs and quantitative restrictions. For the other models, threats do not have as big as impact. Quality controls seem often to have one of the largest effects, but the relative ordering varies quite a bit from model to model.

To conclude, disaggregation of the NTB variable does not dramatically improve the quality of the estimated models, but it does allow for different estimates of the effects of different types of barriers. The relative ordering of the impacts of the four different types of NTBs is not easy to determine confidently from this data set, partly because the estimates vary considerably among models that seem otherwise indistinguishable. Generally though, it is the quality controls that are estimated to have the greatest effect. This reverses the conclusion that the Japanese barriers are ineffective, since they tend to use quality controls most extensively.

Table 13.16   Estimates of effects of barriers: bivariate model. Models with disaggregated NTB variables

	Price	*Quota*	*Contr*	*Threat*	*TAR*	*NTB"*	*TAR"*
A2	0.797	1.005	0.823	0.751	0.670	–	–
A4	0.690	0.848	0.669	0.618	0.577	0.009	0.011
B2	1.134	0.874	0.404	0.893	0.037	–	–
B4	1.066	0.790	0.344	0.813	0.020	0.057	0.0001

– = not available

Table 13.17   Adjusted R^2s and t-values of effects of barriers: bivariate model. Models with disaggregated NTB variables

Model	R^2	k	Price	Quota	Contr	Threat	TAR	NTB"	TAR"
A2	0.7384	189	−1.53	0.03	−1.65	−1.35	−0.67	–	–
A4	0.7428		−2.49	1.03	−3.29	−2.25	−0.74	−6.06	−0.67
B2	0.7157	181	0.84	−0.81	−8.13	−0.54	−5.61	–	–
B4	0.7176	183	0.43	−1.40	−8.99	−0.98	−5.31	−3.60	−1.30

– = not available

Note

1 Actually, the aggregation of barriers that is applied below is based on the assumption that barriers are either non-duplicative or redundant, since the aggregation over different categories is done by $NTB = Max(NTB_1, NTB_2)$. The case of redundance is expressed mathematically by the import function $M = \alpha + \beta\, Max(NTB_1, NTB_2)$. The nonduplicative assumption is $Max(NTB_1, NTB_2) = NTB_1 + NTB_2$.

References

Baldwin, Robert E. 1970: *Nontariff Distortions of International Trade*, Washington, DC: The Brookings Institution.

Leamer, Edward E. 1974: "The Commodity Composition of International Trade in Manufactures: An Empirical Analysis," *Oxford Economics Papers*, 26, 350–74.

Leamer, Edward E. 1984: *Sources of International Comparative Advantage: Theory and Evidence*, Cambridge, MA: MIT Press.

Leamer, Edward E. 1987: "Cross Section Estimation of the Effects of Trade Barriers," in Robert Feenstra (ed.), *Empirical Methods for International Trade*, Cambridge, MA: MIT Press, pp. 52–82.

Leamer, Edward E. 1988: "Measure of Openness," in Robert E. Baldwin (ed.), *Trade Policy Issues and Empirical Analysis*, Chicago: University of Chicago Press.

Leamer, Edward E. and Bowen, H. P. 1981: "Cross-Section Tests of the Heckscher–Ohlin Theorem: Comment," *American Economic Review*, 71, 1040–3.

Nogues, Julio J., Olechowski, Andrzej, and Winters, L. Alan 1986: "The Extent of Nontariff Barriers to Industrial Countries' Imports," *The World Bank Economic Review*, 1 September, 181–99.

United Nations 1983: "Protectionism and Structural Adjustment: the Inventory of non-tariff barriers," UNCTAD: TD/B/940 2 February.

United Nations 1985: "Consideration of the Questions of Definitions and Methodology Employed in the UNCTAD Data Base on Trade Measures," UNCTAD: TD/B/AC.42/2 4 September.

14

A Computational Analysis of Alternative Safeguards Policy Scenarios in International Trade

ALAN V. DEARDORFF AND ROBERT M. STERN

1 Introduction

Nations may at times be subjected to a sudden surge of imports that can be disruptive to firms and workers in an import-competing industry. It is in recognition of the possible adjustment problems that can occur in these circumstances that safeguards or escape clause arrangements have become part of national trade laws and have been incorporated into the Articles of the General Agreement on Tariffs and Trade (GATT). These formal arrangements have often been bypassed by the use of other means of "administered protection" in the importing countries, but it remains the case that an import surge routinely gives rise to some sort of protective response in the affected country or countries. As efforts are renewed in the Uruguay Round of Multilateral Trade Negotiations to agree on a revision of the GATT that will regularize these safeguards responses, we believe it to be useful to examine the implications, both for the world economy and for the protected industries, of the systematic use of safeguards policies of various types. In this paper, therefore, we use the Michigan Model of World Production and Trade to calculate the effects on trade and employment of a variety of safeguards scenarios.

Even though temporary safeguards protection in the form of a tariff or quota is condoned in the event of an import surge, the United States and other industrialized countries have frequently opted instead to rely on special measures of administered protection that bypass the type of investigation, responsibilities, and actions envisaged in escape clause arrangements. Administered protection often includes the investigation of allegations of unfair trading practices and the imposition of antidumping or countervailing duties. In an increasing number of cases, too, it involves the implementation of voluntary export restraints (VERs) that establish limits on market share or the quantities of particular goods that individual countries are permitted to supply to importing nations. In most of these cases, while the administrative procedures tend to be more lax than is required of safeguards actions under the GATT, the end result is a policy that is functionally equivalent to a tariff or quota in its effects on trade and employment. Therefore our analysis in terms of these two policy tools may be understood to encompass both GATT-sanctioned safeguards and administered protection, when the latter is in fact a response to an import surge.

The GATT rules governing emergency protection are contained chiefly in Article XIX, which specifies the criteria to be used in establishing cause and serious injury and allows exporting countries to retaliate in case the importing country does not provide acceptable compensation to exporters for the reduction in trade. Further, it is expected that emergency protection should be applied on a nondiscriminatory basis in accordance with general GATT principles.[1] The decisions by the United States and other industrialized countries to bypass Article XIX procedures and obligations in favor especially of VERs reflect a greater governmental willingness to ease the process by which import-competing industries are able to obtain protection and at the same time to provide compensation on a selective basis to foreign exporters by permitting them to capture the quota rents.

The increasing disregard and devaluation of the GATT rules on safeguards protection have been widely acknowledged for some time. Efforts were made in the 1970s in the Tokyo Round of Multilateral Trade Negotiations to reach an agreement on safeguards, but the issues of selectivity and compensation could not be resolved to the satisfaction of the interested parties, chiefly the European Community (EC), which favored selectivity, and the United States, which favored nondiscrimination. Discussions on safeguards were continued after the conclusion of the Tokyo Round negotiations in 1979, but an agreement was still not possible. The issue of safeguards was thus placed formally on the agenda of the Uruguay Round negotiations that were launched officially in 1986 and are currently under way.

Continuing access to the import markets of the advanced countries is of crucial importance especially to the newly industrializing countries (NICs) that have now become major exporters of manufactured goods, and to other developing countries that may similarly pursue export expansion in manufactures in the not too distant future. If an agreement on safeguards is to be reached in the Uruguay Round, it will be necessary to resolve existing differences among the advanced industrialized countries pertaining to the questions of selectivity or nondiscrimination and compensation. In this connection, Hoekman (1988a, p. 207) has noted that the EC and the United States may have moderated their positions on safeguards taken in the Tokyo Round negotiations. Yet, as he and others have noted, progress on a safeguards agreement would be enhanced if the NICs in particular were to offer reciprocal concessions so that goods and services from the industrialized countries would have increased access to the NIC domestic markets.[2]

While it seems reasonably clear what an agreement on safeguards would involve, what is less clear are the conditions under which safeguards action would be introduced and especially the economic effects that different types of safeguards measures would have when implemented unilaterally or multilaterally. In order to investigate these matters, we have used the Michigan Model of World Production and Trade to analyze the effects of alternative safeguards policies that might be undertaken by the United States and other industrialized countries in response to an exogenous surge in imports of wearing apparel from developing countries. Our objective is to explore the general equilibrium effects of safeguards policies across both industries and countries, taking into account the possibility that an import surge is likely to affect not just one country but many and consequently that safeguards actions will be taken by many countries together. Further, we wish to analyze the differences between alternative trade policies and domestic policies that might be used for safeguards purposes.

The remainder of the paper is structured as follows. In section II, we present a brief description of the essential features of the Michigan Model for the benefit of readers who are not familiar with it and to highlight those features of the Model that pertain to the computational analysis of the alternative safeguards scenarios. In section III, we describe the safeguards experiments and alternative policies in some detail. Our computational results are presented in section IV, and we make some concluding comments in section V.

II Simplified description of the Michigan Model

Since the theoretical structure and equations of the Michigan Model are described in detail in Deardorff and Stern (1986, pp. 9–36 and 235–47), we present here accordingly an overview of the model and call attention to its most important features.

Structure of the Michigan Model

The Model is best thought of as composed of two parts: the country system and the world system. The country system contains separate blocks of equations for individual sectors for each country, and the world system contains a single set of equations for individual sectors for the world as a whole. The country blocks are used first to determine each country's supplies and demands for goods and currencies on world markets, as functions of exogenous variables, such as tariffs, and of world prices and exchange rates. These functions for each country are then combined to provide the input to the world system that permits world prices and exchange rates to be determined. These variables are finally entered back into the separate country blocks to obtain values for other country-specific variables.

The world system is much simpler than the country system. We start with the export-supply and import-demand functions from the country equations that depend on both world prices and exchange rates. To get world prices we simply add these supplies and demands for all countries and set the difference equal to net demand from the rest of the world. To get exchange rates, when these are flexible, we likewise add the values of these excess supplies for a given country for all industries and equate the resulting trade balances to exogenously given net capital flows. As mentioned, once we obtain the world prices for each traded-good industry and the exchange rate for each country, we can enter them into the separate country blocks in order to determine the rest of the relevant country-specific variables.

The aggregate behavior of the Model depends crucially on what is assumed about aggregate expenditure. Since our objective is to concentrate on microeconomic and intersectoral issues, we wanted a neutral characterization of macroeconomic policy such that aggregates would remain largely unaffected when allowing for some policy change. At various times, we have either treated aggregate nominal expenditure as essentially exogenous, or, alternatively, let aggregate expenditure very endogenously so as to maintain aggregate employment unchanged.[3] It is this latter assumption that underlies all of the experiments that are described below.

In designing the Michigan Model, the objective was to take into account as many as possible of the interconnections among industries and countries at the microeconomic level. This enables us to examine a variety of economic issues that most other existing models cannot address, either because they are too highly aggregated, or because they are specified only in partial-equilibrium terms. By the same token, however, the Michigan Model is far too large to be able to say anything concrete without further specification of its parameters. Thus, to implement the Model, we need a realistic selection of countries and industries using, as far as possible, actual data to generate the parameters.

Data and parameters

The current version of the Model includes 22 tradable and seven non-tradable industries in 18 industrialized and 16 developing countries, plus an aggregate sector representing the rest of the world.[4] We use a base of 1976 data on trade, production, and employment for all 34 countries, plus tariffs and constructed measures of NTBs for the 18 industrialized countries.[5]

Trade, production, and employment   The import and export data are adapted from United Nations trade tapes, with concordances that relate the Standard International Trade Classification (SITC) to our International Standard Industrial Classification (ISIC) industry categories. Information on the gross value of production and employment by ISIC sector is directly calculated or estimated from United Nations, *Yearbook of Industrial Statistics*, from Organization for Economic Cooperation and Development (OECD) publications on national accounts and labor statistics, and from various national statistical sources.

Nontariff barriers   NTBs in the Model are represented in two forms: as coverage indexes and as tariff equivalents. The coverage indexes serve to reflect the role of existing NTBs when other barriers are removed. The tariff equivalents, on the other hand, permit analysis of the removal of the NTBs themselves.

The coverage indexes are meant to measure the extent to which imports are subject to nontariff restrictions (e.g., quotas, health regulations, etc.). A value of 100 percent indicates that all trade in a given sector/country is covered by NTBs; zero denotes that no NTBs are present. The calculations are based on data in Murray and Walter (1978), who recorded the value of 1973 imports for a given country and SITC commodity category that was subject to some type of NTB, as identified in underlying documents prepared by the US Department of State and UNCTAD. We in turn aggregated their results and concorded them with our ISIC classification. The indexes were updated to take into account more recent restrictions on such products as footwear, iron and steel, and television receivers. The indexes for textiles (ISIC 321) and wearing apparel (ISIC 322) are based upon the proportion of each country's imports in these sectors from all of the world's nonindustrialized countries. The resulting indexes, which are available from the authors on request, are intended to represent the percentage of trade subject to NTBs of all kinds as of the late 1970s.[6] These indexes are used in the basic version of the Model to generate endogenous implicit tariff variables that serve to limit the responsiveness of trade to changes in policies on the assumption that the NTBs remain in place. We shall return to the interpretation of these indexes in our experiments below.[7]

Exchange rates   In the basic version of the Michigan Model, the exchange regimes of most developing countries are characterized in terms of a system of import licensing with exchange-rate pegging. The purpose was to capture elements of the existing NTBs in these countries.

Input–output tables   Our input–output coverage currently includes the 1972 input–output table for the United States, the 1976 table for Canada, the 1975 table for Japan, and the 1970 national tables for each of the industrialized EC-member countries. The US table is applied to the remaining industrialized countries. We use the 1977 table for Israel and the 1970 table for Brazil. The Brazilian table is applied to the remaining developing countries. Each of the national tables used is of necessity concorded to our ISIC classification.

Coefficients and elasticities   In general, the coefficients of explanatory variables that appear in the Model are calculated from our data on production, trade, and employment by sector in each country, from the input–output matrices, and from relevant published estimates of demand and substitution elasticities. The import-demand elasticities used in the Model are based upon the "best guesstimates" of US import-demand elasticities calculated by Stern et al. (1976).[8] Using the import-demand elasticities together with data on trade we calculate the implied elasticities of substitution in demand between imports and home-produced goods in each country. The implicit import-demand elasticities in other countries are derivable from the common elasticities of substitution and differ across countries due to their differences in shares of trade.[9] We use elasticities of substitution between capital and labor in each sector, based upon Zarembka and Chernicoff (1971). These were estimated from US data, but are assumed in our Model to apply for all countries.

Solution procedure

Given appropriate data and parameter estimates for the countries and sectors noted, solution of the Model is, in principle, straightforward. By differentiating the equations of the Model, we obtain a system of linear equations relating changes in all of the variables of the system. The coefficients in each of these linear equations are evaluated using the data and elasticity information collected. All that remains is to solve the system. Since the system is linear, it can in principle be solved by any of a variety of means.

In our solution procedure, we have devised several Fortran subroutines that process large partitioned matrices in which many of the partitioned blocks contain only zeros, and which avoid costly but meaningless computations involving these zeros. We use a Fortran programming technique known as dynamic dimensioning to avoid wasting computer-memory space on these empty blocks, even as the contents of all blocks change during the course of the solution. We apply these techniques first to each of the 34 countries separately to solve for their net exports in terms of world prices, exchange rates, and exogenous variables. We then use the world system equations to complete the solution.

III   Modeling an import surge and alternative safeguards responses

Our procedure is to assume that there is a surge of imports in a particular sector. We then solve for the effects of this import surge on trade and employment for all sectors and countries in the Model. We use the results of this solution to construct a variety of safeguards policies responding to the import surge, based on the effects that the surge has been calculated to have in the absence of any response. These responses are then introduced into the Model together with the import surge itself, in order to calculate the effects of the two together. In our results, accordingly, we will compare the trade and employment effects of the alternative response scenarios, comparing both among the response scenarios and with the effects of the surge by itself.

The import surge

Just exactly what constitutes an import surge is not altogether clear. It could involve a substantial increase in imports by a single country of a narrowly defined product from an individual supplying country. Alternatively, there could be a substantial increase in imports by several countries at the same time of an entire class of products from several supplying countries. We have chosen this broader conception of an import surge. We thus assume that there is a 10 percent increase in the total imports of wearing apparel (ISIC 322) by all 18 of the industrialized countries included in the Michigan Model. The increased imports are treated as coming from outside the developing countries that are already included in the Model, reflecting our perception that increased competition in the apparel industry is likely to come from countries that are even less developed than those that appear explicitly in our Model.[10]

In addition to modeling a shift in supply, we include a shift in importing-country demand of a size comparable to the import surge itself. The reason for doing this has to do with the structure of the Michigan Model, in which rather aggregated industries are modeled as producing homogeneous products competing together on a single world market. If we model an import surge as a supply shift alone, then we are implicitly having the new imports compete on a par with the goods that are already being exported by all countries in the Model, and this suggests a closeness of competition with exports that we believe to be misleading. What in our view is likely to happen instead is that new imports that give rise to safeguards responses tend to be closer substitutes for goods produced for the domestic market than for exports, and thus there is a sense in which a surge of imports can be thought of as changing the composition or definition of an aggregated imported good. It is to capture this change in composition that we include a shift in demand as a part of the definition of the import surge.

Specifically, for the surge of imports in wearing apparel, we therefore introduce two changes into the model. The first is an outward shift in supply of apparel coming into the world market from the rest-of-world sector, the increase being calculated as 10 percent of the total imports of apparel by all 18 industrialized countries of the model. Second, and simultaneously, we assume a 10 percent upward shift in demand for imports of apparel, at the

expense of demand for domestically produced apparel, in all 18 industrialized countries of the model.

The safeguards responses

In section IV below we report the results for the surge in apparel imports for
each of nine scenarios. The first scenario will be the effects of the surge by
itself, denoted as "no response." The remaining eight scenarios will all
reflect some sort of implicit or explicit response to the import surge, and are
explained as follows.

Existing quotas   As already noted, the Michigan Model includes a facility
by which the presence of existing nontariff restrictions on trade can be taken
into account. This facility makes use of damping coefficients that reduce
the responsiveness of trade to changes in the determinants of trade below
what this responsiveness would be if trade were free or distorted only by
tariffs. As mentioned above, these coefficients have been inferred in an
approximate way from inventories of NTBs and other sources, together
with corresponding trade coverage.

Since these NTB inventories and the calculated trade coverage coefficients include the presence of both orderly marketing arrangements and
VERs that presumably already serve a safeguards function, we have set the
coefficients back to zero in our modeling of an import surge with "no
response" mentioned above. However, our second scenario seeks to
capture the safeguard effects of these existing arrangements by permitting
the damping coefficients to re-assume their values in our data base, while
making no other changes in the form of an explicit safeguards response.
Thus, the scenario headed "existing quotas" reflects the effects of an
import surge, assuming that the changes in imports have been partially
damped by the presence of existing quantitative restrictions. We cannot
determine, unfortunately, how accurate this attempt to model such
restrictions may be, since as noted in Deardorff and Stern (1985) the data on
which these coefficients are based may not clearly capture the price and
quantity effects involved.

Unilateral US tariff   In seeking next to model more deliberate safeguard
responses, we first consider a unilateral US tariff on the industry in which
the surge occurs. Our procedure here is to have policy-makers make a
somewhat naive calculation of the tariff that would be needed to offset the
import surge. Specifically, using the own elasticity of import demand that is
contained in our data base, it is assumed that the US policy-makers
calculate, on a partial equilibrium basis, the tariff that would be needed to
reduce imports by the amount that they rose in the first, no-response,
scenario. This tariff is then included together with the modeling of the
import surge itself in a new run of the Model that produces the effects of

both together. It is to be expected that the actual change in imports under this situation will not be reduced entirely to zero, since the actual change depends on general equilibrium considerations that were absent from the calculation of the policy response itself.

Unilateral US quota   As an alternative to the tariff, we have also modeled a safeguards response that takes the form of a quota. Formally this is done by setting the damping parameter to nearly unity, thus preventing any change in imports at all from occurring. The coefficient cannot be set to exactly unity for technical reasons in the Model, but a value of 0.99 seems close enough to capture the spirit of a comprehensive quota.

It should be noted that there is nothing in the Michigan Model to prevent tariffs and quotas from being equivalent, so long as they are set at appropriate levels. Thus the differences between the quota and tariff safeguards scenarios here are more appropriately regarded as differences arising from the level of protection, rather than the method used. However, the approach does illustrate the important point that the quantitative effects of a tariff may be difficult to ascertain in advance, whereas the quantitative effects of a quota are more likely known. Therefore, as noted in Deardorff (1987a, b), a quota provides a more certain means of achieving a given level of quantitative protection than does a tariff.

Multilateral tariff and quota   Our fifth and sixth scenarios repeat what was done with the US tariff and quota respectively, this time assuming however that all of the countries that were subject to the import surge calculate and use the policies at the same time. In the case of safeguards tariffs, this means that all 18 industrialized countries of the Model implement tariffs that are calculated individually to offset their respective increases in imports from scenario 1. We would expect these tariffs to be even less successful in offsetting the surge than a unilateral tariff, since they are set by each country without regard to the effects that other countries' tariffs will have on themselves.

Unilateral US domestic subsidy   In the preceding scenarios, the assumed safeguard responses to an import surge involved the use of a trade policy, that is, existing quotas or the imposition of explicit tariffs or quotas for safeguards purposes. It is often argued that maintenance of domestic output or employment in an industry would be better accomplished, in terms of economic efficiency and welfare, by the use of a domestic subsidy instead of a trade policy. In addition, there is growing sentiment in the policy community that safeguards remedies should foster adjustment to the changed market conditions, and this too suggests policies that are directed more at the domestic industry than at trade. For both of these reasons we decided to run three additional scenarios in which the safeguard response takes the form of a domestic policy.

Thus scenario 7 assumes that the safeguard response takes the form of a unilateral US subsidy to production for both the home and export sectors that are separately distinguished in our Model. The production subsidy for the home sector is modeled as though it would be fully reflected in a fall in domestic price to demanders. More precisely, the home-sector subsidy is set equal to the percentage decline in home-sector output from the no-response scenario divided by the home-sector elasticity of demand. The subsidy for export production is determined as the percentage change in export-sector output from the no-response scenario divided by the supply elasticity of the sector. This would exactly offset the change in export output assuming partial equilibrium and that the world price is unresponsive to the subsidy.[11]

Multilateral domestic subsidy   Scenario 8 assumes that all 18 industrialized countries respond together to the import surge by providing domestic subsidies to home-sector and export production. These subsidies are calculated for each country as just mentioned for the United States.

Multilateral employment subsidy   We would ideally like to model a subsidy directly to employment, but that is unfortunately not possible given the structure of our Model. What we can do is to have wages in each industry adjust endogenously to maintain industry employment constant. This is equivalent to having endogenous wage subsidies in each industry that maintain constant employment. While our approach here is plausible, it is far from satisfactory for several reasons. First, we are forced to assume that the policy is being applied in all sectors, not just the one that has been subjected to the import surge. Second, the policy is assumed to be applied in all countries, so that we cannot undertaken a unilateral version of this type of response. Finally, since the policy is being designed to be effective ex post, rather than ex ante as in the case of the tariff and production subsidy, it is in this sense too successful. Granting all of these points, this scenario is nonetheless interesting if we interpret it as a kind of benchmark case of complete and perfect safeguards action in all sectors and countries at once.

IV   Computational results

The results of our scenarios are reported in tables 14.1–4. The first column in each table reports results for the import surge alone, while the remaining eight columns report results for the surge together with either existing quotas or one of the alternative safeguards responses discussed above.

Effects of an import surge with no response

As column 1 of table 14.1 indicates, our attempt to increase apparel imports by 10 percent in the industrialized countries did not lead to an increase of exactly 10 percent in all of the countries. The increases varied from a low of 7.14 percent in Belgium–Luxembourg to a high of 11.6 percent in New Zealand. This variation among countries in their response to the cheapening of apparel prices on the world market – which is common to all – is a result of a variety of general equilibrium interactions within the economies, but depends most importantly on differences in the elasticities of import demand among the countries. The decline in world apparel prices is also seen to have had a minor effect in increasing imports into some of the developing countries.

While the imports themselves are often the focus of much discussion in policy circles, it is presumably the effects on employment that are the more direct reason for using a policy response. Thus, in table 14.2 we report the net percentage changes in employment in the wearing apparel industry for all of the countries in the Model for each of the scenarios. In the first column of table 14.2, we see the declines in employment that one would expect to result from an import surge, though the percentage changes are in most cases a good deal smaller than the increases in imports in table 14.1 that appeared to be their cause.

This is not surprising for at least two reasons. First, apparel imports in most of the countries constitute a good deal less than half of the domestic market, so that a 10 percent increase in imports, even if it were to displace an equal amount of domestic production, would displace less than 10 percent of it. And second, imports are less than perfect substitutes for domestically produced goods, so that the displacement of domestic production is even less. Thus, for example, we find the import surge leading to only a 1.65 percent reduction in apparel employment in the United States. This, incidentally, corresponds to an employment reduction of approximately 20,000 workers. These same factors that explain why the employment reductions are often small also explain why some countries experience considerably greater employment reductions in the apparel industry. In Norway, for example, 62 percent of apparel is imported, so that the approximately 9 percent increase in imports there leads to a greater percentage decline in employment of more than 14 percent.

The net employment changes reported in table 14.2 include changes in both the home (or import-competing) sector and the export sector. Because the surge in imports into the world market causes some reduction in the world price of apparel in these calculations, there is some tendency for each country's exports of apparel to drop and for there to be a reduction in employment in the export sector as well as in the home sector. It is the drop in exports of apparel that accounts for the employment reductions that appear in table 14.2 for nearly all of the developing countries. Many of these countries are substantial exporters of wearing apparel, of course, and their declines in exports reduce employment even though in many cases they are protected from the direct effects of the import surge by import licensing. Only in Argentina and Chile, where exports of apparel account for a very

Table 14.1 Percentage changes in imports of wearing apparel (ISIC 322) due to each of nine scenarios in response to a 10 percent surge in imports of wearing apparel

	1 No response	2 Existing quotas	3 Unilateral US tariff	4 Unilateral US quota	5 Multilateral tariff	6 Multilateral quota	7 Unilateral US subsidy	8 Multilateral subsidy	9 Flexible wages
Industrialized countries									
Australia	10.67	5.33	11.54	11.75	3.52	0.06	11.19	8.53	13.52
Austria	9.01	7.60	9.13	9.16	1.41	0.02	9.08	4.21	11.55
Canada	10.50	5.69	11.37	11.57	3.39	0.06	11.02	9.20	12.40
European Community									
Belgium-Luxembourg	7.14	6.97	7.43	7.49	2.33	0.05	7.31	5.34	9.44
Denmark	7.46	5.51	7.85	7.93	2.92	0.06	7.69	5.85	9.41
France	10.51	8.13	11.24	11.41	3.06	0.05	10.94	8.39	12.78
Germany	8.74	5.49	9.33	9.47	3.63	0.06	9.09	7.29	10.38
Ireland	8.15	8.73	8.64	8.76	3.33	0.06	8.44	6.64	10.06
Italy	10.72	7.74	11.54	11.73	3.15	0.05	11.20	11.20	14.14
Netherlands	7.73	6.38	8.04	8.11	2.56	0.05	7.91	5.02	9.65
United Kingdom	9.93	4.77	10.70	10.88	3.62	0.06	10.39	8.53	11.46
Total EC	8.34	7.39	8.86	8.98	3.25	0.06	8.65	6.81	10.25
Finland	9.93	6.57	9.99	10.00	0.64	0.01	9.97	5.59	12.39
Japan	11.04	4.42	11.99	12.21	3.44	0.06	11.60	11.54	15.59
New Zealand	11.16	9.12	12.04	12.24	2.78	0.05	11.69	12.53	14.71
Norway	8.77	7.43	9.12	9.20	2.84	0.04	8.98	4.08	9.94
Sweden	8.87	6.05	9.15	9.21	2.26	0.04	9.04	4.13	11.10
Switzerland	8.99	7.87	9.35	9.43	2.80	0.04	9.20	4.45	11.01
United States	10.82	4.38	1.65	0.02	3.52	0.06	7.48	9.44	14.21
Total industrialized	8.95	7.27	9.44	9.56	3.00	0.05	9.24	6.42	11.05

Developing countries

Argentina	0.23	0.22	0.22	0.22	0.22	0.20	0.22	0.19	0.15
Brazil	0.10	0.09	0.11	0.11	0.08	0.06	0.10	0.07	-0.03
Chile	-0.10	-0.04	-0.25	-0.29	0.07	0.11	-0.24	-0.20	-0.02
Colombia	0.12	0.07	0.09	0.08	0.05	-0.01	0.09	0.04	-0.09
Greece	-0.06	-0.12	-0.05	-0.05	-0.17	-0.26	-0.05	-0.13	-0.31
Hong Kong	0.10	0.31	0.20	0.23	0.42	0.66	0.16	0.36	0.60
India	0.01	-0.10	-0.05	-0.06	-0.16	-0.28	-0.03	-0.13	-0.15
Israel	0.98	2.95	1.92	2.14	4.07	6.48	1.54	3.56	7.45
South Korea	-0.14	-0.54	-0.33	-0.37	-0.75	-1.20	-0.26	-0.65	-0.97
Mexico	0.94	2.96	1.91	2.14	4.10	6.58	1.52	3.59	9.45
Portugal	-0.07	-0.15	-0.08	-0.08	-0.20	-0.30	-0.07	-0.17	-0.28
Singapore	0.21	0.73	0.45	0.51	1.02	1.64	0.36	0.89	2.40
Spain	0.02	0.02	0.05	0.06	0.01	-0.01	0.04	0.01	-0.06
Taiwan	-0.07	-0.35	-0.22	-0.26	-0.49	-0.82	-0.17	-0.43	-0.79
Turkey	-0.02	-0.03	0.01	0.02	-0.05	-0.07	0.01	-0.01	-0.20
Yugoslavia	0.93	2.86	1.85	2.06	3.94	6.29	1.48	3.44	7.11
Total LDCs	0.24	0.67	0.45	0.50	0.91	1.43	0.37	0.80	1.91
All countries	8.67	7.06	9.15	9.26	2.93	0.10	8.96	6.24	10.75

Table 14.2 Net percentage changes in employment in wearing apparel (ISIC 322) due to each of nine scenarios in response to a 10 percent surge in imports of wearing apparel

	1 No response	2 Existing quotas	3 Unilateral US tariff	4 Unilateral US quota	5 Multilateral tariff	6 Multilateral quota	7 Unilateral US subsidy	8 Multilateral subsidy	9 Flexible wages
Industrialized countries									
Australia	−2.08	−1.57	−2.27	−2.32	−1.43	−0.59	−2.19	−0.03	0.0
Austria	−7.13	−12.31	−9.35	−9.86	−16.71	−16.48	−8.47	−1.39	0.0
Canada	−3.05	−2.24	−3.28	−3.34	−1.85	−0.51	−3.19	−1.07	0.0
European Community									
Belgium-Luxembourg	−7.96	−10.35	−9.05	−9.29	−12.08	−10.30	−8.61	−5.95	−0.0
Denmark	−7.04	−8.54	−7.89	−8.08	−9.22	−7.29	−7.55	−4.64	0.0
France	−2.76	−4.36	−3.66	−3.87	−4.93	−5.90	−3.30	−1.99	0.0
Germany	−5.04	−4.80	−5.52	−5.63	−4.65	−2.69	−5.33	−2.46	0.0
Ireland	−4.55	−5.95	−5.26	−5.42	−5.56	−4.76	−4.97	−3.17	0.0
Italy	−1.27	−2.62	−1.95	−2.11	−3.29	−4.64	−1.67	−1.88	0.0
Netherlands	−12.38	−14.49	−13.45	−13.70	−15.40	−10.58	−13.02	−5.90	0.0
United Kingdom	−3.03	−2.71	−3.47	−3.57	−2.85	−2.18	−3.29	−1.76	0.0
Total EC	−5.60	−6.18	−6.25	−6.40	−6.45	−4.75	−5.99	−3.07	0.0
Finland	−3.79	−11.74	−7.09	−7.83	−16.94	−21.65	−5.78	−2.82	0.0
Japan	−1.51	−1.18	−1.74	−1.80	−1.26	−0.98	−1.65	−1.00	0.0
New Zealand	−0.69	−1.76	−1.22	−1.35	−2.27	−3.48	−1.01	−1.21	0.0
Norway	−14.46	−16.17	−15.51	−15.75	−16.12	−9.16	−15.09	−1.03	0.0
Sweden	−11.19	−15.58	−12.92	−13.31	−18.40	−14.61	−12.23	−1.45	0.0
Switzerland	−6.82	−9.29	−8.05	−8.33	−10.07	−9.18	−7.55	−0.36	0.0
United States	−1.65	−1.35	−0.92	−0.34	−1.45	−1.02	0.33	−0.19	0.0
Total industrialized	−5.61	−6.63	−6.31	−6.44	−7.13	−5.65	−5.92	−2.25	0.0

Developing countries

Argentina	0.40	0.37	0.38	0.37	0.37	0.31	0.37	0.31	0.0
Brazil	−0.05	−0.14	−0.09	−0.10	−0.19	−0.30	−0.07	−0.17	0.0
Chile	0.02	−0.03	0.06	0.08	−0.09	−0.14	0.06	0.02	0.0
Colombia	−0.13	−0.44	−0.28	−0.31	−0.62	−0.99	−0.22	−0.54	0.0
Greece	−0.45	−1.54	−0.93	−1.05	−2.15	−3.44	−0.74	−1.88	0.0
Hong Kong	−0.46	−1.50	−0.95	−1.07	−2.06	−3.28	−0.76	−1.84	0.0
India	−0.83	−2.88	−1.80	−2.03	−4.00	−6.35	−1.42	−3.50	0.0
Israel	−0.30	−0.90	−0.58	−0.65	−1.24	−1.96	−0.47	−1.10	0.0
South Korea	−0.87	−3.00	−1.89	−2.13	−4.15	−6.58	−1.49	−3.64	0.0
Mexico	−0.11	−0.34	−0.22	−0.24	−0.46	−0.73	−0.17	−0.41	0.0
Portugal	−0.70	−2.43	−1.49	−1.67	−3.40	−5.44	−1.17	−2.99	0.0
Singapore	−0.83	−2.82	−1.77	−1.99	−3.91	−6.23	−1.40	−3.49	0.0
Spain	−0.15	−0.53	−0.32	−0.36	−0.74	−1.20	−0.26	−0.65	0.0
Taiwan	−0.76	−2.71	−1.71	−1.93	−3.75	−5.99	−1.34	−3.31	0.0
Turkey	−0.27	−0.95	−0.57	−0.64	−1.33	−2.13	−0.45	−1.16	0.0
Yugoslavia	−0.37	−1.17	−0.75	−0.84	−1.62	−2.56	−0.60	−1.42	0.0
Total LDCs	−0.43	−1.49	−0.91	−1.02	−2.09	−3.34	−0.72	−1.83	0.0
All countries	−0.97	−2.02	−1.47	−1.58	−2.61	−3.58	−1.25	−1.87	0.0

Table 14.3 Percentage changes in exports of wearing apparel (ISIC 322) due to each of nine scenarios in response to a 10 percent surge in imports of wearing apparel

	1 No response	2 Existing quotas	3 Unilateral US tariff	4 Unilateral US quota	5 Multilateral tariff	6 Multilateral quota	7 Unilateral US subsidy	8 Multilateral subsidy	9 Flexible wages
Industrialized countries									
Australia	-4.26	-17.77	-9.69	-10.91	-24.10	-34.12	-7.57	-7.72	-6.36
Austria	-1.89	-13.38	-6.38	-7.40	-25.64	-29.42	-4.61	-2.85	9.86
Canada	-1.92	-7.72	-4.41	-4.98	-10.79	-16.69	-3.41	-6.77	2.46
European Community									
Belgium-Luxembourg	-0.12	-2.60	-1.13	-1.36	-5.86	-8.18	-0.72	-2.42	6.44
Denmark	0.02	-2.98	-0.92	-1.13	-5.19	-7.66	-0.54	-2.08	6.18
France	-2.42	-9.30	-5.35	-6.02	-13.64	-19.93	-4.18	-6.13	0.53
Germany	-0.34	-3.50	-1.39	-1.64	-5.25	-8.17	-0.97	-2.41	4.76
Ireland	-0.24	-2.36	-1.21	-1.43	-4.55	-7.16	-0.82	-2.35	3.73
Italy	-0.92	-3.10	-1.88	-2.10	-4.39	-6.77	-1.49	-2.46	-0.94
Netherlands	0.07	-4.85	-1.51	-1.88	-9.85	-12.96	-0.88	-3.20	15.75
United Kingdom	-1.13	-4.65	-2.52	-2.84	-6.42	-9.87	-1.96	-3.44	2.21
Total EC	-0.34	-4.08	-1.68	-1.99	-7.27	-10.38	-1.14	-2.95	7.98
Finland	-3.22	-14.76	-7.86	-8.90	-22.50	-29.15	-6.03	-4.19	0.86
Japan	-1.59	-5.11	-3.15	-3.51	-6.98	-10.87	-2.52	-4.52	-4.71
New Zealand	-5.11	-16.43	-10.60	-11.83	-22.24	-33.26	-8.46	-13.79	-14.15
Norway	-1.76	-16.47	-6.52	-7.59	-31.09	-35.22	-4.65	-2.08	60.38
Sweden	-1.23	-17.63	-5.86	-6.91	-29.43	-32.84	-4.04	-2.66	25.01
Switzerland	-1.90	-14.81	-6.70	-7.77	-25.84	-33.43	-4.78	-3.03	17.02
United States	-4.43	-18.16	-13.45	-13.32	-24.16	-34.56	3.21	-9.39	-10.99
Total industrialized	-0.85	-7.05	-3.05	-3.55	-12.00	-15.89	-2.16	-3.49	10.03

Developing countries

Argentina	−0.28	−1.00	−0.61	−0.69	−1.39	−2.25	−0.48	−1.24	−3.92
Brazil	−0.28	−1.01	−0.63	−0.71	−1.41	−2.28	−0.49	−1.24	−3.24
Chile	−0.34	−1.05	−0.76	−0.86	−1.40	−2.24	−0.62	−1.35	−3.09
Colombia	−0.26	−0.99	−0.62	−0.70	−1.40	−2.26	−0.48	−1.23	−2.52
Greece	−0.28	−0.97	−0.58	−0.65	−1.36	−2.18	−0.46	−1.18	−0.88
Hong Kong	−0.16	−0.52	−0.33	−0.37	−0.72	−1.15	−0.26	−0.64	−0.00
India	−0.29	−1.01	−0.63	−0.71	−1.41	−2.26	−0.50	−1.23	−0.03
Israel	−0.32	−0.97	−0.63	−0.70	−1.32	−2.08	−0.51	−1.16	−1.40
South Korea	−0.30	−1.06	−0.66	−0.75	−1.47	−2.35	−0.52	−1.29	−0.04
Mexico	−0.33	−1.03	−0.67	−0.75	−1.42	−2.24	−0.54	−1.25	−2.71
Portugal	−0.28	−0.98	−0.60	−0.67	−1.37	−2.21	−0.47	−1.21	−0.24
Singapore	−0.29	−0.98	−0.62	−0.69	−1.37	−2.20	−0.49	−1.22	−0.01
Spain	−0.28	−1.00	−0.61	−0.69	−1.40	−2.25	−0.48	−1.23	−2.34
Taiwan	−0.27	−0.95	−0.60	−0.68	−1.32	−2.13	−0.47	−1.17	−0.04
Turkey	−0.28	−1.00	−0.61	−0.68	−1.41	−2.26	−0.48	−1.23	−1.68
Yugoslavia	−0.31	−0.97	−0.63	−0.70	−1.33	−2.10	−0.50	−1.17	−1.20
Total LDCs	−0.28	−0.99	−0.62	−0.70	−1.38	−2.22	−0.49	−1.22	−1.22
All countries	−0.57	−4.13	−1.88	−2.18	−6.90	−9.32	−1.36	−2.40	4.62

small percentage of output, does employment in the apparel industry fail to decline.

Some idea of the importance of changes in exports in the industrialized countries is given in table 14.3, which reports the percentage change in exports for the apparel sector in each country for each of the scenarios. The declines in exports for the "no response" scenario are especially noteworthy for New Zealand, the United States, Australia, Finland, and France. The variations across countries here reflect differences in their assumed supply elasticities, as well as differences in the extent to which reductions in apparel prices on the world market feed through into the input prices of the countries' industries. In the United States and New Zealand, for example, comparatively small import shares in the apparel industry prevent the drop in world price from appreciably reducing the prices of inputs to apparel production from the apparel industry itself, a reduction that moderates the decline in production for export in many of the other countries.

A final thing to consider in a general equilibrium calculation of the effects of an import surge is the effects across other industries. Net percentage changes in sectoral employment are reported in table 14.4 for the United States for each of the 22 tradable and seven nontradable industries of the Michigan Model.[12] Not surprisingly, these percentage changes are quite small for all industries. They are not without interest, however. It is notable, for example, that the import surge in apparel, which reduces employment there, causes a small expansion of employment in almost every other sector of the economy. The chief exception in the "no response" scenario is in textiles, which is closely related to apparel. Thus, since the apparel industry draws almost a quarter of its inputs from the textile industry, when the import surge, coming from outside the system onto the world market, reduces output in the apparel industry it also reduces that industry's purchases from the textile industry and causes employment to decline there as well.

Effects of trade policy safeguards responses

Imports of wearing apparel by the industrialized countries are currently restricted by the Multifiber Arrangement (MFA). We represent the MFA in terms of the damping coefficients for wearing apparel (ISIC 322) that have been calculated for use in the Model. These reflect the proportion of industrialized country (1976) imports of wearing apparel from the developing countries. The effects of these damping coefficients are reflected in the differences between columns 1 and 2 of tables 14.1–4. The US damping coefficient, for example, is 66 percent, and in table 14.1 reduces the import surge into the US from about 11 percent to 4 percent.

The employment effects in table 14.2 suggest that, while in most of the larger industrialized countries the employment reductions are reduced by existing quotas, it is notable that employment reductions are increased in many of the smaller countries. In the Netherlands, Norway, and Sweden, for example, where employment reductions due to the import surge would already have been in excess of 10 percent, the existing quotas make the employment reductions even larger. This is not a result of their small size, however, so much as that these countries are assumed in our Model to have smaller than average coverage by existing NTBs. Thus one can say that the existing quota arrangements put the burden of adjustment to a worldwide import surge more upon those countries whose existing quota arrangements are the least restrictive.

Still more of the burden of this adjustment is put on the developing countries. As indicated also in table 14.2, all of the developing countries suffer a greater loss of employment in the apparel industry (or in the case of Argentina, a smaller gain) when the developed countries use existing quotas as a means of protection. The lesson, of course, in that existing quotas – and safeguards generally, as we shall see – force the burden of adjusting to an import surge onto the countries which do not or cannot make use of these policies, and particularly onto those whose role as exporters renders import protection less meaningful.

Suppose now that we assume that there are no existing quotas and that the object is to design and implement some safeguards trade policy response to mitigate the effects of an import surge. The results of a unilateral US tariff in conjunction with the import surge are shown, for example, in column 3 of tables 14.1–4. This tariff, which has been calculated to offset completely the nearly 11 percent reduction in US imports reported in column 1 if all other things remain constant, does not succeed in reducing the import surge to zero because all other things do not remain constant. In particular, the drop in the world price stimulates US apparel imports somewhat and, together with other general equilibrium interactions, leaves the United States with a 1.65 percent rise in imports.

This is nonetheless a substantial reduction in US imports compared to the "no response" scenario, and what is especially noteworthy is that it comes at the expense of a rise in apparel imports in all of the other industrialized countries. This in turn, in table 14.2, means that while the US tariff lessens the employment effect of the import surge at home, it exacerbates the employment declines abroad. Indeed, the small percentage saving in US apparel employment that is achieved by the unilateral tariff comes at the expense of increased employment dislocations in many other countries that are larger, in percentage terms, than the saving in the United States.

These same effects appear even more strongly when the United States uses a unilateral quota. Here, as indicated in column 4 of tables 14.1–4, the direct control of import quantities prevents the import surge on the world market from causing any change in US imports at all (except for a tiny increase that reflects our Model's technical inability to allow for a 100 percent restriction on trade). The difference between the unilateral tariff

Table 14.4 Net percentage changes in employment in United States due to each of nine scenarios in response to a 10 percent surge in imports of wearing apparel

		1 No response	2 Existing quotas	3 Unilateral US tariff	4 Unilateral US quota	5 Multilateral tariff	6 Multilateral quota	7 Unilateral US subsidy	8 Multilateral subsidy	9 Flexible wages
Traded goods										
Agr., for., & fishing	(1)	0.11	0.10	0.08	0.06	0.10	0.08	0.06	0.06	0.0
Food, bev., & tobacco	(310)	0.01	0.01	0.00	−0.01	0.01	0.01	−0.02	−0.01	0.0
Textiles	(321)	−0.38	−0.38	−0.32	−0.21	−0.41	−0.32	0.01	−0.04	0.0
Wearing apparel	(322)	−1.65	−1.35	−0.92	−0.34	−1.45	−1.02	0.33	−0.19	0.0
Leather products	(323)	−0.01	−0.08	−0.26	−0.32	−0.05	−0.05	−0.14	−0.07	0.0
Footwear	(324)	0.03	0.01	0.00	−0.01	0.01	0.00	−0.01	−0.00	0.0
Wood products	(331)	0.04	0.03	0.00	−0.01	0.04	0.03	−0.00	0.00	0.0
Furniture & fixtures	(332)	0.03	0.02	0.01	−0.00	0.02	0.02	−0.01	0.00	0.0
Paper & paper products	(341)	0.02	0.01	−0.02	−0.03	0.02	0.02	−0.00	0.00	0.0
Printing & publishing	(342)	0.01	0.01	0.01	−0.00	0.01	0.01	−0.01	−0.00	0.0
Chemicals	(35A)	0.01	0.00	−0.02	−0.02	0.00	0.01	0.02	0.02	0.0
Petrol. & rel. prod.	(35B)	−0.01	−0.03	−0.06	−0.08	−0.02	−0.02	−0.06	−0.04	0.0
Rubber products	(355)	0.07	0.06	0.02	0.00	0.07	0.06	0.02	0.03	0.0
Nonmetallic min. prod.	(36A)	0.04	0.03	0.01	−0.00	0.03	0.02	−0.01	0.00	0.0
Glass & glass products	(362)	0.04	0.03	0.01	−0.01	0.04	0.03	0.00	0.01	0.0
Iron & steel	(371)	0.10	0.09	0.05	0.03	0.10	0.09	0.05	0.05	0.0
Nonferrous metals	(372)	0.08	0.07	0.02	−0.01	0.09	0.07	0.02	0.03	0.0
Metal products	(381)	0.07	0.06	0.04	0.02	0.06	0.06	0.02	0.03	0.0
Nonelectric machinery	(382)	0.12	0.11	0.07	0.05	0.12	0.11	0.07	0.07	0.0
Electric machinery	(383)	0.09	0.08	0.05	0.04	0.09	0.07	0.04	0.05	0.0
Transportation equip.	(384)	0.10	0.10	0.08	0.06	0.10	0.09	0.06	0.07	0.0
Miscellaneous manufac.	(38A)	0.07	0.06	0.03	0.01	0.07	0.06	0.04	0.04	0.0
Total traded		−0.04	−0.03	−0.03	−0.01	−0.04	−0.02	0.05	0.02	0.0

Nontraded goods

Mining & quarrying	(2)	0.03	0.01	−0.03	−0.06	0.02	0.01	−0.04	−0.02	0.0
Electric. gas & water	(4)	0.03	0.02	0.02	0.00	0.03	0.02	−0.02	−0.01	0.0
Construction	(5)	0.01	0.01	0.01	0.00	0.01	0.00	−0.02	−0.01	0.0
Wholesale & ret. trade	(6)	0.01	0.01	0.01	0.00	0.01	0.01	−0.01	−0.01	0.0
Transp., stor., & com.	(7)	0.01	0.01	0.01	0.00	0.01	0.01	−0.01	−0.00	0.0
Fin., ins. & real est.	(8)	0.02	0.02	0.02	0.00	0.02	0.01	−0.02	−0.01	0.0
Comm., soc. & pers. serv.	(9)	0.01	0.01	0.01	0.00	0.01	0.01	−0.02	−0.01	0.0
Total nontraded		0.01	0.01	0.01	0.00	0.01	0.01	−0.02	−0.01	0.0
Total, all industries		0.00	0.00	0.00	0.00	0.00	0.00	0.00	0.00	0.0

and quota scenarios is in a sense an artificial one, since it merely means that we did not select a tariff in column 3 that was large enough ex post to prevent an increase in imports. But as we have mentioned before, the difference is also important realistically since it may be impossible to set tariffs in advance to achieve quantitative import targets with any accuracy.

Consider next the two multilateral scenarios in columns 5 and 6 of tables 14.1–4. These scenarios succeed in damping imports still further, in all of the industrialized countries, as compared to the existing quota arrangements noted in column 2 of table 14.1. Here, unlike the existing quota scenario, all of the industrialized countries implement safeguards restrictions that are more or less on a par with one another, differing only to the extent that the initial surge would have affected them differently in column 1.

Not surprisingly, these multilateral safeguards policies put most or all of the burden of adjustment to the import surge onto exports. What is surprising is that almost all of this burden falls on the exports of the industrialized countries themselves, rather than on the developing countries. The latter face a drop in the world price of apparel, and their exports do indeed decline, by a rather uniform amount determined by the elasticity of their response to that world price. In the industrialized countries, on the other hand, much larger reductions in exports show up in table 14.3, and the sizes of these reductions vary considerably across the countries.

The reason for this result is the role that the apparel industry plays in providing inputs to its own production. Restrictions on imports – both tariffs and quotas – raise the prices of these inputs without providing any advantage at all to exporters who must sell on the world market. Thus while safeguards protection may do a reasonable job of protecting output and employment in the import competing part of the industry, exports get squeezed between the lower world price due to the import surge and higher input prices due to the protection. It is therefore perhaps not so surprising after all that the industrialized country exports decline as much as they are shown to in table 14.3.

These declines in exports, in turn, explain why in table 14.2 the overall reductions in employment in the apparel industry are not always improved by multilateral safeguards. The multilateral quota scenario, for example, in column 6 of table 14.2, reduces the employment loss as compared to the "no response" scenario in column 1 for Australia, Canada, Germany, Italy, the Netherlands, the United Kingdom, Japan, Norway, and the United States, but it worsens employment in the industry for all of the other industrialized countries.

The results of scenarios 3–6 thus suggest that the use of import protection as a means of "safeguarding" employment in import-sensitive industries is a questionable practice even when practiced by only one country, since it shifts the burden of adjustment onto other countries. Furthermore, when protective safeguards actions are taken by countries multilaterally in the same industry, then even the beneficial effects in the protecting countries will be to some extent undermined. This is especially the case since the protective policies serve to raise input prices in the protecting countries and thus will also have adverse effects on employment and output in export sectors, perhaps even in the same industry that was initially seeking protection. It is not clear therefore that countries as a group will gain from collectively pursuing protective safeguards policies.

Effects of domestic policy safeguard responses

Suppose now that domestic policies rather than trade policies are to be used for safeguards purposes. The results for the three domestic policy scenarios that we were able to implement are summarized in columns 7-9 of tables 14.1-4. If the United States were to implement a subsidy unilaterally to maintain output in the home and export sectors affected by the 10 percent import surge in wearing apparel, it can be seen in column 7 of table 14.1 that US imports would rise by 7.5 percent. This is in contrast to the effects of the tariff and quota actions that limit the rise in US imports more fully. But, as before, the unilateral US policy shifts the burden of adjustment onto other countries. This action slightly increases US employment in wearing apparel but exacerbates the decline in employment in the other industrialized countries especially in comparison to the "no response" scenario. US exports can be seen in table 14.3 to rise by 3.2 percent while the exports of the other countries decline. Finally, in column 7 of table 14.4, we see that the negative impact on the US textile industry is avoided, although there are some minor negative employment effects in other sectors due to the input-price effects that occur.

When multilateral domestic subsidies are used in the industrialized countries, in scenario 8 in table 14.1, US imports rise by 9.4 percent, only slightly less than in the "no response" scenario, while the imports of many of the other industrialized countries also decline by a small amount in comparison to the "no response" scenario. What is especially striking is that the multilateral domestic subsidies are noticeably more effective in limiting the decline in employment (table 14.2) in the industrialized countries themselves and in the developing countries in comparison to scenarios 5 and 6, which involve multilateral tariffs and quotas. This is apparently because the decline in exports (table 14.3) is now much smaller. The multilateral subsidy thus seems capable of achieving what trade policies could not: a marked improvement in the employment situation in all developed countries.[13]

Finally, in scenario 9, where wage flexibility is permitted so as to keep employment constant in all sectors in all countries, the results in tables 14.2 and 14.4 merely verify what has been assumed. But what is more interesting is the effect of wage flexibility on apparel imports, noted in table 14.1. Imports are greater in all the industrialized countries in this scenario than in all the others, including the "no response" run. What is apparently happening is that the import surge is now being met by a more flexible response in the import-competing sectors of the industrialized countries, where wage reductions permit them to remain competitive. But that means in turn that they continue to supply more apparel to the world market, where the price must therefore fall by more than it did in the other scenarios. This in turn is what stimulates imports. It is interesting though, in table 14.3, that the increases in supplies to the world market are by no means from all countries. There are instead positive and negative changes in apparel exports for different countries, with only the total averaging out to an increase for the group as a whole. In particular, US apparel exports drop noticeably.

V Conclusion

Our conception of an import surge and alternative safeguard responses is perhaps broader than what some observers may have in mind. That is, rather than focusing on the effects of an import surge in a narrowly defined product category involving some particular exporting country and importing country, we view an import surge in sectoral terms coming from an increased supply on the world market by a number of exporting countries and affecting all the major industrialized countries at the same time. Our approach seems suitable for wearing apparel, which is something that many developing countries now apply in large amounts to the industrialized countries and that could be supplied in even larger amounts if conditions permitted. It is becoming apparent that there are also other products that developing countries are capable of producing and exporting in great volume and to many countries, including footwear, iron and steel, electronic products, and automobiles. Even where particular instances of safeguard protection have seemed to be bilateral in nature, there has been a tendency for the exporting country, once constrained, to look for alternative export markets in third countries. It therefore seems plausible to us to conceive of an import surge in broad, sectoral terms coming from a number of supplying countries and impinging on all of the industrialized countries at the same time. Our Model could be used in principle to analyze import surges in other sectors so long as it was assumed that the products involved were perfect substitutes in the world market.

In considering the design of a safeguards agreement in the Uruguay Round negotiations, our analysis suggests that unilateral safeguards measures may shift adjustment burdens onto other countries and that sectoral tariffs and quotas may be particularly detrimental to the importing countries' own interests, insofar as their exports will be adversely affected. The safeguards policy that appears to work best in terms of mitigating employment declines due to a broad import surge is when all the industrialized importing countries act together to subsidize domestic output. In designing a safeguards agreement, it might be desirable accordingly to rule out tariff and quota measures and instead to specify that domestic subsidies be used. Of course, such assistance should be made available only for a limited period of time in order to encourage adjustment and avoid long-lasting protection for any industry. In addition, it would be necessary to coordinate any such recommendation in favor of subsidies with provisions of the GATT subsidies code, which otherwise might lead to a plethora of self-defeating countervailing duties.

Notes

The research underlying this paper was supported by a grant from the Ford Foundation for a program of research in trade policy in the Institute of Public Policy Studies at the University of Michigan. The authors would like to thank John Alfaro for computational assistance and Judith Jackson for editorial and typing assistance.

1   For more extended treatment of safeguards issues and GATT procedures, see Jackson (1986), Richardson (1988), and Hoekman (1988a, b).
2   Note, however, Hindley's (1988) argument that developing countries should be careful what they give up in return for a more viable safeguards code, since they may be better off under the current arrangements that rely on VERs.
3   In both cases, while we do not require equilibrium in individual labor markets, we also do not attempt to model disequilibrium explicitly in terms of which side of the market is rationed and how that rationing may give rise to changes in "effective" supply and demand in other markets.
4   The countries are listed in table 14.1, and the industries are listed in table 14.4.
5   We are currently developing the data base to 1980 and making a number of improvements in the input-output coverage for individual countries.
6   We are currently updating the NTB coverage indexes using more recent information compiled by the UNCTAD Secretariat and made available by the World Bank.
7   We have constructed ad valorem tariff equivalents of existng NTBs by sector for the major industrialized countries and for a subset of the developing countries included in the Model. However, we do not use these ad valorem equivalents for the experiments in this paper. For a description of the procedures that we followed in constructing these estimates and the sources utilized, see Deardorff and Stern (1988, App. B).
8   These are currently being updated using more recent information.
9   Use of these elasticities is subject to the limitation that they are valid, at most, only for the range of prices for which they were estimated. This should not be a problem for the results reported here, however, for which individual prices changed in most cases on average by only a few percent.
10 We have also analyzed import surges of transportation equipment (ISIC 364) and iron and steel (ISIC 371) as coming from the major NICs – Brazil, South Korea, Mexico, Taiwan, and Yugoslavia – included in our Model. In these cases, increased competition is likely to come from countries that have already

become fairly industrialized. Since the analysis of alternative safeguards policies turned out to be broadly similar to what will be presented below for the surge in apparel imports, we decided not to include these other cases in our discussion here. For those interested, the results are available on request.

11 The reason for defining the home-sector subsidy differently from the export-sector subsidy should be explained. Supply and demand elasticities are such that home prices respond more than output to a subsidy, and thus what is needed is a subsidy that will stimulate demand appropriately. That is, when a production subsidy is used in the home sector, it primarily lowers price to demanders, so that the change in equilibrium output depends more on the demand elasticity than on the supply elasticity.

12 The results for other countries are available on request.

13 There is an interesting difference in the employment effects of the trade policies and the subsidy policies that is worth noting. Since trade policies act as taxes on tradable sectors, they tend to cause expansion of employment in the non-tradable sectors. The subsidies do just the opposite. Thus, while the declines in employment are not very large, they are consistent, with all nontradables experiencing a contraction of employment under the two subsidy schemes.

References

Deardorff, Alan V. 1987a: "Safeguards Policy and the Conservative Social Welfare Function," in Henryk Kierzkowski (ed.), *Protection and Competition in International Trade*, Oxford: Basil Blackwell.

Deardorff, Alan V. 1987b: "Why Do Governments Prefer Nontariff Barriers?' *Carnegie-Rochester Conference Series on Public Policy*, Spring.

Deardorff, Alan V. and Stern, Robert M. 1985: *Methods of Measurement of Nontariff Barriers*, Geneva, United Nations Conference on Trade and Development, UNCTAD/ST/MD/28.

Deardorff, Alan V. and Stern, Robert M. 1986: *The Michigan Model of World Production and Trade: Theory and Applications*, Cambridge, MA: MIT Press.

Deardorff, Alan V. and Stern, Robert M. 1988: "A Computational Analysis of Alternative Scenarios for Multilateral Trade Liberalization," in process, 1988.

Hindley, Brian 1988: "GATT Safeguards and Voluntary Export Restraints: What Are the Interests of Developing Countries?" *The World Bank Economic Review*, 1, 689–705.

Hoekman, Bernard M. 1988a: "Services as a Quid Pro Quo for a Safeguards Code," *The World Economy*, 11, 1988, 203–16.

Hoekman, Bernard M. 1988b: *The Uruguay Round of Multilateral Trade Negotiations: Investigating the Scope for Agreement on Safeguards, Services, and Agriculture*. Ph.D. Dissertation, University of Michigan, May.

Jackson, John H. 1986: "The Role of GATT in Monitoring and Promoting Adjustment: The Safeguards System," Research Seminar in International Economics, University of Michigan, Discussion Paper No. 170, May 15.

Murray, Tracy and Walter, Ingo 1978: "Special and Differential Liberalization of Quantitative Restrictions on Imports from Developing Countries," in L. Perez (ed.), *Trade Policies Toward Developing Countries: The Multilateral Trade Negotiations*, Washington, DC: Agency for International Development.

Richardson J. D. 1988: "Safeguards Issues in the Uruguay Round and Beyond," in Robert E. Baldwin and J. David Richardson (eds), *Issues in the Uruguay Round*, NBER Conference Report, Cambridge: National Bureau of Economic Research.

Stern, Robert M., Francis, Jonathan and Schumacher, Bruce F. 1976: *Price Elasticities in International Trade*, London: Macmillan Press.

Zarembka, Paul and Chernicoff, Helen 1971: "Further Results on the Empirical Relevance of the CES Production Function," *Review of Economics and Statistics*, 53, 106–10.

15

Direct Foreign Investment and Trade in East and Southeast Asia

SEIJI NAYA

I Introduction

In the past two and a half decades the Asian newly industrializing economies (NIEs: Hong Kong, Korea, Singapore, and Taiwan) and the four larger members of the Association of Southeast Asian Nations (ASEAN-4: Indonesia, Malaysia, the Philippines, and Thailand) have experienced rapid economic growth as well as substantial economic development. It is generally believed that the openness of these countries to trade and foreign investment has contributed to the overall efficiencies of their economies. Trade accounts for a large share of total output. The relative openness of the trade policies of the countries has attracted a substantial amount of direct foreign investment (DFI). In turn, although difficult to quantify precisely, DFI has contributed to the export expansion of these countries. Thus, the combination of relatively open trade and investment policies has had feedback effects which have worked to enhance the overall economic performance of these countries.

The purpose of this paper is to examine the link between DFI and trade and how this link served to promote economic growth. The analysis begins with a theoretical discussion of the relationship between trade and DFI and then proceeds in four steps which consider (1) the importance of trade in the region, (2) foreign firm activity in the region, (3) the relationship between trade and DFI, and (4) the evolution of policies regarding trade and DFI. Although attention is devoted to isolating a number of factors which have been of key importance in these economies, we will also highlight principles we believe relevant to other developing economies.

II Integrating DFI into trade theory

Linking direct investment and trade flows is not a simple matter. First of all, there is a definitional question: How is DFI different from other capital flows and from domestic investment? In the balance of payments and other statistical sources, the distinction between foreign investment – capital movements which result in foreign control of firms in recipient economies –

and other capital movement – loans, etc., which do not result in control – is rather clear. However, the distinction between direct and portfolio investment is less clear. The distinction is made on the level of ownership control exercised by the foreign investor. But this designated threshold level of control differs among economies and for that reason direction investment figures may not be comparable across countries.

From a conceptual standpoint, it is important to distinguish between direct and portfolio investment. DFI theory suggests that direct investment by multinationals is likely to produce different effects from foreign-procured portfolio investment in domestic firms. The importance of the technology, marketing know-how, and the other intangible assets the foreign firm introduces into the recipient economy, especially in developing countries, is often stressed. Furthermore, the benefits of such transfers accrue not only to recipient firms but to competitors and input suppliers who may benefit from technological spillovers. Indeed, it is sometimes asserted that the primary benefits of DFI are imparted through transfer of intangible assets such as technology and that the transfer of financial capital is of relatively little importance.[1] Thus DFI is not a simple capital flow and the primary channel of DFI–trade interactions may be unrelated to capital transfers but instead to transfers of intangible assets.

Unfortunately, however, very few theoretical analyses of DFI–trade interactions have explicitly integrated these assumptions into their models.[2] Much of the analysis to data has focused on the relationship between factor flows and commodity flows in the modified factor-endowment driven (Heckscher–Ohlin) model of international trade. This approach is perhaps best illustrated in the famous analysis of Mundell (1957) who showed that under certain assumptions a tariff-induced capital flow can be a substitute for commodity trade.

However, allowing for complete specialization, imperfect competition, and differences across economies in technologies and consumer preferences can reverse the Mundell result and generate cases where factor flows lead to greater trade volumes.[3] In addition, although it does not explicitly analyze trade effects, the immiserization literature is of great significance because it illustrates how DFI and other capital flows can lead to suboptimal welfare levels, and even reduce welfare below pre-flow levels, when recipient industries are protected. In short, since protection will result in nonoptimal investment decisions by foreign investors which in turn cause a mis-allocation of resources, the level of social welfare could easily be lower with foreign investment in a protected industry than without it.[4]

Moreover, the potential for complementarity between trade and investment, although not always clearly articulated in the literature on capital flows in general, has been stressed by those trying to analyze direct investment. Schmitz and Helmberger (1970) discussed how natural resource ventures could create trade and Kojima (1978) analyzed the "trade-oriented" nature of Japanese DFI in resources and manufactures, demonstrating how trade-oriented DFI can generate higher levels of welfare than anti-trade-oriented DFI.[5] Other economists have attempted to distinguish between direct investment and other foreign capital movements by assuming DFI capital is sector-specific. This literature does not usually focus explicitly on the DFI–trade relationship but in this framework DFI can impart a variety of effects to trade and welfare depending on the circumstances.[6]

Furthermore, the dynamic effects of DFI need to be considered in trade paradigms. This has been attempted in the product-cycle literature, whose most salient contributors are Vernon (1966) and Akamatsu (1962a, b), in which development is emphasized. In these models, products are initially developed in leading economies and imported by lesser-developed countries. However, as production becomes standardized, it shifts (via DFI) to lesser-developed countries, until the commodity's production takes place entirely in the latter countries. Eventually, these countries begin exporting the product. This "catching-up" process has important policy relevance. For the leading economies, it brings out a concern that heavy foreign investment abroad will eventually lead to lower growth and less economic dynamism. Although economists generally agree that investing economies need not be adversely affected, the political arena is filled with debate about such issues. On the other hand, developing economies are understandably concerned with the implication that they will always be a rung below the developed economies on the product cycle ladder.

In sum, although several problems exist with integrating DFI into trade theory, the analyses do suggest two points of significant policy relevance. First the immiserization literature's demonstration of how DFI flows in protected industries can be welfare-reducing is intuitively clear and of great relevance. In short, stimulating any investment, be it domestic or foreign, in protected sectors can easily lead to a misallocation of resources and a sub-optimal level of welfare; this is a major lesson of economic theory which is exceedingly important to remember. Second, some analyses emphasize the perception that DFI's impacts are generally not related to capital transfers, but rather to transfers of intangibles such as technology. Viewed in this light, the often observed policy emphasis on technology and other intangibles is to be expected and clearly warranted.

III The importance of trade in Asian developing countries

Everyone is familiar with the remarkable export success of the Asian NIEs. These four relatively small countries, accounting for less than 2 percent of world output, have increased their share of world exports to nearly 7 percent in 1986 from less than 2 percent in 1960. This success has been based on a development strategy that has made the NIEs among the most trade-oriented countries in the world. Table 15.1 shows that exports and imports

Table 15.1   Exports and imports of goods and services (percentage of GDP at current prices)

Country	Exports		Imports	
	1970	*1986*	*1970*	*1986*
Developing countries				
Hong Kong	92.9	111.3	89.4	107.0
Indonesia	12.8	20.8	15.8	22.7
Korea	14.0	40.9	23.6	35.1
Malaysia	46.1	56.8	44.4	51.1
Philippines	19.1	24.7	19.4	18.5
Singapore[a]	81.9	129.8	129.8	147.0
Taiwan	29.7	60.4	29.7	40.8
Thailand	16.7	28.2	21.5	25.0
Developed countries				
Japan	11.3	13.2	10.2	13.2
United States	5.6	6.8	5.5	10.2

[a] Merchandise trade only.

Sources: Asian Development Bank, *Key Indicators of Developing Member, Countries of ADB*, vol. 18 (July 1987).
Hong Kong, Census and Statistics Department, 1984.
Hong Kong, Census and Statistics Department, *Hong Kong Monthly Digest of Statistics*, October 1984 and August 1987.
International Monetary Fund, *International Financial Statistics*, Yearbook 1987 and August 1988.
Republic of China, Council for Economic Planning and Development, 1987.

comprise nearly 40 percent of GDP in Korea and more than 100 percent in Hong Kong.[7] Even in Japan, which is considered to be an export-oriented economy, the comparable figure is 13 percent for exports and imports.

The literature discussing the theoretical factors behind the relationship between trade and economic growth is voluminous and will not be addressed in detail here. The welfare gain that accrues to countries when they engage in trade because of improved resource allocation, as well as the positive link between net exports and growth in the Keynesian model are routinely taught in elementary economic theory. Further, the positive effects of economies of scale and increased employment opportunities are often pointed out. In addition, dynamic effects, such as the introduction of new products and new processes, facilitate industrial progress.

Numerous empirical studies have confirmed the strong relationship between export growth and economic performance.[8] In fact, empirical studies examining the sources of economic growth in the NIEs have also found export performance to be a key factor. Using the Chenery (1960) approach to demand decomposition, Kuo (1983) found that, for Taiwan, export expansion accounted for a rapidly increasing share of output growth during the period after 1961. In the 1971–6 period, it contributed to 70 percent of total output growth and 80 percent of growth in manufactures.

She also found that exports contributed to nearly 60 percent of the jobs created in the same period, leading her to conclude that export expansion was a major contributor in bringing the economy to full employment by 1971. In the other countries, the emphasis on labor-intensive manufactured exports in the 1960s and 1970s has also contributed to the remarkably high rate of labor absorption in the manufacturing sector.

In his study of eleven semi-industrial countries, Balassa (1982) also found that export expansion had a beneficial effect on economic growth and contributed to intercountry differences in income growth. In particular, he estimates that Korea's and Taiwan's GNPs would have been 37 and 25 percent smaller, respectively, if their exports had grown at the average rate of the eleven countries. In contrast, he found that countries with below average export growth rates, Chile and India, would have had GNPs 14 and 12 percent higher.

In addition to contributions to overall economic and employment growth in the NIEs, exports both reflect and contributed to the transformation of the economic structures of the economies (Lee and Naya, 1988). In Korea and Taiwan, the rapid growth in manufactures in the 1960s and early 1970s can be seen in the declining share of agriculture and primary commodities in their export structures. Manufactures now account for more than 85 percent of exports in both countries as compared to less than 75 percent in 1970. Moreover, the increasing industrial sophistication of the NIEs in the late 1970s and the 1980s is clear in the changing composition of exports from labor-intensive goods to capital- and technology-intensive goods. Electrical and non-electrical machinery now make up a significant share of exports, ranging from 17 percent in Korea to 29 percent in Singapore. Transport equipment has shown phenomenal growth in Korea, accounting for 21 percent of exports in 1986 from 1 percent in 1970. These sectors in turn were the force behind the rapid growth of manufactures.

The four resource-rich ASEAN countries have been less trade-oriented than the NIEs. In the 1970s, however, exports grew rapidly, resulting in higher shares of trade in total output. Export-to-GDP ratios, though lower than those of the NIEs, are high, averaging 50 percent for Malaysia and about 25 percent for the other countries. With the strong export performance during this period, economic growth rates improved as well.

The export commodity composition of these countries also reflects increasing levels of industrialization. The share of primary commodities has declined significantly in all four countries, while textiles, clothing, and electrical and electronic equipment have become more important.

IV Foreign firm activities and trade

DFI shares of total investment and foreign multinational shares of employment and output are small in most Asian developing economies.

Table 15.2 Foreign investment and Gross Capital Formation (GCF) (annual average amounts in US$ million, shares of GCF in percent)

Country	Total net portfolio investment[a]				Total inflows of direct foreign investment					
	1976–80		1981–6		1967–5		1976–80		1981–6	
	US$m	%	US$m	%	US$m	%	US$m	%	US$m	%
Developing countries										
Hong Kong[b]	–	–	–	–	–	–	253	4.3	614	7.1
Indonesia	42	0.4	138	0.5	99	4.4	253	2.4	230	0.9
Korea	47	0.3	315	1.3	51	1.7	61	0.4	168	0.7
Malaysia	75	1.6	1,047	11.1	173	13.7	559	11.8	991	10.5
Philippines	8	0.1	4	0.1	12	0.5	69	0.9	65	0.8
Singapore	–9	–0.3	74	1.0	233	21.0	644	18.5	1,054	13.8
Taiwan	19	0.2	41	0.3	47	2.0	106	1.2	212	1.7
Thailand	70	1.1	205	2.3	66	2.9	98	1.5	276	3.1
Developed countries										
Japan	1,768	0.6	– 26,899	–7.0	118	0.1	139	0.1	315	0.1
United States	9,226	2.1	34,389	5.2	1,750	0.8	8,947	2.0	20,077	3.0

– = not available.
[a] Positive figures indicate inflows, negative outflows.
[b] Foreign direct investment from DAC countries.

Sources: Asian Development Bank, *Key Indicators of Developing Member Countries of ADB*, vol. 18 (July 1987).
Hong Kong, Census and Statistics Department, 1984.
Hong Kong, Census and Statistics Department, various issues.
International Monetary Fund, *Balance of Payments Statistics Yearbook*, vols 27–38.
International Monetary Fund, *International Financial Statistics Yearbook*, 1987.
Organisation for Economic Cooperation and Development, various years.
Republic of China, Central Bank of China, various years.
Republic of China, Ministry of Economic Affairs, Investment Commission, various years.

In fact, DFI accounts for less than 3 percent of total investment in most Asian developing countries (table 15.2). It exceeded 5 percent only in three cases, Hong Kong, Malaysia, and Singapore.

Nonetheless, DFI has played a significant role in some areas. This is reflected in the tendency for DFI to be concentrated in the leading sectors of the economy. In the NIEs, for example, the foreign share of manufacturing investment is somewhat larger than in the aggregate.[9] In Korea, DFI averaged about 10 percent of fixed investment in manufacturing in the early 1970s, though this dropped to 3 percent or less in 1975–81. In Singapore foreign firms accounted for 66–75 percent of the capital expenditures in manufacturing in 1977–81 but under 63 percent in 1981–5. In Taiwan, the foreign shares of fixed investment in manufacturing averaged 3 to 5 percent in 1972–86, albeit with pronounced fluctuations. Although we have no data to confirm our suspicions, it is also expected that foreign firms accounted for a large portion of manufacturing and resource investments in the ASEAN-4. Foreign shares are likely to be especially large in the oil and gas sectors of Indonesia, Malaysia, and Thailand.

On the investing economy side, it is also interesting to note that in contrast to aggregate figures the ratio of DFI outflows in the manufacturing sector to total manufacturing investment was also relatively large in the United States, reaching 12 percent in 1977–80 and 4 percent in 1981–5.[10] US firms have been particularly active in electronics. In Japan, on the other hand, this ratio for the manufacturing sector was not significantly larger than the aggregate ratio of only 1 percent for the entire 1971–83 period.[11] With the exchange rate realignment, however, there are indications that this figure will increase significantly as Japanese firms move to the Asian developing countries in an attempt to maintain their competitiveness.

Far from dominating the investment and production activities of host economies, the foregoing shows that foreign investors provide only marginal supplements to most domestic activities. However, foreign multinationals are involved in international trade to a much greater extent. One important perspective is provided by host economy survey data on foreign multinational performance (table 15.3), although such data are only available for a limited number of economies. According to these data, foreign firms accounted for about one-fourth of all exports from Korea and Taiwan and an even greater proportion of manufacturing exports. In Singapore, foreign firm shares of manufacturing exports were especially large, exceeding 70 percent throughout the mid-1970s and early 1980s. These shares were smaller in Thailand, fluctuating between 6 and 17 percent for selected years.

It is interesting that shares in Singapore and Taiwan have tended to decline over time while rising in Korea. Since regulations on foreign multinationals were relatively less restrictive in Singapore and Taiwan, existing opportunities may have been exploited relatively early on in these economies with domestic firms growing more rapidly in recent years. On the other hand, Korea did not relax foreign investment regulations until the early 1980s. Consequently, foreign multinational activity has been rising relatively faster in recent years.

Examination of industry level data provided by Taiwanese and Thai surveys also reveals some important patterns. In Taiwan, multinationals have been a particularly important source of exports in textiles, chemicals, and electronics with foreign shares falling significantly over time. The electronics industry generated 16 percent of Taiwanese exports in 1974–9 and 20 percent in 1980–5 and thus is of particular interest. The development of this sector illustrates how foreign multinationals can be a major initiating force in the development of an industry. The Thai survey also shows electronics, textiles, and food and beverage industries to be very important areas of foreign activity, though data are subject to sampling problems.

Information on Japanese and majority-owned US affiliates in Asia (table 15.4) provide a better view of foreign multinational trade in the region as a whole, albeit at the cost of ignoring multinationals from other economies.[12] These data suggest that foreign shares of Korean trade may be somewhat smaller than suggested by Korean data but US and Japanese data correspond closely with host country data in the case of Singapore, Taiwan, and Thailand. US data also show exceedingly large US firm shares of total exports in Hong Kong and Indonesia as well as manufacturing exports in Malaysia and the Philippines.

Multinationals are heavily involved in importing into these economies. In Korea, multinationals imported more than they exported in 1974–8, accounting for over 30 percent of total merchandise imports in this period. By 1984–6 this pattern was reversed and the share of total merchandise imports dropped to 24 percent. In Taiwan imports have always been much lower than exports and multinationals never accounted for more than 20 percent of merchandise imports in the 1974–85 period. Although we have no import data for other economies, heavy involvement of multinationals in trade is also likely. In the final analysis, foreign multinationals probably account for as much as one-third of the trade conducted by the NIEs and the ASEAN-4 economies. On the other hand, the involvement is likely to be much smaller, but growing, in South Asia and China where foreign investment has not been so widespread.

V Trade and DFI: a complementary relationship?

Above we have seen that multinationals, especially those from Japan and the United States, are heavily involved in the international trade of the eight Asian developing countries. But it should be stressed that the heavy involvement of multinationals in trade does not necessarily imply that DFI creates trade. It is entirely possible that multinationals may simply replace previously existing channels and lead to no increase of trade or possibly reduce

Table 15.3 Foreign firm exports and host economy merchandise exports (exports in US$ millions, shares in percent)

Country	Period	Industries covered	Foreign firm exports	Foreign share of exports[a]	Japanese firm exports	Japanese share of exports[a]	US firm exports	US share of exports[a]
Korea	1974–8	All	1,870	23.3	–	–	–	–
		Manufacturing	1,822	24.9	–	–	–	–
Singapore[b]	1984–6	All	8,073	27.9	4,789	16.6	1,443	5.0
	1977–9	Manufacturing	5,535	83.7	552	8.3	1,816	27.5
	1981–5	Manufacturing	7,996	73.6	1,147	10.6	2,326	21.4
Taiwan[c]	1974–9	All	2,740	28.8	1,180	12.4	709	7.4
		Manufacturing	2,607	31.6	1,133	13.7	661	8.0
		Textiles	426	46.9	200	22.1	80	8.9
		Garments, etc.	148	10.4	36	2.5	26	1.8
		Chemicals	311	85.9	54	14.9	39	10.8
		Machinery	104	12.6	69	8.4	14	1.7
		Electronics	1,255	80.0	605	38.6	459	29.2
	1980–5	All	5,480	21.9	2,151	8.6	1,473	5.9
		Manufacturing	5,232	24.8	2,060	9.8	1,369	6.5
		Textiles	622	35.3	181	10.3	226	12.8
		Garments, etc.	210	6.1	36	1.0	44	1.3
		Chemicals	606	56.7	105	9.8	111	10.4
		Machinery	384	20.0	215	11.2	129	6.7
		Electronics	2,675	54.5	1,217	24.8	790	16.1
Thailand (Board of Investment, promoted firms)	1975[d]	Manufacturing	–	–	45	2.6	154	9.1
		Food/Beverages	14	1.9	8	1.2	14	2.1
		Textiles/Apparel	50	27.3	31	17.3	0	0.0
		Basic metals	115	91.8	0	0.0	114	90.8
		Electronics	1	4.1	0	0.6	31	128.6

1979	Manufacturing	598	16.8	152	4.3	270	7.6
	Food/Beverages	97	10.9	–	–	–	–
	Textiles/Apparel	196	31.1	–	–	–	–
	Basic metals	9	1.8	–	–	–	–
	Electronics	219	129.5	–	–	–	–
1984	Manufacturing	329	5.8	82	1.4	61	1.1

– = not available

[a] Total exports as defined in foreign firm survey sources except for Korea (1974–8) where total merchandise exports are taken from balance of payments data. Manufacturing exports defined as the sum of SITC 5–8. Note that industrial classifications used in sources of firm data do not correspond with the SITC; hence these ratios are only rough approximations.

[b] Firms classified by major source of capital.

[c] The foreign total includes overseas Chinese firms.

[d] Manufacturing, Japanese, and US data from Tambunlertchai (1977); all other data from Sibunruang and Brimble (1987). For 1975 Tambunlertchai's (1977) inclusion of a large tin smelter in his sample leads to a large US export figures.

Sources: Asian Development Bank, *Key Indicators of Developing Member Countries of ADB*, vol. 17 (July 1986) and vol. 18 (July 1987).

Koo and Bark, 1988, p. 39.

Koo, B. Y., 1985, pp. 199–200.

Republic of China, Ministry of Economic Affairs, Investment Commission, *A Survey of Overseas Chinese and Foreign Firms and Their Effects on National Economic Development*, 1979–83 issues.

Sibunruang and Brimble, 1987, pp. 335–6, 344.

Singapore, Department of Statistics, *Report on the Census of Industrial Production, 1977–1985* issues.

Tambunlertchai, 1977, pp. 57–8.

Table 15.4   Japanese and US firm exports[a] and host economy exports

Country		Period	Total exports[b] US$m	Total exports[b] % of total	Manufactured exports[c] US$m	Manufactured exports[c] % of total
Hong Kong	Japanese	1972–3	262	4.8	42	1.3
	US	1977	3,822	31.2	600	8.3
	US	1982–5[d]	5,119	16.6	880	6.0
Indonesia	Japanese	1972–3	36	1.4	10	8.7
	US	1977	4,426	40.5	107	27.8
	US	1982–5[g]	7,592	36.4	47	2.2
Korea	Japanese	1972–3	138	4.3	137	6.7
	US	1977	128	1.0	128	1.5
	US	1982–3[e]	296	1.0	303	1.4
Malaysia	Japanese	1972–3	40	1.5	32	5.2
	US	1977	508	7.4	339	21.1
	US	1982–5[g]	2,346	13.9	1,400	33.6
Philippines	Japanese	1973	80	3.2	74	27.8
	US	1977	355	8.4	260	45.1
	US	1982–5	600	7.5	488	35.7
Singapore	Japanese	1972–3	77	1.8	71	5.6
	US	1977	1,423	12.7	822	23.2
	US	1982–5[f]	10,914	35.5	2,224	20.6
Taiwan	Japanese	1972–3	339	7.9	339	11.2
	US	1977	591	5.4	558	7.0
	US	1982–3	1,021	3.7	926	4.4
Thailand	Japanese	1972–3	143	7.6	29	10.8
	Japanese	1972–7	–	–	76	15.6
	Japanese	1977–9	807	15.1	104	8.4
	Japanese	1981–3	780	8.4	134	6.1
	US	1977	104	2.4	–	–
	US	1982–5	460	4.7	–	–

– = not available or not disclosed

[a] For US firms data refer to export sales of majority-owned non-bank affiliates of non-bank parents. Japanese firm data refer to fiscal years ending March 31 of the following calendar year.

[b] Total exports defined as exports of goods and services as reported in the balance of payments except for Hong Kong where exports of goods and non-factor services from national accounts are used.

[c] Manufacturing exports defined as the sum of SITC 5–8. Note that industrial classifications used in sources of firm data do not correspond with the SITC; hence these ratios are only rough approximations.

[d] 1982–4 for manufacturing.

[e] 1982 only for manufacturing.

[f] Excludes 1984 for manufacturing.

[g] 1982–3 for manufacturing.

Sources: Asian Development Bank, *Key Indicators of Developing Member Countries*, vol. 17 (July 1986) and vol. 18 (July 1987).
Hong Kong, Census and Statistics Department, 1984.
Hong Kong, Census and Statistics Department, various issues.
International Monetary Fund, *International Financial Statistics Yearbook 1987*.
Japan, Bangkok Chamber of Commerce, various years.
Japan, Ministry of International Trade and Industry, various issues, *Foreign Activities of National Firms*, Surveys nos 3 and 4 (in Japanese).
United States, Department of Commerce, Bureau of Economic Analysis, 1981.
United States, Department of Commerce, Bureau of Economic Analysis, 1985.
United States, Department of Commerce, Bureau of Economic Analysis, various years

it. Thus a major task remains: to ascertian the degree to which DFI actually substitutes for, or complements, trade.

Trade propensities

As shown earlier, foreign multinationals tend to concentrate in industries with high foreign export shares, for example, Singaporean manufacturing as well as Taiwanese textiles, garments, and electronics. But to judge the relative trade orientation of the multinationals, one must look within the industry to examine the trade propensities of multinational firms as compared to those of other firms. These propensities are most often defined as export–sales (export sales to total sales) and import–content (imported input to total input) ratios. Higher ratios for multinational firms than for other firms indicate that multinationals in the industry are more likely to engage in trade. It is possible to infer from this that the expansion of multinational sales leads to greater trade orientation. Of course, the indirect effects imparted through linkages can be very different from the direct effects; thus, total effects may diverge somewhat from the direct effects measured by these ratios. Nonetheless, such ratios can provide an important first approximation of the relative trade impacts caused by different types of firms.

Export–sales ratios in developing economies indicate that foreign multinationals often do export more of their product than domestic firms (table 15.5). This is highly consistent with the common notion that one of the more important intangible assets possessed by multinationals is easy access to an extensive international marketing network, either internalized within the multinational itself or through other trading firms. On the supply side, the introduction of superior production technologies works to increase competitiveness and, commensurately, the ability to take advantage of such opportunities.

On the import side, Korean import–content ratios declined quite rapidly from a very high 82 percent in 1974 to 70 percent in 1978 (Koo, 1985, p. 195). In Taiwan, these ratios have always been much lower, due primarily to the lower import requirements of industries in which DFI is concentrated. Since 1979, total ratios have fluctuated around 50 percent with those for Japanese firms being slightly lower than those for US firms. Data on the Thai manufacturing sector for 1975 suggest a Japanese ratio of 68 percent and a US ratio of 29 percent; however, if iron and non-ferrous metals are excluded from the sample (eliminating one very large US tin smelter), the US ratio becomes 77 percent and the Japanese one 70 percent.

Investing economy data (table 15.6) again provide more complete regional coverage but recent Japanese data on an economy basis are not available. The regional figures show that Japanese petroleum/mining and trading affiliates in the Asian aggregate are somewhat more export-oriented than US affiliates, while in manufacturing, US firms are significantly more export-oriented, largely due to the extremely high export-orientation of

Table 15.5   Exports–sales ratios for foreign affiliates in selected host economies (export sales as a percent of total sales)

Host economy	Period	Industries covered	Domestic firms	All foreign affiliates	Japanese affiliates	US affiliates
Korea	1974–8	All	–	35.0	–	–
		Manufacturing	23.5	35.1	49.0	21.0
	1984–6	All	–	48.9	73.2	43.9
Singapore	1977–80	Manufacturing	35.4	74.9	68.7	79.8
	1981–5	Manufacturing	43.3	71.9	64.6	70.7
Taiwan[a]	1974–9[b]	All	–	58.1	–	–
		Manufacturing	33.9	58.9	58.2	63.4
		Textiles	33.5	82.5	81.9	75.6
		Garments, etc.	93.2	95.7	96.6	84.1
		Chemicals	9.8	47.4	40.6	27.3
		Machinery	25.8	32.1	69.2	26.3
		Electronics	48.1	68.0	53.0	94.9
	1980–5	All	–	52.5	–	–
		Manufacturing	–	53.3	–	–
		Textiles	–	68.0	–	–
		Garments, etc.	–	93.6	–	–
		Chemicals	–	33.1	–	–
		Machinery	–	29.3	–	–
		Electronics	–	74.3	–	–
Thailand	1975[c]	Manufacturing	–	–	9.7	74.3
(Board of		Food/Beverages	54.7	29.4	22.4	0.2
Investment,		Textiles/Apparel	7.3	28.6	17.2	–
promoted		Basic metals	6.0	19.7	–	98.8
firms)		Electronics	0.0	14.4	0.3	100.0
	1979	Manufacturing	20.9	31.5	17.6	41.7
		Food/Beverages	52.5	53.7	–	–
		Textiles/Apparel	15.9	41.8	–	–
		Basic metals	3.4	9.8	–	–
		Electronics	0.5	16.8	–	–
	1984	Manufacturing	39.0	33.0	21.0	35.0
		Food/Beverages	55.1	56.4	–	–
		Textiles/Apparel	47.3	49.4	–	–
		Basic metals	6.7	2.8	–	–
		Electronics	63.1	28.6	–	–

– = not available or not disclosed
[a] The foreign total includes overseas Chinese firms.
[b] 1976 for domestic firms; 1979–80 for Japanese firms; 1974–8 for US firms. Japanese and US figures are averages of annual ratios; all other figures in table are period averages calculated from export and sales figures.
[c] Manufacturing and sectoral data for Japanese and US firms from Tambunlertchai, 1977, other data from Sibunruang and Brimble, 1987.

Sources: Koo, B. Y., 1985, pp. 199–200.
Koo and Bark, 1988, p. 39.
Lee , C. H., 1983, p. 750.
Liu, T. Y. et al., 1983, p. 111 (in Chinese).
Singapore, Department of Statistics, various years.
Ranis and Schive, 1985, p. 116.
Republic of China, Ministry of Economic Affairs, Investment Commission, *A Survey of Overseas Chinese and Foreign Firms and Their Effects on National Economic Development*, 1979–83 issues.
Republic of China, Central Bank of China, *Financial Statistics, Taiwan District, The Republic of China*, January 1981, February 1982, February 1983, February 1984, February and December 1985, and January and December 1987.
Wu, R. Y. et al., 1980, p. 124 (in Chinese).
Sibunruang and Brimble, 1987, pp. 335–6, 338, 345.

electronics affiliates.[13] On the Japanese side the strong emphasis on security of mineral and petroleum supplies and the large role of trading firms in Japanese business networks lead to large export–sales ratio for affiliates in mining/petroleum and trade. On the US side, the relatively strong tendency for affiliates, especially manufacturing affiliates, to export back to the home market, leads to high ratios in this sector. For example, in 1977 Japan's affiliates in Asia made only 17 percent of their sales to Japan while US Asian affiliates made 34 percent of their sales to the United States. In 1983, the US ratio was 44 percent in all manufacturing and 66 percent in the crucial electronics sector; for Japan in 1981 the corresponding ratios were 10 and 12 percent respectively. Japan's figures, however, are expected to rise as Japanese multinationals become increasingly oriented toward serving the home market.

VI The evolution of trade and DFI policies

The move to outward-looking policies

There is an increasing tendency to accept the proposition that outward-oriented trade regimes encourage greater efficiency and are thus more beneficial than inward-oriented ones. Differences in the nature of trade policy have been a distinguishing characteristic between the NIEs and the ASEAN-4. Actual levels of protection varied significantly even among the NIEs, with higher rates in some Korean and Taiwanese sectors and very little if any protection or subsidy in Singapore and especially Hong Kong. In fact, Korean tariff rates have been on average comparable to those of the ASEAN-4 countries throughout the 1970s and early 1980s. However, one study of tariffs in the Asian developing countries found that, unlike several of the ASEAN-4 countries, tariff escalation was not evident in Korea and tariffs in labor-intensive manufactures were low (Rhee, 1983). Furthermore, there was a concerted effort to see that protected industries became internationally competitive and began exporting in a relatively short period of time. Thus, these firms were forced to quickly become efficient economic units. Owing to their success in developing internationally competitive industries, these NIEs have accumulated large balance of payments surpluses and have effectively graduated from most of the trade preferences offered to developing countries. Taiwan and Korea are also both in the process of further trade liberalization to ease trade tensions with their partners.

In contrast, the ASEAN-4 governments have relied more upon a development strategy emphasizing import substitution, though there was also strong emphasis on developing internationally competitive industries in Malaysian manufacturing and some Thai and Philippine sectors. Yet, in other sectors and especially in the Indonesian manufacturing sector, the primary emphasis was on building up infant industries and promoting

Table 15.6 Export–sales ratios for Japanese and US affiliates in selected industries (export sales–total sales, in percent)

Host region/economy	Investor[a]	Year	All industries	Mining/petroleum[b]	Manufacturing	Textiles	Chemicals	Metals	Machinery	Electronics	Transportation equip.	Trades[c]
World	Japan	1972	48.3	94.5	27.2	32.5	15.1	13.9	9.9	34.1	6.4	27.2
	Japan	1975	36.8	63.0	35.4	38.3	17.2	–	24.7	42.7	19.9	33.7
	Japan	1977	49.3	62.2	21.7	32.0	18.3	8.6	16.0	18.8	10.6	56.6
	US	1981	38.2	49.5	30.8	34.9	26.1	26.8	36.8	33.7	38.8	34.6
	Japan	1982	50.1	77.2	25.9	31.5	25.0	12.7	21.8	21.9	13.5	57.0
	US	1982	34.5	35.4	33.9	42.9	31.7	25.7	40.6	40.7	43.3	41.7
	US	1985	36.2	35.0	38.0	40.2	33.0	29.2	43.4	44.8	49.4	40.5
Asian developing economies[d]	Japan	1972	38.6	73.7	37.6	55.4	14.2	9.0	21.4	39.8	13.4	40.3
	Japan	1975	44.7	31.7	42.6	48.8	17.8	–	27.7	53.7	22.2	45.5
	Japan	1977	38.7	21.0	33.3	37.3	14.1	8.7	33.9	39.6	14.7	48.6
	US	1981	60.9	67.5	57.0	–	15.3	66.3	70.8	–	–	62.4
	Japan	1981	58.8	73.4	34.5	35.2	15.5	16.6	35.8	48.9	20.8	75.5
	US	1982	58.7	63.7	–	–	12.0	29.9	–	87.8	–	56.3
	US	1985	63.3	66.2	68.0	–	–	65.3	–	89.9	–	58.5
Hong Kong	Japan	1972	64.5	–	70.4	76.3	–	0.0	–	40.2	–	61.5
	Japan	1975	45.5	–	35.0	38.9	50.0	0.0	50.0	70.3	0.0	50.7
	US	1977	77.5	–	80.5	–	34.4	–	–	90.0	–	83.4
	US	1982	59.5	55.6	77.4	–	31.0	–	78.3	91.1	–	72.9
	US	1985	65.3	57.3	–	–	32.7	–	89.7	90.1	–	73.9
Indonesia	Japan	1972	23.1	–	4.0	3.6	0.0	0.0	0.0	0.6	0.0	0.0
	Japan	1975	27.8	–	9.6	0.0	4.4	3.3	0.0	–	0.0	–
	US	1977	80.9	–	40.8	–	0.0	0.0	–	–	–	0.0
	US	1982	66.1	73.2	–	–	–	–	0.0	68.6	–	–
	US	1985	82.5	86.6	–	–	1.4	–	–	79.5	–	0.9
Korea	Japan	1972	50.7	–	47.6	66.0	7.5	0.0	59.7	51.0	–	–
	Japan	1975	65.4	45.0	65.3	83.9	18.3	11.8	36.9	67.8	50.0	82.0
	US	1977	58.4	–	68.4	–	25.0	36.9	–	–	–	–
	US	1982	44.0	–	–	–	–	–	–	–	–	–
	US	1985	–	–	–	–	–	–	–	–	–	–
Malaysia	Japan	1972	14.8	10.0	9.3	21.5	0.2	0.0	0.0	0.6	0.0	2.7
	Japan	1975	48.4	50.0	50.0	72.7	16.5	25.9	25.0	71.7	50.0	50.0

Country	Source	Year										
	US	1977	44.3	19.0	76.2	–	12.1	0.0	–	–	–	–
	US	1982	47.4	29.3	81.5	–	14.8	–	–	96.1	–	3.3
	US	1985	95.1	–	83.4	–	18.0	0.0	–	–	–	–
Philippines	Japan	1973	–	–	29.0	55.0	28.3	–	17.0	–	–	–
	Japan	1975	90.0	36.0	52.3	40.6	100.0	–	0.0	1.3	0.0	–
	US	1977	17.2	0.0	25.7	–	8.5	–	0.0	5.7	–	–
	US	1982	15.7	–	26.5	–	5.0	–	–	36.8	–	–
	US	1985	22.2	–	40.5	–	8.8	0.0	–	72.5	0.0	–
Singapore	Japan	1972	35.1	–	37.5	88.4	51.0	1.8	–	31.2	56.3	29.3
	Japan	1975	40.9	–	40.2	73.0	29.6	26.0	–	45.1	49.8	44.8
	US	1977	67.3	30.4	93.2	–	–	–	–	97.0	–	–
	US	1982	82.0	82.9	91.8	–	72.4	80.0	85.4	95.8	98.1	62.0
	US	1985	84.4	87.8	90.7	–	–	90.0	89.0	94.3	95.2	63.3
Taiwan	Japan	1972	53.5	–	54.8	77.6	18.0	5.0	14.8	47.9	17.9	0.0
	Japan	1975	49.5	0.0	50.3	61.9	17.6	52.5	31.1	48.9	39.5	0.0
	US	1977	58.9	–	71.4	–	67.9	–	–	91.7	–	–
	US	1982	49.9	–	59.4	–	10.5	–	–	88.7	–	–
	US	1985	–	–	–	–	17.0	68.8	93.1	89.7	–	–
Thailand	Japan	1972	16.0	–	6.1	9.7	1.3	5.1	–	1.3	0.0	27.9
	Japan	1975	19.9	0.0	13.7	16.4	0.7	4.7	–	16.1	2.0	55.9
	US	1977	11.4	–	–	–	9.4	–	–	–	–	–
	US	1982	17.5	–	–	–	–	–	–	88.2	–	14.8
	US	1985	18.1	6.4	–	–	1.7	–	–	89.5	–	–

– = not available, not disclosed, or zero total sales.

a Data for US affiliates refer to majority-owned non-bank affiliates of non-bank parents. For Japanese affiliate data refer to fiscal years ending March 31 of the following calendar year.

b Mining (including petroleum) for Japan, petroleum only for the United States.

c For the United States, wholesale trade only in 1982, 1985; retail trade included in 1977.

d For the United States investment in developing Pacific island economies is included; note that such activity is very small having little effect on the figures presented.

Sources: Japan, Ministry of International Trade and Industry, Foreign Activities of National Firms, Survey nos 3–12 (in Japanese).
United States, Department of Commerce, Bureau of Economic Analysis, 1981.
United States, Department of Commerce, Bureau of Economic Analysis, 1985.
United States, Department of Commerce, Bureau of Economic Analysis, various years.

However, with the fall of commodity prices in the mid-1980s and the political crisis in the Philippines, balance of payments constraints and rising debts made it more difficult to sustain these inward-oriented trade regimes. Furthermore, the success of the NIEs with outward orientation suggested a more attractive alternative. As a result, trade policies have recently become more outward-oriented in Indonesia, the Philippines, and Thailand.

Thailand has gradually reduced trade barriers and increasingly emphasized export-promotion policies since the mid-1970s (Akrasanee and Ajanant, 1986). Furthermore, despite substantial problems resulting from declines in oil revenues, Indonesia has also worked hard to stimulate growth in export industries other than oil and gas, mainly other primary product industries and light manufacturing. In the Philippines, political problems have overwhelmed efforts at increasing exports. Although there was a substantial reduction of most tariffs in the early 1980s, unfortunately, this tariff liberalization appears to have been largely offset by increased use of nontariff barriers and has been reversed in recent years (World Bank, 1987).

Malaysia is the only country among the ASEAN-4 in which efforts to promote import substitution have increased. Largely in response to rising wages, Malaysia is attempting to build up its heavy industrial base with a strategy similar to Korea's in the 1970s. Increased protection has thus resulted in certain infant industries (e.g., automobiles and related sectors). Nonetheless, Malaysia maintains one of the more open trading regimes among the ASEAN-4 (Lee, 1986).

Thus, by the mid-1980s, most economies in this region were actively involved in promoting exports. Viewed in this context, liberalized foreign investment policies and increased export promotion are part of an overall attempt to instill greater efficiency and competitiveness in these economies.

Changing attitudes toward DFI

In the past, DFI has caused some controversy in several countries. This was clearly shown in Indonesia and Thailand during the anti-Japanese riots coinciding with the 1974 visit of Japanese Prime Minister Tanaka. These riots had many causes but one of them was undoubtedly a reaction against perceived Japanese dominance partially resulting from the rapid increase of Japanese DFI in the region. At that time, the international mood was one of distrust toward multinationals and their motives for investing in developing economies. Policy-makers stressed the need to maintain national control and to regulate foreign investors closely so as to avoid undesirable side effects such as increased market concentration, excessive repatriation of profits, transfer pricing, inappropriate technology transfer, as well as undesirable dependence on imports of foreign technology, capital goods, and intermediate inputs.

Even in the NIEs and the ASEAN-4 where attitudes were relatively pro-

DFI, several countries adopted restrictive regulations. The ASEAN-4 countries and especially Korea enforced the largest number of restrictive regulations, (e.g., limits on foreign ownership shares, local content requirements, and outright bans on foreign investment in certain sectors). At the other end of the scale, Hong Kong and Singapore were the least restrictive, allowing foreign firms to invest largely under the same (rather unrestrictive) conditions as domestic firms. Taiwan's policy was rather unrestrictive but the government often insisted on extensive dialogue with the foreign firm involved before approving a foreign investment.

Starting in the late 1970s and continuing through the mid-1980s, policies toward DFI have undergone a marked change. A major cause of this shift in attitudes was the debt crisis of the early 1980s. Owing to availability of loanable funds and negative real interest rates, foreign borrowing was very inviting for developing economies from the late 1970s through the second oil crisis. However, the unprecedented rise in debt which ensued caused the banks to reassess lending policies, in many cases reducing the availability of capital to developing economies. Although this was a limited problem in Asia (only the Philippines has been subject to really strong pressure from the international banking community), the rising debt caused policy-makers in Indonesia, Malaysia, and the Philippines to adopt austerity measures aimed at slowing the growth of debt. Consequently, development plans were curtailed, imports were restricted, and borrowing fell during the mid-1980s.

DFI and other non-debt-creating forms of financial flows became more attractive sources of foreign capital. This was coupled with an increasing awareness of DFI's benefits as exemplified by the positive role DFI is thought to have played in the NIEs (Galenson, 1985). Policies toward DFI were liberalized in Indonesia, Korea, as well as the Philippines. Major policy changes have not been instituted in other countries, but there have been important changes at the level of implementation. In general, efforts have been made to streamline procedures for foreign investors and to provide a more attractive investment environment. Note that this has also led to greater competition for DFI among the developing economies of this region, the emergence of the open door policy in China being a catalyst to this competition. Indeed, the desire to outcompete China, both in international trade and stimulation of DFI, has been an important factor, especially for the ASEAN-4 countries.

Another and probably more important element of the DFI policy shift is the growing confidence these countries have in their abilities to deal successfully with foreign investors. This reflects (1) increased negotiating skill in host countries which has resulted, in part, from past experience with foreign investors and (2) de facto acceptance of the proposition that host country policy is itself the most important element influencing the nature of impacts imparted by foreign investors. Consequently, policy-makers in these developing economies are not easily intimidated by foreign investors and are often very competent, even shrewd, negotiators representing the interests of their respective countries.

Largely due to this shift in abilities and attitudes, host country policy-makers are now much more concerned with more general investment policy issues than preoccupied with the need to control foreigners *per se*. In short, the critical issues in formulation of DFI policies in the mid-1980s are those common to debates over domestic policy as well. One of the most important issues deals with nature of industrial policy, in particular, industrial targeting. Most governments do this to a greater or lesser degree (Hong Kong being the exception) with a variety of policy measures (e.g., tax policy, subsidies, tariff and quota exemptions, and foreign exchange restriction exemptions). The nature of the incentives offered to foreign investors often differs from those offered domestic firms. However, these differences appear oriented less toward a perceived need to control foreign investors and more toward accounting for the different factors that affect the decisions of foreign investors.

Policy interaction

An important factor in the policy environment affecting foreign investors has been the increasing emphasis on liberal, outward-oriented regimes in the NIE and ASEAN-4 economies. As mentioned above, many countries in the region have moved to liberalize trade by reducing overall tariff rates and the dispersion of protection across industries. The latter is of particular significance when considering DFI because theory suggests that capital will flow into highly protected industries and that this will be immiserizing (welfare-reducing) for the recipient country.

The role of different trade regimes in the overall economy has been the focus of a number of other studies which point out the benefits of outward-oriented policies. However, despite being relatively outward-oriented, the NIE and ASEAN-4 governments have often implemented restrictive measures affecting DFI and trade. Yet, the two countries combining strongly interventionist industrial policies and outward-looking trade regimes, Korea and Singapore, have had strong policy-making bureaucracies which have often demonstrated the ability to make independent decisions based on national goals, not necessarily on the private interests of the bureaucrats involved. Both of these governments have admittedly made large policy mistakes, for example, the over-emphasis on heavy industry in Korea during 1973–80 and the artificial wage hike of the early 1980s in Singapore. The strength and independence of these bureaucracies are illustrated by their abilities to reverse policy decisions and attempt corrections of these mistakes with relatively little political backlash.[14]

A similar ability is not usually present in developing countries which rely on more inward-oriented trade regimes. In contrast, bureaucratic inertia is most common when inward-looking trade strategies are combined with interventionist industrial policies. Policy-makers often secure their positions by dispensing favors to industries that support them politically. In such an environment, the impacts of special interests are often quite extensive and policy-making bureaucracies thus respond more to the needs of individual interest groups rather than to some concept of social welfare maximization. Indeed, one major difference between the NIEs and the ASEAN-4 countries is that policy-making bureaucracies in the ASEAN-4, especially in Indonesia and the Philippines, have historically been weaker and encountered a larger number of corruption-related problems.

It is also highly significant that the increased outward orientation among ASEAN-4 policy-makers during the last two decades has been accompanied by the evolution of increasingly strong and independent policy-making bureaucracies. The greater confidence ASEAN-4 countries have developed in dealing with foreign investors is a case in point. Indeed, one of the primary benefits of developing economy investments in human capital (education, training, and the like) comes in the form of increased efficiency in these policy-making bureaucracies.

VII Conclusion

The outward-oriented strategies pursued by the NIEs and, for the most part, ASEAN countries have undoubtedly contributed significantly to their impressive records of economic growth. By establishing strong export-competitiveness in comparative advantage industries, these economies were able to improve resource allocation and compete formidably on world markets. DFI, which imparts essential intangible assets, was an important catalyst in the dynamism of the export sectors of these economies.

However, it is clear from the experience of the NIEs and ASEAN that correct domestic policies are essential. In fact, DFI itself could inhibit the welfare of a country if its domestic policies are protectionist. Further, the success of DFI and export promotion policies is not exclusively related to the initial policy choice. Rather, success seems to depend more on flexible implementation of policies, which allows for the correction of mistakes. The Korean and Singaporean cases illustrate this point well. Additionally, the probability that mistakes will be corrected seems to be correlated with the degree of openness facilitated by the trade regime. In this context, the movement toward increased openness to trade and investments in the region implies continued strong economic performance.

Notes

The author would like to thank Pearl Imada, Michael Plummer, and Eric Ramstetter for their contributions to this paper.

1   For example, Kojima (1978, p. 104) assumes that "the endowment of K (capital) is not affected (by DFI) significantly because the amount of capital involved is marginal to total capital formation both in investing and receiving countries." Below we will show this to be generally true in the Asia–Pacific although there are a few important exceptions.

2   Kojima and Ozawa (1984) is the only known attempt to explicitly define DFI as a flow of a factor of production other than capital (entrepreneurship). In a related approach Kojima (1978) assumes that DFI-related capital movements are not large enough to shift production-possibilities frontiers in either investing or host economies and that the effects of DFI are realized solely through induced technological progress.

3   Note that trade theorists commonly assume (1) incomplete specialization, (2) perfect competition in all markets, (3) identical production functions which are homogeneous of degree one in all countries, and (4) identical and homothetic preferences in all countries. Although the first assumption may be reasonable, the latter three are extensively violated in the Asia–Pacific region.

4   This proposition originated with the work of Uzawa (1969), Hamada (1974), and Brecher and Díaz-Alejandro (1977). Recently, there have been many extensions of this proposition under a variety of different assumptions; see, for example, Casasa (1985) and Young and Miyagiwa (1986).

5   Note, however, this result depends on the crucial assumption that DFI in comparatively advantaged industries induces greater technological progress than DFI in comparatively disadvantaged industries.

6   In these studies, the nature of the DFI–trade relationship depends crucially on various demand and supply elasticities, those of sector-specific capital being of particular import. See Caves (1982), Ikemoto (1975), and Neary (1978) for summaries of this literature.

7   Note that exports are gross-value and GDP is value-added.

8   Though statistical association does not establish definite causality, and there are many caveats, as Krueger (1984) points out, few observers doubt that this positive relationship between exports and growth exists. See, for example, M. Michaely (1977), Heller and Porter (1978), Balassa (1978), and Krueger (1980).

9   DFI data from Korea Development Institute mimeos (August 1984) and manufacturing investment data from the Republic of Korea, Bank of Korea (1987), and the United Nations, Economic and Social Commission for the Asia and the Pacific (various issues). Data from Singapore, Department of Statistics (various issues). Data from Taiwan, Central Bank of China (various issues) and Ministry of Economic Affairs, Investment Commission (various issues). Since manufacturing DFI data refer to approvals, not actual amounts, the approval figure was multiplied by the ratio of total actual inflows given in the balance of payments to total approvals to obtain an estimate of actual manufacturing inflows. Needless to say, the result is only a rough approximation of the actual ratio.

10 Data from *Survey of Current Business*, August 1987; US Department of Commerce mimeos, November 21, 1986; OECD (1987). Note that US manufacturing DFI picked up again significantly in 1985–6 with the ratio for 1985 being 11 percent.

11 Data from Japan, Ministry of Finance (various issues), Japan, Export–Import

Bank (various issues), and IMF (various issues). Since manufacturing DFI data refer to approvals, not actual amounts, the approval figure was multiplied by the ratio of total actual outflows given in the balance of payments to total approvals to obtain an estimate of actual manufacturing outflows.

12 Note, however, that Japan and the United States account for over half of the DFI in the eight Asian developing countries.

13 However, the predominance of trading firms in Japanese business networks may lead to the underestimation of Japanese export–sales ratios in manufacturing because affiliate exports through trading firms are often recorded as domestic sales by the manufacturer involved, although the eventual destination is an export market. Yet, even if this is taken into account these data do not indicate a pervasive tendency for Japanese firms to be more export-oriented and the patterns observed clearly reflect differences in economic structure in Japan and the United States.

14 Note that considerable political upheaval did coincide with the policy reversal in Korea in 1980. However, the primary cause of this upheaval was not economic policy but rather political demands for democratization.

References

Asian Development Bank, various years, *Key Indicators of Developing Member Countries of ADB*, vol. 15 (April 1984), vol. 16 (April 1985), vol. 17 (July 1986), and vol. 18 (July 1987).

Akamatsu, K. 1962a: "A Historical Pattern of Economic Growth in Developing Countries," *The Developing Economies*, Preliminary Issue, no. 1, 3–25.

Akamatsu, K. 1962b: "A Theory of Unbalanced Growth in the World Economy," *Weltwirtschaftliches Archiv*, 86(2), 196–217.

Akrasanee, N., and Ajanant, J. 1986: "Thailand: Manufacturing Industry Protection Issues and Empirical Studies," in C. Findlay and R. Garnaut (eds), *The Political Economy of Manufacturing Protection: Experiences of ASEAN and Australia*, Sydney: Allen and Unwin, pp. 77–98.

Ariff, M., and Hill, H. 1986: *Export-oriented Industrialization: The ASEAN Experience*, Sydney: Allen and Unwin.

Balassa, Bela 1978: "Exports and Economic Growth: Further Evidence," *Journal of Development Economics*, 5(2).

Balassa, Bela 1982: "Development Strategies and Economic Performance: A Comparative Analysis of Eleven Semi-industrial Economies," in B. Balassa et al., *Development Strategies in Semi-industrial Economies*, Baltimore, MD: Johns Hopkins University Press.

Brecher, R. and Díaz-Alejandro, C. A. 1977: "Tariffs, Foreign Capital and Immiserizing Growth," *Journal of International Economies*, 7(4), 317–22.

Cases, F. R. 1985: "Tariff Protection and Taxation of Foreign Capital: The Welfare Implications for a Small Country," *Journal of International Economics*, 19(1/2), 181–8.

Caves, R. E. 1982: *Multinational Enterprise and Economic Analysis*, Cambridge: Cambridge University Press.

Chenery, H. B. 1960: "Patterns of Industrial Growth," *American Economic Review*, 50(4), 625–54.

Galenson, W. (ed.) 1985: *Foreign Trade and Investment: Economic Growth in the Newly Industrializing Asian Countries*, Madison: University of Wisconsin Press.

Hamada, K. 1974: "An Economic Analysis of the Duty-Free Zone," *Journal of International Economics*, 4(3), 225–41.

Heller, Peter S. and Porter, Richard C. 1978: "Exports and Growth: An Empirical Reinvestigation," *Journal of Development Economics*, 5(2).

Hong Kong, Census and Statistics Department, 1984: *Estimates of Gross Domestic Product, 1966 to 1983*, Hong Kong: CSD.

Hong Kong, Census and Statistics Department, various issues, *Hong Kong Monthly Digest of Statistics*, October 1984, August 1985, August 1986, and February and August 1987.

Ikemoto, K. 1975: "Direct Foreign Investment and the Specific Factors Model," *Kobe University Economic Review*, 21, 29–51.

International Monetary Fund, various issues, *International Financial Statistics*, 1987 and August 1988. Washington, DC: IMF.

International Monetary Fund, various issues, *Balance of Payments Statistics Yearbook*, vols 18–38. Washington, DC: IMF.

Japan, Bangkok Chamber of Commerce, various years, *Survey of Japanese Firm Activities*, Surveys nos 7–9 (in Japanese), Bangkok: Japan Bangkok Chamber of Commerce.

Japan, Export-Import Bank, various issues, *Report of the Institute of Overseas Investment (Kaigai Toshi Kenkyujo Ho)*, November 1986 and July 1987.

Japan, Ministry of International Trade and Industry, various years, *Foreign Activities of National Firms (Wagakuni Kaigai Jigyo no Katsudo)*, Surveys nos 3–9 (1972–1978), 10/11–12/13 (1979/1980–1981/1982), Tokyo: MITI.

Japan, Ministry of Finance, various issues, *Monetary and Financial Statistics Monthly (Zaisei Kinyu Tokei Geppo)*, no. 305 (September 1977), no. 356 (December 1981), no. 380 (December 1983), and no. 404 (December 1985).

Kojima, K. 1978: *Direct Foreign Investment: A Japanese Model of Multinational Business Operations*, London: Croom Helm; New York: Praeger; Tokyo: Tuttle.

Kojima, K. and Ozawa, T. 1984: "Micro- and Macro-economic Models of Direct Foreign Investment: Toward a Synthesis," *Hitotsubashi Journal of Economics*, 25(1), 1–20.

Koo, B. H., and Bark, T. 1988: "The Role of Direct Foreign Investment in Korea's Recent Growth," paper presented at the 1st Conference on Asia–Pacific Relations, April 20–2, 1988, Tokyo, Japan, Foundation for Advance Information and Research.

Koo, B. Y. 1985: "The Role of Foreign Direct Investment in Korea's Economic Growth," in W. Galenson (ed.), *Foreign Trade and Investment: Economic Growth in the Newly Industrializing Countries*, Madison, WI: University of Wisconsin Press, pp. 176–216.

Krueger, Anne O. 1984: "Comparative Advantage and Development Policy 20 Years Later," in M. Syrquin, L. Taylor and L. E. Westphal (eds), *Economic Structure and Performance*, Orlando, FA Academic Press.

Kuo, Shirley W. Y. 1983: *The Taiwan Economy in Transition*. Boulder, CO: Westview Press.

Lee, C. H. 1983: "International Production of United States and Japan in Korean

Manufacturing Industries: A Comparative Study," *Weltwirtschaftliches Archiv*, 119(4), 744-53.

Krueger, Anne O. 1980: "Trade Policy as an input to development," *American Economic Review*, 70, May.

Lee, Chung H., and Naya, Seiji 1988: "Trade in East Asian Development with Comparative Reference to Southeast Asian Experiences," *Economic Development and Cultural Change*, 36(3) Supplement, Chicago: University of Chicago Press.

Lee, Kiong Hock 1986: "The Structure and Causes of Malaysian Manufacturing Sector Protection," in C. Findlay and R. Garnaut (eds), *The Political Economy of Manufacturing Protection: Experiences of ASEAN and Australia*, Sydney: Allen and Unwin, pp. 99-134.

Liu, T. Y., and Chien, C. C. with P. W. Chang, J. H. Chiu, and C. J. Chuang, 1983: *The Effects of Japanese Investment on the National Economy* (in Chinese), Taipei: Taiwan Institute of Economic Research.

Michaely, Michael 1977: "Exports and Growth: An Empirical Investigation," *Journal of Development Economics*, 4(1).

Mundell, R. A. 1957: "International Trade and Factor Mobility," *American Economic Review*, 47(3), 321-35.

Neary, J. P. 1978: "Short-run Capital Specificity and the Pure Theory of International Trade," *The Economic Journal*, 88, 488-510.

Organisation for Economic Cooperation and Development, various years. *Geographical Distribution of Financial Flows to Developing Countries*, 1976-1979 to 1982-1985 issues, Paris: OECD.

Ranis, G., and Schive, C. 1985: "Direct Foreign Investment in Taiwan's Economic Development," in W. Galenson (ed.), *Foreign Trade and Investment: Economic Growth in the Newly Industrializing Countries*, Madison, WI: University of Wisconsin Press, pp. 85-137.

Republic of China, Central Bank of China, various years, *Balance of Payments, Taiwan District, The Republic of China*, 1958-1982 Summary and various quarterlies, Taipei: CBC.

Republic of China, Council for Economic Planning and Development 1987: *Taiwan Statistical Data Book 1987*, Taipei: CEPD.

Republic of China, Ministry of Economic Affairs, Investment Commission, various years, *Statistics on: Overseas Chinese and Foreign Investment, Technical Cooperation, Outward Investment, Outward Technical Cooperation, The Republic of China*, 1983-1985 issues (in Chinese), Taipei: IC.

Republic of China, Ministry of Economic Affairs, Investment Commission, various years. *A Survey of Overseas Chinese and Foreign Firms and Their Effects on National Economic Development*, 1979-1985 issues (in Chinese), Taipei: IC.

Repulic of Korea, Bank of Korea 1987: *National Accounts*, 1987 issue, Seoul: Bank of Korea.

Rhee, H. Y. 1983: "Protection Structures of the Developing Countries in South and East Asia," Pacific Cooperation Task Force Workshop on Trade in Manufactured Goods, Seoul.

Schmitz, A., and Helmberger, Peter 1970: "Factor Mobility and International Trade: The Case of Complementarity," *American Economic Review*, 60, 761-7.

Sibunruang, A., and Brimble, P. 1987: "Foreign Investment and Export Orientation: A Thai Perspective," in S. Naya, V. Vichit-Vadakan, and U.

Kerdpibule (eds), *Direct Foreign Investment and Export Promotion: Policies and Experiences in Asia*, Honolulu and Kuala Lumpur: East-West Center and the South-East Asian Central Banks (SEACEN) Research and Training Centre, pp. 317–56.

Singapore, Department of Statistics, various years, *Report on the Census of Industrial Production*, 1975–1985 issues, Singapore: Department of Statistics.

Tambunlertchai, S. 1977: *Japanese and American Investments in Thailand's Manufacturing Industries: An Assessment of Their Relative Economic Contribution to the Host Country*, Tokyo: Institute of Developing Economies.

United Nations, Economic and Social Commission for Asia and the Pacific, various issues, *Statistical Yearbook for Asia and the Pacific*, 1980–1986 issues, Bangkok: ESCAP.

United States, Department of Commerce, Bureau of Economic Analysis 1981: *United States Direct Investment Abroad 1977*, Washington, DC: BEA.

United States, Department of Commerce, Bureau of Economic Analysis 1985: *US Direct Investment Abroad: 1982 Benchmark Survey Data*, Washington, DC: BEA.

United States, Department of Commerce, Bureau of Economic Analysis, various years, *US Direct Investment Abroad: Operations of US Parent Companies and Their Foreign Affiliates*, Revised Estimates 1983–1984 issues and Preliminary Estimates 1985 issue, Washington, DC: BEA.

Uzawa, H. 1969: "(Foreign) Capital Liberalization and the National Economy (Shihon Jiyuka to Kokumin Keizai)," *Economist (Ekonomisto)*, 47(56), 106–20 (in Japanese).

Vernon, R. 1966: "International Investment and International Trade in the Product Cycle," *Quarterly Journal of Economics*, 80(2), 190–207.

World Bank 1987: *World Development Report*, Washington, DC.

Wu, R. Y., Wong, L. C. H., Chou, T. C., and Li, C. K. 1980: *The Effects of United States Investment on the National Economy* (in Chinese), Taipei: Institute of American Culture, Academia Sinica.

Young, L., and Miyagiwa, K. 1986: "International Investment and Immiserizing Growth," *Journal of International Economics*, 20(1/2), 171–8.

Appendix 1 Robert E. Baldwin – Publications

Books

Economics of Mobilization and War (with Campbell, McKie, Freutel and Scott), Homewood, IL: Richard Irwin, Inc., 1952. ch. 11, pp. 17–90.

Economic Development, Theory, History, Policy (with G. M. Meier), New York: John Wiley & Sons, 1957, 542 pp. seventh printing, 1966. Reprinted 1976 (Krieger Publishing Co., Huntington, NY). Translated into Spanish, Polish, Arabic, Vietnamese and Indonesian.

Economic Development and Growth. New York: John Wiley & Sons, 1966, 2nd edn, 1972. Reprint edn, 1980, 133 pp. Translated into Swedish, Czechoslovakian and Portuguese.

Economic Development and Export Growth: A Study of Northern Rhodesia, 1920–1960, Berkeley, CA: University of California Press, 1966, 264 pp.

Non-Tariff Distortions of International Trade. Washington, DC: The Brookings Institution, 1970, 201 pp. Translated into Swedish.

Disease and Economic Development: The Economic Impact of Parasitic Disease in St. Lucia (with B. Weisbrod, R. Andreano, I. Epstein, and A. Kelly), Madison, WI: University of Wisconsin Press, 1974.

Foreign Trade Regimes and Economic Development: The Philippines, Cambridge, MA: National Bureau of Economic Research, 1975, 165 pp.

Recent Issues and Initiatives in US Trade Policy (ed.), Cambridge, MA: National Bureau of Economic Research, 1984.

The Structure and Evolution of Recent US Trade Policy (with Anne Krueger, co-ed.), National Bureau of Economic Research – University of Chicago Press, 1984.

The Political Economy of US Import Policy, Cambridge, MA: MIT Press, 1985.

International Trade and Finance: Readings (with J. David Richardson), Boston: Little, Brown and Company, 1974, 3rd edn, 1986.

Current US Trade Policy: Analysis, Agenda, and Administration (with J. David Richardson, co-ed.), Cambridge, MA: National Bureau of Economic Research, 1986.

Issues in US–EC Trade Relations (with André Sapir and Carl Hamilton, co-eds), National Bureau of Economic Research–University of Chicago Press, 1988.

Trade Policy Issues and Empirical Analysis (ed.), National Bureau of Economic Research – University of Chicago Press, 1988.

Trade Policy in a Changing World Economy, London: Harvester Wheatsheaf and Chicago: University of Chicago Press, 1988.

Articles

"Equilibrium in International Trade: A Diagrammatic Analysis," *Quarterly Journal of Economics*, November 1948.

"The New Welfare Economics and Gains in International Trade," *Quarterly Journal of Economics*, February 1952. Reprinted in American Economic Association, *Readings in International Trade*, 1968.

"The Secular Change in the Terms of Trade," *Revista Brasileiro de Economia*, December 1952.

"A Vision of American Capitalism," *Explorations in Entrepreneurial History*, May 1952.

"A Comparison of Welfare Criteria," *Review of Economic Studies*, no. 55, (1953–4).

"Some Theoretical Aspects of Economic Development," *Journal of Economic History*, 1954.

"Secular Movements in the Terms of Trade," *American Economic Review*, May 1955.

"Patterns of Development in Newly Settled Regions," *The Manchester School of Economic and Social Studies*, May 1956. Reprinted in Eicher and Witt's *Readings on Development*, in Rosenberg's *The Economics of Technological Change*, and in Bobbs-Merrill's Reprint Series in Economics.

"America's Foreign Aid Policy," Testimony before Subcommittee of Joint Economic Committee of Congress (November 1957). Reprinted in *Economics in Action*, S. M. Mark and D. M. Slate (eds), Belmont, CA: Wadsworth, Inc., 1959.

"The Commodity Compositions of Trade: Selected Industrial Countries, 1900–1954," *Review of Economics and Statistics*, February 1958.

"America's Balance of Payments Position," Part V. *International Influence on the American Economy*, Hearings before the Joint Economic Committee of Congress on Employment, Growth, and Price Levels, Washington, DC: US Government Printing Office, 1959, 972–4.

"The Effects of Tariffs on International and Domestic Prices," *Quarterly Journal of Economics*, February 1960.

"Exchange Rate Policy and Economic Development," *Economic Development and Cultural Change*, July 1961.

"Wage Policy in a Dual Economy – The Case of Northern Rhodesia," *Race*, November 1962.

"Implications of Structural Changes in Commodity Trade," Hearings before the Joint Economic Committee of Congress on Factors Affecting the United States Balance of Payments, Washington, DC: US Govt Printing Office, 57–72.

"Export Technology and Development from a Subsistence Level," *Economic Journal*, March 1963.

"Market Structures and Resource Misallocation in Underdeveloped Countries" (with W. R. Allen), *Economia Internazionale*, November 1963.

"Investment Policy in Underdeveloped Countries," in *Economic Development in Africa*, papers presented to the Nyasaland Economic Symposium, July 1962, E. F. Jackson (ed.), Oxford: Basil Blackwell, 1965.

"Tariff-Cutting Techniques in the Kennedy Round," in *Trade, Growth, and the Balance of Payments: Essays in Honor of Gottfried Haberler*, R. E. Baldwin et al., 1965.

"The Kennedy Round – Troubles and Prospects," *Farm Policy Forum*, 17(4), 1964–65.

"The Role of Capital Goods Trade in the Theory of International Trade," *American Economic Review*, September 1966.

"Substitution and Income Effects on the Supply Side," *Indian Economic Journal*, January–March 1966.

"A New Trade Policy for Developing Countries," *Review of Social Economy*, March 1966.

"Toward the Seventh Round of GATT Trade Negotiations," in *Issues and Objectives of US Foreign Trade Policy*, Joint Economic Committee of Congress, Washington: Government Printing Office, September 1967.

"Comments on Haberler's Reflections on the Trade of Socialist Economies," in *International Trade and Central Planning*, Alan Brown and Egon Neuberger (eds), Berkerley: University of California Press, 1968.

"Non-Tariff Barriers: A Brief Survey," in *Review of US Trade Policy*, US Senate Committee on Finance, Washington: Govt Printing Office, February 1968.

"The Role of Capital Goods Trade in the Theory of International Trade: A Reply," *American Economic Review*, September 1968.

"The Case Against Infant Industry Protection," *Journal of Political Economy*, May–June 1969.

"International Trade in Inputs and Outputs," *American Economic Review*, Papers and Proceedings, May 1970. Reprinted in *Economics of Information and Knowledge*, D. M. Lamberton (ed.), New York: Penguin Books, 1971.

"Adjusting to Increased International Competition," Testimony before

Subcommittee on Foreign Economic Policy, Joint Economic Committee of Congress, September 29, 1970, Washington: Government Printing Office, 1970.

"Determinants of the Commodity Structure of US Trade," *American Economic Review*, March 1971.

"A Multilateral Model of Trade-Balancing Tariff Concessions" (with Gerald Lage), *Review of Economics and Statistics*, August 1971.

"Non-Tariff Barriers to Trade and Investment," in *United States International Economic Policy in an Interdependent World*. Paper submitted to Commission on International Trade and Investment, Washington, DC, 1971.

"Government Purchasing Policies, Other NTBs, and the International Monetary Crisis" (with J. David Richardson), Fourth Pacific Conference on Trade and Development, Ottawa, 1971.

"Customs Unions, Preferential Systems, and World Welfare," *International Trade and Money*, M. Connally and A. Swoboda (eds), London: Allen and Unwin, 1972.

"Export Subsidization," *Bulletin for International Fiscal Documentation*, November 1972.

"Policy Problems in the Adjustment Process (US)" (with John Mutti), in *Prospects for Partnership*, Helen Hughes (ed.), Washington, DC: World Bank, 1973.

"Disease and Labor Productivity" (with B. Weisbrod), *Economic Development and Cultural Change*, Spring 1974.

"International Trade and International Relations" (with David Kay), *International Organization*, Winter 1975.

"International Trade and Economic Growth: A Diagrammatic Analysis," *American Economic Review*, March 1975.

"Der Abban der Nichttarifbichen Beschrankungen des Veethandels als Ziel der Neuen GATT-Verhandlungen," *Europa Archiv*, August 1974.

"The Formation and Effects of US Trade Policy," Research Project for the US Department of Labor, 163 pp., 1975.

"Philippines," in *Trade Strategies for Development*, National Bureau of Economic Research and Asian Development Bank, 1975.

"Industrialization Programme of the Philippines," in *Strategy for Development*, John Barratt, David Collier, Kurt Glaser, and Herman Monnig (eds), London: Macmillan Press, Ltd, 1976.

"Political Economy of Postwar US Trade Policy," *Bulletin* 1976-4, New York University Graduate School of Business, 1976.

"Trade and Employment Effects in the United States of Multilateral Tariff Reductions," *American Economic Review*, May 1976.

"MFN Tariff Reductions and Developing Country Trade Benefits Under GSP," *Economic Journal*, March 1977.

"Trends in World Trade, Limits to Economic and Employment Growth, and the New International Economic Order," in *Trade and Employment in Asia and the Pacific*, Council for Asian Manpower Studies, Manila.

"Crucial Issues for Current International Trade Policy" (with J. David Richardson and John H. Mutti), Report to Trade and Planning Panel, United Nations Association, August 1977.

"Issues in the New International Economic Order," *Portfolio*, 1977, 84.

"World Trade after the Tokyo Round," *Korea International Economic Institute Seminar Series*, no. 18, November 1978.

"The General Design of a Strategy of Industrial Adaptation," in Conference Volume, *Adaptation of Canadian Manufacturing Industry*, sponsored by the Economic Council of Canada, 1978.

"International Resources Flows and Patterns of Trade and Development," presented as V. K. Ramaswami Memorial Lecture, New Delhi, India, December 1977; *Indian Economic Review*, April 1978.

"US Tariff Effects on Trade and Employment in Detailed SIC Industries" (with Wayne E. Lewis), in *The Impact of International Trade and Investment on Employment*, William G. Dewald (ed), Washington, DC: Govt Printing Office, 1978.

"Determinants of Trade and Foreign Investment: Further Evidence," *Review of Economics and Statistics*, February 1979.

"Beyond the Tokyo Round," *Thames Essay* no. 22, London: Trade Policy Research Centre, 1979.

"The Mutlilateral Trade Negotiations: Toward Greater Liberalization?" American Enterprise Institute, Special Analysis, 1979.

"Measuring Trade and Employment Effects of Various Trade Policies," in *Evaluating the Effects of Trade Liberalization* by R. E. Baldwin, R. M. Stern, and Henryk Kierzkowski, nos 3 and 4 in *Commercial Policy Issues*, Gerard and Victoria Curzon (eds), Geneva: Graduate Institute of International Studies, 1979.

"Crucial Issues for Current International Trade" (with J. D. Richardson and John Mutti), in *The New International Economic Order: A US Response*, D. Denoon (ed.), New York: New York University Press, 1979.

"Protectionist Pressures in the United States," in *Challenges to a Liberal International Economic Order*, R. Amacher, G. Haberler, and T. Willett (eds), American Enterprise Institute, 1979.

"Political Economy of Industrialization: The Philippine Case," in *Current Issues in Commercial Policy and Diplomacy*, John Black and Brian Hindley (eds), New York: Macmillan Press, 1980.

"The Economics of the GATT," in *Issues in International Economics*, Peter Oppenheimer (ed.), Oriel Press, 1980.

"Welfare Effects on the United States of a Significant Multilateral Tariff Reduction" (with J. David Richardson), *Journal of International Economics*, August 1980.

"The Political Economy of Protectionism," in *Import Competition and Response*, Jagdish Bhagwati (ed.), Chicago: University of Chicago Press, 1982.

"North American Responses to Imports from New Industrial Countries" (with Malcolm Bale), in *New and Old Industrial Countries*, C. J. Saunders (ed.), University of Sussex – Butterworths, 1981.

"The Political Market for Protection in Industrial Countries: New Empirical Evidence" (with Kym Anderson), World Bank Working Paper no. 492, 1981.

"Adjustment Measures and Adjustment Pressures: The US Case," in *The State of the World Economy: Economic Yearbook 1981*, International Chamber of Commerce, 1981.

"US Political Pressures Against Adjustment to Greater Imports," in *Trade and Growth of the Advanced Developing Countries in the Pacific Basin*, Papers and Proceedings of the Eleventh Pacific Trade and Development Conference, Wontack Hong and Lawrence B. Krause (eds), Seoul: Korea Development Institute, 1981.

"Restricciones No Arancelarias del Comercio Internacional," in *Intercambio v Desarrollo*, Ricardo Ffrench-Davis (ed.), Mexico City: Fondo de Cultura Económica, 1981.

"Hur Kan. vi Föklara och Bemöta de Tiellagande Protektionismen?" *Ekonomisk Debatt*, 1981.

"Gottfried Haberler's Contributions to International Trade Theory and Policy," *Quarterly Journal of Economics*, February 1982.

"The Inefficacy of Trade Policy," Frank D. Graham Memorial Lecture, *Essays in International Finance*, Princeton University, no. 150, December 1982.

"Trade Policies in Developed Countries," in *North-Holland Handbook in International Economics*, R. W. Jones and P. B. Kenen (eds), vol. I, ch. 12, Amsterdam: North-Holland, 1983.

"US Policies in Response to Growing International Trade Competitiveness," *International Policy Research*, National Science Foundation, 1983.

"India and the Tokyo Round" (with André Sapir), *World Development*, 11(7), 1983.

"A Technique for Indicating Comparative Costs and Predicting Changes in Trade Ratios" (with R. Spence Hilton), *Review of Economics and Statistics*, February 1984.

"Trade Policies under the Reagan Administration," in *Recent Issues and Initiatives in US Trade Policy*, R. E. Baldwin (ed.), National Bureau of Economic Research, 1984.

"Responding to Trade-Distorting Policies of Other Countries" (with T. Scott Thompson), *American Economic Review*, Proceedings, May 1984.

"Recent US Trade Policy and its Global Implications" (with J. David Richardson), Conference on the Global Implications of the Trade Patterns of East and Southeast Asia, National Bureau of Economic Research, Kuala Lumpur, 1984.

"The Changing Nature of US Trade Policy Since World War II," in *The*

Structure and Evolution of Recent US Trade Policy, R. E. Baldwin and Anne Krueger (eds), National Bureau of Economic Research–University of Chicago Press, 1984.

"Rent-Seeking and Trade Policy: An Industry Approach," *Weltwirtschaftliches Archiv* (Review of World Economics), 120(4), 1984. Also National Bureau of Economic Research Working Paper no. 1499, November 1984. Also in *Economic Incentives*, Bela Balassa and Herbert Giersch (eds), Macmillan, 1986.

"US Trade Policy and Asian Development," *Asian Development Review*, 2(2), 1984.

"Trade Policy and Employment," in *Employment Growth and Structural Change*, Organisation for Economic Co-operation and Development, Paris, 1985.

"Game-Modelling the Tokyo Round of Tariff Negotiations" (with Richard N. Clarke), National Bureau of Economic Research Working Paper no. 1588, March 1985; *Journal of Policy Modelling*, 9(2), 1987.

"Sectoral Adjustment Implications of Current US Trends in Trade Competitiveness" (with Stephen Parker), in *Structural Adjustment in Developed Open Economies*, Douglas Hague (ed.), International Economic Association, 1985.

"Ineffectiveness of Protection in Promoting Social Goals," *The World Economy*, 8(2), June 1985.

"Lobbying for Public Goods: The Case of Import Protection," presented at the National Bureau of Economic Research conference on The Political Economy of Trade Policy, Dedham, Massachusetts, January 10–11, 1986.

"Toward More Efficient Procedures for Multilateral Trade Negotiations," *The Swiss Review of International Economic Relations (Aussenwirtschaft)*, 41(II/III), September 1986. Also in *Protection and Structural Adjustment*, Heinz Hauser (ed.), Verlag Rügger, 1986.

"Fashioning a Negotiating Package Between Developing and Developed Countries," Council on Foreign Relations Study Group on "The Integration of Developing Countries into the World Economy," October 16–17, 1986.

"Alternative Liberalization Strategies," in *Free Trade in the World Economy: Towards an Opening of Markets*, Herbert Giersch (ed.), Kiel: Kiel Institute of World Economics, 1987. Also National Bureau of Economic Research Working Paper no. 2045.

"The New Protection: A Response to Shifts in National Economic Power," in *The New Protectionist Threat to World Welfare*, Dominick Salvatore (ed.), Amsterdam: North-Holland, 1987. Also National Bureau of Economic Research Working Paper no. 1823.

"GATT Reform: Selected Issues," in *Protection and Competition in International Trade: Essays in Honor of Max Corden*, H. Kierzkowski (ed.), London: Basil Blackwell, 1987.

"The Political Market for Protection in Industrial Countries: New Empirical Evidence" (with Kym Anderson), in *Protection, Cooperation, Integration and Development: Essays in Honor of Professor Hiroshi Kitamura*, Ali M. El-Agraa (ed.), London: Macmillan Press, 1987. Also World Bank Working Paper no. 492.

"Current North-South Trade Issues and Negotiations," presented at conference, "GATT and the Developing World: Agenda for a New Trade Round," East-West Center, Honolulu, June 24-29, 1987.

"US International Competitiveness," presented at Annual Meeting of Minnesota Economic Association at Federal Reserve Bank of Minneapolis, October 23, 1987.

"Multilateral Liberalization," in *The Uruguay Round: A Handbook on the Multilateral Trade Negotiations*, J. Michael Finger and Andrzej Olechowski (eds), Washington, DC: World Bank, 1987.

"US and Foreign Competition in the Developing Countries of the Asian Pacific Rim," in *The United States in the World Economy*, Martin Feldstein (ed.), Chicago: University of Chicago Press, 1988. Also National Bureau of Economic Research Working Paper no. 2208.

"Increasing Access to Markets for Manufactured Goods: Opportunities in the Uruguay Round," in Anne O. Krueger, *Developing With Trade: LDCs and the International Economy*, San Francisco: Institute for Contemporary Studies Press, 1988.

"Structural Change and Patterns of International Trade," in J. Black and Alasdair McBean (eds), *Causes of Changes in the Structure of International Trade*, London: Macmillan, 1989.

"The Effects of Protection on Domestic Output" (with Richard Green), in *Trade Policy Issues and Empirical Analysis*, Robert E. Baldwin (ed.), National Bureau of Economic Research-University of Chicago Press, 1988.

"Other Issues: North-South Trade, Intellectual Property Rights, and Subsidies," in *Issues in the Uruguay Round*, Robert E. Baldwin and J. David Richardson (eds), NBER Conference Report, 1988.

"US Trade Policy, 1945-1988: From Foreign to Domestic Policy," presented at Symposium in Honor of Isaiah Frank, Johns Hopkins School for Advanced International Studies, Washington, DC, October 21, 1988.

"The Political Economy of Trade Policy," *Journal of Economic Perspective*, forthcoming.

"US Trade Policy: Recent Changes and Future US Interests," *American Economic Review, Papers and Proceedings*, forthcoming.

"Measuring Nontariff Trade Policy," for OECD Experts Group on Trade and Employment, Organization for Economic Cooperation and Development, Paris, 1988.

"The Microfoundations of Political Economy" for NBER conference on Global and Domestic Factors in International Cooperation, Trento, Italy, April 1989.

Appendix 2   Robert E. Baldwin – Curriculum Vitae

AB, University of Buffalo, 1945; PhD, Harvard University, 1950

1945–6	Instructor, University of Buffalo
1950–2	Instructor, Harvard University
1952–7	Assistant Professor, Harvard University
1957–62	Associate Professor, University of California, Los Angeles
1962–4	Professor, University of California, Los Angeles
1964-present	Professor, University of Wisconsin, Madison
1975–8	Chairman, Department of Economics, University of Wisconsin
1974-present	F. W. Taussig Research Professor, University of Wisconsin
1960–1	Ford Foundation Foreign Area Training Fellowship, Federation of Rhodesia and Nyasaland
1963–4	Chief Economist, Office of Special Trade Representative, Executive Office of the President, Washington, DC
1967–8	Research Professor, The Brookings Institution, Washington, DC
1969–70	Ford Faculty Research Fellowship
1974–5	US Department of Labor, Bureau of International Labor, Washington, DC, Research Contrast
1975, Summer	United Nations Conference on Trade and Development (UNCTAD), Geneva, Switzerland, Consultant
1978–9	Consultant, World Bank, Washington, DC
1982-present	Hilldale Professorship, University of Wisconsin
1982-present	Research Associate and Director of US Trade Relations Project, National Bureau of Economic Research
1986-	Chair, Social Systems Research Institute, University of Wisconsin
1988, Summer	Shelby Cullom and Katheryn Davis Visiting Professor, Graduate Institute of International Studies, Geneva

Index

Note: page references in *italics* indicate tables.

Index compiled by Meg Davies (Society of Indexers)